Metabolomics

METHODS IN MOLECULAR BIOLOGY™

John M. Walker, SERIES EDITOR

METHODS IN MOLECULAR BIOLOGY™

Metabolomics

Methods and Protocols

Edited by

Wolfram Weckwerth

Department of Metabolic Networks, Max Planck Institute of Molecular Plant Physiology, Potsdam-Golm, Germany

HUMANA PRESS ✳ TOTOWA, NEW JERSEY

© 2007 Humana Press Inc.
999 Riverview Drive, Suite 208
Totowa, New Jersey 07512

www.humanapress.com

This publication is printed on acid-free paper. ⊚
ANSI Z39.48-1984 (American Standards Institute)

Permanence of Paper for Printed Library Materials.

Production Editor: Erika J. Wasenda

Cover design by Patricia F. Cleary

For additional copies, pricing for bulk purchases, and/or information about other Humana titles, contact Humana at the above address or at any of the following numbers: Tel.: 973-256-1699; Fax: 973-256-834; E-mail: orders@humanapr.com; or visit our Website: www.humanapress.com

Printed in the United States of America. 10 9 8 7 6 5 4 3 2 1

eISBN:1-59745-244-0

ISSN: 1064-3745

Library of Congress Cataloging in Publication Data

Metabolomics : methods and protocols / edited by Wolfram Weckwerth.
    p. ; cm. -- (Methods in molecular biology, ISSN 1064-3745 ; 358)
  Includes bibliographical references and index.
  ISBN 1-58829-561-3 (alk. paper)
  1. Metabolism--Laboratory manuals.
  [DNLM: 1. Metabolism--physiology--Laboratory Manuals. 2. Spectrum Analysis, Mass--methods--Laboratory Manuals. 3. Magnetic Resonance Spectroscopy--methods--Laboratory Manuals. QU 25 M587 2007]
  I. Weckwerth, Wolfram. II. Series: Methods in molecular biology (Clifton, N.J.) ; v. 358.
  QP171.M48 2007
  612.3'9078--dc22
                            2006007129

Dedication

To all, who speculate the elements.

Preface

With the onset of full-scale DNA sequencing projects, biologists began to look at organisms in an entirely new way. In contrast to last century's paradigm, genes are not the be-all and end-all of investigations into the workings of life. Sequencing is just the first step in understanding organisms at a molecular level; most of the questions remain unanswered. To really get at the function of genes, biological systems must be analyzed at multiple levels of control—external parameters (environment, developmental stage, molecular signals, etc.) and internal parameters (transcription and mRNA degradation, posttranslational modification, protein dynamics, and metabolite concentrations and fluxes).

Metabolomics, the unbiased identification and quantification of all metabolites in a biological sample, is playing a substantial role in this process. The technology provides high analytical precision, comprehensiveness, and sample throughput. However, the physicochemical diversity of metabolites necessitates the application of different complementary analytical methods. High throughput and unmatched comprehensiveness for different compound classes makes gas chromatography–mass spectrometry (GC–MS) technology a superior technique for metabolomics. Most metabolites can be partitioned into polar and nonpolar fractions, and after specific derivatization to make each fraction volatile, analyzed using GC–MS. A major portion of *Metabolomics* focuses on different GC–MS techniques and their applications to real-world samples, such as analysis of blood samples (Chapter 1), plant metabolite analysis, and mass spectral and retention time index libraries of known and unknown metabolites (Chapter 2), headspace trapping of volatile compounds (Chapter 3), and the integration of GC–MS metabolite profiling with protein and transcript profiling (Chapters 4 and 5) for systems biology approaches. In this context, data integration and biostatistics, especially multivariate data mining, are addressed and fundamental techniques for the analysis of multivariate datasets described (Chapters 6 and 7).

GC–MS, however, has severe limitations. Measurements of higher sugar-phosphates, cofactors, and nucleotides have to be carried out using other techniques. Moreover, the analyses of secondary plant metabolites and metabolites with relative molecular masses exceeding m/z 600–800 (after derivatization) are not reasonable using GC–MS techniques. Sensitive alternative techniques involve the coupling of capillary electrophoresis and mass spectrometry for the analysis of the polar metabolite fraction (Chapter 8) and classical reversed-phase liquid chromatography–mass spectrometry (Chapter 9).

In the future, the structural elucidation of unknowns detected in metabolomic studies and their compilation in mass spectral libraries will be vital. There is no routine procedure, but the methods demonstrated in this book point the way to future efforts in this field, such as LC–MS techniques for polar metabolite fractions (HILIC) and hydrophobic metabolite fractions (C18) (Chapter 9). Liquid chromatography coupled to electrochemical detection and mass spectrometry reveals the redox-active metabolite fraction, which is important in the investigation of diseases in biomedical applications (Chapter 10).

All these techniques lead to measurements of metabolite steady state levels. An important complementary approach is the measurement of metabolic fluxes, which perhaps can be extended to whole heterogeneous pathway networks. Chapter 11 gives some clues about flux measurements in accessible systems like bacteria or cell cultures. In this context, Chapter 12 provides a theoretical framework for the analysis of metabolic pathway networks and relative fluxes between metabolite compartments based on mass conservation and reaction stoichiometries.

Besides the applications of MS in metabolomics, the establishment of unbiased metabolite analysis as a postgenomic top-down analysis tool has been pioneered with nuclear magnetic resonance spectroscopy. These techniques are the focus of three chapters (Chapters 13–15).

I would like to cordially thank all the contributing authors for providing state-of-the-art procedures, detailed protocols, and tips and tricks to avoid pitfalls. I am grateful to series editor, John Walker, for inviting me to edit this volume. I would also like to thank Megan McKenzie for revising parts of the book, and Katja Morgenthal for continuous help. The result is a compendium of analytical technologies with a focus on intelligibility and applicability. My hope is that researchers from all disciplines will find this a useful aid in their metabolomic approaches.

Wolfram Weckwerth

Contents

Contributors

NELLY ARANIBAR • *Pharmaceutical Research Institute, Bristol-Myers Squibb, Princeton, NJ*

ALEXANDER ERBAN • *Department of Molecular Physiology, Max Planck Institute of Molecular Plant Physiology, Potsdam-Golm, Germany*

ALISDAIR R. FERNIE • *Department of Molecular Physiology, Max Planck Institute of Molecular Plant Physiology, Potsdam-Golm, Germany*

OLIVER FIEHN • *Genome Center, University of California-Davis, Davis, CA*

TOBIAS FUHRER • *Institute for Molecular Systems Biology, ETH Zürich, Zürich, Switzerland*

ROBERT D. HALL • *Department of Bioscience, Plant Research International, Wageningen, The Netherlands*

TAKASHI HIRAYAMA • *Environmental Molecular Biology, RIKEN Yokohama Institute, Yokohama, Japan*

RIMA KADDURAH-DAOUK • *Department of Psychiatry, Duke University Medical Center, Durham, NC*

JUN KIKUCHI • *Advanced NMR Metabolomics Research Unit, RIKEN Plant Science Center, Yokohama, Japan*

TOBIAS KIND • *Genome Center, University of California-Davis, Davis, CA*

JOACHIM KOPKA • *Department of Molecular Physiology, Max Planck Institute of Molecular Plant Physiology, Potsdam-Golm, Germany*

BRUCE S. KRISTAL • *Dementia Research Service, Burke Medical Research Institute, White Plains, NY and Department of Neuroscience, Weill Medical College of Cornell University, New York, NY*

WAYNE R. MATSON • *Department of Systems Biochemistry, Bedford Veterans Administration Medical Center, Bedford, MA*

KATJA MORGENTHAL • *Department of Metabolic Networks, Max Planck Institute of Molecular Plant Physiology, Potsdam-Golm, Germany*

ANNIK NANCHEN • *Institute for Molecular Systems Biology, ETH Zürich, Zürich, Switzerland*

KARL-HEINZ OTT • *Pharmaceutical Research Institute, Bristol-Myers Squibb, Princeton, NJ*

MIKHAIL PACHKOV • *Department of Bioinformatics, Friedrich-Schiller University of Jena, Jena, Germany*

UWE SAUER • *Institute for Molecular Systems Biology, ETH Zürich, Zürich, Switzerland*

NICOLAS SCHAUER • *Department of Molecular Physiology, Max Planck Institute of Molecular Plant Physiology, Potsdam-Golm, Germany*

MATTHIAS SCHOLZ • *Institute of Biochemistry and Biology, University of Potsdam, Potsdam, Germany*

STEFAN SCHUSTER • *Department of Bioinformatics, Friedrich-Schiller University of Jena, Jena, Germany*

JOACHIM SELBIG • *Institute of Biochemistry and Biology, University of Potsdam, Potsdam, Germany*

YEVGENIYA I. SHURUBOR • *Dementia Research Service, Burke Medical Research Institute, White Plains, NY*

TOMOYOSHI SOGA • *Institute for Advanced Biosciences, Keio University and Human Metabolome Technologies Inc., Yamagata, Japan*

RALF STEUER • *Institute of Biochemistry and Biology, University of Potsdam, Potsdam, Germany*

NOBUO TANAKA • *Department of Polymer Science and Engineering, Kyoto Institute of Technology, Kyoto, Japan*

YURY M. TIKUNOV • *Center for BioSystems Genomics, Wageningen, The Netherlands*

VLADIMIR V. TOLSTIKOV • *Genome Center, University of California-Davis, Davis, CA*

EWA URBANCZYK-WOCHNIAK • *Department of Molecular Physiology, Max Planck Institute of Molecular Plant Physiology, Potsdam-Golm, Germany*

FRANCEL W. A. VERSTAPPEN • *Department of Bioscience, Plant Research International, Wageningen, The Netherlands*

MARK R. VIANT • *School of Biosciences, University of Birmingham, Birmingham, UK*

AXEL VON KAMP • *Department of Bioinformatics, Friedrich-Schiller University of Jena, Jena, Germany*

WOLFRAM WECKWERTH • *Department of Metabolic Networks, Max Planck Institute of Molecular Plant Physiology, Potsdam-Golm, Germany*

STEFANIE WIENKOOP • *Department of Metabolic Networks, Max Planck Institute of Molecular Plant Physiology, Potsdam-Golm, Germany*

LOTHAR WILLMITZER • *Department of Molecular Physiology, Max Planck Institute of Molecular Plant Physiology, Potsdam-Golm, Germany*

FLORIAN WOLSCHIN • *Department of Metabolic Networks, Max Planck Institute of Molecular Plant Physiology, Potsdam-Golm, Germany*

I

Metabolome Analysis Using Gas Chromatography Coupled to Mass Spectrometry

1

Metabolite Profiling in Blood Plasma

Oliver Fiehn and Tobias Kind

Summary

Metabolite profiling has been established as a multiparallel strategy for relative quantification of a mixture of compounds or compound classes using chromatography and universal detection technologies (gas chromatography–mass spectrometry [GC–MS], liquid chromatography–MS). Despite its origins dating back to the late 1960s, it was only in the 1980s that its use was acknowledged to diagnose metabolic disorders in men, especially for rapid screening of inborn errors. Even faster electrospray ionization–MS/MS screening methods replaced longish chromatographic methods, and method development had stopped despite its potential use for other, less imminent diseases such as likelihood assessments of type II diabetes mellitus or cardiovascular risk factor evaluation. In addition to its diagnostic use, profiling blood samples can be employed to investigate specific biochemical responses. The broader scope of analysis outweighs the disadvantages by taking compromises in method development and the reduced accuracy for specific metabolites. This chapter exemplifies the strategies in metabolite profiling by GC–MS. It gives experimental details on basic steps like blood plasma withdrawal, storage, protein precipitation, extraction, concentration, derivatization, data acquisition, raw data processing, and result data tranformation. A major difference to profiling plant tissues is that no fractionation step is utilized, enabling the analysis of primary metabolites like sugars and amino acids concomitant with lipids such as sterols and free fatty acids.

Key Words: Mass spectrometry; GC–MS; metabolomics; data mining; diabetes.

1. Introduction

Metabolite profiling is an analytical method for relative quantification of a selected number of metabolites from biological samples (1), i.e., members of specific pathways or compound classes. In plant biology, samples have been garnered from a specific tissue or a part of a tissue of interest, but for biomedical purposes, analysis of metabolite profiles in body fluids such as blood, urine,

From: *Methods in Molecular Biology, vol. 358: Metabolomics: Methods and Protocols*
Edited by: W. Weckwerth © Humana Press Inc., Totowa, NJ

or saliva, is equally important. Metabolite profiling is distinguished from other
analytical procedures by its scope:

1. Target analysis is constrained to one or a very few target compounds (such as
   hormones). Such targets are usually quantified in an absolute manner using calibration curves and/or stable isotope-labeled internal standards.
2. Metabolite profiling restricts itself to a certain range of compounds or even to
   screening a predefined number of members of a compound class. Within these
   constraints, a single analytical platform may be sufficient. Examples might be
   the analysis of carotenoid intermediates by high-performance liquid chromatog-
   raphy/diode array ultraviolet detection (HPLC-UV), or sugars, hydroxy acids,
   and amino acids by fractionation and gas chromatography–mass spectrometry
   (GC–MS), or vitamin profiling by HPLC–MS/MS. Quantification in m1etabolite
   profiling is usually carried out relative to comparator samples, such as positive
   and negative controls.
3. Metabolomics seeks a truly unbiased quantitative and qualitative analysis of all
   biochemical intermediates in a sample. It must not be restricted by any physicochemical property of the metabolites, such as molecular weight, polarity, volatility, electrical charge, chemical structure, and others. Because there is currently
   no single technology available that would allow such comprehensive analysis,
   metabolomics is characterized by the use of multiple techniques and unbiased
   software. Metabolomics also uses relative quantification. In addition, it must
   include a strong focus on *de novo* identification of unknown metabolites whose
   presence is demonstrated (*see* Chapter 9).
4. Metabolite fingerprinting is different from the other three approaches in that it
   does not aim to physically separate individual metabolites. Instead, spectra from
   full-sample extracts are acquired by a single instrument (such as ^{1}H-nuclear magnetic resonance [NMR]) (*see* Chapters 13 and 14). Spectra are then compared by
   multivariate statistics in order to find spectral regions that discriminate samples
   by their biological origin. In some instances, these regions may again point
   toward specific metabolites; in general, however, one-dimensional methods are
   restricted in resolving complex mixtures.

Metabolite profiling, therefore, must be seen as a compromise between
truly quantitative target analysis and completely unbiased metabolomics.
Each metabolite profiling method is directed toward a chemically different
compound class, hence, there are various methods published depending on
the actual task. In itself, each procedure will be a compromise between several parameters, such as compound stability, solubility, influence of the cellular matrix, time needed to carry out the protocol, constraints given to garner
samples (blood withdrawal), extraction (potentially followed by fractionation), submission to analytical instruments, raw data analysis, and statistics.
For example, a protocol found to be well suited for the analysis of oxylipids in
urine will be very different from one that aims at hydrophilic sugars and amino
acids in blood plasma. Validation criteria for metabolite profiling and

metabolomics protocols are, therefore, different from target analysis: (1) reproducibility (precision of relative metabolite levels) is more important than absolute recovery. (2) Robustness and practicability are more important than accuracy (correctness in absolute metabolite concentrations). (3) Comprehensiveness is more important than inclusion of a certain metabolite that might be missed. (4) Overall dynamic range for the majority of compounds is more important than the detection limit for a specific substance. (5) On the contrary, the ability to include important known key metabolites may still be more important than the detection of unidentified peaks that might be biochemical side products of enzymes with low substrate specificity.

Obviously, these considerations can only serve as guidelines and must be weighed for importance when new methods are developed, explicitly stating which criteria were regarded most important and why. This refers to the need of exact definitions of the scope of an analytical method *(2)*, which is dependent on the research area to which it is applied.

In this chapter, a validated method for metabolite profiling of primary metabolites and sterols is elaborated for blood plasma matrix. Analysis of lipophilic components, such as (unsaturated) free fatty acids and sterols, is regarded equally important to sugars and hydroxy acids in medical diagnostics, therefore, classical metabolite profiling techniques that made use of inexpensive and mature technologies (such as GC/quadrupole MS) needed to be replaced by more sophisticated setups. The basic steps in the process can be summarized as:

1. Design an experiment according to the biological question. Use randomization wherever possible. Use pre-existing knowledge to target the number of individuals to be tested; generally, biological variation among humans exceeds greatly the variation found in animals. If there is not enough information available about (metabolic) variation in your test populations, consider small test experiments to gather such values. Consult statisticians *before* carrying out the experiments.

2. Collect as much background information about your individuals or animals as possible, as this will later aid in the interpretation of data. This includes any data that potentially may have an effect on the measured variables, for instance: genotype (gender, ethnicity/line, SNPs, progeny, and others), phenotypic descriptions (e.g., images, weight, body mass index, waist–hip ratio, size, and others), and environmental impacts (food/nutrition, health status, drug treatments, physical exercise, mental status/stress, fasting state, and others).

3. Withdraw blood using standard procedures into EDTA-containing tubes. Freeze at −20°C after blood withdrawal. Do not use samples that have been thawed more than twice.

4. Extract blood plasma in a comprehensive and mild way concomitant with enzyme inactivation and addition of internal standards.

5. Dry down an aliquot of extract and keep the other aliquots frozen for record purposes.
6. Derivatize the extract by first adding methoxyamine in an aprotic basic solvent, and then adding a trimethylsilylating agent.
7. Analyze the derivatized sample by direct thermodesorption GC-time-of-flight (TOF) MS.
8. Process the raw GC-TOF data.
9. Normalize and transform the result data, and perform statistical evaluations.

The basic theoretical considerations behind this process are quite simple. The measured metabolite levels should reflect the in vivo state which needs background information for interpretation of metabolic changes (and variation). Therefore, any metabolic variation by formation of chemical or post-harvest biochemical artifacts must be prevented. Biochemical inactivation can be ensured by coagulation of enzymes, either using heat- or cold-shock methods, with the help of organic solvents such as chloroform, acetone, isopropanol, or acetonitrile that force protein precipitation. Conversely, chemical artifact formation depends on the stability of each specific compound and is therefore hard to predict. Generally, any harsh treatment of the metabolome mixture should be avoided. Instead, conditions for extraction, storage, chemical derivatization, and analysis should be as mild, comprehensive, and universal as possible. In this respect, cold treatments are generally preferred over heat treatments.

2. Materials

2.1. Blood Plasma Collection

1. A notebook in electronic or paper format is needed to keep track on sample identity numbers, fasting state, day, time, and physiological parameters.
2. Vacutainer safety equipment for collection of blood plasma samples should be used, withdrawing blood directly into K_3EDTA lavender-top tubes.
3. Spare tubes and a centrifuge capable of $3000g$ centrifugation to separate plasma from blood cells are needed.
4. Microcentrifuge tubes and a vortexer are employed for aliquotation and homogenization.
5. Dewars with liquid nitrogen will ensure the immediate arrest of residual biological activity after centrifugation.
6. Dry ice and an −80°C freezer are needed to ensure plasma stability during storage and transportation.

2.2. Extraction

1. For rinsing or cleaning dishes, only ultra-pure water with a level of total organic carbon (TOC) less than 10 ppb should be employed (standard deionized water still contains large amounts of organic contaminants).

2. For preparing the extraction mixture, degassing devices (such as vacuum/ultrasonic bath, or pure argon or nitrogen gas bombs) and a liquid cooling system must be available. A freshly prepared, chilled (–15°C), and degassed mixture of acetone and isopropanol is prepared at a ratio of 2:1 (v/v). For each solvent, the highest quality (e.g., >99% ultra-pure HPLC–MS gradient-grade purity) is used and stored at room temperature in the dark.
3. A pH measurement device will be needed to check neutrality of solvents.
4. Volumes are measured using calibrated pipets whose accuracies are subjected to quality control (QC) routines at least once every 6 mo.
5. An ice bath and liquid nitrogen dewars are used for temporarily storing samples during the process. Large twisters are useful to operate in nitrogen dewars. Extraction is performed in a microcentrifuge tube shaker.

2.3. Derivatization

1. A speed vacuum concentrator or lyophilizer is used for drying extracts to complete dryness. A mixture of 40 mg/mL of methoxyamine HCl in pyridine (p.a. quality) is freshly prepared using an ultrasonicator.
2. In case ATAS (NL) liners are used, pyridine must be exchanged against dimethylformamide as polar, aprotic, and basic solvent.
3. *N*-methyl-*N*-trimethylsilyltrifluoroacetamide (MSTFA) is used from freshly opened 1-mL bottles.
4. Reagents and solvents are stored in a desiccator in the dark. Derivatizations are carried out in thermoshakers, which are set to 45 and 37°C for the first and second reaction step, respectively.

2.4. Mass Spectrometric Analysis

GC–MS analysis is carried out on a quadrupole or a TOF–MS equipped with autosampler and electron impact ionization. Samples must be injected in randomized order or appropriate block designs. For each injection sequence, the analysis of QC samples is a prerequisite (e.g., reagent blanks, method blanks, reference compound mixture, and reference design sample).

Low-bleeding injector septa or septum-free injector systems are prerequisite. Standard 10-µL GC injection needles are mounted into the autosampler.

Chromatography is carried out on a 30-m long, 0.32-mm I.D., and 0.25-µm (35%-phenyl)-methylpolysiloxane column. The GC oven must be temperature programmable up to 360°C. The MS must be capable of a data acquisition rate of at least 20/s and a mass range of at least 83–500 Da. Raw GC–MS data files are transferred to servers. Long-term data safety is ensured by back up routines on DVDs or by mirrored server space. Data analysis is carried out on office personal computers using the vendor's GC-TOF software that is able to carry out multitarget analysis, including compound identity checks based on mass spectral and retention index matching (e.g., ChromaTOF 2.25). The software must be capable of quantitation by area and height on user-defined ion traces.

3. Methods

3.1. Blood Plasma Withdrawal (see Note 1)

1. Take patient metadata and store them.
2. Collect 2 mL blood plasma into K₃EDTA tubes.
3. Separate cells from plasma by centrifugation within 15 min after blood withdrawal.
4. After centrifugation store plasma in a separate tube.
5. Ensure homogeneity by vortexing for 10 s.
6. Aliquot samples in six 30-µL batches into microcentrifuge tubes, storing the residual plasma in a 2-mL centrifuge tube.
7. If plasma is not directly extracted, close tubes and store at 4°C for up to 24 h, otherwise place into liquid nitrogen and store at –20°C for up to 10 d.

3.2. Protein Precipitation and Metabolite Extraction (see Note 2)

1. Take out 30-µL sample aliquots one-by-one and add internal standards, e.g., U-¹³C-sorbitol (200 ng per vial) for normalization and vortex for 10 s.
2. Add 0.4 mL of cold extraction solvent mixture (–15°C, degassed) to each (3) and vortex vigorously for 20 s.
3. Shake the samples in batches of 10 for 5 min in a 4°C room. When taking out the samples, place them in an ice bath.
4. Centrifuge samples at 14,000g for 2 min.
5. Collect the liquid supernatant of each sample and store in clean microcentrifuge tubes. The cell debris pellet can be discarded.
6. Repeat **steps 1–5** until all samples are extracted.
7. For storage, extracts must be degassed with a gentle stream of nitrogen or argon gas for 1 min prior to tube closure. Tubes can then be stored in the dark at –80°C for approx 4 wk.
8. Dry the extracts in a speed vacuum concentrator or a lyophilizer to complete dryness.
9. For storage, deoxygenate the dried samples with a gentle stream of nitrogen or argon gas for 1 min before closing the tubes. Tubes can then be stored in the dark at –80°C for at least 4 wk.

3.3. Derivatization (see Note 3)

1. Take out dried samples from store and allow them to warm up to room temperature for at least 15 min before the start of derivatization.
2. Add 10 µL of methoxyamine solution (40 mg/mL in dimethylformamide) to each dried extract, and immediately close tubes afterwards.
3. Shake extracts for 90 min at 28°C.
4. Add 180 µL silylating agent (MSTFA) to each tube, and immediately close tubes afterwards.
5. Shake samples for 30 min at 37°C.

6. Transfer sample reaction solutions to glass vials suitable for the GC–MS autosampler. Immediately close each sample with crimps that contain a Teflon rubber seal. Wait 2 h before injecting the first sample into the GC–MS.

3.4. Data Acquisition by GC–MS (see Note 4)

1. The mass spectrometer must be tuned according to the manufacturer's manuals for optimal parameters for ion lenses, detector voltage, and other settings. Usually, this can be performed in autotune operation.
2. Change or clean the liner with every sample, otherwise data for lipids and aromatic compounds will not be reliable. If an ATAS direct thermodesorption/automatic liner exchange system is used, *see* extended **Note 5**.
3. Check that manufacturer's recommended maintenance routines have all been carried out.
4. Inject 1 µL (1.5 µL for ATAS liners) of each sample in splitless, depending on the metabolite concentrations and eventual signal-to-noise ratios in the GC–MS profiles. Injection temperature is set to 230°C (*see* extended table in **Note 4** for ATAS liners). Injection programs have to include syringe washing steps before and after the injection, a sample pumping step for removal of small air bubbles, and an air buffer for complete sample removal during injection.
5. Separate metabolites using a GC temperature ramping program. Reasonable values are: GC start conditions at 80°C, 2 min isothermal, ramp with 5°C/min up to 330°C, 5 min isothermal, cool down to initial conditions. The ion source should be turned off during the solvent delay.
6. Detect metabolites by setting the ion source filament energy to 70 eV. Scan a mass range of at least 83–500 Da, or 40–500 Da, if low mass-to-charge (*m/z*) fragment ions are to be recorded. At least two scans per second should be recorded in full-scan mode.
7. Transfer raw GC–MS profile chromatograms to a server station.

3.5. Data Analysis (see Note 5)

1. For raw data processing, use appropriate software. First choice is the GC–MS manufacturer's software (**Fig. 1**). For general quadrupole mass spectrometers, data deconvolution by the freely available software AMDIS is recommended (http://chemdata.nist.gov/mass-spc/amdis) (*4*).
2. For TOF instruments, LECO's ChromaTOF software is superior (v2.25 and higher). Define target peaks that are to be included in the metabolite profiles.
3. Define optimal peak-finding thresholds and quantification ion traces for each target compound. Peak identifications have to be carried out by matching retention indices and mass spectral similarity against a user-defined metabolite library.
4. Quantify metabolite peaks by area of target ion traces. Export result peak tables of all chromatograms to a database or a PC office table calculation software (e.g., MS Excel 2000).
5. Organize peak area results in a matrix of metabolites vs chromatograms.

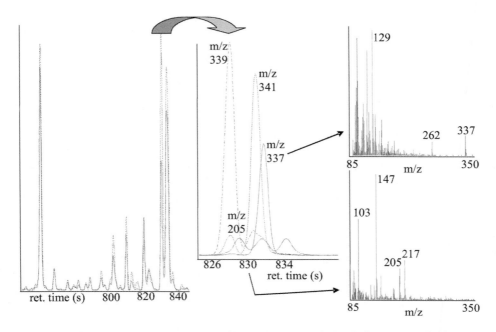

Fig. 1. Mass spectral deconvolution for comparison of blood plasma metabolite profiles. (Left panel) total ion chromatogram (TIC) overlay of two profiles revealing differences in regulation. (Middle panel) enlarged view of ion trace chromatograms for dotted TIC blood profile. (Right panel) spectra are automatically deconvoluted despite dense coelution of stearic (*m/z* 341), oleic (*m/z* 339), and linoleic acid (*m/z* 337), even for low abundant compounds like an unknown sugar alcohol at 829 s (*m/z* 205).

6. Count the number of detected metabolites per chromatogram. In case one or a few chromatograms show an unexplainable large deviation in the number of detected peaks, check the chromatograms visually and delete them from the resulting table.

7. For each target metabolite, count the number of chromatograms in which the metabolite could be positively identified. In case one or a few metabolites show an unexplainable large deviation in the number of positive peak findings, check the chromatograms visually, especially for the thresholds that were used for peak finding. Delete the metabolites from the resulting table that have lots of negative peak findings (missing values).

8. For each chromatogram, divide all peak areas by the area of the internal standard (e.g., U-^{13}C-sorbitol) and the sample weight. Log10 transform all data to down weight outliers and ensure a more Gaussian-type frequency distribution.

9. Calculate univariate statistics (e.g., *t*-test in Excel, ANOVA in MATLAB®).

10. Calculate multivariate statistics. Often, such calculations do not accommodate missing values for metabolites so suitable strategies must be employed for

dealing with such occurrences. The results of multivariate statistics from two strategies have to be compared: (1) calculations that were carried out on all metabolites that had no missing values. (2) Calculations that were carried on all metabolites after replacement of missing values.

4. Notes

1. Blood plasma collection: metabolite profiling starts with the experimental design of the study. It is a rather inexpensive technique compared to proteomics or transcript expression analysis. Therefore, larger numbers of individual analyses can be carried out allowing rigid statistical assessments of the quantitative results. This allows the adequate addressing of the issue of natural biological variability, which usually contributes more to the standard deviation of metabolite mean levels than technical errors. Especially for human blood plasma, the individuality of samples must not been neglected. In this respect, the first issue to consider is the accurate description of blood donors with respect to underlying metadata, most importantly the fasting state. Without such well-defined metadata, no interpretation of metabolic levels will be possible. Depending on the biological question underlying a study, pooling strategies may be designed to counteract this variability.

   Proteins in full blood will coagulate quickly by clotting factors, so it is of utmost importance to stop coagulation by complexation with EDTA (or other chemicals). There are protocols using coagulated and centrifuged blood, however, the process of coagulation is uncontrollable and coprecipitation of metabolites seems unavoidable. Blood plasma further contains metabolically active cells, therefore, cells need to be quickly centrifuged out to preserve the metabolic state at sampling time.

2. Extraction and protein precipitation: many protocols exist for protein precipitation, mostly with chilled (−15 to −40°C) organic solvents. If solvents are used that are water miscible, this mixture may not only precipitate proteins but concurrently extract metabolites. No comprehensive test has been published so far that tests a multitude of solvents and mixtures with the objective to quantitatively extract an array of different metabolites of different classes. Therefore, the solvent composition given in this chapter has been validated only for the mixtures that have been tested in the author's laboratory after thorough experimental design, but is likely not the final solution for this task. Ultimately the idea of metabolomics has to be kept in mind that demands for ruggedness, precision, and comprehensiveness (for various chemical classes) rather than accuracy for any given target molecule.

   It is important that for any solvent mixture both the chilling temperature and the solvent:sample ratio must be followed. We suggest that the latter ratio should always be larger than 10:1. Another important point is the working time needed per sample, especially when a multitude of samples is to be handled like in cohort studies. For example, it might be tried to re-extract the protein precipitate pellet two or three times. However, more time would be needed per sample and it does not seem very likely to extract relevant amounts of soluble metabolites from such a condensed pellet. With the single extraction/precipitation method suggested here, repeatability was found to be around 20% CV for most compounds. The high water content in blood plasma renders it unnecessary to add further water for polar compounds (such as glucose) to the mixture; however, when chloroform was added both recovery and precision declined dramatically. In addition to stopping enzymatic activity by cold temperatures and protein coagulation, avoiding oxidation is necessary. Solvents will contain huge amounts of oxygen if they are not degassed by vacuum/ultrasonicator or by bubbling inert gases through it (argon or nitrogen are most convenient). If deoxygenation is performed by gas exchange, great care must be taken to use ultrapure gases and clean bubble tips (e.g., rinsed Pasteur pipets). It is somewhat less important to avoid light; some metabolites, such as catecholamines, will decompose if exposed to light for too long. In initial method development, no difference was found for blood samples that were strictly kept in the dark throughout the sample preparation and samples that were handled under regular laboratory conditions. We generally recommend to specifically care for reactive metabolites such as cysteine, the ratio of ascorbate/dehydroascorbate, and tocopherol. Loss of (low abundant) organic phosphates points to inappropriate sample handling causing partial enzymatic activity. Classical compounds, such as glucose and cholesterol, will always be the dominant metabolites in blood profiles because these metabolites also mark different metabolic pathways, and octanol/water partition coefficients can be used as important marker compounds for assessing general reproducibility. If extracts are concentrated to complete dryness in a speed vacuum concentrator, caution should be taken to avoid sample losses, spilling, or cross-contamination owing to boiling retardation. For this reason extracts need be dried with punctured plastic tube caps.

3. Derivatization: during derivatization, access of moisture to the reaction solution must be totally avoided. The amount of water during the silylation reaction can be assessed by the occurrence and abundance of polysiloxanes which are degradation (hydrolysis) products of the reactant MSTFA. Polysiloxanes are recognized by their typical spectra with abundant ions m/z 221 and m/z 281. We have not found it to be necessary to perform the derivatization in a dry atmosphere. The most likely step to reload significant amounts of water is when samples are opened too early after cold storage, which would cause severe water condensation. For the same reason we do not recommend storing samples longer than 48 h, and even if this is needed they must not be stored in the cold but just kept dark. Reanalysis of samples that have already been injected into the GC–MS does not result in reproducible data, most likely again a result of air (moisture) access after punctuation of the vial septa. Temperatures and times of derivatization steps can be kept flexible because they present a compromise between completeness of reaction, time, and efforts needed to perform the reactions, and breakdown of certain compounds (e.g., chemical conversion of glutamine to oxoproline). The basic and apolar solvent pyridine serves as a catalyst in the methoximation procedure, which is used to avoid sugar ring cyclization. Generally it has been proven

Table 1
Injector Program for Direct Thermal Desorption

Method name	DTD-analysis	DTD-deactivation
Method type	Splitless	Split
Equilibration time (s)	5	5
End time (s)	1440	470
Initial temperature (°C)	45	85
Ramp rate (°C/s)	4.0	50.0
Final temperature (°C)	290	340
Temperature control	Keep current temperature	Keep current temperature
Solvent cooling effect	No	No
Cooling valve mode	No	No
Transfer column flow (mL/min)	2.0	2.0
Transfer time (s)	150	0
Initial column flow (mL/min)	2.0	2.0
Final column flow (mL/min)	2.0	2.0
Split flow (mL/min)	50	—
Vent mode	—	Fixed time
Vent time	—	0
Vent flow (mL/min)	—	150

as the most suitable solvent for this purpose, however, if ATAS direct thermo-desorption liners are used, dicarboxylic acids were found to be highly uncontrollable and irreproducible. Instead dimethylformamide (DMF) can be used, however, the volume ratio of DMF to the silylation agent MSTFA must be strictly kept at ≤1:20.

4. GC–MS: the most critical part of GC–MS is largely unknown to many people. It is neither the gas chromatograph nor the mass spectrometer *(5)*, but in greater than 80% of cases it is the injection process, especially if full extract metabolomics is aimed for (such as suggested in this protocol). Sample cross contamination of lipids is basically unavoidable with standard split/splitless liners. Because lipids, such as sterols and arachidonic acid, are presumed to have high indicative values for diseases, the integration of polar and lipophilic components seems to be highly advantageous. For this reason this proposal suggests an automatic liner exchange, for example by ATAS' direct thermodesorption unit. Specialized (large volume) glass liners with small inserted microvials are used herein. Samples are then injected in the cold and flash heated so that only volatile compounds will reach the surfaces of the liner and injector body before eventually getting refocused at the GC column start. We have found that peak shapes for low-boiling compounds are hard to control with these liners, however, with the gas flow, injection volumes, and heat rates given in **Table 1**, acceptable reproducibilities can be achieved.

These ratios have been found optimal for a combination of a CTC Twin-Pal dual robotic autosampler with direct thermodesorption/Optic3 injector unit (ATAS GL, Zoetermeer, NL) and an Agilent 6890 GC oven. Other conditions may be found suitable for similar equipment purchased from other vendors. Care has to be taken that liner caps are tight; caps should be hardly movable by hand in order to avoid gas or humidity exchange during storage, and to avoid evaporation of reagents during derivatization. Take out desiccated samples in glass vials, crimped with magnetic caps, from store. Do not open samples or punch septa. Most of the DTD failures are because of skewed caps. Exclusively close liners with an electric crimper device prove that the microliner faces the liner top with its opening upside. When placing the liners into the multilinker tray, turn them around one full turn to see whether any crimp cap is skewed. A second test for a straight horizontal cap is to hang it onto the magnetic liner displacement arm.

Actual GC–MS run conditions may be found to be adjustable; however, we found use of a 35% phenyl-coated fused silica capillary column of 30-m length, 0.32-mm I.D., and 0.25-μm film thickness to be more reproducible than standard 5 or 50% coatings.

In addition to these parameters, high scrutiny in maintenance and QC checks is proposed.

The following rules can serve as guidelines or parts of Standard Operation Procedures in GC–MS:

a. Read the log file from the last 24 h to check for hardware error messages or autotune/calibration problems. No injections are performed before hardware errors are removed. Copy/paste log file and sample log readings into the corresponding Excel sheets, and save files.

b. Before each large sample sequence run mass calibrations.

c. Vacuum pump air filters are cleaned if there is an unpleasant odor.

d. Vacuum oil pump maintenance: check oil level, color, and viscosity quarterly.

e. If a gas leakage is suspected, all connections and gas lines are to be checked using a gas leakage detector.

f. O-rings for liners, filters for injector tubings, injector gold plates, filaments, and other replacement parts are exchanged if necessary, i.e., once lower intervention limits in corresponding QC charts are violated.

g. Exchange GC column to 10-m DB5 column (0.18-mm I.D., 0.18-μm film thickness), inject and record signal-to-noise ratios for a hexachlorobenzene standard if all intervention measures (specifically filament change) have not restored the "in-control" status. If QC still reports the instrument to be out of control, report findings and call GC–MS technicians for detector replacement after consulting the supervising scientist.

h. Use a QC standard mixture composed of compounds of different chemical properties and classes. Inject a dilution series of 10, 30, 50, 100% of the mix in splitless and split 1:3 mode. After QC injections, reagent blank and method blank control injections are carried out. The splitless 100% QC injection is evaluated right after the run. No sample injection is performed if the upper or lower intervention limits are violated.

   i. Check for peak shape and occurrence of double peaks for low boiling point (early eluting) compounds. If peak width is larger than 6 s with deteriorated peak shape ("mountain-like"), stop injection of samples and clean the direct thermodesorption injector port. Check for peak shape and detectability for high boiling point (last eluting) compounds at 100% QC splitless injection. If these are undetectable (S/N < 10), stop all further injections, disconnect, and cut GC column by 10 cm. Readjust the total length of the column for gas flow calculations in the GC–MS software.

   j. Randomize the injection sequence with respect to classes of your biological question/experimental design in order not to compromise later statistical analysis.

It is generally suggested to refer to retention indices instead of retention times. Retention indices are calculated from retention times of internal marker peaks; usually alkanes are added to the samples to serve as retention anchor points, however, in principle other peaks can also be used. In the protocol previously presented, an unusual scan range of 85–500 Da is proposed for mass spectrometric detection. Reasons for this choice are found in the properties of silylated compounds, which often have characteristic ions between 100 and 370 Da. Additionally, at m/z 79, bleeding of pyridine may infer mass spectra of low-boiling compounds. For almost all peaks, m/z 73 is the most abundant ion — although this is helpful that for lower limits of detection for pure compounds, m/z 73 does not have any selectivity power in metabolic profiles.

5. Data analysis: some metabolomic laboratories have missed the importance of data analysis as part of the process. This process includes raw data cleaning, alignment, reporting, and primary statistical analysis. Standard software of the leading MS vendors does not include a suitable data deconvolution software that alone can ensure valid peak identification in high-throughput routine operations. This is especially important for low abundant metabolites that might coelute with abundant major peaks (**Fig. 1**). As a general solution, we here propose use of AMDIS (www.nist.gov). However, we regard the integrated deconvolution software of Leco Corp. to be more dedicated for complex samples. In any of these two software packages, model ions will be determined that best describe the presence of a peak in its local environment, e.g., next to a coeluting abundant metabolite. Such model ions may serve as a valid default choice for calculating peak areas from ion traces (**Fig. 2**). Defining thresholds for peak finding is more delicate if the thresholds for mass spectrum matching, retention index windows, abundance, and peak widths are set too high. A lot of peaks will not be taken as metabolite targets, although these are actually present in the chromatograms. Such instances are called false-negatives and would result in missing values in the resulting experiment data matrix. However, if these thresholds are set too low, peaks might be falsely taken as true target metabolites, although these are actually absent from the chromatograms (false-positives). The only way to rem-

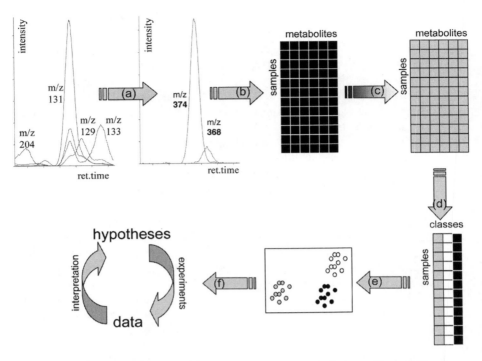

Fig. 2. Data analysis flowchart after mass spectrometric recording of blood profiles. (**A**) Select optimal quantifier ions. (**B**) Export peak areas or peak heights from multiple samples to receive a data matrix. (**C**) Normalize and transform data by, e.g., vector normalization or z-transformation. (**D**) Structure data according to "hypotheses" or background data such as "survival rate." (**E**) Get significance and hidden data structures by univariate and multivariate statistics. (**F**) Interpret findings, generate new hypotheses, and verify new hypotheses by better experiments.

edy this situation is to store as much mass spectral metadata as possible to allow other research to verify peak identification claims.

After compiling a result data matrix, statistical analysis will need to be performed to test that actual results are interpretable. Certain multivariate tools will require that there are no missing values, which might be caused by either false- or true-negatives. This cannot be decided without manual chromatogram investigation, a task that is hardly doable in high-throughput metabolomics. Therefore, mock up data will be needed to fill these "missing values," but great care must be taken that these mock up values do not skew or bias the statistical analysis. For example, all statistical routines may be performed by several means to replace "missing values," e.g., by zeroes, arithmetic averages, random generated numbers, or others. If a given metabolite is not positively detected in 0–20% of all samples of a given experimental design class, it may be suspected that it is indeed not present in this class. In this case, entering half of the detection limit might be a sensible way. In any case, the means to replace missing values need be detailed when reporting such data to the scientific community. Usually such data matrices are further transformed to ensure better data homogeneity and adequacy for statistical analyses (**Fig. 2**). Among others, z-transformations are used to normalize all data-to-unit variances around zero means. We further suggest a log of 10 transformation in order to down weigh outliers and to transform the data matrix into a more Gaussian-type distribution. Similar logarithmic transformations are also used when analyzing transcriptomic data. In any case, data need to be retransformed when x-fold average values are to be computed, e.g., in comparisons of blood plasma samples of healthy vs diseased individuals. For any interpretation of these univariate or multivariate statistical tests, samples need to have a clear description by biological metadata describing the actual experimental design, otherwise no novel hypotheses can be generated. Data without metadata are irrelevant.

Acknowledgments

Blood plasma samples were provided by Dr. Joachim Spranger, German Institute for Human Nutrition (DIfE), Potsdam-Rehbruecke, Germany. This work was funded by the Max-Planck Society and the German Ministry of Education and Research (BMBF), BioProfile Nutrigenomics Berlin/Brandenburg, BMBF project number 0313036C.

References

1. Fiehn, O. (2002) Metabolomics: the link between genotypes and phenotypes. *Plant Mol. Biol.* **48,** 155–171.
2. Krull, I. S. and Swartz, M. (1999) Analytical method development and validation for the academic researcher. *Anal. Lett.* **32,** 1067–1080.
3. Weckwerth, W., Wenzel, K., and Fiehn, O. (2004) Process for the integrated extraction, identification and quantification of metabolites, proteins and RNA to reveal their co-regulation in biochemical networks. *Proteomics* **4,** 78–83.
4. Stein, S. E. (1999) An integrated method for spectrum extraction and compound identification from gas chromatography/mass spectrometry data. *J. Am. Soc. Mass. Spectrom.* **10,** 770–781.
5. Oehme, M. (1998) *Practical Introduction to GC-MS Analysis With Quadrupoles,* 1st Ed. Hüthig, Heidelberg, Germany.

2

Nonsupervised Construction and Application of Mass Spectral and Retention Time Index Libraries From Time-of-Flight Gas Chromatography–Mass Spectrometry Metabolite Profiles

Alexander Erban, Nicolas Schauer,
Alisdair R. Fernie, and Joachim Kopka

Summary

Gas chromatography–mass spectrometry (GC–MS) is routinely applied to the metabolite profiling of biological samples. Time-of-flight (TOF)-GC–MS metabolite profiling is based on highly reproducible electron impact ionization. Single chromatograms may comprise 200–1000 mass spectral components. The nature and composition of these mass spectral components depend on the choice of metabolite extraction, type of biological sample, and experimental condition. The components represent mass spectral tags (MSTs) of volatile metabolites or metabolite derivatives. Identification of MSTs is the major challenge in GC–MS metabolite profiling. We describe methods suitable for the automated construction of mass spectral and retention time index databases from large sets of TOF-GC–MS profiles. Application of these libraries for automated identification by pure reference compounds and classification of hitherto unidentified MSTs from biological sources is demonstrated.

Key Words: Metabolite profiling; electron impact ionization; time-of-flight GC–MS; mass spectral matching; retention time index; metabolite classification.

1. Introduction

One of the major challenges in gas chromatography–mass spectrometry (GC–MS)-based metabolite profiling is the identification of the multitude of hitherto

From: *Methods in Molecular Biology, vol. 358: Metabolomics: Methods and Protocols*
Edited by: W. Weckwerth © Humana Press Inc., Totowa, NJ

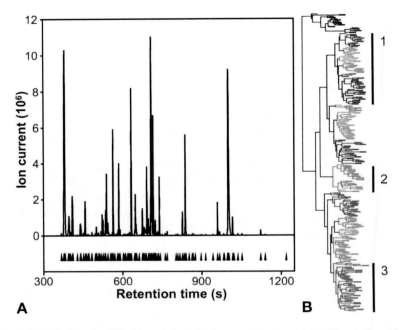

Fig. 1. Metabolite profile of an intercellular yeast extract (**A**). Tics below the chromatogram trace indicate positions of automated deconvolutions of mass spectra. Mass spectral components obtained from yeast metabolite profiles were clustered with mass spectra of pure reference metabolites (**B**). Major clusters represent (1) sugars, polyols, and polyhydroxy acids, (2) phosphorylated compounds, and (3) amino acids.

unidentified metabolic components from extracts of diverse biological samples *(1,2)*. Automated deconvolution of single GC–MS chromatograms generates hundreds of mass spectral tags (MSTs) (**Fig. 1**). MSTs were previously defined as mass spectra of metabolites or metabolite derivatives *(3,4)*, which can be unambiguously identified by mass abundance or fragment composition and chromatographic retention behavior. As a rule of thumb, less than 30–40% of the detected MSTs can currently be linked to known metabolites. Unidentified MSTs are not necessarily artifacts of the GC–MS profiling technology. These MSTs can be shown to represent metabolites by in vivo labeling of organisms with stable isotopes, for example, labeling of microbial cultures by U-^{13}C-glucose *(5)* or feeding of $^{13}CO_2$ to photoautotrophic organisms. Thus, efforts to identify MSTs will be crucial for the further development and general applicability of GC–MS-based metabolite profiling *(1–3)*.

Identification of MSTs is performed through two complementary approaches. The "top down" approach whereby metabolite identities are unravelled by taking, for example, a single MST of interest and establishing its structure through stepwise purification and complete structural elucidation. This approach is highly time consuming. "Top down" identification is only recommended if the biological function of the unknown MST is clearly established and if the importance of the hitherto unknown metabolite justifies the task. The second, i.e., "bottom up," approach in which metabolites of interest to a particular researcher are analyzed by the purchase or synthesis of authentic standards is certainly less time demanding and, thus, appears to be more efficient. Identification is easily performed through standard addition experiments of pure reference compounds *(6–9)*. Both mass spectral matching and cochromatography can routinely be established in different laboratories and can thus meet the general prerequisites of unambiguous chemical identification *(3)*. In summary, metabolite identification can be repeated with all GC–MS equipment and is easy to cross-validate between many laboratories across the world.

We describe a largely automated method for the highly reproducible generation of MSTs and mass spectral/retention time index (MSRI) libraries. The method is designed to suppress artifacts of chemical derivatization by timed and automated in-line derivatization of metabolic extracts. Furthermore, the high degree of automation supports increased reproducibility of retention time behavior, as determined by Kovàts' retention time indices (RI) *(10)*. In parallel, mass spectral characteristics are quality controlled by in-build auto-tuning routines of the time-of-flight (TOF)-GC–MS system *(11)*.

The availability of curated MSRI libraries as well as nonsupervised MSRI libraries, i.e., automated generation of MST compendia from well characterized and defined biological samples, facilitates identification of metabolites in diverse biological samples *(3,12)* and integrates use of commercially available mass spectral libraries *(13,14)*, which lack retention time characteristics. The aim of this method description is to enable mass spectral library searches with single bait mass spectra of a reference substance that allow clear identification by mass spectral match and RI **(Fig. 2)**. Moreover, the hit lists of these mass spectral searches are utilized to discover candidate component MSTs of highly similar chemical nature as compared with the bait and, thus, facilitate classification of as yet unidentified MSTs **(Fig. 3)**.

2. Materials
2.1. Sampling and Metabolite Extraction

1. Methanol gradient grade for liquid chromatography (Merck, Darmstadt, Germany; cat. no. CAS 67-56-1).
2. Chloroform for liquid chromatography (Merck; cat. no. CAS 67-66-3).
3. Bidistilled water approx 0.055 µS/cm (USF Deutschland GmbH, Ransbach-Baumbach, Germany; cat. no. USF 800).

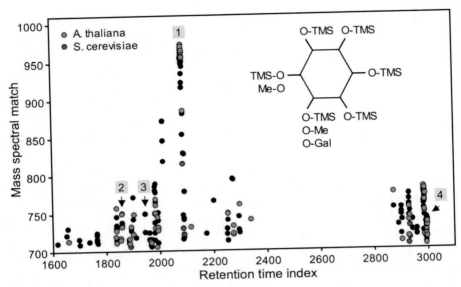

Fig. 2. Mass spectral hit list of myo-inositol (6TMS). Identified mass spectral tags were (1) myo-inositol (6TMS), (2) 3-*O*-methyl-D-chiro-inositol (5TMS), (3) 4-*O*-methyl-myo-inositol (5TMS), and (4) α-D-galactopyranose-(1,3)-myo-inositol (9TMS). Occurrence in *Arabidopsis thaliana* and *Saccharomyces cerevisiae* is color coded. Mass spectral matching was performed without limits or constraints.

4. Ribitol (Sigma, Munich, Germany; cat. no. CAS 488-81-3).
5. DL-Alanine, 2,3,3,3-d$_4$ (Sigma; cat. no. CAS 53795-92-9).
6. D(−)-Isoascorbic acid (Sigma; cat. no. CAS 89-65-6).
7. Methyl nonadecanoate (Sigma; cat. no. CAS 1731-94-8).
8. 1.5-mL Safe-lock, tapered-bottom microvial (Eppendorf, Hamburg, Germany).
9. 2.0-mL Safe-lock, round-bottom microvial (Eppendorf).
10. Microcentrifuge 5417 (Eppendorf).
11. Oscillating ball mill MM200 (Retsch GmbH and Co. KG, Haan, Germany).
12. Teflon adaptor for 1.5- to 2.0-mL microvials (Retsch GmbH and Co. KG).
13. VA 5-mm steel balls (Th. Geyer Berlin GmbH, Berlin, Germany).
14. VR Maxi standalone vacuum concentrator with rotors R96-13 and R120-111 (Jouan Nordic, Allerod, Denmark).
15. HBP hold-back vacuum pump (Ilmvac GmbH, Ilmenau, Germany).
16. Polystat K6-1 cycling thermostat (P. Huber GmbH, Offenburg, Germany).
17. 15- and 50-mL plastic tubes with screw caps (Falcon™ Conical Centrifuge Tubes, BD Biosciences, San Jose, CA).
18. Orange silica gel (Carl Roth GmbH, Karlsruhe, Germany; cat. no. 77.1).
19. Argon 5.0 (Messer-Griesheim GmbH, Krefeld, Germany).

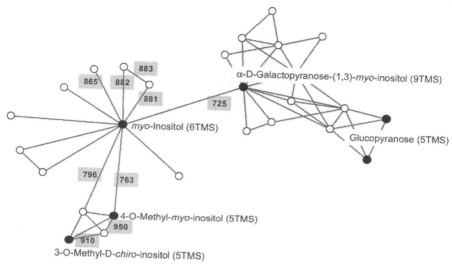

Fig. 3. Proximity map of a search for mass spectral similarity among identified and unidentified mass spectral tags from GC–MS profiles of biological sources. The search was initiated at myo-inositol (6TMS). Open circles represent hitherto unclassified mass spectra, and connecting edges represent best mass spectral match as partially indicated in shaded boxes. Mass spectral matching was performed in the mass range, *m/z* 85–600, with minimum abundance set to 50.

2.2. Chemical Derivatization

1. CTC Combi PAL autosampler and PAL cycle composer software v1.5.0 (CTC Analytics AG, Zwingen, Switzerland). The chosen configuration comprises an agitator–incubator oven, a 98-sample tray for 2.0-mL vials, a 32-sample tray for 10- to 20-mL vials, three 100-mL solvent reservoirs, i.e., a syringe wash station, and a liquid version 25-µL syringe kit mounted to the robotic autosampler arm.
2. Methoxyamination reagent: methoxyamine hydrochloride (Sigma; cat. no. CAS 593-56-6) is dissolved at 20 mg/mL in pure pyridine (Merck; cat. no. CAS 110-86-1). This reagent is prepared immediately before analysis in 1-mL aliquots and loaded into the first reagent reservoir of the CTC Combi PAL autosampler (*see* **Note 1**).
3. Per-silylation reagent: 1-mL vials of *N*-methyl-*N*-(trimethylsilyl)trifluoroacetamide (MSTFA; Macherey and Nagel, Düren, Germany; cat. no. CAS 24589-78-4) is loaded into the second reagent reservoir (*see* **Note 1**).
4. Solvents for syringe washes were *n*-hexane (Fisher-Scientific GmbH, Schwerte, Germany; cat. no. CAS 110-54-3) and ethylacetate (Merck; cat. no. CAS 141-78-6).
5. RI standard mixture: *n*-alkanes are dissolved in pyridine (Merck; cat. no. CAS 110-86-1) at a final concentration of 0.22 mg/mL each and loaded into the agitator–incubator oven of the CTC Combi PAL autosampler (*see* **Note 2**). The following

substances are combined: *n*-decane (RI 1000; cat. no. CAS 124-18-5), *n*-dodecane (RI 1200; cat. no. CAS 112-40-3), *n*-pentadecane (RI 1500; cat. no. CAS 629-62-9), *n*-octadecane (RI 1800; cat. no. CAS 593-45-3), *n*-nonadecane (RI 1900; cat. no. CAS 629-92-5), *n*-docosane (RI 2200; cat. no. CAS 629-97-0), *n*-octacosane (RI 2800; cat. no. CAS 630-02-4), *n*-dotriacontane (RI 3200; cat. no. CAS 544-85-4), and *n*-hexatriacontane (RI 3600; cat. no. CAS 630-06-8). All substances were obtained from Sigma.

6. 1.1 CTVG crimp-cap vial (Chromacol, Trumbull, CT).
7. R11-Sil-r/w magnetic crimp cap (CS-Chromatography Service GmbH, Langerwehe, Germany).
8. Adjustable 11-mm crimp-cap sealer (Supelco, Munich, Germany).

2.3. TOF-GC–MS

1. Pegasus III TOF mass spectrometer (LECO Instrumente GmbH, Mönchengladbach, Germany).
2. Agilent 6890N gas chromatograph, split/splitless injector with electronic pressure control up to 150 psi (Agilent, Böblingen, Germany).
3. Conical single taper split/less liner with glass wool (Agilent), deactivation reagent (DMDCS, Restek GmbH, Bad Homburg, Germany), toluene (Sigma; cat. no. CAS 108-88-3), methanol (Merck; cat. no. CAS 67-56-1) (*see* **Note 3**), 7-mL glass tubes (cat. no. 23 175 11 59) with screw caps (cat. no. 29 990 12 04) (Schott, Mainz, Germany).
4. Precolumn (Restek GmbH) or VF-5ms capillary column, 30-m length, 0.25-mm inner diameter, 0.25-μm film thickness, and a 10-m EZ-guard precolumn (Varian Inc., Lake Forest, CA).
5. Helium 5.0 carrier gas (Air Liquide, Magdeburg, Germany).

2.4. GC–MS Data Processing

1. ChromaTOF chromatography processing and mass spectral deconvolution software, v1.00, driver 1.61 (LECO Instrumente GmbH).
2. Automated mass spectral deconvolution and identification system AMDIS (National Institute of Standards and Technology [NIST], Gaithersburg, MD).
3. NIST mass spectral search and comparison software v2.0 (NIST).
4. Microsoft Office Word 2003 (Microsoft Corporation), Excel 2003 (Microsoft Corporation), software package for exploratory data analysis and statistical modelling, S-Plus 2000 standard edition release 3 (Insightful, Berlin, Germany).

3. Methods

Metabolite turnover is extremely rapid as compared to mRNA or protein turnover. Analysis of metabolite composition and changes in pool sizes, therefore, requires fast and reproducible metabolic inactivation. Samples are best shock-frozen and kept below –60°C until extraction. Maintenance of metabolic inactivation during extraction and workup procedures is essential for a robust and repeatable representation of *in situ* metabolite composition *(15)*. We describe two exemplary protocols of metabolite extraction from plant material and liquid microbial cultures. We are fully aware that the choice of metabolic inactivation and extraction protocol may influence and indeed determine the scope of metabolites that can be monitored by subsequent metabolite profiling. Variations of extraction protocols may be pursued to broaden the spectrum of metabolites that are accessible to metabolite profiling (*see* **Note 4**) or to perform integrated analyses of metabolome, proteome, and transcriptome *(16)* (*see* Chapter 5).

The essence of metabolite profiling is discovery of novel marker metabolites and determination of relative changes of metabolite pool sizes in comparison to reference samples *(1,2)*. This approach necessitates thorough control experiments, monitoring of GC–MS system performance, and check of laboratory contaminations, which may arise from solvent and reagent impurities or leakage of vial and septum material. For these reasons, nonsample control experiments are indispensable. All chemicals and containers need to be of the highest available purity. Please consider that autoclaved material, although sterile, may nevertheless be chemically contaminated.

3.1. Experimental Design and Preparation of Samples for Metabolite Profiling

Make sure to include a set of nontreated control samples in each experiment and analysis. For a large series of analyses prepare and store a large batch of reference material. Take an additional set of control samples from this batch of reference material for each subset of analyses. Results from this reference material allow the experimenter to control for day-to-day and week-to-week variability. Thus, discovery of marker metabolites and relative changes in metabolite levels can be distinguished from accidental contaminations or changes in instrumental sensitivity.

Provide at least 6 (better 8–16) replicate samples of each experimental condition. Perform replications at the level of individual plants or cell cultures rather than repeating assays of the same sample *(6–9,15)*. Pooling of samples from a set of plants or cell cultures and repeated analyses of this pool is advised when sample size is small. Analysis of sample pools, however, is less informative with respect to the underlying variability inherent to the experiment and nature of biological samples.

3.1.1. Metabolic Inactivation and Extraction of Plant Material

1. Shock-freeze plant material in liquid nitrogen and keep below –60°C throughout processing. Use precooled 2.0-mL safe-lock microvials or wrap samples in precooled aluminium foil. Store either in liquid nitrogen or at –80°C until further processing. The amount of required sample may vary depending on species and plant organ. Always perform test analyses when analyzing previously unknown

samples or novel experimental conditions. The following protocol describes a typical analysis that is optimized for 60-mg fresh weight (±5–10%) of dicot leaves. Monocot leaves or root material may require more material (factor 2–4), whereas storage organs, flowers, or cold-stressed material may be performed with smaller amounts (factor 0.1–0.5). The optimum sample load is best determined by adjusting the major metabolic components to the upper detection limit of GC–MS, while still avoiding peak overload (*see* **Subheading 3.4.**).

2. The preparation of representative aliquots from large samples, greater than 125 mg (fresh weight), requires homogenization using a precooled mortar and pestle and subsequent generation of small aliquots of the desired amount of material. Keep samples in liquid nitrogen throughout the process. Avoid condensing ice and be careful not to spill the final powder by boiling liquid nitrogen. The powder may be stored in liquid nitrogen or in a –80°C freezer using screw-cap or safe-lock vials. Be careful to evaporate residual liquid nitrogen at –80°C before caps are sealed.

3. Small samples, 5–125 mg (fresh weight), are homogenized using steel balls that fit into 2.0-mL round-bottom microvials. Sets of 5–10 microvials are mounted onto an oscillating ball mill and exposed to two 3-min bursts at 15/s frequency. Steel balls, microvials, and the mounting adaptor need to be precooled in liquid nitrogen. Homogenized samples are extracted within microvials without removal of the steel balls. Sample weight is best determined after shock-freezing. Differential weighing of frozen powder or nonhomogenized material can be performed in cooled 2.0-mL microvials before adding steel balls. Avoid high air humidity and use dry ice for cooling to obtain stable zero point calibration.

4. Take frozen 2.0-mL microvials with homogenized samples from the freezer and add 360 μL of extraction mixture (*see* **Notes 5** and **6**). The extraction mixture needs to be precooled to –20°C and is best degassed by bubbling argon or nitrogen gas. Use an oil filter between gas supply and high-performance liquid chromatography bubbling device. Shake samples thoroughly using a vortex mixer and keep on ice until all samples are processed.

5. Shake all samples simultaneously for 15 min at 70°C and subsequently cool to room temperature. Solvent evaporation may generate excess pressure. Vent microvials after a 1-min incubation at 70°C and reclose vials thoroughly.

6. Add 200 μL $CHCl_3$, shake thoroughly using a vortex mixer, and incubate at 37°C.

7. Add 400 μL H_2O to induce phase separation, shake thoroughly using a vortex mixer, and separate liquid and solid phases in a microcentrifuge for 5 min at approx 22,000g. Addition of H_2O may be omitted for a joined analysis of the lipophilic and polar metabolic complement of the sample.

8. Take a 10-μL aliquot of the upper phase, which contains the polar metabolic complement of the sample, and transfer into a crimp cap-tapered glass vial suitable for GC–MS analyses (*see* **Note 7**). In the following, we describe automated analysis of 10 μL of the polar or a combined liquid extract. In case of manual processing, 1.5–2.0 mL safe-lock microvials may be used to dry, transport, and store metabolic extracts (*see* **Subheading 3.2.**). For analysis of the lipophilic

metabolic complement, take a 100-μL aliquot of the lower liquid phase and process manually. The analysis of the lipophilic complement induces strong chromatographic memory effects and is not recommended for high-throughput split or splitless GC–MS injection.

9. Dry 10-μL samples in a vacuum concentrator for a minimum of 2 h at room temperature or lyophilize larger sample volumes overnight.

3.1.2. Metabolic Inactivation and Extraction of Yeast Liquid Cultures

The major challenge in metabolite profiling of microbial cultures is the separation of intracellular metabolites from secreted metabolites and residual components of liquid growth media, the so-called footprint, while rapidly inactivating metabolism during sampling. Typically, cell suspensions are rapidly sprayed into precooled polar organic solvents, such as methanol, which dilute the media and shock-freeze the cells *(17–19)*. We recommend growth media spiked with nonmetabolized low molecular weight compounds for the control of residual liquid medium, which is unavoidably trapped in the cellular periplasm. In the case of yeast we successfully used lactose, which cannot be utilized by yeast, at 1–10% (w/w) concentration of the major carbon source in the growth medium. We furthermore suggest use of synthetic-defined growth media (SD) instead of complex media. Complex media contain numerous compounds in high concentrations. These substances will obscure intracellular metabolites even in cases of only small medium contaminations.

1. Prepare 5-mL yeast batch cultures in SD medium and time the sampling to the late logarithmic or to the stationary growth phase ($OD_{595} = 1.8$). Follow general recommendations for yeast growth *(17–19)*. Make sure to prepare noninoculated samples for nonsample control of the experiments. Avoid unwanted chemical contaminations of the liquid cultures. Sterilized glassware and media are devoid of microbial contaminations but might nevertheless have received chemical deposits from the autoclave. Media components may decompose while exposed to high temperatures.

2. Sample the complete culture at routine growth temperature, 28°C, by rapid decanting or use temperature equilibrated disposable pipet tips for sampling 5-mL aliquots from larger batches. Avoid slow temperature changes before sampling. Continue to agitate batch cultures until sampling. Thus, sedimentation of cells and changes in mechanical stress are circumvented.

3. Rapidly mix 5 mL medium with 20 mL precooled 60% methanol, methanol:water, 6:4 (v/v). 60% methanol is best prepared as a large batch and partitioned into 50-mL screw-cap plastic tubes, which are kept before and after sampling in a methanol/dry ice bath at approx –60°C.

4. Spin down cells no longer than 5 min at approx 3200g in a temperature-controlled centrifuge preset to –20°C.

5. Immediately after centrifugation, collect plastic tubes into the methanol/dry ice bath. Decant supernatant cautiously and perform an optional gentle rinse with a

small volume of precooled 60% methanol. During temperature adjustment the supernatant might get slightly turbid but should not freeze solid.

The following steps can be downscaled according to the initial concentration of cells in suspension culture as determined by OD_{595} of diluted samples. The following volumes are as required for a 5-mL culture of $OD_{595} = 1.8$.

6. Add 374 μL extraction mixture for yeast intercellular metabolites immediately (*see* **Note 8**). The extraction mixture needs to be precooled to −20°C and is best degassed (*see* **steps 4** and **5**). At this step the cells should easily resuspend. If cells form a semi-solid viscous pellet, the temperature control was inadequate for metabolite profiles and needs to be optimized. Critical steps are centrifugation and time between decanting of the supernatant and resuspension into the extraction mixture. Slightly viscous yeast pellets may be resuspended in small droplets of ice-cold water prior to adding the extraction mixture. Metabolite profiling of these samples is not recommended.

7. Transfer resuspended samples from 50-mL plastic tubes into 7-mL screw-cap glass tubes for simultaneous extraction, 15 min at 70°C. Shake glass tubes intermittently and depressurize at least once. Allow to cool for 5 min at room temperature.

8. Add 188 μL $CHCl_3$ and extract 10 min at 30°C with intermittent vigorous shaking using a vortex mixer.

9. Add 75 μL of bidistilled H_2O, spin down cellular debris, and transfer a 10-μL aliquot of the combined polar and lipophilic extract into a crimp cap-tapered glass vial suitable for GC–MS analyses. Phase separation into a polar and lipophilic metabolic complement may be induced by adding 400 μL H_2O prior to centrifugation. Subsequent steps are as previously described (*see* **Subheading 3.1.1.**).

3.2. Storage and Transport of Metabolite Extracts

Metabolite extracts are best stored at low temperatures and under nonoxidizing conditions. If possible, long periods of storage and transport should be avoided. Samples can be transported and stored for up to 4 wk. Longer periods have not been tested.

1. After drying samples in a vacuum concentrator or lyophilization, flush the vacuum system with an inert gas, such as argon or nitrogen, instead of ambient air before removing samples.

2. Seal GC vials under inert gas using magnetic crimp caps and an adjustable crimp-cap sealer. Seal vials in plastic bags with silica gel. Combine the full number of vials comprising one experiment in single bags.

3. Transport sealed bags for short periods at room temperature otherwise on dry ice and store at −20 or −80°C.

4. Allow temperature equilibration at room temperature before opening bags for further analysis.

3.3. TOF-GC–MS Metabolite Profiling

Profiling of metabolite extracts involves a two-step chemical derivatization, which (1) substitutes carbonyl moieties through methoxyamination and (2) comprises a per-silylation prior to the GC–MS analysis of the reaction products *(6–9)*. Samples are injected while dissolved in silylation reagent. Major sources of analytical variability are the imprecise dispensing of reagent volumes and the variable timing of the per-silylation reaction. In typical experiments, 50–100 samples are processed. Chemical derivatization was hitherto performed simultaneously on a batch of samples prior to injection. Thus the exposure time to the silylation reagent of the first and last sample within a batch differed considerably, i.e., 50–100 h in setups of 60 min per single GC–MS run. As a result, instable derivatives discomposed, side products of silylation reagents accumulated, and slow evaporation caused notable sample concentration. An optimization of the chemical reaction and GC–MS analysis was, therefore, in high demand.

We employ a CTC Combi PAL with a single syringe autosampler for automated and timed in-line derivatization, vial transport, and injection for GC–MS analysis. Vials are transported from the vial tray to positions within the agitator–incubator oven and finally back to the injection position by means of magnetic crimp caps. In short, in-line chemical derivatization requires samples to be dried within GC glass vials and sealed under nitrogen or argon. Each sample is processed in four equal time intervals of 45 min each. The first two intervals are assigned to methoxyamination (90 min), the third to per-silylation (45 min), and the fourth to a single slow or alternately two fast GC–MS runs per sample (total time <45 min). A typical TOF-GC–MS profile of a preparation of intracellular yeast metabolites is shown in **Fig. 1**.

3.3.1. In-Line Chemical Derivatization

1. The following instructions require 10 µL of metabolic extracts to be dried in 1.1 CTVG crimp-cap vials. The sealed vials are positioned on the sample tray and kept at ambient temperature (*see* **Note 9**).
2. Methoxyamination: the first vial is moved to position 1 of the agitator–incubator oven, which is set to constant 40°C. A 10-µL volume of methoxyamination reagent is dispensed into the vial. The vial is then agitated twice for 45 min.
3. Per-silylation: after 90 min, agitation is interrupted by dispensing 17.5 µL per-silylation reagent. Then 2.5 µL of a retention time standard mixture are added. Agitation is resumed for an additional interval of 45 min at 40°C.
4. At the end of the last interval the GC vial is moved back to the initial position on the sample tray and 1 µL is injected for GC–MS analysis (*see* **Note 10**). Processed vials are kept on the sample tray until discarded.

5. For automated high-throughput analysis, samples are processed in parallel with a time lag of 45 min each. Four positions of the agitator–incubator oven are used, three for derivatization of samples and one to store the retention time index standard mixture of *n*-alkanes (*see* **Note 2**). The most recent sample in the process is always subject to the first methoxyamination interval. Prior samples are in the second methoxyamination period, the per-silylation interval, or in the process of GC–MS analysis, respectively.

6. Syringe washes are performed between all dispensing procedures (*see* **Note 11**).

7. Automation using the Combi PAL autosampler can be performed with three basic programming parts. The first part primes the in-line derivatization process and ends with injecting the first sample, while the following two samples are already under derivatization. The second part comprises three methods that allow an "endless" cycle, each cycle ending with an injection. The final programming part contains methods that end in-line derivatization by processing the last samples of an analysis series and then safely shuts down the system.

3.3.2. TOF-GC–MS

1. Injection parameters: injection of a 1-µL sample is performed at 230°C in splitless mode with helium carrier gas flow set to 0.6 mL/min. Purge time is 1 min at 20 mL/min flow. The flow rate is kept constant with electronic pressure control enabled. Optionally and especially recommended in cases of high metabolite concentrations, injection is performed in split mode with the split ratio adjusted 1:25. As a rule of thumb, split injection may be prone to discrimination of high-boiling metabolic components, whereas splitless injection may, in rare cases, result in peak shape artifacts for low-boiling components. These artifacts occur in few chromatograms and result in different degrees of peak splitting and shoulder formation. For suppression of this peak shape artifact either inject at decreased flow or apply a 2-min pressure pulse at 110 psi during injection. However, a robust suppression of this artifact for all biological samples can currently not be recommended.

2. Chromatography parameters: chromatography is performed using a 30-m RTX-5Sil MS capillary column with an integrated guard column. The temperature program starts in isothermal mode set to 1 min at 70°C. The isothermal step is followed by a 9°C/min ramp to 350°C. The final temperature is kept constant for 5 min. Cooling is performed as fast as instrument specifications allow. The transfer line temperature is set to 250°C and matches ion source conditions.

3. Mass spectrometer parameters: the ion source is set to maximum instrument specifications, 250°C. High-boiling metabolic components exhibit increased peak tailing at lower temperature settings. The recorded mass range is $m/z = 70$–600 at 20 scans/s. Mass spectrometric solvent delay with filaments turned off is 6.6–7.5 min, the remaining chromatography is fully monitored with omission of cool down periods. Manual mass defect is set to 0, filament bias current is –70 V, and detector voltage is approx 1700–1850 V depending on detector age. The instrument tune is automated and performed without EPA tune compliance.

3.4. Automated Deconvolution of Mass Spectra

Automated deconvolution of MSTs from GC–MS metabolite profiles is crucial for increased accuracy of metabolite identification and detection (**Fig. 1**). Deconvolution is the process of locating MSTs, also called mass spectral components, in GC–MS chromatograms and the subsequent automated purification of the mass spectral scans at peak apex from electronic and chemical background noise and cross-contaminating fragments of coeluting compounds. Both the ChromaTOF software of LECO TOF-GC–MS systems and the technology platform-independent automated mass spectral deconvolution and identification system, AMDIS, may be used to this purpose *(3,13–14)*. When using AMDIS, files are best exported in CDF file format after baseline correction within the ChromaTOF software. Large TOF-GC–MS files, such as those with fast scanning acquisition rates, may be impossible to load into AMDIS using standard desktop computers. Here, we describe the use of the ChromaTOF software for automated deconvolution and construction of MSRI libraries. MSRI libraries may contain either manually curated and selected entries of identified compounds or have the purpose to provide full automatically generated collections of mass spectra from single or multiple TOF-GC–MS profiles. This process we would like to term nonsupervised construction.

1. Chromatograms are processed by ChromaTOF software with activated baseline tracking and offset set to "just above noise," smoothing and peak width are set to 20 and 6, respectively. The signal-to-noise threshold is set to minimum 2.0 and the number of deconvolutions is unlimited.

2. RI are generated for each individual chromatogram in two steps: first a mass spectral library search is conducted to identify all expected *n*-alkanes in each chromatogram. Then retention times of the *n*-alkanes are used for chromatogram-specific RI calculation. The mass spectral library search for *n*-alkane identification is restricted to the mass range *m/z* = 80–600 and threshold signal to noise set to 20. Further criteria for identification are expected peak height and area in total ion chromatography (TIC) mode, as well as occurrence of respective molecular ions for each *n*-alkane. The retention times of the expected and verified *n*-alkanes are transferred into a chromatogram specific retention index method and the chromatogram subsequently processed with the same settings. Overloaded peaks must be avoided or excluded in order to maintain high RI accuracy.

3. Chromatogram processing results are exported to text files. All available information for each deconvoluted peak or MST is exported including auxiliary information, such as retention time index, retention time, unique mass, total signal to noise, and full mass spectrum in absolute intensity format.

4. These text files can be imported and modified in Microsoft Excel and Word. More efficient is a customized automated programmed conversion into the MSP format for import into NIST02 and AMDIS software, which needs to add RI information for the generation of MSRI libraries. During this process auxiliary

information, such as user comments, can be tagged as synonyms. MSTs can be removed or selected by signal to noise, peak purity, peak width, or RI thresholds. Thus, data can be specifically selected for import into NIST02 software and information can be added. A typical example of an identified mass spectrum is shown in the following:

Name: EITTMS_163001-101_METB_1627.14_L-Glutamic acid (3TMS)
Synon: SOURCE_CHROMATOGRAM:1185EK12_1627.1
Synon: NAME:L-Glutamic acid (3TMS)
Synon: MATCH:[834; L-Glutamic acid (3TMS)]
Synon: MPIMP-ID:163001-101-1
Synon: QM:246|363|128|348|156
Synon: ROLE:METB
Synon: METABOLITE:DL-Glutamic acid
Synon: KEGG:C00025|C00302|C00217
Synon: TECHNOLOGY:GC-TOF-MS (EITTMS)|GC [M1]
Synon: RI:1627.1
Synon: RT:10.253 min
Synon: SP:Standard| Sigma| G-1251
Synon: DATE:2001.06.01
Comments: Kopka J, Max Planck Institute of Molecular Plant Physiology, Am Muehlenberg 1, D-14476 Golm, Germany
Formula: C14H33NO4Si3
MW: 363
CAS no.: 15985-07-6
DB no.: 799
Num Peaks: 151
70 11; 71 6; 72 38; 73 999; 74 102;
75 454; 76 33; 77 79; 78 6; 79 7;
80 2; 81 1; 82 5; 83 6; 84 164;   ...

5. Chromatogram processing results can also be exported directly from the peak table of the ChromaTOF software to NIST02 without the need of programming skills. Deconvoluted MSTs can be either added to NIST02 user libraries or exported as MSP files. Customization of library entries within ChromaTOF software before export is highly restricted. However, NIST02 offers a full toolbox for editing mass spectral information. Thus, mass spectral libraries of manually selected, identified, and curated MSTs can be easily generated and maintained with the tools and options provided by NIST02 and ChromaTOF software.

6. Examples of annotated MSRI libraries comprising identified compounds as well as unidentified MSTs and MSRI libraries, which were fully generated in the non-supervised mode, may be found at CSB.DB (http://csbdb.mpimp-golm.mpg.de/csbdb/gmd/gmd.html).

3.5. Comparison and Classification of Mass Spectra

The NIST02 mass spectral search and comparison software represents the most widely accepted standard tool for analysis of mass spectra generated by GC–MS systems *(13,14)*. Systems' manufacturers optimize automated MS tuning with the aim to produce comparable mass spectra. NIST02 is mature in automation, algorithm, as well as user friendliness. However, the great challenge of identifying or at least classifying all hitherto unidentified metabolic components from GC–MS profiles of biological samples requires additional features that are not provided by NIST02. One of the most useful additional features for mass spectral comparisons is the integration of retention time index information into mass spectral comparisons. Only information on chromatographic retention will allow unambiguous identification of those stereo- and conformational isomers, which cannot be distinguished by mass spectral criteria alone *(3)*. In addition, mass spectral classification needs to be reconsidered for those MSTs that cannot immediately be linked to a known metabolite. Here, we demonstrate first attempts to systematically deal with the challenge of identifying multiple unknown mass spectral tags from TOF-GC–MS profiles. Our present analyses are all performed using a single technology platform and a set of chromatograms that were produced on identical GC capillary columns. Transfer of our results to other technology platforms appears to be feasible but still awaits thorough investigation.

3.5.1. Clustering

Mass spectra can be directly clustered using hierarchical clustering of Euclidian distance or any other algorithm of commercially or publicly available software packages for statistical analysis. An alternative approach is clustering based on the generally accepted matching value generated by NIST02 mass spectral comparison software instead of Euclidian or other statistical distances. For "nonstandard" mass spectral distance measures and queries that incorporate RI information refer to our web pages, http://csbdb.mpimp-golm.mpg.de/csbdb/gmd/gmd.html *(12)*. For the purpose of clustering a full matrix of pairwise similarity, measures of all MSTs and identified mass spectra needs to be defined through automated comparison and data export using NIST *(3)*. We performed a combined analysis of identified and all MSTs that occur in yeast metabolite profiles (**Fig. 1A**). Clustering was performed as described using the S-Plus 2000 standard edition statistical software package. Clustering demonstrated the presence of major metabolite classes in TOF-GC–MS profiles, such as carbohydrates, amino acids, and organic phosphates (**Fig. 1B**). The mass spectrum of myo-inositol (6TMS), which we subsequently use as a test case, classifies to the sugar cluster. Most of the hitherto nonclassified MSTs sorted into clusters of identified metabolites. Thus, simple hierarchical clustering provides means to link unidentified MSTs to major metabolite classes. Some major clusters formed clear subdivisions. For example the carbohydrate cluster had disaccharide, monosaccharide, noncyclic polyol, and polyhydroxy carbonic acid branches. In total, up to 18 clear minor mass spectral clusters were found.

However, clustering might lack resolution within the terminal branches of hierarchical trees.

3.5.2. Visualization of MSRI Search Results

For the resolution of mass spectral similarity at the level of single mass spectra, the NIST02 hit lists are unsurpassed, but are lacking in visualization. The additional RI information is best shown in bi-plots with axes of RI and mass spectral match (**Fig. 2**). These plots easily accommodate auxiliary information, for example, on occurrence of MSTs in different sample types and frequency of occurrence in cases of redundant mass spectral libraries, such as nonsupervised MSRI libraries from GC–MS profiles. These visualizations allow discovery of MSTs that exhibit similarity to the bait mass spectrum. In addition, structural similarities of identified mass spectra become apparent as mass spectral similarity can be accessed. In our test case myo-inositol (6TMS) had among the top scoring identified mass spectra, methyl-substituted inositols, ononitol (5TMS) (4-*O*-methyl-myo-inositol), pinitol (5TMS) (3-*O*-methyl-D-chiro-inositol), and an inositol conjugate, galactinol (9TMS) (α-D-galacto-pyranose-[1,3]-myo-inositol). Conformational isomers of myo-inositol, such as chiro- or scyllo-inositol, rank highest but are not yet included in this and the subsequent analysis.

3.5.3. Generation of Mass Spectral Proximity Maps

Hit lists of single MSTs present good means of discovery of best matching mass spectra but do not convey an overview of similarities between many MSTs. For this purpose proximity maps are best suited (**Fig. 3**). Proximity maps visualize the journey through the "space" of mass spectral matches present within a MSRI library. The process of generating a proximity map can be manually performed by starting a mass spectral search with a mass spectrum of interest, such as myo-inositol (6TMS). The aim of this process is to discover groups of related compounds based on mass spectral similarity. The initial hit list will contain redundant mass spectra of myo-inositol (6TMS) and one best hit, which as judged by RI or already known identity, represents a different compound. We travel to this compound along the best match (865 in **Fig. 3**) and will not use this connection in the same direction again throughout the remaining journey. Instead, we perform a mass spectral search with the found best hit. In our test case, the best match of this second search was myo-inositol (6TMS). Thus, we return to myo-inositol (6TMS) and close the connection in the reverse direction as well. We then continue with the next best match of myo-inositol (6TMS) (882 in **Fig. 3**). The proximity map is subsequently generated using the same rules. The journey can be terminated after a limited number of steps, a number of visited mass spectra, or at a threshold match value.

Visualization of a proximity map can performed using network visualization tools such as Pajek software *(20)*. The resulting map clearly shows that myo-inositol (6TMS) has a set of 11 directly linked MSTs in our present MSRI library within a similarity range of 725 to 865. Among those we found a set of four MSTs with high "internal" similarity (910–950), which represent two methyl-substituted inositols and two putative still unidentified other methyl-inositols. Furthermore, we found an inositol conjugate, galactinol (9TMS), and a group of highly similar (match values not shown) MSTs, which form connections to glucopyranoses that are highly similar in structure to the second conjugation partner, i.e., galactopyranose, of galactinol (9TMS).

4. Notes

1. Reagents are stored in 1-mL crimp-cap sample glass vials. These vials contain excess reagent but are replaced after 24 h in order to avoid aging and accumulation of contaminations.

2. The retention time index standard mixture contains high molecular weight *n*-alkanes, which tend to precipitate at low ambient temperature. The *n*-alkane mixture is best prepared at elevated temperature and during use is kept at 40°C within the heated agitator.

3. Deactivation of the glass insert liners reduces the number of cleaning cycles, which are required after liner exchange and increases column lifetime. For glass liner deactivation, dissolve 20 mL of DMDCS in 400 mL toluene and treat liners for 15 min in this solution. Then rinse twice with toluene and, finally, keep liners 15 min in methanol and rinse clean with methanol. Liners are dried, heated, and stored under inert gas and in sealed-glass tubes.

4. We describe the analysis of polar methanol and chloroform-soluble metabolites without and in combination with the lipid metabolite complement. Major additional variants are selective enrichment of acidic or basic compounds, permutations of temperature and extraction time for improved coverage of labile compounds, and application of other solvents for selective extraction. Descriptions of alternate extraction protocols may be found elsewhere within this book.

5. The internal standard premixture for the analysis of polar compounds contains ribitol, 2,3,3,3-d_4-DL-alanine and D(-)-isoascorbic acid. Each component is prepared separately at 10 mg/mL in bidistilled water except for ribitol, which is dissolved in methanol. These stock solutions are combined into 50 mL bidistilled water and, thus, diluted to 0.02, 0.10, and 0.05 mg/mL final concentration, respectively. Diluted stocks can be stored at –20°C for a limited time. The internal standard solution for the analysis of the lipophilic metabolic complement needs to be freshly prepared and contains 2 mg/mL nonadecanoic acid methyl ester in chloroform. The internal standard premixtures can be extended to contain any set of stable isotope-labeled or synthetic internal standards.

6. The extraction mixture for plant material contains 300 parts methanol, 30 parts internal standard premixture for the polar metabolic complement (*see* **Note 5**),

and 30 parts of the internal standard premixture for the lipophilic metabolic complement.

7. Back-up samples for in-line or manual derivatization can easily be generated by preparing additional aliquots from the surplus extracts and subsequent vacuum concentration. Note that rotors R96-13 and R120-111 require customized adaptors to accommodated tapered GC vials. Disposable 10-mL pipet tips, which are cut down to fit, may serve the same purpose.

8. The extraction mixture for yeast intercellular metabolites contains 350 parts methanol, 12 part internal standard premixture for the polar metabolic complement (*see* **Note 5**), and 12 parts internal standard premixture for the lipophilic metabolic complement.

9. The reagent volumes of the in-line derivatization steps are adjusted to 10-μL sample volume. Increased sample volumes may not be fully redissolved in the 10-μL volume of methoxyamination reagent and result in nonmethoxyaminated but subsequently per-silylated side products, such as silylated hexopyranoses. The source of these side products is residual dried extract that sticks to the walls of the GC vials. These dried residues are not accessible through high-intensity shaking by the CTC agitator–incubator oven, but do not present a problem during manual agitation. For automated processing of extract, the aliquot volumes must not exceed 10 μL and need to be deposited at the bottom of the vial before vacuum centrifugation.

10. For continuous operation the GC–MS program needs to last less than 45 min. It is essential to either operate the GC–MS system under constant ambient temperature or check that increased ambient temperature owing to seasonal changes does not unexpectedly prolong the GC cycle time resulting in extended cooling times.

11. For the complete process of in-line derivatization a single syringe is used. This setup puts high demands on syringe cleanliness and mechanical performance. We mount a 25-μL syringe for best mechanical robustness of plunger and needle. Reagent and sample cross-contaminations may occur with inadequate wash protocols. Major contaminants from microbial and plant extracts are disaccharides, such as sucrose and trehalose, or lipids and chlorophyll. When permanently present at high concentrations, these compounds are best removed by sequential treatment with polar and apolar solvents. The type of syringe cleaning cycle is best adjusted to the subsequent syringe task. We use hexane immediately before transferring MSTFA reagent and discard each first draw from the MSTFA reagent reservoirs taking care not to contaminate the reagents. Syringes are cleaned by maximum volume draws from the ethylacetate and *n*-hexane reservoirs.

Acknowledgments

The authors would like to thank Professor Lothar Wilmitzer and Dr. Oliver Fiehn, Max-Planck Institute of Molecular Plant Physiology (MPI-MP), Potsdam, Germany, and Professor Le Tran Binh, Institute of Biotechnology (IBT), Hanoi, Vietnam, for valuable advice, encouragement, and discussions. This work was supported by the Max-Planck society and the Bundesministerium für Bildung und Forschung (BMBF), grant PTJ-BIO/0312854.

References

1. Bino, R. J. Hall, R. D, Fiehn, O., et al. (2004) Potential of metabolomics as a functional genomics tool. *Trends Plant Sci.* **9,** 418–425.
2. Fernie, A. R., Trethewey, R. N., Krotzky, A. J., and Willmitzer, L. (2004) Metabolite profiling: from diagnostics to systems biology. *Nat. Rev. Mol. Cell Biol.* **5,** 763–769.
3. Wagner, C., Sefkow, M., and Kopka, J. (2003) Construction and application of a mass spectral and retention time index database generated from plant GC/EI-TOF-MS metabolite profiles. *Phytochem.* **62,** 887–900.
4. Colebatch, G., Desbrosses, G., Ott, T., et al. (2004) Global changes in transcription orchestrate metabolic differentiation during symbiotic nitrogen fixation in *Lotus japonicus. Plant J.* **39,** 487–512.
5. Birkemeyer, C., Luedemann, A., Wagner, C., Erban, A., and Kopka, J. (2005) Metabolome analysis: the potential of *in vivo* labeling with stable isotopes for metabolite profiling. *Trends Biotechnol.* **23,** 28–33.
6. Fiehn, O., Kopka, J., Trethewey. R. N., and Willmitzer., L. (2000) Identification of uncommon plant metabolites based on calculation of elemental compositions using gas chromatography and quadrupole mass spectrometry. *Anal. Chem.* **72,** 3573–3580.
7. Roessner, U., Wagner, C., Kopka, J., Trethewey, R. N., and Willmitzer, L. (2000) Simultaneous analysis of metabolites in potato tuber by gas chromatography-mass spectrometry. *Plant J.* **23,** 131–142.
8. Fiehn, O., Kopka, J., Dormann, P., Altmann, T., Trethewey, R. N., and Willmitzer, L. (2000) Metabolite profiling for plant functional genomics. *Nat. Biotechnol.* **18,** 1157–1161.
9. Roessner, U., Luedemann, A., Brust, D., et al. (2001) Metabolic profiling allows comprehensive phenotyping of genetically or environmentally modified plant systems. *Plant Cell* **13,** 11–29.
10. Kovàts. E. S. (1958) Gas-chromatographische characterisierung organischer verbindungen: Teil 1. Retentionsindices aliphatischer halogenide, alkohole, aldehyde und ketone. *Helv. Chim. Acta* **41,** 1915–1932.
11. van Deursen, M. M., Beens, J., Janssen, H. -G., Leclercq, P. A., and Cramers, C. A. (2000) Evaluation of time-of-flight mass spectrometric detection for fast gas chromatography. *J. Chromatogr. A* **878,** 205–213.
12. Kopka, J., Schauer, N., Krueger, S., et al. (2005) GMD@CSB.DB: The Golm Metabolome Database. *Bioinformatics* **21,** 1635–1638.
13. Ausloos, P., Clifton, C. L., Lias, S. G., et al. (1999) The critical evaluation of a comprehensive mass spectral library. *J. Am. Soc. Mass Spectrom.* **10,** 287–299.
14. Stein, S. E. (1999) An integrated method for spectrum extraction and compound identification from gas chromatography/ mass spectrometry data. *J. Am. Soc. Mass Spectrom.* **10,** 770–781.

15. Kopka, J., Fernie, A. R., Weckwerth, W., Gibon, Y., and Stitt, M. (2004) Metabolite profiling in plant biology: platforms and destinations. *Genome Biol.* **5,** 109–117.

16. Weckwerth, W., Wenzel, K., and Fiehn, O. (2004) Process for the integrated extraction, identification and quantification of metabolites, proteins and RNA to reveal their co-regulation in biochemical networks. *Proteomics* **4,** 78–83.

17. De Koning, W. and van Dam, K. (1992) A method for the determination of changes in glycolytic metabolites in yeast on a subsecond time scale using extraction at neutral pH. *Anal. Biochem.* **204,** 118–123.

18. Gonzalez, B., Francois, J., and Renaud, M. (1997) A rapid and reliable method for metabolite extraction in yeast using boiling buffered ethanol. *Yeast* **13,** 1347–1355.

19. Castrillo, J. I., Hayes, A., Mohammed, S., Gaskell, S. J., and Oliver, S. G. (2003) An optimized protocol for metabolome analysis in yeast using direct infusion electrospray mass spectrometry. *Phytochemistry* **62,** 929–937.

20. Batagelj, V. and Mrvar, A. (1998) Pajek: program for large network analysis. *Connections* **21,** 47–57.

3

Metabolomic Profiling of Natural Volatiles

Headspace Trapping: GC–MS

Yury M. Tikunov, Francel W. A. Verstappen, and Robert D. Hall

Summary

Plants are a fabulously rich source of naturally volatile metabolites, which are derived from a range of contrasting biochemical pathways (e.g., mono-, di-, and sesquiterpenoids, benzoates, alcohols, esters). Such volatiles may immediately be released from the plant or they may be stored, e.g., in glycosylated form for release later "on demand." Certain roles for these molecules have already been determined in that they can function as attractants (e.g., to pollinators, seed dispersers, and others) or as protectants (repellants, pathogen inhibitors, and so on). The flavor and fragrance of plant materials to humans and other animals are also, to a great extent, determined by natural volatiles. Other more sophisticated roles have also been elucidated where plant volatiles have been shown to be involved either as signal molecules to attract the predators of damaging herbivorous insects or potentially even as signal molecules warning other plants of imminent danger. As such, detailed knowledge of these components can be valuable in relation to breeding crop varieties for enhanced product quality or for achieving improved resistance to pathogens and insects. Furthermore, knowledge of the metabolites can result in a corresponding knowledge of the genes responsible for their synthesis and this can lead to dedicated strategies for their in vitro production through, e.g., reverse genetics in heterologous microbial expression systems in fermentors for the production of high-value fine chemicals. Various analytical techniques based on gas chromatography–mass spectrometry have been devised for the analysis of this complex group of metabolites. Two of these key methods are detailed in this chapter.

Key Words: Headspace trapping; GC–MS; natural volatiles.

1. Introduction

A significant part of the plant cell metabolome—comprising the volatile metabolites—is of particular interest not only in fundamental research into, e.g.,

From: *Methods in Molecular Biology, vol. 358: Metabolomics: Methods and Protocols*
Edited by: W. Weckwerth © Humana Press Inc., Totowa, NJ

signaling mechanisms and interorganism interactions *(1)*, but also are equally important in applied research as these metabolites play an important role in plant product quality in terms of, e.g., flavor and fragrance *(2)*. Headspace trapping techniques combined with gas chromatography–mass spectrometry (GC–MS) are analytical approaches that are suitable for metabolomics studies of natural volatiles. Specially designed porous polymers, used as the adsorbant to fill flow-through cartridges (e.g., Tenax), or to coat solid-phase microextraction (SPME) fibers, are used to collect and concentrate the volatiles released into the air space above the plant material. These technologies have high sensitivity, reproducibility, and robustness *(3–10)*. Such approaches can be used to collect and concentrate naturally released volatiles from either parts of, or whole plants, over a period of time—so-called headspace analysis. In addition, similar approaches can be applied after, e.g., plant material has been pretreated (frozen, ground to a powder, and so on) where certain procedures can be applied in order to drive off (purge) the major volatile fraction from the plant matrix for subsequent collection and detection. Headspace trapping includes several basic steps: (1) sample preparation, which is aimed at stabilizing the biological material (for example plant tissue) and inducing the release (purging) of volatiles from the material into the air above (the headspace); (2) the volatiles are then extracted (trapped) from the headspace using a solid-phase adsorbant in the form of a fiber (in the case of SPME; **Fig. 1**) or of a flowthrough cartridge filled with a porous polymer (e.g., Tenax). Different adsorbants are available that have different affinities to different classes of volatile metabolites. As such, polymer choice can be used to give preference to those groups of metabolites of greatest interest; (3) the trapped volatiles are subsequently released from the solid phase for analysis. In the case of SPME this only happens after the fiber has been inserted into the injection port of the gas chromatograph at which time it is exposed to a high temperature. When using cartridges, the volatiles can either be chemically extracted using organic solvents and then be concentrated further prior to injection into the GC or alternatively, they may, using direct thermal desorption, be released directly into the GC using dedicated equipment supplied with the machine; and (4) chromatographic separation then occurs using a long capillary column, usually in combination with a suitable temperature gradient. During the analysis the individual molecules are first separated as they pass through the chromatography column at different rates, and, on entry into the mass spectrometer, they are fragmented into characteristic fragments that are then detected as charged molecular ions. These ions are qualified on the basis of their mass-to-charge ratios (m/z value) and are quantified based on relative abundance, which results in a distinct spectrum for each compound. These spectra can then be used to interrogate existing databases (e.g., National Institute of Standards and Technology [NIST] and Wiley compound libraries) to assist in compound identification.

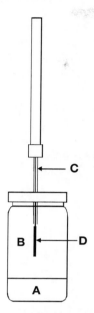

Fig. 1. Schematic representation of a solid-phase microextraction fiber exposed in the headspace of a glass vial containing biological material. The fiber (**D**) has been removed from the protective sheath (**C**) into the headspace (**B**) of the pulped plant material and CaCl$_2$/EDTA (**A**).

Modern investigations in the field of metabolomics require (1) reliable profiling of the metabolic composition of large numbers of biological samples and (2) an unbiased comparative (statistical) analysis of the datasets obtained. In some cases (e.g., SPME), the samples are often not subjected to any pretreatment procedures using organic solvents and, thus, the components remain as native as possible and the majority of natural volatile components that the living plant tissue consists of, are represented in the analysis as a sort of metabolic snapshot. However, in certain cases it may be desirable to choose a modified approach in order to maximize volatile release while avoiding potential artifacts caused by, e.g., many biological processes moving into senescence or complicating matrix effects. Undesirable effects may also be initialized owing to cell disruption altering the original metabolic composition, thus failing to provide a true picture of the living material. In this respect, the most important step in the procedure is making the correct decision concerning sample preparation. This should be made with the aim of stabilizing the biological matrix during the period of volatile collection and/or to drive off all volatiles into to headspace so that they can be extracted.

In this chapter, we describe reliable protocols for automated, sequential metabolomic profiling of volatile metabolites released from plant material. The first example chosen, by way of illustration, uses readily available tomato fruits in combination with a headspace SPME-GC–MS approach involving a pre-treatment strategy to maximize volatile release. In a second example, a method is presented where natural *Arabidopsis* flower volatiles, which are inevitably released in small amounts, are collected and concentrated over an extended period for subsequent further concentration and analysis. Information on how to proceed with an unbiased comparative analysis of metabolic data obtained from such an analysis is also presented.

2. Materials

2.1. Natural Volatiles

2.1.1. SPME Adsorption

1. Red ripe tomato fruits.
2. A supply of liquid N_2.
3. Freezer at –70°C.
4. MilliQ water or the double distilled equivalent.
5. NaOH/EDTA water solution: 100 mM EDTA adjusted to pH 7.5 using 1 M NaOH.
6. $CaCl_2$ powder.
7. 50-mL Plastic centrifuge/storage tubes (e.g., Corning, Corning, NY).
8. 4-mL Glass screw-cap vials, 15–45 mm (e.g., Bester, Amstelveen, The Netherlands).
9. 10-mL Polypropylene bimetal crimp-cap vials (e.g., Bester), with silicon/Teflon septa, 20 mm (Interscience, Breda, The Netherlands).

2.1.2. Headspace Trapping/Tenax Adsorption

1. Flowering plants of *Arabidopsis thaliana*.
2. 2-mL Glass vials containing 1 mL tap water.
3. Teflon tape.
4. Pentane, redistilled.
5. Diethyl ether, redistilled.
6. Tenax, TA, 20/35 mesh (Alltech, Breda, The Netherlands).
7. Glass cartridges, 140 × 4 mm with reduced diameter at one end to assist loading.
8. Flexible Teflon tubing.
9. 1-mL Pipet tips with the points removed to create a wider opening.
10. Glass jar (ca. 500 mL) sealed with a Teflon-lined lid equipped with inlet and outlet ports.
11. Flow meters and a vacuum pump.
12. 4-mL Screw-cap vials (Bester).
13. Polypropylene screw caps with polytetrafluoroethylene (PTFE)-lined rubber septa.
14. 2-mL Wide-mouth crimp-cap vials with crimp caps equipped with polytetrafluoro-ethylene (PTFE)-lined septa (Bester).
15. 250-μL Vial inserts (Bester).
16. Source of N_2 gas.

2.2. Equipment

2.2.1. Natural Volatiles

2.2.1.1. SPME

1. Metal electric grinder, basic analytical mill A11 (IKA, Staufen Germany).
2. Shaking water bath at 37°C.
3. Ultrasonic bath.
4. SPME fiber assembly (65-μm polydimethylsiloxane-divinylbenzene [PDMS-DVB]) (Supelco, Zwijndrecht, The Netherlands) (*see* **Note 1**).
5. Gas chromatograph (e.g., Fisons 8060) coupled to a MD 800 mass spectrometer (Fisons, Beverly, MA) and fitted with a CombiPAL auto-sampler (CTC Analytics, Zwingen, Switzerland) (*see* **Note 2**).
6. Capillary column: HP-5 (50 m × 0.32 mm, 1.05-μm film thickness; Hewlett Packard, Amstelveen, The Netherlands) with a supply of helium as carrier gas (*see* **Note 3**).

2.2.1.2. HEADSPACE TRAPPING/TENAX ADSORPTION

1. Gas chromatograph (e.g., Hewlett Packard 5890 series II) coupled to a mass spectrometer (e.g., Hewlett-Packard 5972A).
2. Capillary column: HP-5MS, 30 m × 0.25 mm, 0.25-μm film thickness (Boom, Meppel, The Netherlands); retention gap 5 m × 0.32 mm, deactivated (Alltech).

3. Methods

3.1. SPME: GC–MS of Tomato Fruit Volatiles

3.1.1. Tomato Fruit Sampling (see **Note 4**)

1. Preferably, use freshly harvested undamaged tomato fruits of similar age and developmental stage. Use at least five fruits per sample. Cut each fruit into quarters with a sharp knife and immediately freeze one one-fourth part of each fruit in liquid N_2 (*see* **Note 5**).
2. Grind the five-pooled frozen tomato parts in liquid N_2 in a metal electric grinder. Keep the powder deep-frozen at all times and transfer it to 50-mL storage tubes, again using a precooled spatula (*see* **Note 6**).
3. Store the pooled powder sample obtained in the freezer at approx –70°C until all samples are ready to be analyzed together.

3.1.2. Preparation of Samples for SPME-GC–MS

1. Samples removed from the freezer should be placed conveniently available for use but nevertheless must remain deep-frozen (in liquid N_2 or in a –70°C freezer) until being used one at a time for the following steps.
2. Quickly but carefully weigh out 0.5 g of frozen powder using a metal spatula with the end prefrozen in liquid N_2 into a prefrozen 4-mL screw-cap vial.
3. Immediately close the vial with its screw cap and incubate in a preheated water bath at 37°C with gentle agitation for 10 min (*see* **Note 7**).

4. Open the vial and quickly add 0.5 mL of NaOH/EDTA (100 mM EDTA, pH 7.5) and then immediately after 1.1 g CaCl$_2$ powder (*see* **Note 8**). Immediately close the vial and shake thoroughly. Sonicate in an ultrasonic bath for 5 min.

5. Transfer the pulp obtained using a 1-mL pipet tip into a 10-mL crimp-cap vial and immediately close it (*see* **Note 9**). The samples are now ready to be analyzed by SPME-GC–MS.

3.1.3. SPME-GC–MS Analysis (see **Note 10**)

1. Set the GC–MS parameters to the following values:
   a. Helium pressure is maintained at 37 kPa.
   b. The GC interface and MS source temperatures are 260 and 250°C, respectively.
   c. Set up the following GC temperature gradient program: start at 45°C (2 min), raise to 250°C at a rate of 5°C/min and finally, hold at 250°C for 5 min.
   d. After each run the column is automatically cooled from 250°C back to the starting temperature.
   e. The total run time including the final oven cooling back to the starting temperature is 60 min.

2. Prior to volatile adsorption, incubate the vials containing the plant material at 50°C for 10 min with continuous agitation (*see* **Note 11**).

3. Insert the SPME fiber (**Fig. 1D**) through the septum and into the headspace of the vial, and expose the coating to the air above the sample (**Fig. 1B**). Incubate for 20 min while maintaining the temperature at 50°C with continuous agitation (*see* **Note 12**).

4. Insert the fiber into the GC injection port and desorb the volatiles for 1 min at 250°C.

5. Run the temperature gradient and record the mass spectra in the 35–400 *m/z* range using the MS set at a scanning speed of 2.8 scans/s with an ionization energy of 70 eV (*see* **Fig. 2**).

6. Use the commercial software supplied with the mass spectrometer for subsequent data analysis (*see* **Note 13**).

3.2. Headspace Trapping Analysis of Arabidopsis Flower Volatiles

3.2.1. Sampling of Plant Material

1. For each glass jar to be used, fill two glass cartridges each with 150 mg Tenax (*see* **Note 14**).

2. Cut the inflorescence and part of the stem of a healthy *Arabidopsis* plant with a scapel blade and place in a 2-mL vial containing 1 mL tap water. Seal the vial neck with Teflon tape (*see* **Fig. 3**) (*see* **Note 15**).

3. Place the sample in the glass jar and replace the lid bearing the two outlet ports.

4. Connect up the two Tenax-filled cartridges using Teflon tubing to the inlet and outlet ports (*see* **Note 16**).

5. Connect the other end of the outlet port cartridge to the vacuum pump and establish an air-flow rate through the system of 100 mL/min and keep running for 24 h (*see* **Note 17**).

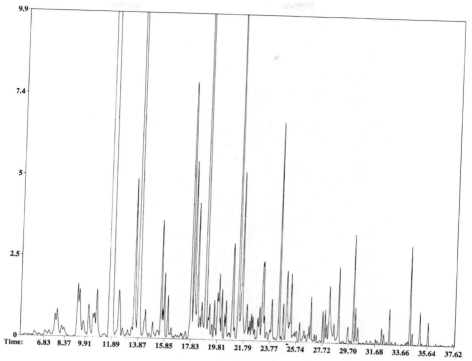

Fig. 2. A typical gas chromatography–mass spectrometry profile of tomato volatiles.

6. Repeat for the other samples and include one empty jar as negative control (*see* **Note 18**).
7. After 24 h make a mixture of pentane:diethylether (80:20) and elute the Tenax from the outlet cartridge with 1 mL of the mixture. Collect the run-through in a 4-mL screw-cap vial and repeat twice to give in total a 3-mL of eluant (*see* **Notes 19** and **20**).
8. Concentrate the eluant down to 50 μL using a gentle flow of N_2 in a fume hood.
9. Transfer the eluant into a vial insert and place into a 2-mL crimp-cap vial and seal with a crimp cap for GC analysis (*see* **Note 21**).

3.2.2. GC–MS Analysis of Purge and Trap Eluates

1. Use the following gradient for the GC run: 45°C for 1 min, increase the temperature to 280°C at a rate of 10°C/min, maintain the temperature at 280°C for 5 min. After each run the column temperature will automatically be returned to the starting temperature. Set the injection port to 250°C, the interface to 290°C, and the MS source to 180°C.

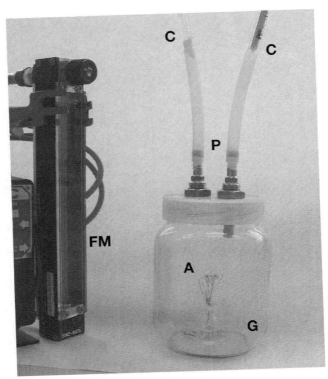

Fig. 3. Glass jar (G) containing a piece of *Arabidopsis* inflorescence (A). The inlet and outlet ports (P) are both connected by Teflon tubing to glass cartridges (C) containing Tenax. Air is then sucked through the system by a vacuum pump connected to a flowmeter to control the flow rate (FM).

2. Set the helium inlet pressure with the electronic pressure control to give a constant flow rate of 1 mL/min. Set the ionization potential to 70 eV.
3. When the equipment is stabilized, inject a 2-μL aliquot of the Tenax eluate in splitless mode into the GC.
4. Repeat for all the samples and the control.
5. Analyze the data further using the commercial software supplied with the mass spectrometer (*see* **Note 22**; **Fig. 4**).

Fig. 4. (*opposite page*) (**A**) Typical headspace volatile fingerprint of natural volatiles released from *Arabidopsis* flowers. (**B**) Enlargement of a section of the upper trace showing characteristic peaks present in the sesquiterpene region of the chromatogram.

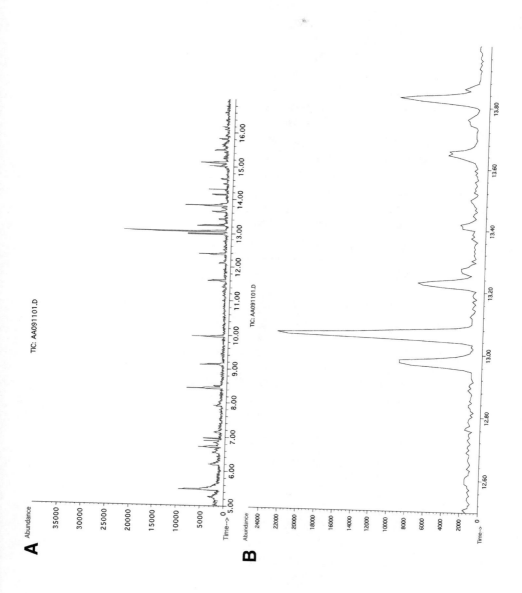

3.3. Data Analysis

When unfamiliar with GC–MS data it is recommended to begin data analysis using the packages supplied with the equipment used. You can then proceed to export the differential mass peaks into programs such as AMDIS, and databases such as the NIST mass spectral library (http://www.nist.gov) to help identify interesting compounds. For large-scale metabolomic comparisons of many datasets, premanipulation of the data is likely to be required. Packages such as metAlign™ (www.metalign.nl) can be used for this data preprocessing. This involves, e.g., baseline correction and noise elimination, full spectral alignment of datasets, that is, alignment of every mass peak (*m/z*) situated in a particular retention time throughout all datasets analyzed, and searching for statistically significant metabolic differences between datasets. An example of the results of one such comparative analysis of the volatile composition of two tomato lines is presented in **Fig. 5**. The difference chromatograms represent mass peaks (molecular fragments), which are either more, or less, abundant in one line compared with the other. Using AMDIS and NIST, known volatile metabolites corresponding to these peaks can then be determined.

4. Notes

1. Different SPME fiber types are available. For nontargeted metabolomics, fiber assemblies that have a more universal adsorption capacity should be chosen. The one listed has been chosen for its broad affinity to volatiles with different chemical origins. When a more targeted approach is desired, more specific fiber types can be selected to give maximal preference to specific compound classes (*see*, e.g., http://www.sigmaaldrich.com/Brands/Supelco_Home).
2. There are many different producers and models of GC–MS available. Much manufacturer information is available to help you chose which machine is most appropriate to meet your needs and budget.
3. A range of different types and lengths of columns are available from several different manufacturers and the information these supply can be used to make choices. The HP-5 column used here is often a good starting point and its use is frequently reported in the literature. There is a lot of information on KI values available for this type of column, which helps to facilitate compound identification.

Fig. 5. (*opposite page*) Difference chromatograms of fruit volatiles from two contrasting tomato cultivars (**A,B**). **Figure 3A** contains those peaks of volatiles that are more abundant in fruit of the cultivar A compared with the cultivar B. **Figure 3B** contains the peaks of volatiles that are more abundant in fruit of the cultivar B compared to the cultivar A. **Figure 3C** represents the mass spectrum of one of the differential peaks. When compared with the National Institute of Standards and Technology mass spectral library the mass spectrum 3-C represents *trans*-geranylacetone.

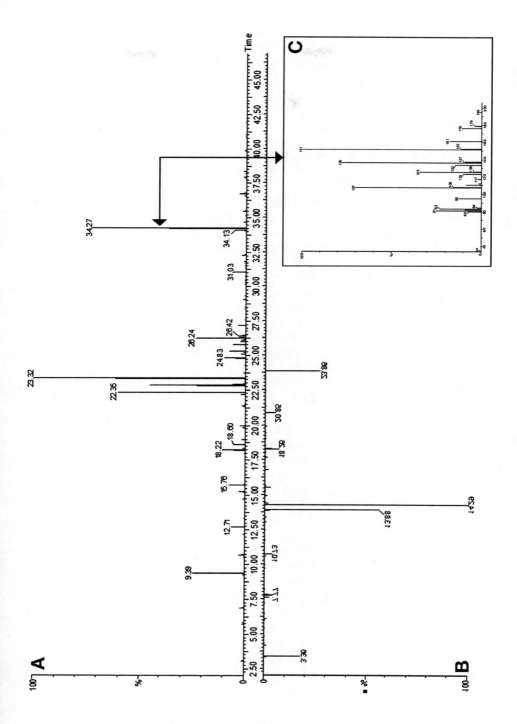

49

4. A significant level of biological variation will always be present between different replicate plants of the same genotype, or even different samples from the same plant (fruits for example). Consequently, to reduce the intersample variation it is strongly recommended to work with pooled materials taken from several comparable sources. In addition, a number of biological replicates of each sample to be analyzed (e.g., genotype, developmental stage, tissue type—depending on what is to be compared) must be taken to get statistically reliable information. Actual numbers are dependant on the type of material used and the uniformity of its prehistory. However, a good rule of thumb is to use five replicates each comprising of five-pooled tissue samples. Experience will then tell if more or less is required. In the case of truly high-throughput screening where perhaps hundreds of samples are to be screened, each genotype can initially be represented by a single sample obtained by pooling of a number of biological replicates. Nevertheless, analysis of such pooled samples should again be repeated two to three times randomly throughout the entire period of analysis to assess and compensate for any analytical (instrumental) variation.

5. It is essential to obtain the most reliable and reproducible overview of the metabolic fingerprint of the living material. Unfresh or damaged material is, therefore, to be avoided as some volatile compounds are only produced as a consequence of damage or senescence. Very sharp knives should be used for cutting and the cut segments should be plunged carefully into the liquid nitrogen within seconds. Subsequent uniformity in handling is also essential and when working with multiple samples the whole process needs to be streamlined to ensure uniform treatment.

6. We use this type of analytical mill as it is capable of withstanding the extreme temperatures of liquid nitrogen. If such a grinder is not available then a large pestle and mortar can readily be used. Both should be prefrozen by pouring in liquid nitrogen and allowing everything to cool down before use. Grinding should also take place in the presence of liquid nitrogen to ensure the sample remains frozen at all times. As liquid nitrogen is being used, appropriate safety precautions should be taken at all times (eye and hand protection, protective clothing, and others). Follow the exact recommendations of your organization.

7. Normally, the chemical composition of biological material should be preserved from any undesirable changes occurring before and during experiments. However, some volatile compounds are only released after cell disruption through enzymatic and nonenzymatic processes. Such compounds can be of considerable relevance specifically in flavor and fragrance studies. Consequently, a strictly controlled incubation of fixed duration and temperature is used prior to analysis to enable these compounds to be included in the analysis. After the incubation period all reactions must be immediately stopped (*see* **Note 8**).

8. When analyzing a series of biological materials in a sequential automated mode, their chemical composition must be preserved during the entire analytical procedure. This means that any enzymatic and nonenzymatic processes occurring in a biological matrix and, thus, altering its chemical composition must be controlled in a uniform manner and terminated on demand. Several ways have been described

to achieve a relative stability of a biological material in time, e.g., boiling, short microwave treatment, and saturation with salts *(11)*. Here, we use probably the most popular way — saturation of the material with $CaCl_2$, which not only inactivates the enzymes but also facilitates driving off the volatiles into the headspace above. $CaCl_2$ can be added either as a powder — in the case of material like fruit, which normally contains greater than 90% water, or in an aqueous solution when using completely, or relatively dry, material. In both cases, the final concentration of $CaCl_2$ must be not less than 5 *M*. To prevent a nonenzymatic oxidation of the volatiles an aqueous solution of EDTA and NaOH is used. Both have a chelating effect while at the same time increasing the pH from 4.5 (a typical pH of tomato fruit) up to 6.2–6.3. Such a procedure has been found to preserve the volatile composition of tomato fruit pulp for at least 12 h.

9. The easiest way to transfer the pulp is to use a pipet fitted with a 1-mL tip that has had the end cut off to create a wider opening. Avoid getting any material to be analyzed onto the vial wall — such material will slowly dry out and subsequently change its polarity, which can then alter the composition of volatiles in the headspace.

10. When analyzing a series of samples, the steps of the headspace extraction and the injection of extracted compounds into GC should be performed by a CombiPAL auto-sampler or its equivalent. In this way, all steps can be made uniform. This is essential to obtain reliable and reproducible results.

11. Agitation and heating to drive off the volatiles is appropriate for the material used here but when using living plant material (e.g., intact leaves, whole small fruits, or unground fruit parts) agitation and heating are usually to be avoided.

12. Make sure no plant material gets deposited on the inside of the vial septum and never allow the fiber (**Fig. 2D**) to touch the plant material at the bottom of the vial (**Fig. 2A**) during headspace extraction.

13. In the case of the SPME analysis, the method described for tomato samples has been shown to give stable mixtures for 12 h after sample preparation. With, e.g., run times of 60 min only ≤ 12 samples should, therefore, be prepared at one time. For other plant materials, sample stability should first be thoroughly checked before planning large-scale analyses of multiple samples. As analytical conditions can vary slightly during longer runs, and often unexpected changes in data acquisition can occur, it is strongly recommended to have a monitoring system in place to check for this. To monitor for such divergences and to be able to use this information to estimate the degree of reliability of the data, a constant amount of a standard compound (one not present in your sample and which has a retention time different to the sample components) should be added to your samples prior to analysis. In addition, a reference mixture (a collection of standard compounds related to the chemical composition of your sample) should be routinely analyzed at regular intervals (e.g., every tenth run). Information from these runs can both be used to test for abnormalities in data acquisition and also can be useful for subsequent statistical analysis of the whole dataset. SPME is known as a semi-quantitative analysis method. It is useful for the reliable detection of qualitative differences between samples and for larger quantitative differences. This

is because the dynamic range for individual components is limited (linearity in response is usually limited to a fourfold difference) and the adsorption properties can be dependent on chemical composition of the sample. This complicates quantification when using this method but relative amounts can be used reliably for comparative analysis of the biological composition of related biological samples.

14. Depending on the chemical properties of the compounds of greatest interest it is possible to chose different adsorbants with differing affinities. *See*, e.g., http://www.sigmaaldrich.com/Brands/Supelco_Home or http://www.markes.com for details of the range of possible materials that are available.

15. Cut plant material may give off extra volatiles owing to the wounding effect. Avoid, therefore, any unnecessary damage to the explant and seal in the stem into the vial fully with Teflon tape. Chose plants with a number of open flowers and few dying/dead ones.

16. It is imperative to only use inert materials such as glass, stainless steel, and Teflon. All connections should be made using Teflon tubing (although the final connection between the outlet cartridge and the vacuum pump may be made of, e.g., silicone tubing. Plastics must be avoided. Noninert materials may release contaminating volatiles which interfere with the analysis. Their contact with organic solvents will also result in irreversible contamination of your spectra through, e.g., the dissolution of the softners often used in plastics (e.g., phtalates).

17. The chosen flow rate should be in relation to the size of the glass jar used—a total sample chamber purge time of 5 min is recommended. The inlet port cartridge is essential to clean the air entering the system of all environmental volatiles adsorbed by the polymer used. In this way all the volatiles trapped in the outlet cartridge must have come specifically from the plant material in the sample chamber.

18. These are best set up in parallel to ensure maximum uniformity in experimentation.

19. Trapping is essentially a chromatographic process, which is influenced by the amount of Tenax, the trapping time, temperature, and gas-flow rate. If you are worried that saturation might be achieved early or that leaching through the system may be occurring you can test for this in an initial trial run by connecting two Tenax inserts in series. Under the right conditions the second insert should still be empty of volatiles at the end of the sampling period chosen.

20. Release of volatiles, especially from flowers, is often regulated or at least influenced by circadian or light/dark cycles. This must be taken into account when wishing to measure volatile release for shorter periods than 24 h. In these cases, a proper time series must be performed prior to experimentation in order to characterize volatile release. Only then can the right choice of adsorbance time be made to ensure uniformity of sampling.

21. Again, at all stages avoid the use of plastics for any of the handling steps and always take the required precautions when dealing with these highly volatile solvents.

22. Depending on the scientific goal there are different ways to analyze the data. For compound identification, peak comparison with spectra in commercial databases (NIST, Wiley) is a useful starting point. For definitive confirmation of identity,

running authentic standard compounds is necessary. If you wish to proceed to fully quantify individual interesting components it is also necessary to run a dilution series of each authentic reference compound to make the necessary calibration curve. *See also* **Note 13** for comments on spiking samples and reproducibility tests.

Acknowledgments

Y. T. acknowledges a grant from the Centre for BioSystems Genomics (CBSG) which is part of the Netherlands National Genomics Initiative (NGI).

References

1. Seskar, M., Shulaev, V., and Raskin, I. (1998) Endogenous methyl salicylate in pathogen-inoculated tobacco plants. *Plant Physiol.* **116,** 387–392.
2. Baldwin, E. A., Scott, W. J., Shewmaker, C. K., and Schuch, W. (2000) Flavor trivia and tomato aroma: biochemistry and possible mechanisms for control of important aroma components. *HortScience* **35,** 1013–1022
3. Augusto, F., Valente, A. L. P., Tada, E. S., and Rivellino, S. R. (2000) Screening of Brazilian fruit aromas using solid-phase microextraction–gas chromatography–mass spectrometry. *J. Chromat. A* **873,** 117–127.
4. Yang, X. and Peppard, T. (1994) Solid-phase microextraction for flavor analysis. *J. Agric. Food Chem.* **42,** 1925–1930.
5. Matich, A. J., Rowan D. D., and Banks, N. H. (1996) Solid phase microextraction for quantitative headspace sampling of apple volatiles. *Anal. Chem.* **68,** 4114–4118.
6. Song, J., Gardner, B. D., Holland, J. F., and Beaudry, R. M. (1997) Rapid analysis of volatile flavor compounds in apple fruit using SPME and GC/time-of-flight mass spectrometry. *J. Agric. Food Chem.* **45,** 1801–1807.
7. Song, J., Fan, L., and Beaudry, R. M. (1998) Application of solid phase microextraction and gas chromatography/time-of-flight mass spectrometry for rapid analysis of flavor volatiles in tomato and strawberry fruits. *J. Agric. Food Chem.* **46,** 3721–3726.
8. Augusto, F., Valente, A. L. P., Tada, E. S., and Rivellino, S. R. (2000) Screening of Brazilian fruit aromas using solid-phase microextraction–gas chromatography–mass spectrometry. *J. Chromat. A* **873,** 117–127.
9. Verdonk, J. C., de Vos, C. H. R., Verhoeven, H. A., Haring, M. A., van Tunen, A.J., and Schuurink, R. C. (2003) Regulation of floral scent production in petunia revealed by targeted metabolomics. *Phytochemistry* **62,** 997–1008.
10. Verhoeven, H. A., Beuerle, T., and Schwab, W. (1997) Solid-phase micro extraction: artefact formation and its avoidance. *Chromatographia* **46,** 63–66.
11. Bezman, Y., Mayer, F., Takeoka, G. R., et al. (2003) Differential effects of tomato *(Lycopersicon esculentum* Mill) matrix on the volatility of important aroma compounds. *J. Agric. Food Chem.* **51,** 722–726.

II ———————————————————————

METABOLOMICS:
DATA INTEGRATION AND DATA MINING

4

Integrative Profiling of Metabolites and Proteins

Improving Pattern Recognition and Biomarker
Selection for Systems Level Approaches

Katja Morgenthal, Stefanie Wienkoop, Florian Wolschin, and Wolfram Weckwerth

Summary

Methods such as mRNA expression profiling have provided a vast amount of genomic and transcriptomic information about plants and other organisms. However, there is explicit indication that considerable metabolic control is executed on the metabolite and on the protein level including protein modifications, thereby constituting the phenotypic plasticity. Consequently, the analysis of the molecular phenotype demands the step toward mass spectrometry (MS)-based postgenomic techniques such as metabolomics and proteomics. This chapter describes a straightforward protocol for simultaneously extracting metabolites and proteins from the same biological sample in preparation for MS analysis. Furthermore, protocols for profiling polar metabolites using gas chromatography time-of-flight MS and for shotgun proteomics using liquid chromatography–MS are discussed. A practical course is laid out that outlines all the basic steps, from harvesting to data analysis. These steps enable the correlative study of metabolite and protein dynamics with minimal technical variation. Biological variability of independent samples is exploited for variance analysis and pattern recognition.

Key Words: Metabolomics; proteomics; multivariate data mining; biomarker discovery; pattern recognition; systems biology; correlation.

1. Introduction

Plants can be investigated at a variety of levels, from the organismic to the molecular, the genomic to the biochemical, the whole plant to the organ, tissue, organelle, or cell. Some 400,000 plant species are estimated to occur on earth. Because all flowering plants are closely related, studying models

From: *Methods in Molecular Biology, vol. 358: Metabolomics: Methods and Protocols*
Edited by: W. Weckwerth © Humana Press Inc., Totowa, NJ

like *Arabidopsis thaliana*, the first plant to have its genome sequenced, helps researchers learn about the jobs genes do in flowering plants in general. Even though the *Arabidopsis* genome is relatively small, about 30% of its genes are of unknown function and only 9% of its annotated genes have been characterized experimentally *(1)*. However, recent advances in functional genomics, like metabolite profiling and concomitant developments in statistical analysis, are making it possible to breach this gap *(2–4)*. A systematic analysis of metabolic networks promises to provide new insights into the response of biological systems to genetic and/or environmental changes. The coupling of gas chromatography to time-of-flight mass analyzers (GC-TOF-MS), allows large quantities of metabolic data to be generated in short periods of time (25 min per chromatographic run) *(5–10)*.

Nucleic acid-based technologies have been widely used in studies of comparative gene expression profiling for biomarker discovery. However, it is essential that these studies also be carried out at the protein level. Proteins are the functional readout of genetic information and, therefore, there can be substantial discordance between transcript abundance and protein expression levels. Even the parts list of mature proteins, including splice variants and posttranscriptional modifications, cannot be predicted from the genome sequence. Furthermore, protein expression is a function of the cellular state, subcellular compartment, extracellular milieu, and metabolic level fluctuations. Thus, protein profiling brings insight into regulatory mechanisms not discernible based on transcript profiling.

Because quantitative protein analysis remains challenging, especially with respect to sample throughput and reproducibility, to date, few researchers have attempted to combine metabolomic and proteomic data for integrative profiling. Recently, we published a novel strategy for such an approach, identifying time-dependent system regulation and biomarkers using correlative metabolite and protein profiling *(5,9)*. Protein and metabolite samples were obtained from the same plant material using an integrative extraction protocol described in this chapter. The two leading technological platforms for quantitative protein profiling are two-dimensional gel electrophoresis (2DE) followed by MS and a one- or multidimensional liquid chromatography (LC)/MS/MS analysis called shotgun proteomics *(11,12)*. We used the shotgun approach because, compared to 2DE, it has a higher-throughput capacity and less bias against protein classes.

Here, we describe our strategy for generating quantitative data from highly complex biological samples to identify metabolite and protein biomarkers in the context of dynamic biochemical networks. This combination of metabolomics and proteomics is especially well suited to open up new vistas to understanding how metabolism works at a systems level. The following sections will illustrate the steps involved from harvesting plant material all the way up to producing a final data matrix containing relative compound concentrations. The focus is metabolite profiling via a GC-TOF-MS application from LECO®/Pegasus® and shotgun proteomics using an LC-ion trap-MS system. The metabolite profiling techniques presented can be applied to all kinds of biological material. Shotgun proteomics, however, is optimally performed with well-annotated organism-specific genomic databases.

2. Materials

2.1. Equipment

1. Retsch mill (ball mill), alternative mortar.
2. Centrifuge.
3. Speed-vac concentrator.
4. Thermo shaker.
5. GC–MS setup, preferentially equipped with a Pegasus II TOF mass analyzer from LECO and corresponding software (LECO, St. Joseph, MI).
6. LC–MS setup, preferentially equipped with an Agilent nano LC system 1100 (Agilent, Waldbronn, Baden-Wuerttemberg, Germany), a Finnigan Linear Ion Trap mass spectrometer (LTQ) (ThermoElectron Corp., San Jose, CA) and corresponding software Chemstation (Agilent), and Xcalibur 1.4 and Bioworks 3.1 (ThermoElectron).
7. Statistical data analysis software MATLAB® 6.5 (Mathworks, Natick, MA).

2.2. Extraction and Analysis of Metabolites

1. Metabolite extraction buffer: methanol/chloroform/water (2.5:1:0.5 [v/v/v]).
2. 40 mg/mL Methoxyamine hydrochloride in dry pyridine. Store pyridine in a tightly closed vessel in a cool dry place with adequate ventilation (i.e., a hood suitable for flammable liquids). Exposure levels of 3600 ppm are immediately dangerous to life and health. Because material is readily adsorbed through skin, immediately remove contaminated clothing.
3. N-methyl-N-trimethylsilyltrifluoroacetamide (MSTFA). MSTFA should be stored in tinted glass bottles under nitrogen. Contact with water or moist air generates highly toxic and corrosive hydrogen fluoride gas, which, in contact with metal, may produce flammable or explosive hydrogen gas.
4. Internal standard solution: leucine-2,3,3-d_3, aspartic acid-2,3,3-d_3, sorbitol-$^{13}C_6$ (each 200 µg/mL in H_2O).
5. Retention time index marker: odd-numbered *n*-alkanes ranging from C_8 to C_{30} (each 200 µg/mL in pyridine), alternatively *n*-fatty acid methyl esters (n-FAMEs) (each 200 µg/mL in $CHCl_3$).

2.3. Extraction and Analysis of Proteins

1. Protein extraction buffer: 50 mM HEPES-KOH, 40% sucrose (w/v), pH 7.2–7.5.
2. TE buffer equilibrated phenol, pH 7.5–8.0 (TE buffer: 10 mM Tris, 1 mM EDTA-Na_2). Store phenol in original container and protected from light. Phenol is highly

flammable. The vapor has a narcotic effect and in high concentrations induces unconsciousness. Use only in areas with appropriate exhaust ventilation.

3. 2-Mercaptoethanol: 2-mercaptoethanol is slightly hygroscopic. Store protected from air and moisture. Yellowing is possible on prolonged storage. 2-Mercaptoethanol is corrosive to the skin and eyes. Inhalation of vapors or mists may irritate the respiratory tract. Laboratory experiments have shown mutagenic effects.

4. Ice-cold acetone.

5. Ice-cold methanol.

6. Lys-C digestion buffer: 50 mM Tris-HCl, 8 M urea, and 100 mM methyalamine, pH 7.5.

7. Trypsin digestion buffer: 50 mM Tris-HCl, 10% acetonitrile (ACN), and 10 mM CaCl$_2$, pH 7.5.

8. Iodoacetamide (IAA) (Sigma, St. Louis, MO): IAA is light sensitive. Store refrigerated and protected from light. IAA is highly toxic and may act as a human carcinogen. Take precautions to protect skin. Wash thoroughly after handling.

9. Dithiothreitol (DTT) (Sigma): DTT causes respiratory tract, skin, and eye irritation, and may affect the central nervous system. Avoid breathing dust and use only with adequate ventilation.

10. Endoproteinase Lys-C, sequencing grade (Roche Applied Sciences, Penzberg, Germany).

11. Poroszyme™ bulk immobilized trypsin (Applied Biosystems, Darmstadt, Germany).

12. SPEC C18 96-well plates (Varian, Darmstadt, Germany).

13. High-performance liquid chromatography (HPLC)-solvent A: 2.5% methanol, gradient grade (Merck, Darmstadt, Germany) and 0.1% formic acid (FA).

14. HPLC-solvent B: 100% methanol gradient grade (Merck) and 0.1% FA.

3. Methods

Metabolome and proteome analyses are difficult, particularly with regard to the identification/quantification of all compounds present in a specific tissue. The basic steps include sample collection, extraction of metabolites and proteins from a matrix, separation of the analytes (chromatography), detection and quantification, and data analysis. The following guidelines can serve as a code of practice for the extraction of metabolites and proteins, and subsequent profiling from the same tissue. A schematic view of the proceedings described in the following sections is depicted in **Fig. 1**.

3.1. Plant Material and Harvest

Before starting the experiment, define the conditions (e.g., photoperiod, light intensity, and temperature) under which to grow the plants.

Make sure that the number of replicate plants is sufficient to your experimental setup (*see* **Notes 1** and **2**).

Define the time-points of harvest, with consideration to the fact that plants pass through several developmental stages. This is a critical point, particularly

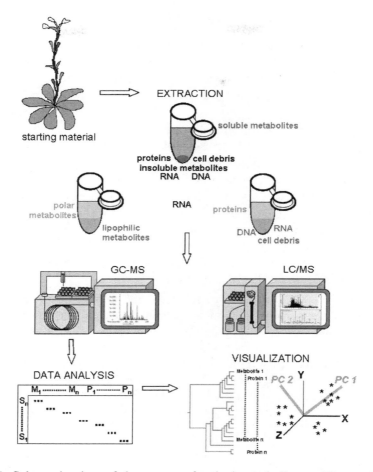

Fig. 1. Schematic view of the strategy for dual metabolite profiling and protein profiling of the same sample material, from harvesting to data analysis. M1...Mn: Metabolite 1 to n. P1...Pn: Protein 1...n.

if one wants to compare different species. For *A. thaliana*, a convenient growth stage-based classification is given by Boyes et al. *(13)*.

Plant metabolism is a highly dynamic system and the response to environmental (or other) changes (e.g., wounding) can occur in seconds or milliseconds. To avoid undesired artifactual changes on the metabolite and/or protein level, any further metabolism must be prevented. This holds especially true for the harvest process; here one has to work quickly and systematically. Freeze the harvested leaf tissue immediately in liquid nitrogen in order to quench enzyme activity and store the tissue at −80°C until further use.

3.2 Integrative Extraction of Metabolites and Proteins

The applied extraction method should be as simple and rapid as possible. Compared to proteins, metabolites show a remarkable variability regarding their chemical structures and physiological properties, which complicates the extraction procedure. All compounds which are to be analyzed must be recovered to avoid bias.

If strong differences on the metabolite and/or protein level are expected between samples that are to be compared, build a master sample. A master sample is an average sample reflecting all states of the sample set that is generated either by the extraction of pooled plant material or by combining relevant extracts. Use the master sample in order to build reference chromatograms (*see* **Fig. 2**) and master lists for metabolite and protein identification. However, averaging destroys information; thus, in some cases this may result in false-negative outcomes owing to dilution below the detection limit.

Here, a proposed method for the extraction of soluble metabolites and proteins from the same plant leaf tissue is given.

1. Grind harvested leaf tissue using a Retsch mill or prechilled mortar. Ensure a similar homogeneity for tissues that are to be compared. Make sure that the material remains frozen during grinding. Thawing will affect the results dramatically and, therefore, *must* be avoided.
    a. Retsch mill: prepare 2-mL Eppendorf tubes each containing a Retsch ball. Use an appropriate hole punch (3–5-mm I.D.) and place one to three tissue disks in the prepared tubes. Immediately freeze samples in liquid nitrogen and then homogenize the samples for 20 s with a frequency of 20/s.
    b. Mortar: weigh out an appropriate amount (10–50 mg) of homogenized material into prechilled 2-mL Eppendorf tubes.
2. Add 1.0–1.5 mL of the prechilled metabolite extraction buffer and 10 µL of the internal standard solution (*see* **Note 3**).
3. Vortex samples thoroughly for 10 s and subsequently shake samples for 8 min at 4°C.
4. Centrifuge at 14,000g for 4 min.

This will result in nongreen pellets containing cell debris, RNA, DNA, and proteins, which also can be used for further analysis (*see* **Subheading 3.6.**). Soluble metabolites are extracted into the supernatants.

3.3. Preparation of the Metabolite Fraction for GC-TOF-MS Analysis

3.3.1. Fractionation

1. Separate the green supernatants into polar and lipophilic phases by adding 0.5 mL ddH$_2$O, vortexing, and centrifuging for 2 min at 14,000g (*see* **Note 4**).
2. Collect the upper polar phases and dry them completely in a speed-vac concentrator. Dried samples can be stored at –80°C until GC–MS analysis.

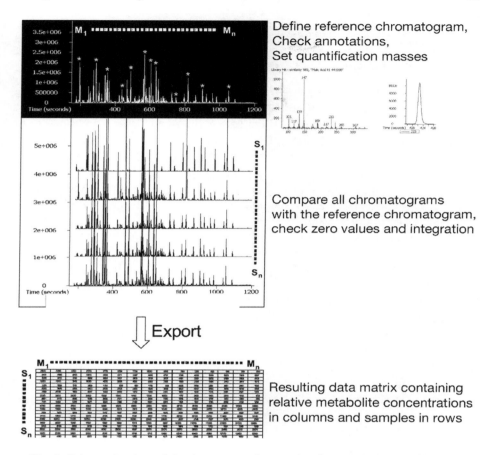

Define reference chromatogram,
Check annotations,
Set quantification masses

Compare all chromatograms
with the reference chromatogram,
check zero values and integration

Export

Resulting data matrix containing
relative metabolite concentrations
in columns and samples in rows

Fig. 2. Schematic view of the data processing routine for metabolite profiling using gas chromatography-time-of-flight-mass spectrometry, starting with the selection of a reference chromatogram, followed by matching of all chromatograms against the reference, and then construction of a data matrix containing relative metabolite concentrations.

3.3.2. Derivatization

1. Prepare a fresh solution of 40 mg/mL methoxyamine hydrochloride in dry pyridine.
2. Add an appropriate volume of this solution to the dried metabolite pellets. Guidance level: 20 µL per 20 mg fresh weight (FW). Incubate for 90 min at 30°C with rigorous shaking.
3. Subsequently add 180 µL MSTFA per 20 mg FW and incubate for an additional 30 min at 37°C with rigorous shaking. Centrifuge at 14,000*g* for 2 min and transfer the samples into GC vials.

4. Add 1 μL of the retention time index marker prior to injection into the GC to provide an additional criteria for compound identification (*see also* **Notes 5–7**).

3.4. GC-TOF-MS Setup for Metabolite Profiling

In principal, each kind of GC–MS setup can be used for metabolite profiling assuming a high data acquisition speed and mass range. Scan rates of at least 20/s and mass ranges of 80 to 600 Da are recommended. The prerequisite to achieve valuable data is the compliance with the maintenance routine as recommended by the manufacturer of the system. For finding optimal parameters, the manufacturer's auto-tune functions are of great benefit.

In this section, a typical setup for plant metabolite profiling via GC coupled to a LECO Pegasus II TOF mass analyzer according to Morgenthal et al. *(9)* is described. The major advantage of the Pegasus is its capability to acquire full-range spectra at high scan rates without sacrificing data quality, thus allowing for the resolution of highly complex mixtures without the need for further separation or fractionation techniques, as in the case of polar plant metabolite extracts.

The GC-TOF-MS analysis is performed on an HP 5890 gas chromatograph with deactivated standard split/splitless liners containing glass wool. One microliter of sample is injected in the splitless mode at a 230°C injector temperature. GC is operated on a MDN-35 capillary, 30 m × 0.32 mm I.D., 25 μm film (Supelco, Bellefonte, PA), at a constant flow of 2 mL/min helium. The temperature program starts with 2 min isocratic at 85°C, followed by temperature ramping at 15°C/min to a final temperature of 360°C, which is held for 8 min. Data acquisition is performed on a Pegasus II TOF mass spectrometer with an acquisition rate of 20 scans/s in the mass range of $m/z = 85$–600.

3.5. Metabolite Detection and Quantification

Compared to target analyses where the compounds of interest are clearly defined and their number is clear-cut, metabolite profiling deals with a much larger number of analytes in an unbiased manner. Thus, unambiguous identification and quantification represent a special challenge. Beside this, a high data acquisition speed goes along with the production of large amounts of data in short periods of time. The limiting factor today is the data evaluation rather than the data acquisition.

For compound identification two criteria are at the user's disposal: on the one hand the fragmentation pattern resulting in mass spectra specific for almost every compound and on the other, the retention time and the retention time index *(14,15)*. Generally, only the combination of these two criteria provides evidence sufficient for identification. In particular, carbohydrates, whose chemical structures often differ only in the configuration of a single hydroxyl group, yield similar mass spectra. Such metabolites are only distinguishable on the basis of their retention time. Hence, the existence of a user-defined spectra library containing additional information about the retention behavior alongside the fragmentation pattern of the analytes of interest is indispensable. Owing to the variety of derivatization methods, freely available online scientific databases like the National Institute of Standards and Technology (NIST) Standard Reference Database (www.nist.gov) are often insufficient. A big drawback of such databases is the absence of information regarding retention time or retention index.

Additionally, the integration of a defined quality control mixture into the analysis routine can serve as basis for the identification and quantification of compounds (*see* **Notes 8–10**).

General steps in data analysis using the ChromaTOF software package from LECO that enables automated data processing routines are described here (*see also* **Fig. 2**).

1. Process all chromatograms of your sample set by computing the baseline for each mass, finding peaks above the baseline, and identifying all peaks found with a valuable signal-to-noise threshold (*see* **Note 11**).
2. Use the master chromatogram as a reference or define a reference chromatogram depending on the number of detected peaks. Calculate retention time indices with the help of the retention time index marker added prior to injection into the GC.
3. Manually check the annotation in the reference chromatogram obtained by the data processing routine; here one has to count with mismatches (*see* **Fig. 3**). Compare the peaks detected to a user-defined spectra library containing retention time indices (*see* **Notes 12** and **13**).
4. Define ion traces specific for each analyte to be quantified.
5. Compare all chromatograms of your sample set to your reference chromatogram with valuable match factors (*see* **Note 11**) and calculate the peak areas and/or heights (*see* **Note 14**).
6. Export chromatography data to a spreadsheet program (e.g., Microsoft Excel).
7. Normalize the data either to leaf area (if a hole puncher was used) or to milligram FW (if a mortar was used) and subsequently to endogenously added stable isotope-labeled internal standard compounds.

Presumably, the obtained data matrix will contain a couple of zero values. These zero values are in most cases caused by deconvolution failings (*see* **Fig. 3**) and are, therefore, not of biological relevance. Unfortunately, this limitation can still not be overcome by an automated procedure. Thus, manual evaluation of these data points is strongly recommended.

3.6. Preparation of the Protein Fraction for LC–MS Shotgun Analysis

3.6.1. Fractionation

1. Solubilize pellets obtained from **Subheading 3.2.** in 200 µL protein extraction buffer per 50 mg FW and add 2-mercaptoethanol to a final concentration of 1% (v/v).

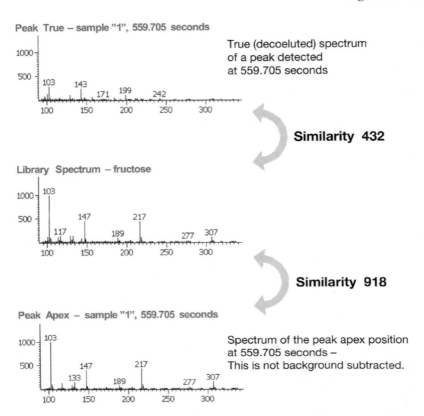

Fig. 3. Example of a deconvolution failure of a detected fructose peak. Peak True and Peak Apex spectrum of the identical peak from the identical chromatogram show a strong discrepancy. The low similarity between the Peak True spectrum and the library spectrum (similarity factor of 432) may result either in nonidentification of fructose, or in zero values in the resulting data matrix. The strong similarity of the Peak Apex spectrum to the library spectrum indicates "nonsense deconvolution."

2. Add 600 μL (3 vol) TE buffer equilibrated phenol and shake for 30 min at 4°C
3. Centrifuge at 4000*g* for 8 min. Soluble proteins are now dissolved in the *upper* phenolic phase (*see* **Note 15**). Separate the phenolic phase.
4. Precipitate proteins overnight in 5 vol ice-cold acetone.
5. Centrifuge at 4000*g* for 8 min.
6. Wash pellet three times with ice-cold methanol.

Protein pellets can be stored at −80°C until further use (*see* **Note 16**).

The precipitated proteins can directly be used for further analysis via 2D-PAGE. For shotgun proteomics, further enzymatic digestion is necessary.

3.6.2. Enzymatic Digestion

1. Redissolve pellet in an appropriate volume of Lys-C digestion buffer (approx 50 μL per 50 mg FW).
2. Determine protein amount according to **ref. 16**.
3. Reduce proteins with DTT in a final concentration of 5 mM with gentle shaking for 30 min at 37°C.
4. For alkylation, add an appropriate amount of a freshly prepared IAA solution to a final concentration of 100 mM, and incubate for 1 h in the dark at room temperature with gentle shaking.
5. To quench IAA activity, add further DTT to 10 mM final concentration.
6. Digest proteins with endoproteinase Lys-C with an enzyme:substrate ratio of 1:1000 for 5 h at 37°C with gentle shaking.
7. Dilute proteins fourfold with trypsin digestion buffer resulting in a final urea concentration of 2 M.
8. Add poroszyme bulk immobilized trypsin to an exact ratio 1:20 enzyme:substrate (trypsin is used as internal standard) and digest proteins for 10 h to no more than 15 h at 37°C with gentle shaking.
9. Desalt the protein digest solution using a SPEC C18 96-well plate according to the manufacturer's instructions.
10. After lyophilization of the tryptic peptide eluate, pellets can be stored at −80°C until use.

3.7. LC–MS Setup for Protein for Shotgun Proteomics

Although the instrumentation may vary, in addition to adequate chromatographic separation of the peptides, shotgun proteomics requires fast scanning mass analyzers. Unlike metabolite profiling, shotgun proteomics is mostly applied to reversed-phase C18 columns. Thereby polymeric monolithic capillary columns, consisting of a continuous polymeric porous stationary phase, offer the best separation efficiencies because of the lack of interparticular void volumes compared to packed particle columns (*see also* **Note 17** and Chapter 9).

In this section, a detailed example of shotgun proteomic analysis of plant leaf protein extracts on a Finnigan LTQ linear ion trap mass spectrometer equipped with an Agilent nano-HPLC system is given. Sample separation was performed on a reversed-phase C18 monolithic silica-based capillary column (1 m × 100-μm I.D.; manufactured in the lab of Professor Nabuo Tanka, Kyoto, Japan) *(12)*.

1. Prior to MS analysis, pellets of the protein digests are dissolved in 5% FA. ACN can be added (up to 10% [v/v]) to increase solubilization of hydrophobic peptides.
2. 200 μg protein per sample are loaded onto a peptide-trap column (Michrom, Auburn, CA) with a flow rate of 10 μL/min. After 10 min of washing the peptide-trap column with solvent A, the sample is eluted to a RV C18 monolithic

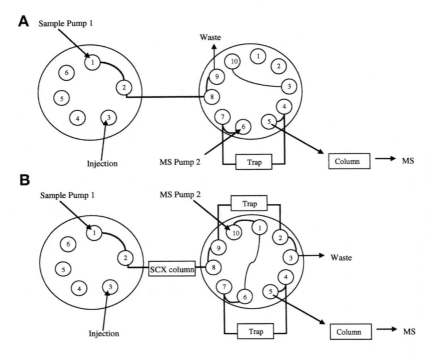

Fig. 4. Schematic configuration of one-dimensional and a two-dimensional (2D) nano column switching liquid chromatography–mass spectrometry (LC–MS) system for shotgun proteomics. **(A)** Shown are switching valves and a preconcentration column (peptide trap). The tryptic digest of a complex protein sample is loaded onto a peptide trap column, washed, and then by valve switching eluted to the analytical column connected to MS. Two pumps are needed for this setup, a sample pump loading the sample and a MS pump delivering a solvent gradient to the analytical column and the MS. **(B)** Setup of a 2D nano-LC–MS with a strong cation exchange (SCX) column as the first dimension and two preconcentration columns as peptide traps. During loading and washing steps of salt fractions from the SCX column to the peptide traps, the MS pump enables the parallel analysis on the analytical column (for details *see* **ref. *13***).

column (1 m × 100-µm I.D.) *(12)*, which is coupled to the mass spectrometer (Iontrap MS, *see* **Subheading 2.1.** and **Fig. 4** for details). Peptides are eluted by increasing solvent B (*see* **Subheading 2.3.**) from 0 to 100% within 4 h using the Agilent nano-HPLC system with a flow rate of 300 nL/min (*see* **Fig. 4** for details). Eluting peptides are analyzed with the LTQ mass spectrometer using a triple play where the three most abundant ions are selected for MS^2 and subsequently put on an exclusion list for the next 3 min (*see* **Notes 18–21**).

3. After MS analysis, DTA files are created from RAW files and searched against a database (*see* **Note 22**) using a search algorithm such as Sequest (Bioworks 3.1).

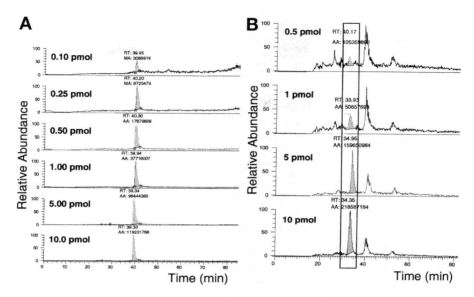

Fig. 5. Quantitative nano-liquid chromatography–mass spectrometry (LC–MS) analysis of a spiked *Arabidopsis* leaf extract protein sample. A recombinant purified protein was spiked into the complex sample to demonstrate the quantification process and matrix effects. **(A)** Extracted ion chromatograms of a tryptic peptide from the digested recombinant protein with increasing concentrations from 0.1 to 10 pmol. The resulting calibration curve for the determination of the absolute concentration of the tryptic peptide/corresponding protein is shown below with a correlation coefficient of 0.99. **(B)** Extracted ion chromatograms of the same peptide after spiking the recombinant protein in the complex *Arabidopsis* leaf protein sample with increasing concentrations from 0.5 to 10 pmol. The protein complex (leaf protein and recombinant protein) was digested, analyzed by nano-LC–MS, and the resulting calibration curve for the concentration of the spiked peptide/corresponding protein was determined. The correlation coefficient is 0.9.

4. With DTASelect (*see* **Note 23**), redundancies are filtered out and using following criteria Xcorr: –1 2.0, –2 2.0, –3 3.5 (*17*), ΔCn value greater than 0.08, a list of identified proteins is obtained. At least two different peptides fulfilling these criteria are required for unambiguous protein identification.

3.8. Protein Quantification

For quantitative analysis, Contrast (*18*) allows one to compare peptides identified in different runs (*see* **Note 24**). These peptides can be used for the extraction of specific ion traces from full MS chromatograms. Subsequent peak areas can be integrated using Bioworks 3.1 Qual Browser (*see* **Fig. 5A,B**). In a manner similar to that employed in metabolite identification and quantification (*see* **Subheading 3.5.**), the retention time is an important criterion for unambiguous identification and subsequent quantification of proteins and/or peptides present in different biological samples (*see* **Note 25**). It is necessary to detect at least two peptides and to integrate their specific ion traces. Averaging different peptide integrals of the same protein then results in accurate quantification. Deviations in electrospray ionization efficiency are normalized to internal standard peptides (*see* **Note 26**).

3.9. Statistical Data Analysis

The subsequent analysis of metabolites and proteins in one dataset enables the ranking of proteins based on their impact on the metabolite dynamics (*see* **Fig. 6**). This is an extension of existing methods ranking protein differences based on their changes to a reference.

1. All data were normalized to milligram FW and stable isotope-labeled standard compounds. All statistical tests were performed in MATLAB 6.5.
2. Data normalization enables the comparison of profiling data originating from different instruments, such as GC-TOF-MS data and LC–MS data. The signal intensities of the instruments represent arbitrary units. To ensure a comparable scale the measurements of each metabolite and protein were first divided by the median. This allows for a direct comparison of different metabolite or protein levels. A high relative change in concentration is then still represented by a high variance. Subsequent log-transformation increases the importance of low-intensity metabolites and compresses the upper end of measurement scale and thus leads to more balanced variables. Furthermore, the influence of potential outliers is reduced.
3. Independent component analysis (ICA) was applied in combination with principal component analysis (PCA) as preprocessing and the measure of kurtosis was used as an evaluation criterion. The dimensionality of the data was first reduced by PCA to a set of three principal components. ICA was then applied to this reduced dataset and the extracted independent components were ranked by the kurtosis measure. The contributions of each metabolite/protein to a independent component can be obtained by combining the transformation matrix W of PCA with the transformation matrix V of ICA to a direct transformation $U = W*V$. The elements of the i-th vector in U represent the individual contributions to the i-th independent component (ICi). (For more details, *see* Chapter 6.)

4. Notes

1. Each measurement has errors; the value determined never fully corresponds to the ideal "true value." Errors can be "random errors" or "systematic errors." "Random errors" are avoided easily by replicate measurements. "Systematic errors" are often revealed by standardization.

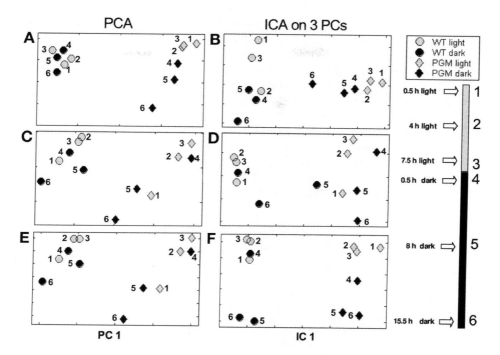

Fig. 6. Principal components analysis (PCA) and independent component analysis (ICA) of the protein data, the metabolite data, and the integrative protein/metabolite data matrix. The improvement of pattern recognition with focus on the discovery of sets of biomarkers reflecting the genetic background (WT or PGM mutant), as well as the physiological state (different time-points throughout a diurnal rhythm) is clearly visible in (**F**), where ICA was performed on the integrated metabolite/protein dataset (for more details *see* **ref. 10** and Chapter 6). (**A**) PCA proteins, (**B**) ICA proteins, (**C**) PCA metabolites, (**D**) ICA metabolites, (**E**) PCA metabolites/proteins, (**F**) ICA metabolites/proteins.

2. Reproducibility is not a guarantee for accurate results; wrong results may be reproducible.
3. Degassing of solvents minimizes the formation of byproducts.
4. Phase separation is a subtle step; semipolar metabolites such as tryptophan are often incompletely extracted into the polar phase. The recovery can be checked by adding internal standards before and after the extraction procedure.
5. The KOVATS retention time index system vastly simplifies the identification of compounds. Commonly used *n*-alkanes may provide poor peak shapes on some polar phases. In such cases, *n*-FAMEs can be used as references.
6. The classical KOVATS retention time index for a linear alkane is by definition equal to 100 times the number of carbon atoms. Using the same instrumental

setup (identical column, unchanged temperature program, and other), the KOVATS retention time index remains constant. Changes in the instrumental setup may lead to considerable alterations of the KOVATS retention index.

7. In nature, exclusively even-numbered n-alkanes or n-FAMEs are found. Basic ester hydrolysis of even-numbered FAMEs occurring during the derivatization may result in false-positive identification of free fatty acids.

8. As a rule of thumb in GC, 10 ng is an appropriate injection level.

9. A quality control mix should contain metabolites representing all compound classes in defined concentrations. Calibration curves can be constructed by measuring dilution series of this mixture.

10. In GC–MS analysis, no significant matrix effects arise. Calibration curves can be constructed from measurements of standards; there is no need for spiking into the matrix.

11. Thresholds set during data processing may affect the outcome dramatically. The match threshold is more important for the assignment of compound in the reference chromatogram than for comparison of chromatograms with the reference. Peaks below a signal to noise of five frequently provide peak shapes objectionable for quantification. Benchmarks for the data analysis using the ChromaTOF sofware package from LECO: match threshold 700 (for assignment in the reference) and 500 (for comparison with the reference), signal-to-noise 10, RI deviation 5.

12. GC-TOF-MS identifies peaks within chromatograms. The number of detected peaks does not necessarily correspond to the number of metabolites. Carbohydrates and related compounds form anomers during derivatization (methoximation) yielding at least two peaks. The derivatization of acidic protons (silylation) is incomplete, leading to multiple detection of the corresponding derivatives (singly, doubly, or triply silylated functional groups).

13. Some metabolites tend to degrade. Ascorbic acid, for example, can be oxidized yielding dehydroascorbic acid, and pyroglutamic acid is often formed by glutamic acid breakdown. Hexose phosphates, like glucose-6-phosphate or fructose-6-phosphate, can be present in an open-chain configuration and are therefore very reactive. Degradation of labile compounds can be checked by adding two internal standards, one being stable, the other being of similar stability as the compound.

14. Quantification via peak area is superior to quantification via peak height.

15. The high sucrose concentration in the protein extraction buffer causes a phase reversal, thus the phenol fraction, which is usually the bottom phase, is now separated into the upper phase. Water residuals in the protein pellet may prevent this phase reversal. In this case, additional supplementation of sucrose-containing protein extraction buffer converts the phases.

16. Protein degradation is extremely rapid. Pellets can be stored for a maximum of 4 wk at −80°C until further use. Although a high amount of protein is needed, provide at least 3 (5–10 is even better) replicate samples of each experimental condition.

17. The use of monolithic silica-based C18 columns clearly improves the resolving power of the chromatography (19). In addition, back-pressure is significantly

lower and loading capacity and lifetimes are increased. Clogged or chapped capillary ends may affect the chromatographic power. Perfectly square cut capillary ends can be polished by fingers to minimize band broadening and tailing.

18. To avoid carry-over, a blank gradient between each sample is recommended strongly.

19. To check spray and chromatographic conditions, 100 fmol Glufibrino peptide (Sigma) is injected and the peak shape monitored. This can be done instead of using a blank gradient between the samples.

20. Methanol instead of ACN often offers better peak separation (*see also* **ref. 20**).

21. The two-dimensional vs one-dimensional HPLC chromatography (*see* **Fig. 5**) for quantitative analysis is more time consuming. Instead of peak integration, the use of spectrum count data may be preferred in this case as a fast and comprehensive semiquantitative approach *(21)*.

22. The Arabidopsis protein database may be downloaded at ftp://ftpmips.gsf.de/cress/.

23. DTASelect and Contrast *(18)* may be found at http://fields.scripps.edu/DTA Select/.

24. To generate a list of peptides for peak integration, a DTAselect software package was used that assembles SEQUEST identifications and highlights the most significant matches. The accompanying Contrast tool compares DTASelect results from multiple experiments *(18)*.

25. Peptides in complex mixture generally elute earlier than in purified samples. A RT shift of approx 5 min can be observed (compare **Fig. 6A** with **Fig. 6B**). It may well be useful to implement a retention time index based on a series of internal retention time markers.

26. It is possible to normalize to specific trypsin peptides (internal standard) with the following precursor masses 1081.5, 1136.5, and 1144.5 (data not shown). This results in a coefficient of variation of about 25%. Therefore, an exact trypsin/protein ratio has to be ensured. For future applications, the optimum is a set of stable isotope-labeled peptides distributed over the whole chromatography range.

Acknowledgments

We thank Megan McKenzie for revising the manuscript. We thank the Max Planck Society for financial support.

References

1. The Arabidopsis Genome Initiative (2000) Analysis of the genome sequence of the flowering plant Arabidopsis thaliana. *Nature* **408,** 796–815.
2. Fiehn, O., Kopka, J., Dormann, P., Altmann, T., Trethewey, R. N., and Willmitzer, L. (2000) Metabolite profiling for plant functional genomics. *Nat. Biotechnol* **18,** 1157–1161.
3. Fiehn, O. (2002) Metabolomics: the link between genotypes and phenotypes. *Plant Mol. Biol.* **48,** 155–171.

4. Weckwerth, W. (2003) Metabolomics in systems biology. *Ann. Rev. Plant Biol.* **54,** 669–689.
5. Weckwerth, W., Wenzel, K., and Fiehn, O. (2004) Process for the integrated extraction identification, and quantification of metabolites, proteins and RNA to reveal their co-regulation in biochemical networks. *Proteomics* **4,** 78–83.
6. Boldt, R., Edner, C., Kolukisaoglu, U., et al. (2005) D-Glycerate 3-kinase, the last unknown enzyme in the photorespiratory cycle in Arabidopsis, belongs to a novel kinase family. *Plant Cell* **17,** 2413–2420.
7. Weckwerth, W., Tolstikov, V., and Fiehn, O. (2001) Metabolomic characterization of transgenic potato plants using GC/TOF and LC/MS analysis reveals silent metabolic phenotypes. *Proceedings of the 49th ASMS Conference on Mass spectrometry and Allied Topics, American Society of Mass Spectrometry, Chicago,* 1–2.
8. Weckwerth, W., Loureiro, M. E., Wenzel, K., and Fiehn, O. (2004) Differential metabolic networks unravel the effects of silent plant phenotypes. *Proc. Natl. Acad. Sci. USA* **101,** 7809–7814.
9. Morgenthal, K., Wienkoop, S., Scholz, M., Selbig, J., and Weckwerth, W. (2005) Correlative GC-TOF-MS based metabolite profiling and LC-MS based protein profiling reveal time-related systemic regulation of metabolite-protein networks and improve pattern recognition for multiple biomarker selection. *Metabolomics* **1,** 109–121.
10. Morgenthal, K., Weckwerth, W., and Steuer, R. (2006) Metabolomic networks in plants: transitions from pattern recognition to biological interpretation. *Biosystems* **83,** 108–117.
11. Whitelegge, J. P. (2004) Mass spectrometry for high throughput quantitative proteomics in plant research: lessons from thylakoid membranes. *Plant Physiol. Biochem.* **42,** 919–927.
12. Wienkoop, S., Glinski, M., Tanaka, N., Tolstikov, V., Fiehn, O., and Weckwerth, W. (2004) Linking protein fractionation with multidimensional monolithic reversed-phase peptide chromatography/mass spectrometry enhances protein identification from complex mixtures even in the presence of abundant proteins. *Rapid Commun. Mass Spectrom.* **18,** 643–650.
13. Boyes, D. C., Zayed, A. M., Ascenzi, R., et al. (2001) Growth stage-based phenotypic analysis of arabidopsis: A model for high throughput functional genomics in plants. *Plant Cell* **13,** 1499–1510.
14. Peng, C. T. (1994) Retrieval of structure information from retention index. *J. Chromatogr. A* **678,** 189–200.
15. Kovats, E. (1958) Gas-chromatographische charakterisierung organischer verbindungen .1. Retentionsindices Aliphatischer Halogenide, Alkohole, Aldehyde Und Ketone. *Helvetica Chimica Acta* **41,** 1915–1932.
16. Bradford, M. M. (1976) Rapid and sensitive method for quantitation of microgram quantities of protein utilizing principle of protein-dye binding. *Anal. Biochem.* **72,** 248–254.
17. Peng, J., Elias, J. E., Thoreen, C. C., Licklider, L. J., and Gygi, S. P. (2003) Evaluation of multidimensional chromatography coupled with tandem mass spectrom-

etry (LC/LC-MS/MS) for large-scale protein analysis: the yeast proteome. *J. Proteome Res.* **2,** 43–50.

18. Tabb, D. L., McDonald, W. H., and Yates, J. R. (2002) DTASelect and contrast: Tools for assembling and comparing protein identifications from shotgun proteomics. *J. Proteome Res.* **1,** 21–26.

19. Tanaka, N. and Kobayashi, H. (2003) Monolithic columns for liquid chromatography. *Anal. Bioanal. Chem.* **376,** 298–301.

20. Giorgianni, F., Cappiello, A., Baranova-Giorgianni, S., Palma, P., Trufelli, H., and Desiderio, D. M. (2004) LC-MS/MS analysis of peptides with methanol as organic modifier: improved limits of detection. *Anal. Chem.* **76,** 7028–7038.

21. Liu, H., Sadygov, R. G., and Yates, J. R., 3rd (2004) A model for random sampling and estimation of relative protein abundance in shotgun proteomics. *Anal. Chem.* **76,** 4193–4201.

5

Integrating Profiling Data

Using Linear Correlation to Reveal
Coregulation of Transcript and Metabolites

Ewa Urbanczyk-Wochniak, Lothar Willmitzer, and Alisdair R. Fernie

Summary

Recent advances in the medical and biological sciences have been characterized by a major paradigm shift from reductionism to integrated and holistic systems approaches. Such approaches are characterized at the experimental level by the multiparallel analysis of a multitude of parameters of a given biological system at a range of different molecular levels, following the systematic perturbation of the system in question. Although a multitude of studies have been carried out to assess the transcript, protein, and metabolite complements of cells under various conditions, to date, few have been attempted that encompass the profiling of more than one of these entities. In this chapter, we describe combined analysis of data obtained from transcript and metabolic profiling, and detail advantages of using both approaches in parallel.

Key Words: Data preprocessing; gene expression profiling; metabolite profiling; correlation analysis; biotechnology.

1. Introduction

Developments in high-throughput measurement technologies for biological samples have created a paradigm shift in modern life science research. Advances in nucleotide sequencing techniques have made possible the large-scale sequencing of several genomes including those of the plant species *Arabidopsis thaliana* *(1)* and rice *(2)*, and the expression analysis of complete genomes (or large proportions thereof) at the transcript level *(3)*. Similar strategies to allow comprehensive studies of protein and metabolite complements of the cell are still at a

From: *Methods in Molecular Biology, vol. 358: Metabolomics: Methods and Protocols*
Edited by: W. Weckwerth © Humana Press Inc., Totowa, NJ

relatively early stage in their development. That said, rapid progress has been made in proteomic *(4)* and metabolomic *(5)* analyses in recent years, but for a better understanding of systems regulation, transcriptomics, proteomics, or metabolomics data need to be garnered in parallel (*see also* Chapter 4 for integration of metabolite and protein data). Examples of combined studies on the transcriptome and a subset of the proteome have been performed in *Saccharomyces cerevisiae (6–8)*, whereas Askenazi et al. *(9)* presented a parallel analysis of complex gene expression with a limited number of metabolites. More comprehensive analysis of transcriptome and metabolome data was, however, presented recently in elegant studies of the response of plants to nutritional stress *(10)*.

We previously presented a broad parallel analysis of metabolites and transcripts using gas chromatography–mass spectrometry (GC–MS)-based metabolic profiling in tandem with gene expression data analysis using classical array technology to investigate genetically and developmentally distinct potato tuber systems *(11)*. We chose to analyze five developmental stages of potato tuber and two well-characterized transgenic lines exhibiting altered sucrose mobilization. Parallel samples were used to analyze the expression of approx 2000 expressed sequence tags (ESTs) encoding a wide variety of biosynthetic genes, whereas the levels of the major primary metabolites were determined using a GC–MS protocol. To go beyond a conventional description of the transcriptomic and metabolomic changes we decided to combine the datasets in order to ascertain if we could use them in the generation of novel hypotheses of metabolic regulation. As a first approach, we decided to apply simple correlation analysis *(11)* because this has proven to be effective in analyzing correlations within the datasets of a given phenotyping platform. Transcript:transcript correlations have frequently been used to determine patterns of gene regulation and coexpression of genes of the same metabolic pathway (for an example *see* **refs.** *12–14*). Similarly, applications of correlation analysis to large-scale metabolite datasets have highlighted a wide number of relationships ranging from those of metabolites clearly linked by a single, reversible enzyme to nonlinearly associated metabolites of pathways known to be under feedforward and feedback control *(15,16)*. Because we determined the relative levels of transcripts and metabolites within the same samples, we checked the level of each transcript against that of each metabolite. The number of significant correlations that we obtained via this approach was well above those that would be conventionally expected to be owing to chance. Examples of significant correlations are given in **Figs. 1–3**. That said, the parallel analysis of metabolite and transcript data is clearly a powerful tool in the generation of clear and testable hypotheses, and such approaches are likely to be of immense interest to the metabolic engineering.

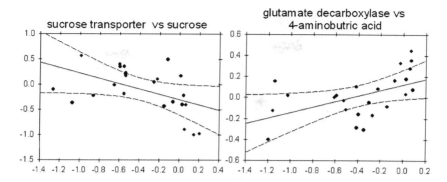

Fig. 1. Correlation between metabolite and transcript levels of the analyzed systems. Correlation between the level of chemically defined metabolites and the level of selected clones was assessed, and then was plotted using the logarithimic scale. r_s Values are given in parenthesis. (**A**) Sucrose transporter vs sucrose ($r_s = -0.52$). (**B**) Glutamate decarboxylase vs 4-aminobutric acid ($r_s = 0.55$). (Reproduced with permission from **ref. 11**.)

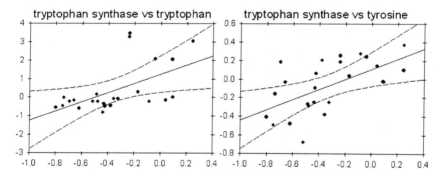

Fig. 2. Correlation between metabolite and transcript levels of the analyzed systems. Correlation between the level of chemical-defined metabolites and the level of selected clones was assessed, and then there are plotted using the logarithimic scale, r_s values are given in parenthesis: (**A**) tryptophan synthase β chain 1 vs tryptophan ($r_s = 0.61$); (**B**) tryptophan synthase β chain 1 vs tyrosine ($r_s = 0.65$). (Reproduced with permission from **ref. 11**.)

2. Materials

2.1. Plant Materials and Growth Conditions

To produce comparable material, all plants should be grown in tightly controlled environmental and developmental conditions. For potato (*Solanum tuberosum*), plants initially are maintained in tissue culture with a 16 h-light/8 h-dark regime on Murashige and Skoog (*17*) medium containing 2% sucrose.

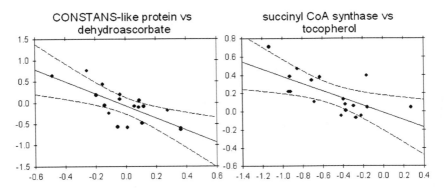

Fig. 3. Correlation between metabolite and transcript levels of the analyzed systems. Correlation between the level of chemical-defined metabolites and the level of selected clones was assessed, and then there are plotted using the logarithimic scale, r_s values are given in parenthesis: (A) CONSTANS-like protein vs ascorbate ($r_s = -0.72$); (B) succinyl-CoA synthetase α subunit vs tocopherol ($r_s = -0.64$). (Reproduced with permission from ref. *11*.)

After transfer to a greenhouse, plants are grown under the same light regime with a minimum of 250 μmol photons m^{-2} s^{-1} at 22°C with days starting at 6 AM and ending at 10 PM. Healthy, similar-sized, developing tubers of the same shape and color are selected for experimental purposes. For each replicate, a pool of tuber tissue is taken. Sample tuber slices are cut with a cork bore (10 mm) and immediately snap-frozen in liquid nitrogen. Tissues samples are stored at –80°C, and after homogenization of frozen material, divided into aliquots for transcript and metabolite analysis.

2.2. Data From Gene Expression Analysis

For transcript profiling, several methods have become available recently (comprehensively reviewed in **ref. 3**). In the method described here, about 1000 biosynthetic genes can be analyzed on a custom array constructed on nylon filters (*11*). Each array contains about 2000 tomato ESTs picked up from the cDNA libraries constructed in the laboratories of Dr. Steve Tanksley, Cornell University Solanaceae Genome Network; Dr. Greg Martin, Boyce Thompson Institute; and Dr. Jim Giovannoni, Boyce Thompson Institute and provided by TIGR (*see* **Note 1**). Using the website annotation http://www. tigr.org/tdb/tgi/lgi/ form LeGI Release 7.0–May 22, 2001, approx 1000 interesting tentative consensus (TCs) were selected, and for each, at least two ESTs were picked to form our Solanaceous library (*see* **Note 2**). The "raw" datasets obtained from microarray analysis are submitted to our in-house *Haruspex* database (http://www.mpimp-golm.mpg.de/haruspex/index-e.html). Within

Haruspex, the raw data are annotated, rearranged, and normalized in a way that makes them comparable between hybridizations. *Haruspex* is optimized to handle expression profiles derived from hybridizations on nylon membranes performed with radioactively labeled mRNA probes *(11,18,19)*. In order to normalize the raw data fully, a two-step procedure is followed. To quantify the PCR products spotted on the membrane, a hybridization with short oligonucleotides specific for the vector part of the product is performed. This reference hybridization has to be done once for every new filter. Subsequent hybridizations with complex probes (complex hybridization) need to be correlated to their corresponding reference hybridization in order to retrieve fully normalized data, which can be used for further correlation analysis.

2.3. Metabolite Profiling

Parallel samples are used for the determination of the level of primary metabolites including sugars, sugar alcohols, organic acids, amino acids, as well as the nutritionally important ascorbate and tocopherol using a GC–MS protocol. Metabolite analyses can be carried out using a GC–MS system consisting of an AS 2000 autosampler, a GC 8000, and a Voyager quadrupole mass spectrometer (ThermoQuest, Manchester, UK) *(15)*. Chromatograms and mass spectra can be evaluated using the MASSLAB program (ThermoQuest). For evaluation of relative metabolite levels, the peak areas derived from a specific ion trace indicative of each analyzed compound are normalized by the peak area derived from an internal standard added to the sample. The resulting values, termed response ratios, are subsequently converted to relative response ratios through division by the fresh weight of each sample. The relative response ratio of each metabolite from each chromatogram can subsequently be used for correlation analysis.

3. Methods

3.1. Preprocessing of Data

3.1.1. Standardization

Given that there is a fair degree of natural variation at the levels of both transcripts and metabolites, all individual values (replicates) measured are used for correlation analysis rather than the mean of replicate samples. In fact, evaluating correlations in natural as well as experimental variables adds to the robustness of any subsequently identified coregulation. Furthermore, from a pragmatic approach it allows statistically valid experiments to be carried out at slightly lower sample size—an important fact given the expense incurred in these experiments. A consequence of taking this approach is that before a comparison of several arrays or GC–MS runs can be made, variations between the experiments caused by technical and biological factors must be corrected by mathematical standardizations (*see* **Note 3**).

After primary normalization of microarray data (*see* **Subheading 2.2.**), each value for each specific EST obtained following a hybridization is divided by the average value for this EST achieved after hybridizations with control samples (be these wild-type samples in comparison to mutant samples or untreated in comparison to treated samples). Similarly, metabolite data is standardized by dividing the relative response of each ion of a sample by the relative response of that ion in the control samples.

For all subsequent statistical tests, data are log-transformed, resulting in Gaussian-type distributions.

3.1.2. Finding Outliers

The normalized data are then subjected to Grubbs' test *(20,21)* in order to detect outliers in the dataset (*see* **Note 4**), which are then removed prior to further statistical analyses.

3.1.3. Preselection of Relevant Genes

For EST pairs representing the same gene, nonparametric Spearman's rank-order correlation and parametric Pearson's linear correlation analyses can be applied (*see* **Note 5**). For ease of analyses all of the algorithms can be implemented in PERL programming script. Correlation analysis is used to select ESTs that give highly reproducible results with respect to other ESTs of the consensus sequence (*see* **Subheading 2.2.**) from which they were derived. For this purpose the significance threshold was set to $p = 0.001$. Only ESTs that were below this threshold according to the Spearman method and which appeared reliable during every experiment were selected for subsequent analysis.

3.2. Coresponse Analysis

Correlated expression of the set of preselected genes and changes in metabolites levels can be detected by nonparametric Spearman's rank order correlation analysis with a significance threshold of $p = 0.01$ (*see* **Note 6**).

3.3. Scatter Plots

For selected pairs, scatter plot are performed using Sigma plot 2000 (SYSTAT Software Inc., Chicago, IL) (*see* **Notes 7** and **8**).

4. Notes

1. Because of high similarity at the genome level *(22)*, tomato EST clones were used to create a universal Solanum library, and then used for experiments with potato RNA.

2. TC sequences are created by assembling ESTs into virtual transcripts. In some cases, TCs contain full or partial cDNA sequences (ETs) obtained using classical methods. TCs contain information on the source library and abundance of ESTs and, in many cases, represent full-length transcripts. Alternative splice forms are built into separate TCs. Having two ESTs corresponding to one TC provides the opportunity to select relevant genes (*see* **Subheading 3.1.3.**).

3. The purpose of transcript data normalization is to minimize systematic variations in the measured gene expression level of different mRNA samples, which are hybridized as replicates, so that biological differences can be more easily distinguished, as well as to compare expression levels among different hybridizations *(23)*. Similarly, metabolic datasets measured at different times are not directly comparable because of varying tuning parameters of the GC–MS machine over time. Another goal of standardization is to make possible the comparison from one platform (transcript profiling) to another (metabolite profiling).

4. Outliers are by definition atypical or infrequent observations, data points that do not appear to follow the characteristic distribution of the rest of the data, and they are often excluded from the data after a superficial analysis with quantitative methods.

5. Because there are no EST/gene libraries publicly available for crop plant systems, including the potato tuber system, the relationships between ESTs and potential genes are checked. Relevant genes for a meaningful coresponse analysis are required to exhibit significant changes in gene expression under the experimental conditions analyzed, and ESTs representing the same gene have to exhibit equal hybridization behavior.

6. Rank-order correlation should be chosen because mRNA and metabolite levels may be correlated in a nonlinear manner. Nonparametric methods for correlation analysis are also appropriate in our case, because from relatively few data points it cannot be estimated whether they follow a normal distribution, an assumption for the application parametric methods like Pearson correlation analysis. Spearman's rank-order method is preferred to Kendall test statistics because the latter demand more data points.

   The Spearman correlation uses ranks rather than raw expression levels, which makes it less sensitive to extreme values in the data. The possibility existed that extreme values in the dataset might significantly influence the Pearson calculation and, thereby, enable a small number of microarray experiments to have a disproportionately large effect on our gene similarity measure.

7. The number of obtained correlations should be well above the number of correlations expected to arise by chance. These correlations fall into three classes: (1) confirmatory correlations that are in line with correlations identified in previous experiments (**Fig. 1**), (2) correlations that seem to have a functional basis that can be retrospectively assigned (**Fig. 2**), and (3) novel correlations unrelated to the biochemical pathways in which the gene products participate (**Fig. 3**). Interestingly, in our experiment *(11)*, the majority of the transcript:metabolite correlations observed fell in the third class, and included correlations with nutritionally relevant metabolites such as lysine, methionine, tocopherol, and ascorbate. As

previously mentioned, however, it is clear that correlation analysis merely identifies the co- (or anti)-regulation of parameters and does not allow discrimination of mechanism and a further round of experimentation is required for this purpose. Scanning for the best coresponses among changing (transcript and metabolite) levels allows us to infer hypotheses regarding the functional interaction of transcripts with transcripts, metabolites with metabolites, and especially transcripts with metabolites.

8. The scatter plot is an important graphical tool for studying the spread and linearity of data. In its simplest form, two variables are plotted along the axes, and marks are drawn according to these coordinates.

Acknowledgments

The authors would like to thank the Max Planck Gesellschaft for financial support of this work and Megan McKenzie for critical revision of this chapter.

References

1. The Arabidopsis Genome Initiative. (2000) Analysis of the genome sequence of the flowering plant *Arabidopsis thaliana*. *Nature* **408,** 796–815.
2. Goff, S. A., Ricke, D., Lan, T. H., et al. (2002) A draft sequence of the rice genome (*Oryza sativa L.* ssp. *japonica*). *Science* **296,** 92–100.
3. Aharoni, A. and Vorst, O. (2002) DNA microarrays for functional plant genomics. *Plant Mol. Biol.* **48,** 99–118.
4. Hirano, H., Islamb, N., and Kawasakia, H. (2004) Technical aspects of functional proteomics in plants. *Phytochemistry* **65,** 1487–1498.
5. Fernie, A. R., Trethewey, R. N., Krotzky, A., and Willmitzer, L. (2004) Metabolite profiling: from diagnostics to systems biology. *Nat. Rev. Mol. Cell. Biol.* **5,** 763–769.
6. Futcher, B., Latter, G. I., Monardo, P., McLaughlin, C. S., and Garrels, J. I. (1999) A sampling of the yeast proteome. *Mol. Cell Biol.* **19,** 7357–7368.
7. Gygi, S. P., Rochon, Y., Franza, B. R., and Aebersold, R. (1999) Correlation between protein and mRNA abundance in yeast. *Mol. Cell Biol.* **19,** 1720–1730.
8. Ideker, T., Thorsson, V., Ranish, J. A., et al. (2001) Integrated genomic and proteomic analyses of a systematically perturbed metabolic network. *Science* **292,** 929–934.
9. Askenazi, M., Driggers, E. M., Holtzman, D. A., et al. (2003) Integrating transcriptional and metabolite profiles to direct the engineering of lovastatin-producing fungal strains. *Nat. Biotechnol.* **21,** 150–156.
10. Hirai, M. Y., Yano M., Goodenowe, D. B., et al. (2004) Integration of transcriptomics and metabolomics for understanding of global responses to nutritional stresses in *Arabidopsis thaliana*. *Proc. Natl. Acad. Sci. USA* **101,** 10,205–10,210.
11. Urbanczyk-Wochniak, E., Luedemann, A., Kopka, J., et al. (2003) Parallel analysis of transcript and metabolic profiles: a new approach in systems biology. *EMBO Rep* **4,** 989–993.

12. Niehrs, C. and Pollet, N. (1999) Synexpression groups in eukaryotes. *Nature* **402**, 483–487.
13. Carrari, F., Urbanczyk-Wochniak, E., Willmitzer, L., and Fernie, A. R. (2003) Engineering central metabolism in crop species: learning the system. *Metab. Eng.* **5**, 191–200.
14. Bono, H. and Okazaki, Y. (2002) Functional transcriptomes: comparative analysis of biological pathways and processes in eukaryotes to infer genetic networks among transcripts. *Curr. Opin. Struct. Biol.* **12**, 355–361.
15. Roessner, U., Luedemann, A., Brust, D., et al. (2001) Metabolic profiling allows comprehensive phenotyping of genetically or environmentally modified plant systems. *Plant Cell* **13**, 11–29.
16. Weckwerth, W., Loureiro, M. E., Wenzel, K., and Fiehn, O. (2004) Differential metabolic networks unravel the effects of silent plant phenotypes. *Proc. Natl. Acad. Sci. USA* **101**, 7809–7814.
17. Murashige, T. and Skoog, F. (1962) A revised medium for rapid growth and bioassays with tobacco tissue cultures. *Physiol. Plantarum* **15**, 473–497.
18. Thimm, O., Essigmann, B., Kloska, S., Altmann, T., and Buckhout, T. J. (2001) Response of arabidopsis to iron deficiency stress as revealed by microarray analysis. *Plant Physiol.* **127**, 1030–1043.
19. Colebatch, G., Desbrosses, G., Ott, T., et al. (2004) Global changes in transcription orchestrate metabolic differentiation during symbiotic nitrogen fixation in *Lotus japonicus*. *Plant J.* **39**, 487–512.
20. Grubbs, F. (1969) Procedures for detecting outlying observations in samples. *Technometrics* **11**, 1–21.
21. Stefansky, W. (1972) Rejecting outliers in factorial designs. *Technometrics* **14**, 469–479.
22. Tanksley, S. D., Ganal, M. W., Prince, J. P., et al. (1992) High density molecular linkage maps of the tomato and potato genomes. *Genetics* **132**, 1141–1160.
23. Yang, Y. H., Dudoit, S. Luu, P. et al. (2002) Normalization for cDNA microarray data: a robust composite method addressing single and multiple slide systematic variation. *Nucleic Acids Res.* **30**, 1–10.

6

Visualization and Analysis of Molecular Data

Matthias Scholz and Joachim Selbig

Summary

This chapter provides an overview of visualization and analysis techniques applied to large-scale datasets from genomics, metabolomics, and proteomics. The aim is to reduce the number of variables (genes, metabolites, or proteins) by extracting a small set of new relevant variables, usually termed components. The advantages and disadvantages of the classical principal component analysis (PCA) are discussed and a link is given to the closely related singular value decomposition and multidimensional scaling. Special emphasis is given to the recent trend toward the use of independent component analysis, which aims to extract statistically independent components and, therefore, provides usually more meaningful components than PCA. We also discuss normalization techniques and their influence on the result of different analytical techniques.

Key Words: Data normalization; feature extraction; dimensionality reduction.

1. Introduction

A good visualization of a dataset provides useful information for understanding how experimental conditions affect transcript, metabolite, or protein levels. The large set of variables (genes or metabolites) is reduced to two or three new variables, thereby maintaining most of the information from the original large dataset. The results depend significantly on the normalization technique and on the optimized criteria of the visualization or analysis method.

The new variables are denoted as components, which are usually obtained by a linear combination of all original variables. Thus, a component explains a specific direction in the original data space, which should have some meaning. Ideally, the component is related to a biological or experimental factor such as temperature, experimental time, or to a factor for discriminating different

From: *Methods in Molecular Biology, vol. 358: Metabolomics: Methods and Protocols*
Edited by: W. Weckwerth © Humana Press Inc., Totowa, NJ

ecotypes or different experimental conditions. Sometimes the components are called factors or features.

The methods described are unsupervised techniques, meaning that the group identifier (class labels) are not taken into account by the algorithm. Thus, the extracted components explain the major or global information, or the most important characteristics of the data independently from the experimental conditions, which are unknown to the algorithm. This can tell us whether the investigated experimental conditions are well reflected by the data as expected, or whether there are stronger artifacts owing to badly controlled technical or environmental factors.

A technique is referred to as a dimensionality reduction technique if the main emphasis is on reducing the number of variables, whereas the focus of a feature extraction technique is to obtain meaningful components (features). The classical principal component analysis (PCA) is more likely an example of dimensionality reduction, which is its most widely used application, than of feature extraction. The closely related independent component analysis (ICA), by contrast, aims to extract meaningful components with a high amount of information, the number of variables is usually not reduced. However, often it cannot be well distinguished. Feature extraction means that each extracted component (feature) is a combination of all original variables. The similar term feature selection, by contrast, means that simply a subset of variables is selected from the original variable set, but this is not considered further in this chapter.

2. Materials

The techniques are, in general, applicable to gene expression as well as metabolite or protein profiles. As an example, in this chapter the techniques are applied to metabolite data from a crossing experiment of *Arabidopsis thaliana*. There are four groups, two parental lines Columbia "Col-0" and "C24," and two crosses "Col-0 × C24" and "C24 × Col-0." For each group there are 24 samples (observations), hence, 96 samples altogether. The samples were analyzed using a direct infusion mass spectrometer without chromatographic separation, thus, each spectrum reflects the composition of all metabolites in a given sample (*see* **Fig. 1**). Each sample is characterized by 763 variables, which contain the intensities at 763 different masses (*m/z*), *see* **ref. *1*** for more details. The purpose of the analysis is to investigate how the biological background is reflected in the metabolite data.

3. Methods

Not only the analysis technique affects the quality of the result, a previous normalization has a strong impact as well. Therefore, we also discuss differ-

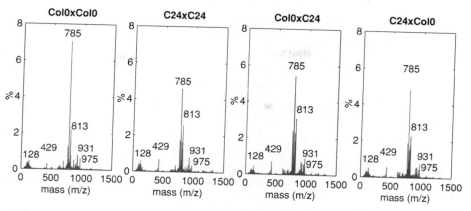

Fig. 1. Mass spectra of *Arabidopsis thaliana* crosses, analyzed to investigate the response at the metabolite level.

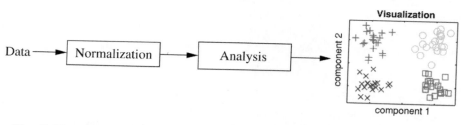

Fig. 2. Normalization and analysis techniques are both important for an optimal visualization or feature extraction result. The plot on the right illustrates samples from different experimental conditions.

ent normalization techniques and their impact on the analysis techniques. The choice of analysis technique depends mainly on the aim of the analysis or the kind of information we are searching for, whereas the normalization technique can be used to make the individual samples comparable for such joint analysis (**Fig. 2**).

3.1. Normalization

Normalization attempts to remove nonbiological contributions or systematic bias from the data. It is a convenient way to include prior knowledge, such as additional technical or biological knowledge, and assumptions about how the generated data can also be taken into account.

Consider a set of n experimental samples, each characterized by d measurements (one for each variable), e.g., d different genes. The data can be arranged in a $d \times n$ matrix where rows represent variables (genes) and columns correspond to different samples. The data matrix can be normalized row- or column-wise, such that either the variables or the samples are normalized to make them more comparable. The variables can be rescaled to a uniform distribution or the total intensity amount of sample vectors can be set constant. One advantage of a sample normalization is that in case of additional samples, the new samples can be normalized individually, and no renormalization of all samples is required, which is important, for example, for diagnostic tasks. Variable normalization, however, is important when the exact contribution of each variable (gene) to a component or visualization result is interesting. Log fold change as variable and unit vector norm as sample normalization are both convenient normalization techniques for molecular data. Nevertheless, it is often useful to preselect the usually very large number of variables in advance, e.g., by absolute variance or by mean intensity. Although a small intensity or variance might have a large biological impact, small observed values are usually strongly corrupted by the relatively large amount of background noise and, therefore, are normally of no use. A comprehensive discussion of data matrix normalization in respect of microarrays can be also found in **ref. 2**.

3.1.1. Log Fold Change (Log Ratio)

Here, it is assumed that the relevant information is the relative change in expression or concentration with respect to the average or to control samples. These ratios should be transformed by logarithm, e.g., to base two log_2, to obtain symmetric values of positive and negative changes. Any other logarithm could be used instead as the difference is only given by a global scaling factor c, which does not affect the directions of components in PCA or ICA, e.g., $log_2 (x) = c * log_{10} (x)$ with $c = 3.32 = log_2 (10)$. However, to obtain a normalized variable $\tilde{x}_i$, the elements of the variable $x_i = \left(x_i^1, ..., x_i^n \right)$ are divided by the median of x_i and subsequently transformed by logarithm.

$$\tilde{x}_i = log \left[\frac{x_i}{median(x_i)} \right] \qquad (1)$$

Now, a high variance would point out a high relative change, useful for variance considered analysis techniques, such as PCA. It is convenient to use the median as it is more robust to outliers than the mean. Where control samples are available (e.g., the wild-type in a mutant experiment or the zero time point in a time series) the samples can be divided by the median of the control samples alone.

$$\tilde{x}_i = log \left[\frac{x_i}{median\left(x_i^{control} \right)} \right] \qquad (2)$$

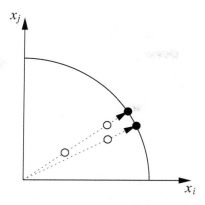

Fig. 3. Geometrical illustration of l_2-vector norm. The samples ('○') are projected onto a hypersphere. This strongly affects the pairwise distances. Highly correlated samples end up close to each other, even if they had a large distance beforehand. Geometrically, high correlated samples are located in the same direction from the origin, but with possibly different intensities.

As the meaning is quite similar, the results are expected to be very close, though a division by control might be easier to interpret.

3.1.2. Unit Vector Norm

It is assumed that the total amount of a sample vector $v = (v_1, v_2, \ldots, v_d)$ is nonrelevant, and can, therefore, be removed by scaling the power or intensity of this vector to a fixed value, usually one, $\|\tilde{v}\| = 1$. The normalized sample vector is obtained by

$$\tilde{v} = \frac{v}{\|v\|} \tag{3}$$

Vector normalization emphasizes the ratios between the different measurements (genes) of one sample. The l_1-vector norm transforms the data into percentages, whereas the l_2-vector norm is geometrically interesting as it projects the samples onto a unit hypersphere, *see* **Fig. 3**.

$$l_1\text{-norm } \|v\|_1 = \sum_i |v_i|$$

$$l_2\text{-norm } \|v\|_2 = \sqrt{\sum_i |v_i|^2}$$

$$l_p\text{-norm } \|v\|_p = \sqrt[p]{\sum_i |v_i|^p}$$

$$l_\infty\text{-norm } \|v\|_\infty = \max_i |v_i| \tag{4}$$

Scaling the sample vector to a unit vector is closely related to correlation analysis, as highly correlated samples are projected close to each other (small Euclidean distance).

With gene expression data it might be convenient to reduce the number of genes by a kind of filtering (feature selection), where those genes are removed that fall below a certain threshold of a specific criterion, e.g., the variance. Otherwise, the high expected rate of irrelevant noisy genes might confuse the vector norm.

3.1.3. Unit Variance

Here, it is assumed that the variance σ_i^2 of each variable x_i, e.g., of each metabolite, has no relevance (which is often not the case), and can therefore be rescaled to one. As the variance σ_i^2 is the square of the standard deviation σ_i, it is identical to unit standard deviation.

$$\tilde{x}_i = \frac{x_i}{\sigma_i} \tag{5}$$

This brings out the correlations between variables. The covariance matrix, e.g., used in PCA, is then identical to the correlation matrix. The covariance between two variables x_i and x_j

$$cov\left(x_i, x_j\right) = \frac{1}{n-1}\left(x_i - \overline{x}_i\right)\left(x_j - \overline{x}_j\right)^T \tag{6}$$

with mean

$$\overline{x}_i = \frac{1}{n}\sum_{l=1}^{n} x_i^l \tag{7}$$

is equal to the correlation $corr(x_i, x_j)$ when normalized by the standard deviations σ_i and σ_j

$$corr\left(x_i, x_j\right) = \frac{corr\left(x_i, x_j\right)}{\sigma_i \sigma_j} \tag{8}$$

Thus, covariance is equal to correlation when unit variance $\sigma^2 = 1 = \sigma$.

For a variance optimization technique such as PCA, all variables have the same opportunity to get a high rank to the important first components, as they all have the same variance. The first component of PCA, which usually depends on variables of high variance and correlation, now solely depends on the largest group of highly correlated variables, which jointly form the direction (component) of highest variance in the data space.

A similar normalization is termed z-score

$$z\text{-}score \; \tilde{x}_i = \frac{x_i - \overline{x}_i}{\sigma_i} \tag{9}$$

where the standard deviation σ_i is also set to one and additionally the mean $\bar{x}$ is set to zero. However, whether the mean is zero or not is usually not important for PCA or ICA as the algorithms remove the mean automatically.

Although unit variance or z-score are standard normalization methods in many areas, there are strong limitations when applied to molecular data. This is caused by an important difference in the experimental design. In many areas, these observed variables are usually expected to be related to the investigated factor and, hence, we can assume that a high percentage of these variables give us useful information. Molecular data, by contrast, are usually obtained by high-throughput screening techniques, where as many variables (e.g., genes) as possible are measured. The attempt is mostly to find some relevant candidates within the large number of measured variables. Most variables are usually not related to our experiment and, therefore, show a low concentration or activation level that has a low effect in many analysis techniques. The disadvantage of unit variance, however, is that by scaling up these nonrelevant variables, the impact on the analysis result is increased dramatically. Unit variance normalization should, therefore, not be used without any preselection (filter), especially with gene expression data. After such preselection, we can assume that most of the selected genes are experimentally relevant and so unit variance might be reasonable. Caution is also required because of the limited number of samples, where high correlations might occur by chance.

3.2. Analysis

To analyze an experimental dataset, a convenient approach would be to obtain a set of "interesting" components (new variables). These components can be plotted against each other such that the plotted dots represent the individual samples, *see* **Fig. 2**. With these plots, a meaningful component can be identified which best reflects the investigated experimental condition. Now we can estimate the most important original variables with the highest influence on these components by ranking the variables by their weights (loadings), given by the corresponding vector of a transformation matrix.

First, we explain the classical PCA and closely related techniques such as singular value decomposition (SVD) and multidimensional scaling (MDS). Special emphasis is given to ICA, which recently became popular in molecular biology. A procedure is explained to apply ICA to high-dimensional datasets from molecular biology.

3.2.1. PCA

The main application of PCA *(3,4)* is to reduce the dimensionality (the number of variables) of the dataset, thereby maintaining as much variance as possible. It is, therefore, important that the required information is strongly related to the variance in the data. This would be the case when the experimental environment could be perfectly controlled, which it mostly can not. However, even if PCA sometimes gives a less than optimal result, it still gives a good first impression of the data.

PCA transforms a d-dimensional sample vector $x = (x_1, x_2, \ldots, x_d)^T$ into a usually lower dimensional vector $y = (y_1, y_2, \ldots, y_k)^T$, where d is the number of variables (metabolites or genes) and k is the number of selected components. The PCA transformation is given by the $k \times d$ matrix V, such that

$$y = Vx \qquad (10)$$

Each row vector of matrix y contains values (scores) of a new variable y_j termed principal component (PC). The component PC j, given by the new variable $y_j = (y_{j1}, y_{j2}, \ldots, y_{jn})$, is a linear combination of all original variables $x_i = (x_{i1}, x_{i2}, \ldots, x_{jn})$, weighted by the elements of the corresponding transformation vector $y_j = (y_{j1}, y_{j2}, \ldots, y_{jd})$,

$$y_j = \sum_{i=1}^{d} v_{ji} x_i = v_{j1} x_1 + v_{j2} x_2 + \ldots + v_{jd} x_d \qquad (11)$$

n is the number of samples and d is the number of original variables. The weights v_{ji} (sometimes referred to as loadings) give us the contribution of all original variables x_i to the jth component. Geometrically seen, PCA is a rotation of the original data space. The new axes are the PCs. The vector v_j gives the direction of the jth PC (PC j). The first component (PC 1), represented by the variable y_1, is in the direction of highest variance, the second component (PC 2) is in the direction of highest variance from the first component in all orthogonal directions. The first and second component together explain the two-dimensional plane of highest variance. A column vector $y = (y_1, y_2, \ldots, y_k)^T$ contains the k new coordinates in the space of PCs of the corresponding sample x.

The transformation or rotation matrix V can be estimated by different algorithms. The classical way is to calculate the eigenvectors of the $d \times d$ covariance matrix between variables,

$$cov(X) = \frac{1}{n-1} \sum_{l=1}^{n} \left(x^l - \bar{x} \right) \left(x^l - \bar{x} \right)^T \qquad (12)$$

where the vector $\bar{x}$ contains the mean of all variables, n is the number of samples, and x^l is a sample vector. The eigenvectors are sorted by their corresponding eigenvalues. The matrix V is then given by the first k eigenvectors v_j to the largest eigenvalues. Sometimes the correlation matrix is used instead of the standard covariance matrix. However, this is identical to normalizing the data by unit variance in advance (*see* **Subheading 3.1.3.**). As the possibly large number d of variables in molecular data can be problematic for solving the eigenvalue problem of a $d \times d$ covariance matrix, the required PCs can be more easily obtained by SVD, MDS, or an adaptive PCA method.

3.2.2. SVD

A different approach for obtaining the same PCs is SVD, *see*, e.g., **ref. 5**. SVD is more efficient than the PCA covariance approach, especially when there is a large number of variables and a small number of samples, as is typical in molecular datasets.

The SVD of a $d \times n$ data matrix X is

$$X^T = USV^T \tag{13}$$

The columns u_j of U are termed left singular vectors, the columns v_j of V are termed right singular vectors, and the diagonal elements s_j of the diagonal matrix S are the singular values.

If we consider a centered dataset X, where the rows, the variables x_i, have zero mean, then the PCs (the scores) y_j are given by the columns of the matrix multiplication $Y = US$. The columns v_j of V are equivalent to the eigenvectors of the covariance matrix.

A comprehensive description of SVD in relation to PCA with respect to gene expressions is given by **ref. 6**. Other applications of SVD to gene expressions can be found in **refs. 7–9**.

3.2.3. MDS

Another convenient way to obtain the PCs is to use a basic approach of MDS based on eigenvalue decomposition. MDS (*see* **ref. 10**) gives a projection or visualization of the data by use of a distance matrix D alone. It is, therefore, useful in cases where only relative distances d_{ij} from one sample i to another sample j are available, and not the exact position in a multidimensional space. Such a distance can be, e.g., a similar measure between two sequences. Nevertheless, the distances or similarities can also be derived from a data matrix, e.g., by use of Euclidean distance, covariance, correlation, or mutual information. The aim is to project the data into a two- or low-dimensional space such that the pairwise distances $\| y_i - y_j \|$ are as similar as possible to the distances d_{ij} given by the distance matrix, thus, minimizing the function

$$\sqrt{\sum_{i \ne j} \left(d_{ij} - \| y_i - y_j \| \right)^2} \tag{14}$$

There exists a wide variety of methods for performing MDS, where nonlinear projections are usually more efficient. However, to explain the relation to

PCA, we consider a simple linear MDS by eigenvalue decomposition of the covariance matrix as a distance matrix, $D = cov(X)$. Here, the two eigenvectors to the largest eigenvalues of the distance matrix give the required projections (components). For a dataset X where the variables x_i have zero mean, it is shown, e.g., by **ref. *11***, that by use of the $n \times n$ covariance matrix between samples (not between variables as in PCA), the eigenvectors of this covariance matrix are the required PC scores y. This is advantageous in case of a small number of samples where only a relatively small sample covariance matrix is obtained.

3.2.4. Adaptive Algorithms

With the currently small number of samples, the estimation of the PCs can be efficiently calculated by use of SVD or MDS, even with a very large number of variables (genes). However, with a decrease in measurement costs, the number of samples will increase rapidly. Then it will be impossible to estimate all PCs. Instead we have to use adaptive algorithms which extract the PCs in a deflationary (sequentially) manner, meaning that the components are extracted one after the other starting from the component of highest variance. Consequently, only the first k desired components are extracted instead of all components.

Convenient algorithms for this include: Sanger's learning rule *(12)* linear auto-associative neural networks *(13)*, or the APEX network by Diamantaras and Kung *(4)*.

3.2.5. Application of PCA

Although PCA is often a very useful technique, it fails to give optimal projections when applied to our metabolite dataset of *A. thaliana* crosses (*see* **Fig. 4**). The first PC 1, the component of highest variance, contains no information for discriminating the lines or crosses. The components PC 2 and PC 3 give a better result, although they are of smaller variance. This means that the required experimental information is not related to the highest variance in the data. In **Subheading 3.2.6.**, we show that ICA gives better projections of the data by maximizing an information criterion (entropy) and not the variance as in PCA.

3.2.6. ICA

To use the ICA model we make the assumption that the measured gene expression levels, or metabolite or protein concentrations depend on some biological or environmental factors (e.g., temperature, light) that are assumed to be statistically independent. The aim is to identify these factors in the measured data automatically by searching for independent components (ICs). Independence

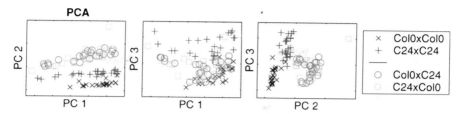

Fig. 4. Principal component analysis applied to metabolite data of *Arabidopsis thaliana* crosses. The best projection is given by the second and third principal components (PC 2, PC 3) and not by the first (PC 1) as expected.

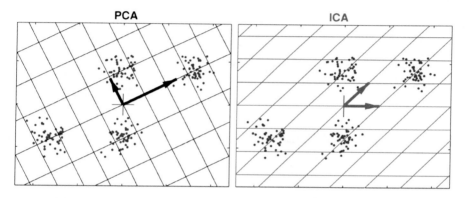

Fig. 5. Principal component analysis (PCA) and independent component analysis (ICA) applied to an artificial dataset. The grid represents the new coordinate system after PCA or ICA transformation. The identified components are marked by an arrow. The components of ICA are better related to the cluster of the data. They have an independent meaning. One ICA component contains information solely to separate clusters above from clusters below, whereas the other component can be used to discriminate the cluster on the left from the cluster on the right.

means that the values of one component provide no information about the values of other components. This is a stronger condition than the noncorrelation condition in PCA, where the values of one component can still provide information about the values of another component. Furthermore, the components are not restricted to being orthogonal in ICA (*see* **Fig. 5**).

Applied to high-dimensional molecular data, ICA can outperform the classical PCA (**Fig. 6**). However, this higher informative power can be achieved only when ICA is combined with PCA as a preprocessing step and the measure of kurtosis as the ranking criterion (*see* **Fig. 7**).

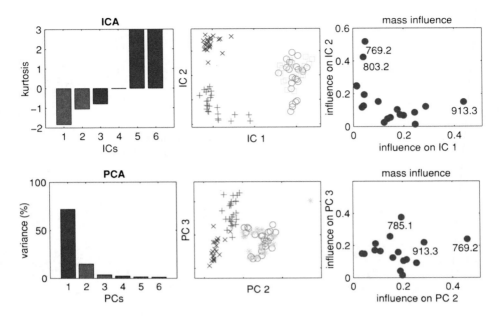

Fig. 6. Independent component analysis (ICA) vs principal component analysis (PCA). In the middle, ICA visualization shows a higher discrimination of the samples than PCA visualization. Furthermore, in ICA the different discriminations are optimal given by the two axes, the first two independent components (ICs) when ranked by the kurtosis measure. The best PCA result is only given by the second and third principal component (PC) ranked by variance (**Fig. 4**). The bar plots on the left show the respective values of the ranking criteria of the first six components for both variance in PCA and kurtosis in ICA. On the right, the absolute contributions (loadings) are plotted against each other for the top 20 masses of highest contribution. In PCA, the masses are more likely to make a contribution to both components, whereas in ICA the masses are involved differently, contributing to one or to the other IC, confirming that different ICs represent independent biological processes where different metabolites are involved.

Fig. 7. The proposed independent component analysis (ICA) procedure. First, the dataset is reduced by principal component analysis thereby maintaining all of the relevant variances. ICA is applied to this reduced dataset and the extracted independent components are sorted by their kurtosis value.

3.2.6.1. COMPONENT RANKING

One difficulty in applying ICA to high-dimensional molecular data is that the number of extracted components equals the number of variables in the dataset. The components have no order as in PCA, and, hence, we need a criterion to rank the components to our interest. For that the kurtosis measure is a suitable measurement. It is a classical measure of non-Gaussianity, it indicates whether the data are peaked or flat relative to a Gaussian (normal) distribution.

$$\text{kurtosis}(z) = \frac{\sum_{i=1}^{n}(z_i - \mu)^4}{(n-1)\sigma^4} - 3 \qquad (15)$$

where $z = (z_1, z_2, \ldots, z_n)$ represents a variable or component with mean μ and standard deviation σ, n is the number of samples. The kurtosis is the fourth auto-cumulant after mean (first), variance (second), and skewness (third).

Negative kurtosis can indicate a cluster structure (different experimental conditions) or a uniformly distributed factor (temperature). Thus, the components with the most negative kurtosis can give us the most relevant information.

3.2.6.2. PCA PREPROCESSING

Applying ICA directly to this high-dimensional dataset is questionable and the results are usually of no practical relevance. It is therefore necessary to reduce the dimensionality in advance by PCA. By doing this we assume that the relevant information is still related to a significantly high amount of variance but not necessarily to the highest amount. The PCA preprocessing step attempts to preserve all of the relevant variances and removes only the noise given by small variances. On this reduced dataset, ICA is then applied to optimize criteria other than variance, namely information theoretic criteria such as entropy or kurtosis. The optimal number of PCs or the optimal reduced dimensionality can be found by considering the aim of our analysis to find as many relevant components as possible. As a negative kurtosis indicates relevant components, the optimal dimensionality is then given by the dimensionality where the highest number of independent components with negative kurtosis can be extracted (*see* **Fig. 8**).

3.2.6.3. CONTRIBUTIONS OF EACH VARIABLE

As the detected independent components often have a biological interpretation, it would be important to know which variables (genes/metabolites/proteins) are most involved in the components. These contributions are given by the transformation matrices of PCA and ICA and are also termed loadings or weights.

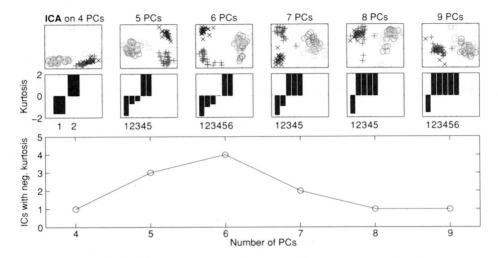

Fig. 8. Independent component analysis (ICA) is applied to reduced datasets with different numbers of principal components. At six components of principal component analysis, ICA extracts the highest number of relevant independent components (ICs), i.e., ICs with negative kurtosis.

PCA transforms a d-dimensional sample vector $x = (x_1, x_2, \ldots, x_d)^T$ into a usually lower dimensional vector $y = (y_1, y_2, \ldots, y_k)^T$, where d is the number of variables and k is the number of selected components. The PCA transformation is given by the eigenvector matrix V, $y = Vx$. Similarly, ICA transforms this vector y into the required vector $z = (z_1, z_2, \ldots, z_k)^T$, containing the independent values z_i for each IC i. For that a demixing matrix W is estimated by ICA, $z = Wy$. V gives the contributions of each variable to each of the PCs, whereas W gives the contributions of each PC to each of the ICs. We can combine both matrices $U = W * V$ into a direct transformation $z = Ux$, where U gives vector-wise the contributions of each variable to each of the ICs.

3.2.6.4. APPLICATION

ICA, applied to our test case of *A. thaliana* crosses, could identify three relevant ICs, i.e., three ICs with a significantly negative kurtosis value. For this, a prior reduction of dimensionality to five or six PCs was necessary (**Fig. 8**). The extracted independent components could be interpreted with biological meaning. The first component, IC 1, can be used to discriminate between the crosses from the background parental lines, the second component, IC 2, contains information to discriminate between the two parental

Table 1
Freely Available ICA Algorithms

• Web-Based Analysis Tool	
MetaGeneAlyse *(1)*	metagenealyse.mpimp-golm.mpg.de/
• MATLAB® Packages	
FastICA *(16)*	www.cis.hut.fi/projects/ica/fastica/
JADE *(32)*	www.tsi.enst.fr/icacentral/Algos/cardoso/
Infomax *(15)*	www.cnl.salk.edu/~tewon/ICA/Code/ext_ica_download.html
TDSEP *(33)*	wwwold.first.fhg.de/~ziehe/download.html
CuBICA *(34)*	itb.biologie.hu-berlin.de/~blaschke/code.html
Kernel-ICA *(35)*	www.cs.berkeley.edu/~fbach/kernel-ica/

lines (**Fig. 6**). The third component, IC 3, is not related to the biological experiment, however, there is a relation to the identifier of the samples, representing the order over time of measurement in the mass spectrometer (**Fig. 9**). Hence, IC 3 is an experimental artifact resulting from increasing contamination of the QTOF skimmer along the analytical sequence. This technical factor was not detected by PCA.

3.2.6.5. BIBLIOGRAPHIC NOTES

ICA was first introduced by Comon *(14)*, with subsequent developments by Bell and Sejnowski *(15)*. Since then a wide variety of ICA algorithms have been developed, *see* **Table 1**. Good introductions to ICA can be found in **refs. *16* and *17***, and in several books published in recent years *(18–22)*.

One of the first motivations for development of ICA was sound signal separation. Now, a major field of application of ICA in biomedical science is in computational neuroscience, with the aim of identifying artifacts and signals of interest from magnetoencephalograms *(23,24)* and from electroencephalograms *(25,26)*. ICA has also become important in the field of molecular biology. It has been applied by Liebermeiser *(27)* to analyze gene expression patterns during the yeast cell cycle and in human lymphocytes. Martoglio et al. *(28)* applied ICA to ovarian cancer data. In Lee and Batzoglou *(29)*, different ICA algorithms were compared and applied to yeast cell cycle, *Caenorhabditis elegans*, and human gene expression data. Saidi et al. *(30)* showed that clustering on components from ICA give more biologically reasonable groupings than clustering on components from PCA. In Scholz et al. *(1)* ICA was applied to metabolite data from *A. thaliana* crosses. It was found that ICA extracts more meaningful and interpretable components than PCA, and even an unexpected

Scholz and Selbig

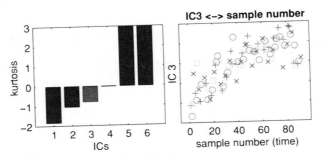

Fig. 9. Three components with clearly negative kurtosis are detected. The third component (IC 3), an almost uniformly distributed factor, could be interpreted as an experimental artifact, related to the order over time, when the samples were measured.

experimental artifact was detected. Also, when applied to enzymatic activities *(31)*, ICA was able to provide components of greater discriminating power and with greater meaning than components of PCA.

Acknowledgments

The authors thank Thomas Altmann and Rhonda Meyer for initiating and stimulating the *Arabidopsis* hybrid vigour (heterosis) project, which aims to use recombinant inbred and near isogenic lines for functional genomics. We are very grateful to Oliver Fiehn, Stephan Gatzek, and Alistair Sterling for providing us with the mass spectra of *A. thaliana* crosses. We also thank John Lunn for helpful comments on the manuscript.

References

1. Scholz, M., Gatzek, S., Sterling, A., Fiehn, O., and Selbig, J. (2004) Metabolite fingerprinting: detecting biological features by independent component analysis. *Bioinformatics* **20**, 2447–2454.
2. Quackenbush, J. (2002) Microarray data normalization and transformation. *Nat. Genet.* **32**, 496–501.
3. Jolliffe, I. T. (1986) *Principal Component Analysis.* Springer-Verlag, New York, NY.
4. Diamantaras K. I., and Kung, S. Y. (1996) *Principal Component Neural Networks.* Wiley, New York, NY.
5. Golub, G. and van Loan, C. (1996) *Matrix Computations,* 3rd Ed. The Johns Hopkins University Press, Baltimore, MD.
6. Wall, M. E., Rechtsteiner, A., and Rocha, L. M. (2003) Singular value decomposition and principal component analysis. In: *A Practical Approach to Microarray*

Data Analysis, (Berrar, D. P., Dubitzky, W., and Granzow, M., eds.), Kluwer, Norwell, MA, pp. 91–109.

7. Alter, O., Brown, P. O., and Botstein, D. (2000) Singular value decomposition for genome-wide expression data processing and modeling. *PNAS* **97,** 10,101–10,106.

8. Holter, N. S., Mitra, M., Maritan, A., Cieplak, M., Banavar, J. R., and Fedoroff, N. V. (2000) Fundamental patterns underlying gene expression profiles: simplicity from complexity. *PNAS* **97,** 8409–8414.

9. Liu, L., Hawkins, D. M., Ghosh, S., and Young, S. S. (2003) Robust singular value decomposition analysis of microarray data. *PNAS* **100,** 13,167–13,172.

10. Cox, T. F. and Cox, M. A. A. (2001) *Multidimensional Scaling.* Chapman and Hall, London, England.

11. Burges, C. J. C. (2004) Geometric methods for feature extraction and dimensional reduction-a guided tour. In: *Data Mining and Knowledge Discovery Handbook* (Rokach, L. and Maimon, O., eds.), Springer Verlag, New York, pp. 59–92.

12. Sanger, T. D. (1989) Optimal unsupervised learning in a single layer linear feedforward network. *Neural Networks* **2,** 459–473.

13. Baldi, P. F. and Homik, K. (1995) Learning in linear neural networks: a survey. *IEEE Trans. on Neural Networks* **6,** 837–858.

14. Comon P. (1994) Independent component analysis, a new concept? *Signal Processing* **36,** 287–314.

15. Bell, A. J. and Sejnowski, T. J. (1995)An information-maximization approach to blind separation and blind deconvolution. *Neural Computation* **7,** 1129–1159.

16. Hyvärinen, A. and Oja, E. (2000) Independent component analysis: algorithms and applications. *Neural Networks* **4–5,** 411–430.

17. Stone, J. V. (2002) Independent component analysis: an introduction. *Trends Cogn. Sci.* **6,** 59–64.

18. Haykin, S. (2000) *Unsupervised Adaptive Filtering, vol. 1: Blind Source Separation.* Wiley, New York, NY.

19. Haykin, S. (2000) *Unsupervised Adaptive Filtering, vol. 2: Blind Deconvolution.* Wiley, New York, NY.

20. Hyvärinen, A., Karhunen, J., and Oja, E. (2001) *Independent Component Analysis.* Wiley, New York, NY.

21. Cichocki, A. and Amari, S. (2003) *Adaptive Blind Signal and Image Processing: Learning Algorithms and Applications.* Wiley, New York, NY.

22. Stone, J. V. (2004) *Independent Component Analysis: A Tutorial Introduction.* MIT Press, Cambridge, MA.

23. Vigário, R., Särelä, J., Jousmäki, V., Hämäläinen, M., and Oja, E. (2000) Independent component approach to the analysis of EEG and MEG recordings. *IEEE Trans. Biomed. Eng.* **47,** 589–593.

24. Tang, A. C., Pearlmutter, B. A., Malaszenko, N. A., Phung, D. B., and Reeb, B. C. (2002) Independent components of magnetoencephalography: Localization. *Neural Comput.* **14,** 1827–1858.

25. Jung, T. -P., Makeig, S., Lee, T. -W., et al. (2000) Independent component analysis of biomedical signals. In: *Proc. Int. Workshop on Independent Component Analysis and Blind Signal Separation* (ICA2000), (Pajunen, P. and Karhunen, J., eds.), IEEE Signal Processing Society, Helsinki, Finland, pp. 633–644.

26. Makeig, S., Westerfield, M., Jung, T. -P., et al. (2002) Dynamic brain sources of visual evoked responses. *Science* **295**, 690–694.

27. Liebermeister, W. (2002) Linear modes of gene expression determined by independent component analysis. *Bioinformatics* **18**, 51–60.

28. Martoglio, A. -M., Miskin, J. W., Smith, S. K., and MacKay, D. J. C. (2002) A decomposition model to track gene expression signatures: preview on observer-independent classification of ovarian cancer. *Bioinformatics* **18**, 1617–1624.

29. Lee, S. -I. and Batzoglou, S. (2003) Application of independent component analysis to microarrays. *Genome Biol.* **4**, R76.

30. Saidi, S. A., Holland, C. M., Kreil, D. P., et al. (2004) Independent component analysis of microarray data in the study of endometrial cancer. *Oncogene* **23**, 6677–6683.

31. Scholz, M., Gibon, Y., Stitt, M., and Selbig, J. (2004) Independent component analysis of starch deficient *pgm* mutants. In: *Proceedings of the German Conference on Bioinformatics*, (Giegerich, R. and Stoye, J., eds.), GI, Bielefeld, Germany, pp. 95–104.

32. Cardoso, J. -F. and Souloumiac, A. (1993) Blind beamforming for non Gaussian signals. *IEE Proceedings-F* **6**, 362–370.

33. Ziehe, A. and Müller, K. -R. (1998) TDSEP: an efficient algorithm for blind separation using time structure. In: *Proc. ICANN'98, Int. Conf. on Artificial Neural Networks*, (Niklasson, L., Boden, M., and Ziemke, T., eds.), Springer Verlag, London, UK, pp, 675–680.

34. Blaschke, T. and Wiskott, L. (2004) CuBICA: independent component analysis by simultaneous third- and fourth-order cumulant diagonalization. *IEEE Trans. Image Process* **52**, 1250–1256.

35. Bach, F. R. and Jordan, M. I. (2002) Kernel independent component analysis. *J. Mach. Learn. Res.* **3**, 1–48.

7

A Gentle Guide to the Analysis of Metabolomic Data

Ralf Steuer, Katja Morgenthal, Wolfram Weckwerth, and Joachim Selbig

Summary

Modern molecular biology crucially relies on computational tools to handle and interpret the large amounts of data that are generated by high-throughput measurements. To this end, much effort is dedicated to devise novel sophisticated methods that allow one to integrate, evaluate, and analyze biological data. However, prior to an application of specifically designed methods, simple and well-known statistical approaches often provide a more appropriate starting point for further analysis.

This chapter seeks to describe several well-established approaches to data analysis, including various clustering techniques, discriminant function analysis, principal component analysis, multidimensional scaling, and classification trees.

The chapter is accompanied by a webpage, describing the application of all algorithms in a ready-to-use format.

Key Words: Metabolomics; data analysis; clustering techniques; data visualization.

1. Introduction

Recent advances in experimental methodology, as described in Chapter 4, allow for the generation of large quantities of metabolomic data in best time. Clearly, and similar to other "-omic" technologies aiming to measure many variables simultaneously, this experimental progress sets an ever increasing demand on the development of sophisticated and powerful methods to evaluate and analyze the data—and eventually turn it into biological knowledge *(1)*.

The purpose of this chapter is, thus, to review and describe several typical approaches to the analysis of metabolomic data. Although our focus will not be on the latest advances of specific algorithms, we aim to describe well-established statistical methods that can be the starting point of any analysis. This includes such issues as data normalization, the detection of outliers, and basic

From: *Methods in Molecular Biology, vol. 358: Metabolomics: Methods and Protocols*
Edited by:W. Weckwerth © Humana Press Inc., Totowa, NJ

statistical tests, as well as higher order analysis, such as clustering, discriminant function analysis, principal component analysis, and decision trees. In this chapter, we will largely omit computational details, but rather focus on the practical applicability of the described concepts. Appropriate implementations of the described methods can be found on a webpage (http://bioinformatics. mpimp-golm.mpg.de/), ready to use on one's own data.

2. Materials
2.1. Availability of Algorithms

All methods described here were performed using the MATLAB™ package (Mathworks, Natick, MA), though other programs, like R, SPSS, or octave, are likewise applicable and offer a similar functionality. Details on the usage of particular functions in MATLAB are given on the accompanying webpage (http:// bioinformatics.mpimp-golm.mpg.de/), including all scripts used in the analysis.

2.2. Biological Background

The working example throughout this chapter will be a dataset obtained from *Arabidopsis thaliana*, a small plant in the mustard family that has become the organism of choice for research in plant biology.

The dataset consists of more than 80 classified metabolites measured from leaf extracts obtained from tissue of wild-type (WT) and a starchless mutant (phosphoglucomutase-deficient mutant [PGM]) *(2)*. The PGM considered here is lacking in starch synthesis, resulting in an increased level of glucose, fructose, and sucrose.

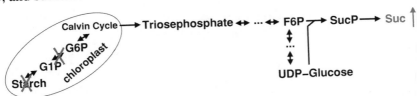

Measurements were taken at six distinct time-points during short day (8 h light [L]) growth conditions. Harvest was 8 wk after sowing.

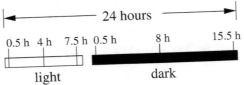

At each time-point 10 samples were taken for both genetic strains (with the exception of "PGM 15.5 h dark [D]," where only 9 measurements are available), resulting in 119 measurements.

3. Methods

3.1. Prearrangements and Basic Analysis

In most cases, a data matrix obtained directly from metabolomic measurements has to be suitably prepared for the application of higher order methods and algorithms. As a first step, it is necessary to check the data for missing values and possible outliers. Also, normalization techniques and data transformations will affect the results and validity of the subsequent analysis.

3.1.1. Treatment of Missing Values

A common phenomenon in metabolomics measurements (as well as for most other "-omic" approaches) is that the data matrix frequently contains missing values, i.e., empty cells where the respective metabolite has not been assigned to any numerical value. As many multivariate methods require a fully defined matrix, or become computationally ineffective for incomplete data, estimation and treatment of missing values has become an important step in the preparation of the data.

The most straightforward solution to tackle this problem is, of course, to discard an entire row of observations, whenever a missing value is present. However, this comes at the cost of losing valuable information contained in the remaining (nonempty) entries of the row. Consequently, several methods have been proposed to estimate missing values, usually exploiting local similarity structures within the data.

The simplest methods include:

1. Replace by means: a missing metabolite value is simply replaced by the average (or median) of the metabolite level across different samples.
2. Replace by means of nearest neighbors: slightly more sophisticated is to replace a missing value by the average of this metabolite across the k nearest neighbors, as determined by the remaining entries. This is visualized in **Fig. 1**, a suitable script is available in the supporting online material.

It is emphasized that replacement of missing data is mostly an issue of computational convenience and will *not* contribute to an improved significance or improved discriminatory power of the results (**Notes 1–4**).

3.1.2. Detection of Outliers

Closely related to missing values is the detection of possible outliers within the data. As the term itself is not unambiguously defined, we treat as outliers individual (or small sets of) data points, whose values are not concordant with those of the vast majority of the remaining data points. Such a situation usually warrants checking again the respective peak areas in the chromatogram (*see* **Subheading 3.5.** in Chapter 4) and might require discarding the values.

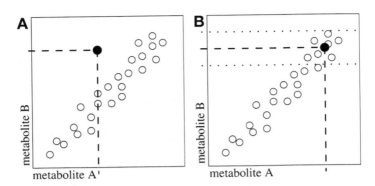

Fig.1. Imput of missing values. Replacement by the average across all samples can be improved by taking local similarity structures into account. In this example, the missing value of metabolite A is replaced by the average of the nearest neighbors, as determined by the remaining (nonmissing) metabolite values.

A rather quick and dirty way to detect outliers in metabolomic data is to look at the (relative) ratio of the mean and median of the distribution. Because, for unimodal distributions, the median is considered more robust with respect to outliers, large deviations between mean and median call for a more detailed examination. This is demonstrated in **Fig. 2** for our dataset of *A. thaliana* WT plant leaf extracts. To assess the impact of outliers on estimated values, such as the average, a "relative influence" of each data point can be determined. **Figure 2C** shows the relative change in the average value of tartronic acid (2-methyl-aminomethyl) when each data point (of a total of 60) is successively omitted. Ideally, all data points should have approximately the same impact, the deviations again indicate the presence of outliers. Similar strategies are employed in robust estimation, where the weights of data points are adjusted to circumvent the dominating effect of a few heavily influential points (**Notes 5** and **6**).

3.1.3. Normalization and Data Transformations

Another crucial step in the preparation of the data is often an appropriate transformation and normalization of the measured values. In general, there is no such thing as the correct or optimal normalization, but its adequacy in a particular case also depends on the methods and algorithms one intends to use. For a proper interpretation of the results, recall that any data normalization will serve several distinct objectives (**Note 7**).

The most common choices include (but *see also* Chapter 6):

1. Z-score: the *z*-score is defined as the deviation of each point from the mean, divided by the standard deviation. In this case, it is assumed that neither mean

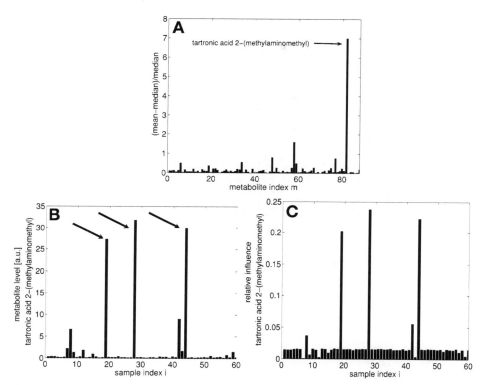

Fig. 2. Detection of outliers. (**A**) A comparison of median to mean of the wild-type samples for all 88 metabolites. Tartronic acid-2-(methylaminomethyl) indicates a large deviation. (**B**) Measured (relative) abundance of tartronic acid-2-(methylaminomethyl) across all wild-type samples (six time-points each with 10 samples). Indeed three values deviate strongly from the remaining measurements. (**C**) This is consistent with the "relative influence" of each data point on the estimation of the average of the metabolite.

    nor variance contains any valuable information. Note that in this way, variables with a very small (and possibly noise-corrupted) variance will get an equal impact on the results.

2. Division by mean or median: if one wants to retain the (relative) variance of the variables, it is more appropriate to divide only by the mean, median, or any other reference concentration. A subsequent log-transformation ensures that the data is still (approximately) evenly distributed and centered about zero.

3. Transformation of the distribution: as many statistical tests assume an approximately Gaussian distribution, a highly skewed distribution of the data sometimes needs to be adjusted accordingly. Possible transformations include to take the

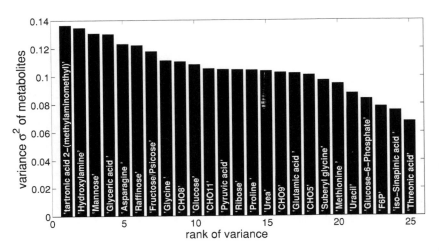

Fig. 3. The relative variances of metabolite abundance in *Arabidopsis thaliana* wild-type leaf tissue (after division by median and subsequent log-transformation), sorted according to their rank.

logarithm of the data. To obtain a constant probability density, a rank transformation, i.e., a transformation that projects the N measurements into equally spaced numbers in the interval [0,1], while preserving their original order, can be used. Note that any of these transformations also reduce the impact of outliers.

In the case of metabolomic data, the absolute value of the metabolite level is only given up to a multiplicative constant. Thus, we transform the values to relative fold changes by division of the mean (or median) and a subsequent log-transformation. This also accounts for the skewed distribution of the measurements and reduces the effect of outliers. **Figure 3** shows the resulting relative variances of metabolite abundance in *A. thaliana* WT leaf tissue, which can now be compared also between different metabolites.

Note that owing to $log(a/b)=log(a)-log(b)$, the division by the mean or median is essentially an additive constant and can be omitted if further analysis is invariant with respect to an additive constant (as are, for example, principal component analysis [PCA] and correlation coefficients).

3.1.4. Some Basic Statistical Tests

Once the normalization is done, the next step in any analysis should be to test for some basic statistical properties of the data. First, we are interested in the overall differences in metabolite abundance between the WT and the PGM mutant.

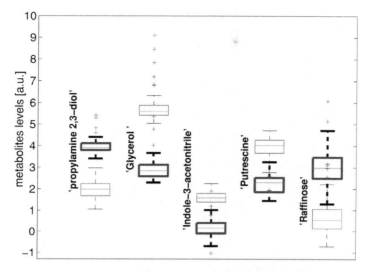

Fig. 4. The metabolites with the most significant differences in their average levels between wild-type (WT) and phosphoglucomutase-deficient mutant leaf tissue. The boxplots denote the upper and lower quartile of the data and are depicted in bold for the WT. The data was log-transformed prior to the test, all depicted metabolites match a significance level $p < 0.0001$.

To test for the hypothesis that two samples (drawn from a Gaussian distribution) have the same mean, a two-sided t-test can be used. Note that in its standard form, the t-test assumes unknown, but equal variances, a restriction that must not always be fulfilled. **Figure 4** shows those metabolites with the most significant differences in their average levels between WT and PGM leaf tissue, as determined by a two-sided t-test assuming that both samples come from Gaussian distributions with unknown and possibly unequal variances.

Likewise, we can ask for the overall differences between light and dark conditions. **Figure 5** shows the time course of glyceric acid and glycine, the two metabolites with the most significant differences in light (pooled 4 h L and 7.5 h L) vs dark (pooled 8 h D and 15.5 h D) conditions for both genetic strains. Based on these results, a scatterplot of the respective metabolites, as shown in **Fig. 6**, already reveals a first indication of a clear separation between the experimental conditions.

Another biologically relevant question concerns those metabolites, for which the PGM mutant shows a significant difference between light and dark conditions, but not the WT (or vice versa). Such a situation is depicted in **Fig. 7**.

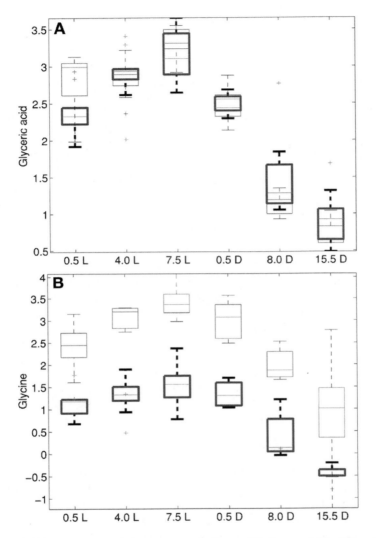

Fig. 5. Time courses of the two metabolites with the most significant differences (in wild-type [WT], as well as for phosphoglucomutase-deficient mutant tissue) in light (4 h L and 7.5 h L) vs dark (8 h D and 15.5 h D) conditions. The WT is depicted in bold.

In accordance with biological intuition, glucose and sucrose show a strongly increased level during light conditions in the PGM mutant as compared with WT.

More appropriate for multivariate data, however, are usually explicitly multivariate extensions, designed for cases when several dependent variables (metabolites) are measured simultaneously across several experimental conditions.

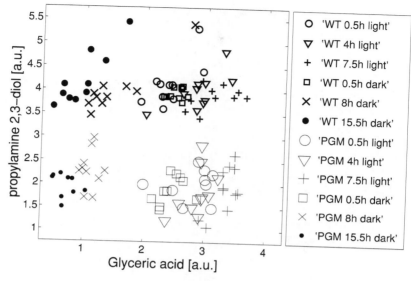

Fig. 6. A scatterplot of propylamine-2,3-diol vs glyceric acid. The plot shows a clear distinction between wild-type and phosphoglucomutase-deficient mutant, as well as between dark (8 h D and 15.5 h D) and the remaining conditions.

Among the most important methods of this kind is multivariate analysis of variance (MANOVA). It is emphasized that multivariate tests are, in general, not equivalent to multiple univariate tests. In particular, MANOVA takes into account possible dependencies between variables, resulting in an improved performance compared to a multiple application of univariate methods:

1. For multiple univariate tests, one has to take into account the inflation of false-positive results (type 1 error), in particular when the number of tests is high. Because for multivariate methods only one test is performed, one obtains a better control of the significance.
2. Strongly correlated dependent variables will lead to redundant results, thereby also inflating the type 1 error.
3. Sometimes individual metabolites might not show any significant differences, whereas their combination does. Multivariate methods are thus more powerful in revealing discriminatory structure within the data.

Intimately connected to MANOVA is discriminant function analysis (DFA), aiming to predict group membership (here given by the experimental conditions) based on linear combinations of the measured variables (metabolites). In particular, DFA constructs a new set of (orthogonal) variables chosen to maximize the separation between groups. The first canonical variable is, thus,

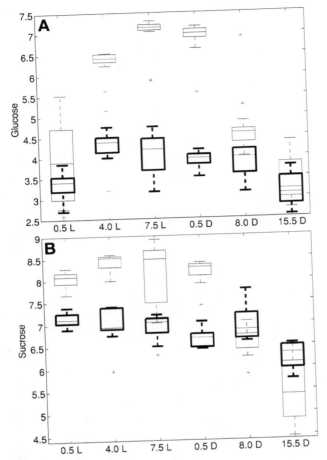

Fig. 7. Glucose shows a significant difference between light (4 h L and 7.5 h L) and dark (8 h D and 15.5 h D) in the phosphoglucomutase-deficient mutant ($p < 10^{10}$), but not in the wild-type ($p > 0.01$). A similar situation holds for sucrose, though the differences are less significant.

defined as the linear combination of original variables that maximizes the separation of group means with respect to variance, or equivalently, that gives the most significant result in a univariate one-way analysis of variance (ANOVA). The second canonical variable is then defined analogously and subject to being orthogonal to the first.

In general, DFA is useful to determine whether (and which) groups can be predicted from the variables and, more importantly, provide insight into which

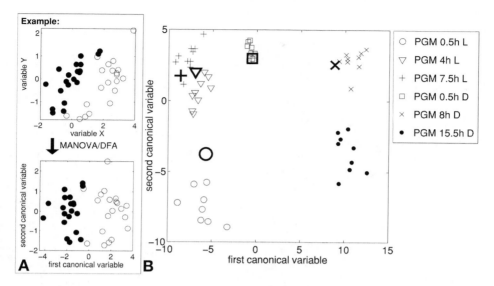

Fig. 8. Discriminat function analysis. (**A**) A simple example. Note that neither of the original variables can clearly distinguish between the two groups (given as black and white circles, respectively). DFA seeks to find a linear combination that separates best between the two groups (the first canonical variable). (**B**) DFA performed on 12 preselected metabolites of the PGM mutant. The first canonical variable is dominated by glyceric acid (with a larger weight than all other metabolites combined), separating between late dark conditions (8 h D and 15.5 h D) vs all others. The second canonical variable is mostly dependent on glucose, with contributions from alanine and ascorbic acid. The bold symbols denote test cases that were not used in the initial computation.

variables are used to predict group membership. **Figure 8** shows the result of a DFA on our dataset, using only 12 preselected metabolites. Note that DFA belongs to the class of supervised methods, i.e., the group membership has to be known beforehand and rests on some rather strong assumptions about the data. The validity of the predication can be tested using leave-one-out cross-validation (**Notes 8–11**).

3.2. Explorative Analysis of Metabolomic Data

Having obtained a first glance of the basic properties of the measured dataset, we may now proceed to a higher order explorative analysis. On that score, commonly used methods include PCA, clustering algorithms, as well as classification methods.

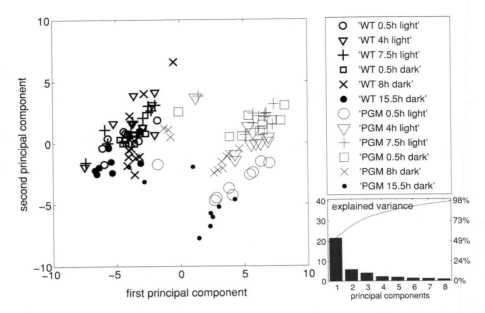

Fig. 9. Principal component analysis of measurements of *Arabidopsis thalina* leaf extracts. Each dot corresponds to a 2-d projection of a metabolite profile (the first two principal components). As can be observed, the experiments are clearly separated into two distinct groups, reflecting the two distinct genetic strains (wild-type vs phospho-glucomutase-deficient mutant). Examining the associated weight loadings reveals which metabolites have the largest impact on the first two principal components. Among the top scoring 15 metabolites, we find again glucose, fructose, raffinose, glycerol, glycine, glyceric acid, and sucrose (**Note 12**).

3.2.1. Principal Component Analysis

Among the oldest and most widely used methods to visualize and reveal discriminatory structure within a given dataset is PCA *(3)*. The objective of PCA is to reduce the dimensionality of the data while retaining as much information (identified with variance here) as possible. The first principal component is thus defined as the linear combination of the original variables that explains the greatest amount of variation. The second principal component is then defined as the linear combination of the original variables that accounts for the greatest amount of the remaining variation subject of being orthogonal (uncorrelated) to the first component. Subsequent components are defined likewise. A more detailed synopsis of PCA is given in Chapter 6.

Figure 9 depicts the results of the principal components analysis for the dataset of *A. thalina* leaf extracts. Sometimes it can be beneficial to repeat the

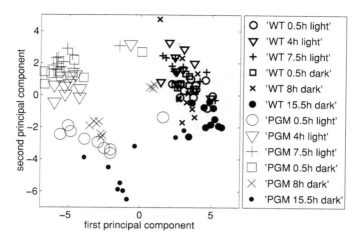

Fig. 10. A principal component analysis based only on the 20 top-scoring metabolites, given by the associated weight loadings of **Fig. 9**. Again, the two genetic strains wild-type and phosphoglucomutase-deficient mutant (PGM) are clearly separated. Additionally, tissue obtained from the PGM mutant seems to separate further into two distinct subgroups, corresponding to different time of harvest. Interestingly, the first group consists of the late light phases (4 h L and 7.5 h L) together with early dark (PGM 0.5 h D), whereas the early light condition (PGM 0.5 h L) is attached to the second group (8 h D and 15.5 h D).

analysis, using only a smaller number of preselected metabolites. **Figure 10** shows a PCA based only on the 20 top-scoring metabolites, determined by the associated weight loadings in **Fig. 8**. Intuitively, the first principal component seems to (approximately) discriminate between the two genetic strains, with glycerol being the metabolite with the highest loading on this component, i.e., having the largest contribution on this component. On the other hand, the second component, at least for the PGM mutant, seems to discriminate between light and dark conditions, with glucose and glyceric acid having the largest impact on this component. This can be visualized more systematically in a biplot of components and weights, as shown in **Fig. 11**. Importantly, the results of the PCA are largely consistent with the findings of **Subheading 3.1.**

Closely related to PCA are a number of methods and computational techniques. In particular these are:

1. Singular value decomposition (SVD): in most implementations, including the one used here, the principal components are actually determined using a SVD of the data matrix. For a brief discussion of SVD and its relationship to PCA *see also* Chapter 6.

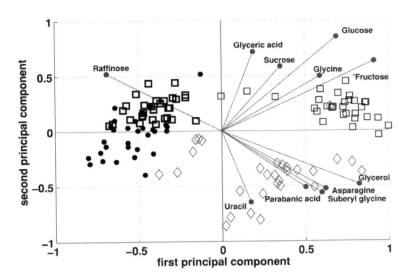

Fig. 11. A biplot of a principal component analysis (based on a reduced number of 11 preselected metabolites). Again, the two genetic strains, as well as light and dark conditions, separate into distinct groups (wild-type [WT] light condition [0.5 h D, 4 h L, 7.5 h L]): bold squares, WT dark condition (0.5 h L, 8 h D, 15.5 h D): bold circles, PGM light conditions: squares, PGM dark conditions: diamonds). Additionally, each of the 11 metabolites is represented by a vector, with the direction and length indicating how the respective metabolite contributes to the first two principal components.

2. Factor analysis (FA): computationally closely related to PCA is also FA. Being likewise a dimension reduction technique, FA assumes that the measured variables depend on a (much) smaller number of unobserved common factors plus some independent random variability for each variable. There is no unique way to obtain the common factors, some variants of FA explicitly involve a PCA. Note that, in contrast to PCA, the factors do not necessarily have to be orthogonal.

3. Multidimensional scaling (MDS): a more general approach to dimension reduction, and thus also to the visualization of multivariate data, is MDS. MDS seeks to project the data onto a lower dimensional space, while retaining the pairwise interpoint distances as good as possible. As input, it accepts almost any measures of similarity or dissimilarity (including nonlinear measures such as mutual information), making it more flexible than PCA. If the distance matrix between objects (here the experimental conditions) is given by the correlation or covariance, classical MDS proceeds similar as PCA (*see* Chapter 6). **Figure 12** shows a classical MDS of the experimental conditions of *A. thaliana* leaf extract data, using the Pearson correlation as a measure of proximity.

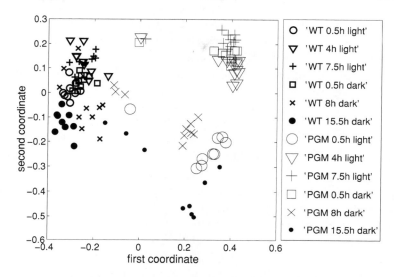

Fig. 12. A multidimensional scaling of the 12 experimental conditions of the dataset obtained from *Arabidopsis thaliana* leaf tissue considered here. Distances between the experimental conditions were determined using the Pearson correlation. Note the close correspondence to **Figs. 9–11**.

4. Noise reduction: PCA is also frequently used as a noise reduction technique. As previously described, it seeks to find a linear combination of the original variables that (successively) accounts for as much variance as possible. Assuming that directions in the data space with little variance are essentially inflated by inevitable measurement errors, these directions can be discarded and set to zero. In this way, PCA serves as a noise reduction either implicitly, by performing a subsequent analysis on the first principal components only, or explicitly, by projecting the reduced dimensions back into the original data space.

5. Independent component analysis (ICA): in contrast to PCA, which assumes orthogonal (i.e., uncorrelated) components, ICA requires the components to be statistically independent. The extension of PCA to ICA with respect to metabolomic data is detailed in Chapter 6.

3.2.2. Clustering of Metabolomic Data

Although PCA is frequently used to reveal and visualize disjoined "groups" in the data, as already observed in **Figs. 8–11**, it does not perform any actual partitioning of the points into distinct sets. Probably the most well-known approach to investigate groupings in data is to perform a cluster analysis. Clustering methods explicitly aim to assign objects (rows or columns of the data matrix) to a low number of distinct groups, based in their pairwise similarity.

There is a wide variety of distinct algorithms, among the most common are hierarchical clustering, *k*-means clustering, and self-organizing maps (SOM). Their particular details and possible applications are well covered in the literature, and will not be given here. However, it is crucial to distinguish between three essential steps:

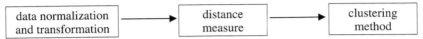

Most, if not all, clustering methods rely on the definition of similarity measure, giving a quantitative account of the similarity between objects. The clustering method then builds on these similarities to compile groups of similar objects.

Unfortunately, as most clustering algorithms also have a multitude of internal parameters that can be adjusted, the diversity of possible data normalizations and distance measures makes a systematic comparison of clustering methods a notoriously tedious task.

The validity of a clustering result can either be checked by comparison with a given *a priori* grouping, or by internal measures of consistency, e.g., comparing the within-cluster distances to those between points in different clusters.

Figure 13 shows a *k*-means clustering of the *A. thaliana* metabolite data matrix in comparison with the original labeling. As can be observed, the data-generated labeling seems to reflect some of the (known) grouping according to experimental conditions. However, the overall correspondence is not too good, which can also be verified using a contingency table and more quantitative measures (data not shown). Similar results are obtained for the case of WT data.

A slightly different approach, though strictly no genuine clustering as the experimental conditions need to be known, is the construction of a dendrogram of the group means after a multivariate analysis of variance. In particular, when the number of experimental conditions is large, a hierarchy, like the one depicted in **Fig. 14**, provides a quick and easy insight into the proximity and organization of experimental conditions.

In general, clustering approaches are more useful when applied to a situation where an *a priori* labeling is not available (or even not meaningful) to reveal groups with "similar" behavior. This is usually the case when, instead of the metabolite profiles as rows, the metabolites themselves (columns) are clustered. **Figure 15** shows a hierarchical clustering of 40 metabolites, constructed using the correlation distance on data in light conditions (pooled 4 h L and 7.5 h L). The dendrogram visualizes the relationship between metabolites in terms of their pairwise correlations. Note that the dendrogram does not only represent a single clustering, but rather a multilevel hierarchy. An actual grouping of the metabolites can be obtained by cutting the dendrogram at some defined depth (**Note 13**).

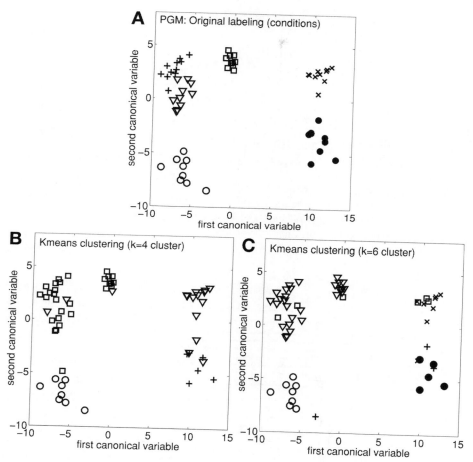

Fig. 13. A *k*-means clustering of the *Arabidopsis thaliana* leaf tissue for the phosphoglucomutase-deficient mutant (59 data points). For visualization all points are assigned the same positions as in **Fig. 8**. (**A**) The original labeling according to the experimental conditions (*see* legend of **Fig. 8**). (**B,C**) The labeling obtained by a *k*-means clustering using the correlation distance and *k* = 4 and 6 cluster, respectively.

3.3. The Interpretation of Metabolite Cluster

The clustering of objects into distinct groups plays a major role in the analysis of gene expression. The common assertion is that genes sharing a similar pattern of expression are likely to be involved in the same regulatory processes *(4)*. This proposition, commonly referred to as "guilt-by-association,"

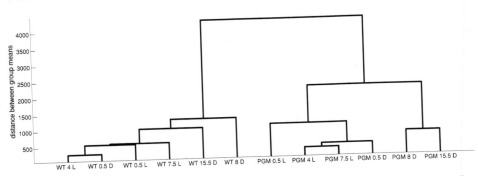

Fig. 14. Dendrogram showing the clusters of group means after MANOVA for phosphoglucomutase-deficient mutant and wild-type. Both genetic strains clearly separate, with an additional partition between dark phase (8 h D and 15.5 h D) and the remaining experimental conditions.

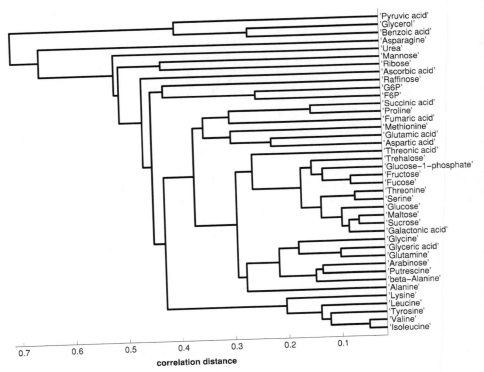

Fig. 15. Hierarchical clustering of 40 metabolites in light conditions (pooled 4 h L and 7.5 h L) for wild-type data, using the correlation distance and average linkage.

has already proven successful for the inference of putative functional annotations, as well as the extraction of regulatory motifs in the upstream regions of genes.

However, a similar reasoning does not straightforwardly apply to metabolomic data. Here, the interpretation of correlations between metabolites, and, thus, their assignment to different clusters, is more complicated and subject to recent debate *(5)*. Moreover, the objectives of metabolomic analysis are profoundly different. In this respect, clustering of metabolites has, as yet, only played a minor role in the literature.

3.3.1. Classification and Decision Trees

Yet a different approach to the classification of samples, based on measured metabolite profiles, are classification or decision trees. Decision trees are among the most popular classification algorithms in data mining and machine learning. Importantly, they are a heuristic method and do not rest on particular assumptions about the data, such as normally distributed data.

Although the objectives are similar to discriminant function analysis, the means are different: a decision tree represents a hierarchical tree-structured plan to predict the class membership (in our case experimental condition), based on a set of attributes (here metabolite levels). At each node, the attribute which has the highest predictive power (measured in terms of information gain) is chosen. For real-valued data, as is usually the case in metabolomic experiments, this decision is based on a (usually binary) threshold, i.e., whether the metabolite level is above or below a certain value.

Figure 16 depicts a decision tree for the *A. thaliana* WT data to predict the six distinct experimental conditions. The final result is a set of thresholds t_i and logical rules of the form

if [(metabolite A $> t\_1$) and (metabolite B $< t\_2$)] g class

Note that decision trees, similar to DFA, belong to the group of supervised methods, i.e., the class membership has to be known in advance for a set of training data. Consequently, we also run into the problem of overfitting: the algorithm will produce a tree, independent of whether the samples actually possess statistically significant differences with respect to class membership. To assess the validity of the tree, cross-validation techniques can be used.

In general, decision trees represent a very quick and easy strategy to look for metabolites that classify between different samples. Among their advantages are a straightforward and intuitive interpretation in terms of "logical rules," as well as rather cheap computational costs, making them applicable even for large datasets. Also, in terms of predictive power, they often perform qualitatively similar to more complicated classification methods, such as support vector machines (**Note 14**).

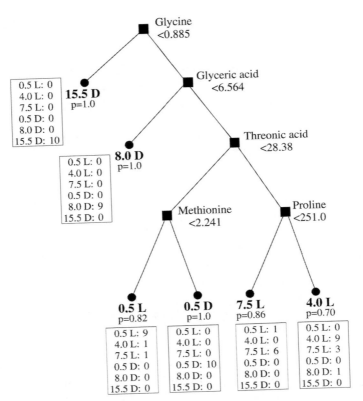

Fig. 16. Decision tree for *Arabidopsis thaliana* wild-type data. The box at each endpoint gives the class membership, along with the probability of correct classification. Note that the tree has been pruned, i.e., we allow for some misclassifications in favor of a more compact tree (pruned at two of five possible levels).

4. Notes

1. The most important step in any analysis is, of course, a visual inspection of the results. We strongly advise against taking the output of any program or algorithm for granted.
2. Sometimes a missing value is not "missing," but actually indicates that the level of the respective metabolite was below the detection limit. In this case, the value can still be used in algorithms that rely only on a categorization of the data, i.e., whether the level of a metabolite is above or below some threshold, such as decision trees.
3. Instead of deleting an entire row of observations whenever a missing value is present, many quantities (like the correlation coefficient or the covariance) require only a pairwise deletion of missing values. However, this comes at the cost that

the resulting correlation matrix is no longer a "true" correlation matrix, i.e., it will not satisfy some properties associated with correlation matrices.

4. In particular, when using online tools to replace missing values with some more-or-less sophisticated algorithms, check the result manually (*see also* **Note 1**).

5. Of course there is no computational way to decide whether an outlier is indeed a measurement artifact or represents true biological information. A large number of outliers might indicate the presence of an additional "state" or "condition" that was not intended in the experiment.

6. Whether or not a data point must be considered as an outlier depends also on the normalization or transformation of the data.

7. Most methods of data normalization can be applied row- or column-wise. Whichever way is appropriate depends also on the matter of interest, i.e., whether one is interested in relationships between experimental conditions or between metabolites.

8. The denotation "analysis of variance" sometimes causes confusion, as the objective of MANOVA is actually to compare the group means. However, this can only be done with respect to their variances, hence the name.

9. MANOVA, and likewise DFA, rests on some rather strict assumptions about the data. While in practice these can not always be strictly fulfilled, the results are mostly robust with respect to minor violations of the assumptions.

10. For MANOVA, and likewise DFA, it is not always advisable to include as many dependent variables (metabolites) as possible to avoid overfitting. Often one can reduce the number of variables, based on intuitive reasoning or preprocessing method (e.g., a sufficient variance that exceeds technical variability).

11. Given enough dependent variables, DFA, as most other supervised methods, will always provide a "result" even when it just amounts to fitting noise. Just because the discrimination between experimental conditions works well on the training set, it does not mean that new experiments can be classified correctly.

12. Though **Figs. 8** and **9** superficially appear somewhat similar, PCA makes no use of the (known) classification of samples into distinct experimental conditions. It is an unsupervised method, working solely on the data.

13. The results of some clustering algorithms, such as *k*-means, depend on the initial conditions. In particular for large datasets, different runs might thus produce different results. It is always recommended to check for the robustness of the solution with respect to different initial conditions and other parameters.

14. Last, we strongly advise to always run through a number of standard methods and algorithms to obtain a first picture about the properties of the dataset. Unfortunately, as statistical testing is often perceived as tedious, there is a growing tendency to jump far too swiftly to the application of some latest "evolutionary agent-based kernel-fuzz transform method using adaptive global network programming." Although the development of new or improved methods is undoubtedly important, these should be used as a last, not as a first, resort. Often well-known and accepted methods, though maybe not as fancy in name, will provide equal, if not better, results.

References

1. Weckwerth, W. and Morgenthal, K. (2005) Metabolomics: from pattern recognition to biological interpretation. *Drug Discov. Today* **10**, 1551–1558.
2. Morgenthal, K., Wienkoop, S., Scholz, M., Selbig, J., and Weckwerth, W. (2005) Correlative GC-TOF-MS based metabolite profiling and LC-MS based protein profiling reveal time-related systemic regulation of metabolite-protein networks and improve pattern recognition for multiple biomarker selection. *Metabolomics* **1**, 109–121.
3. Everitt, B. S. and Dunn, G. (1991) *Applied Multivariate Data Analysis*. Edward Arnold, London, England.
4. Quackenbush, J. (2001) Computational analysis of microarray data. *Nat. Rev. Genet.* **2**, 418–427.
5. Steuer, R., Kurths, J., Fiehn, O., and Weckwerth, W. (2003) Observing and interpreting correlations in metabolomic networks. *Bioinformatics* **19**, 1019–1026.

III

CAPILLARY ELECTROPHORESIS
COUPLED TO MASS SPECTROMETRY

8

Capillary Electrophoresis–Mass Spectrometry for Metabolomics

Tomoyoshi Soga

Summary

A new approach for the comprehensive and quantitative analysis of charged metabolites by capillary electrophoresis–mass spectrometry (CE–MS) is described. Metabolites are first separated by CE based on charge and size, and then selectively detected using MS by monitoring ions over a large range of m/z values. This technique enables the simultaneous determination of over 1000 charged species, and it can readily be applied to various types of biological samples originating from bacteria, plants, mammals, body fluids, and others. This chapter highlights detailed practical procedures for using this technology.

Key Words: Metabolome; metabolic pathway; capillary electrophoresis; mass spectrometry; bacteria; *Bacillus subtilis*; rice plant.

1. Introduction

Metabolomics, the measurement of the levels of all intracellular metabolites, is rapidly becoming an important tool for gaining functional insight into cell biology. Spatial and temporal information about specific metabolite increases and decreases complements gene expression and proteome studies, and provides direct information on metabolic phenotypes.

Despite its importance, so far only a few methodologies for metabolomics have been reported, mainly because most cellular metabolites are highly polar, poorly detected, and similar in their physicochemical characteristics. In addition, the fact that several hundred metabolites coexist in cells complicates the analysis. Recently, several large-scale methods for metabolite analysis have been developed using gas chromatography–mass spectrometry (GC–MS) (*1*),

From: *Methods in Molecular Biology, vol. 358: Metabolomics: Methods and Protocols*
Edited by: W. Weckwerth © Humana Press Inc., Totowa, NJ

liquid chromatography–mass spectrometry (LC–MS) *(2)*, nuclear magnetic resonance (NMR) *(3,4)*, and Fourier transform ion cyclotron resonance mass spectrometry (FT-ICRMS) *(5)*.

To complement these methods, capillary electrophoresis–mass spectrometry (CE–MS) has proven to be a powerful analytical new tool for charged species. In this marriage of techniques, CE combines rapid analysis and efficient separation, whereas MS provides excellent detection selectivity and sensitivity. The main advantage of CE–MS over the other methods previously described resides in its ability to separate most small and highly polar, charged metabolite species, which form the bulk of the cellular metabolome. Recently, our group has developed a direct and quantitative metabolome analysis method using CE–MS *(6,7)*, and its utility was demonstrated in the analyses of various kinds of biological samples on a very large scale *(7,8)*. This chapter describes the technical details of these metabolome analysis methods using bacteria.

2. Materials
2.1. Bacterial Strains and Culture

1. *Bacillus subtilis* 168 cells (*trpC2*) were inoculated in 100 mL of modified nutrient sporulation medium (2X SG medium; 1.6% Difco nutrient broth, 0.1% KCl, 1 mM MgSO$_4$, 1 mM Ca(NO$_3$)$_2$, 1 µM FeSO$_4$, 10 µM MnCl$_2$, and 0.1% glucose) and were incubated at 37°C with shaking *(7)*.
2. Cell growth was monitored by measuring optical density at 660 nm.

2.2. Buffers for Cation Analysis

1. Capillary conditioning and run buffer: 1 M formic acid. Store at room temperature.
2. Sheath liquid: 5 mM ammonium acetate in 50% (v/v) methanol water. Store at room temperature.

2.3. Buffers for Anion Analysis

1. Capillary conditioning A and run buffer: 50 mM ammonium acetate solution, pH 8.5. Store at room temperature.
2. Capillary conditioning buffer B: 50 mM ammonium acetate solution, pH 3.4. Store at room temperature.
3. Sheath liquid: 5 mM ammonium acetate in 50% (v/v) methanol water. Store at room temperature.

2.4. Buffers for Nucleotide and Coenzyme A Compound Analysis

1. Capillary conditioning and run buffer: 50 mM ammonium acetate solution, pH 7.5. Store at room temperature.
2. Sheath liquid: 5 mM ammonium acetate in 50% (v/v) methanol water. Store at room temperature.

2.5. Metabolite Standard Mixture

1. Individual stock solutions of chemical standards, at a concentration of 10 or 100 mM should be prepared in Milli-Q water, 0.1 N HCl or 0.1 N NaOH, depending on the nature of the compound. Store at 4°C.
2. The working standard mixture is prepared by diluting these stock solutions with Milli-Q water just prior to injection.
3. All chemicals should be of analytical or reagent grade. Water should be purified with a Milli-Q purification system (Millipore, Bedford, MA) (*see* **Note 1**).

3. Methods

Precise metabolite extraction procedures, as well as a comprehensive and quantitative analytical method, are indispensable to accurately measure metabolites in cells. The metabolite extraction procedures from cells must meet several requirements. First, rapid enzyme inhibition (quenching) and quantitative metabolite extraction are necessary to precisely quantify the level of intercellular metabolites because turnover can occur rapidly. Second, samples should be concentrated to facilitate detection. Third, simultaneous extraction of both cationic and anionic metabolites is desirable. Finally, the recovered metabolites should be dissolved in a low-conductivity solution to ensure maximum performance of CE–MS.

To achieve high throughput and quantitative analysis of most metabolites, three CE–MS systems (**Fig. 1**) are used in parallel *(7)* for cationic metabolites, anionic metabolites, and nucleotides.

Figure 1A illustrates the cation analysis system, where cations are separated by CE based on their charge and size using a fused-silica capillary and then detected by MS. In order to analyze all cations simultaneously, a very low pH electrolyte, 1 M formic acid (pH 1.8) *(9)*, is used to confer a positive charge on the metabolites, thus, making them amenable to MS analysis.

Analysis of anions by CE–MS is performed in negative mode, where the inlet of the capillary is at the cathode and the outlet at the anode. Under normal conditions, because the CE–MS system does not possess an outlet vial, the electro-osmotic flow (EOF) *(10)* is directed toward the cathode (opposite to MS direction) and creates a gap in the liquid phase at the capillary exit, resulting in a current drop and failure to analyze by MS *(6)*. This problem can be overcome by reversing the direction of EOF *(6)* using a SMILE(+) *(11)*, cationic polymer-coated capillary, as illustrated in **Fig. 1B**.

One remaining problem is that using the above anion analysis system, significant adsorption of multivalent ions (e.g., nucleotides and CoA compounds) on the cationic-coated capillary is observed. To prevent their adsorption and allow precise quantification, a pressure-assisted CE–MS technique using a non-charged polymer-coated capillary *(12)* is used (**Fig. 1 C**). Altogether, the three

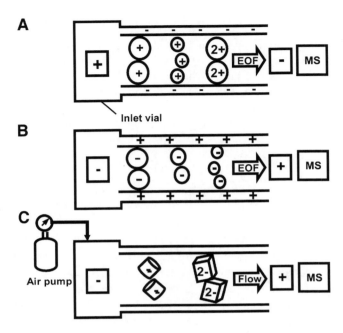

Fig. 1. Schematic of the various capillary electrophoresis–mass spectrometry configurations. Method for (**A**) cationic metabolites, (**B**) anionic metabolites, and (**C**) nucleotides and CoA compounds. (Reproduced with permission **ref. 7** © [2003] American Chemical Society.)

CE–MS methods allow the analysis of almost all charged metabolites in a sample (*see* **Fig. 2**) *(7)*.

3.1. Metabolite Extraction

1. To rapidly isolate metabolites from *B. subtilis* cells, 10 mL of culture medium is passed through a 0.45-µm pore size filter. Residual cells on the filter are washed with 10 mL of Milli-Q water and the filter is then rapidly plunged into 2 mL of methanol, containing internal standards (5 µ*M* methionine sulfone for cations and 5 µ*M* 2-monopholinoethanesulfornic acid [MES] for anions), to inactivate enzymes.

Fig. 2. *(opposite page)* Capillary electrophoresis–mass spectrometry analysis of cationic metabolites extracted during the late logarithmic growth phase of *Bacillus subtilis* 168, in the range of 101 to 150 *m/z*. The numbers in the upper left corner of each trace represent the ion intensity associated with the tallest peak in the electropherogram for each *m/z*, and the numbers on top of peaks are relative migration times normalized with methionine sulfone. (Reproduced with permission from **ref. 7** © (2003) American Chemical Society.)

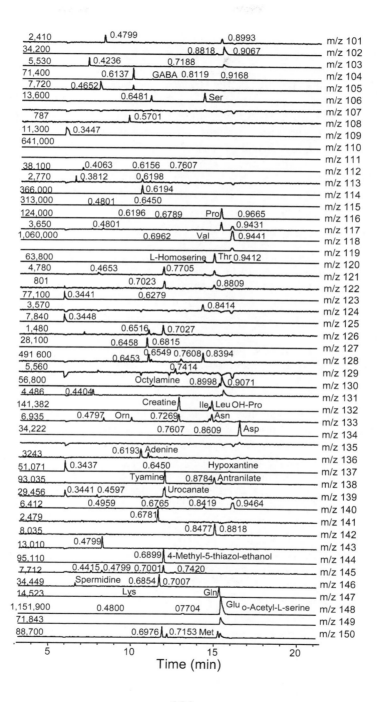

2,410	0.4799		0.8993	m/z 101
34,200		0.8818	0.9067	m/z 102
5,530	0.4236	0.7188		m/z 103
71,400	0.6137	GABA 0.8119	0.9168	m/z 104
7,720	0.4652			m/z 105
13,600	0.6481		Ser	m/z 106
				m/z 107
787	0.5701			m/z 108
11,300	0.3447			m/z 109
641,000				m/z 110
				m/z 111
38,100	0.4063	0.6156 0.7607		m/z 112
2,770	0.3812	0.6198		m/z 113
366,000		0.6194		m/z 114
313,000	0.4801	0.6450		m/z 115
124,000	0.6196 0.6789	Pro	0.9665	m/z 116
3,650	0.4801		0.9431	m/z 117
1,060,000	0.6962	Val	0.9441	m/z 118
63,800	L-Homoserine	Thr 0.9412		m/z 119
4,780	0.4653	0.7705		m/z 120
801	0.7023	0.8809		m/z 121
77,100	0.3441	0.6279		m/z 122
3,570		0.8414		m/z 123
7,840	0.3448			m/z 124
1,480	0.6516 0.7027			m/z 125
28,100	0.6458 0.6815			m/z 126
491,600	0.6453 0.6549 0.7608 0.8394			m/z 127
5,560	0.7414			m/z 128
56,800	Octylamine 0.8998	0.9071		m/z 129
4,486	0.4404			m/z 130
141,382	Creatine	Ile Leu OH-Pro		m/z 131
6,935	0.4797 Orn 0.7269	Asn		m/z 132
34,222	0.7607 0.8609	Asp		m/z 133
				m/z 134
3243	0.6193 Adenine			m/z 135
51,071	0.3437 0.6450	Hypoxantine		m/z 136
93,035	Tyamine	0.8784 Antranilate		m/z 137
29,456	0.3441 0.4597	Urocanate		m/z 138
6,412	0.4959 0.6765	0.8419 0.9464		m/z 139
2,479	0.6781			m/z 140
8,035		0.8477 0.8818		m/z 141
13,010	0.4799			m/z 142
95,110	0.6899	4-Methyl-5-thiazol-ethanol		m/z 143
7,712	0.4415 0.4799 0.7001 0.7420			m/z 144
34,449	Spermidine 0.6854 0.7007			m/z 145
14,523	Lys	Gln		m/z 146
1,151,900	0.4800	07704	Glu o-Acetyl-L-serine	m/z 147
71,843				m/z 148
88,700	0.6976 0.7153 Met			m/z 149
				m/z 150

5   10   15   20

Time (min)

2. After a 5-min incubation at room temperature, 1.6 mL of chloroform and 640 μL of Milli-Q water are added to the solution and the mixture is thoroughly mixed to remove phospholipids liberated from cell membranes, which can adsorb on the capillary wall and dramatically reduce CE performance.

3. The separated 1.6 mL methanol–water layer is then centrifugally ultrafiltrated (2500*g*) through a Millipore 5-kDa cutoff filter to remove proteins. The ultrafiltrate can be lyophilized, stored frozen, and dissolved in 50 μL of Milli-Q water prior to CE–MS analysis (*see* **Note 2**). Overall, this procedure results in a 200-fold enrichment of metabolites.

4. The metabolite extraction procedures can be applied to any other biological species with some modifications. Sato et al. *(8)* reported details of the extraction procedures from rice plants.

3.2. Instrumentation

1. We routinely perform CE–MS experiments using an Agilent Technolgies (Waldbronn, Germany) CE capillary electrophoresis system equipped with an air pressure pump, an Agilent 1100 series MSD mass spectrometer, an Agilent1100 series isocratic HPLC pump, a G1603A Agilent CE–MS adapter kit, and a G1607A Agilent CE-electrospray ionization (ESI)-MS sprayer kit (Agilent) (*see* **Notes 3** and **4**).

2. System control, data acquisition, and MSD data evaluation are performed using the G2201AA Agilent ChemStation software for CE-MSD.

3.3. CE–MS for Cations

1. Prior to use, a new capillary should be equilibrated with the running buffer (1 *M* formic acid) for 20 min (*see* **Note 5**). In addition, before each injection, the capillary is preconditioned for 5 min by flushing with the same buffer.

2. Separations are carried out on a fused-silica capillary (50 μm I.D. × 100 cm total length) (*see* **Notes 6** and **7**). The sample is injected using a pressure of 50 mbar for 3 s (3 nL) (*see* **Notes 8** and **9**). The applied voltage is set at 30 kV. The capillary temperature is maintained at 20°C using the CE thermostat and the sample tray should be cooled below 5°C.

3. The sheath liquid, 5 m*M* ammonium acetate in 50% (v/v) methanol–water, is delivered at 10 μL/min using the LC pump. ESI–MS is conducted in the positive ion mode and the capillary voltage set at 4000 V. The flow of heated dry nitrogen gas (heater temperature of 300°C) should be maintained at 10 L/min. In MS using the selective ion monitoring (SIM) mode, sets of 30 protonated $[M+H]^+$ ions *m/z* are analyzed successively to cover the whole range of *m/z* values from 70 through 1027 *(7,9)*.

3.4. CE–MS for Anions

1. A new capillary should be flushed successively with the running buffer (50 m*M* ammonium acetate solution, pH 8.5), 50 m*M* acetic acid (pH 3.4), and running buffer again, for 20 min each (*see* **Note 5**). In addition, before each injection, the

capillary should be equilibrated for 2 min by flushing with 50 mM acetic acid (pH 3.4) and then for 5 min with the running electrolyte.

2. Separation is carried out on a SMILE (+) cationic capillary coated with successive multiple ionic polymer layers *(11)* (Nacalai Tesque, Kyoto, Japan) (*see* **Notes 6** and **7**). The standard capillary dimensions are 50 µm I.D. × 100 cm total length. The sample is injected using a pressure of 50 mbar for 30 s (30 nL) (*see* **Notes 8** and **9**). The applied voltage is set at –30 kV.

3. ESI–MS is conducted in the negative ion mode and the capillary voltage set at 3500 V. In MS using with SIM mode, sets of 30 deprotonated [M–H]⁻ ions are analyzed successively to cover the whole range of m/z values from 70 through 1027 *(6,7)*.

4. Other conditions are the same as in cationic metabolite analysis.

3.5. CE–MS for Nucleotides and CoA Compounds

1. A new capillary should be equilibrated with the running buffer (50 mM ammonium acetate solution, pH 7.5) for 20 min (*see* **Note 5**). Before each injection, the capillary should be equilibrated for 5 min by flushing with the running buffer.

2. Separations are carried out on a GC capillary, polydimethylsiloxane (DB-1) (50 µm I.D. × 100 cm total length) (Agilent) (*see* **Notes 6** and **7**). The applied voltage is set at –30 kV and a pressure of 50 mbar is applied to the capillary inlet, during the whole run, to maintain a conductive liquid junction at the capillary outlet *(12)*.

3. Other conditions are the same as for anionic metabolite analysis.

4. Notes

1. All solutions should be prepared in Milli-Q water that has a resistivity of 18.2 MΩ–cm.

2. For samples, it is recommended to use polypropylene sample vials rather than glass vials.

3. The type of ESI–MS instrument is important in successfully employing CE–MS. The electrospray probes of most ESI- time-of-flight (TOF)–MS systems are maintained at a potential of several kV, which result in the generation of EOF, the bulk flow of liquid through the capillary, toward the capillary inlet in CE–MS. This phenomenon causes the injected sample to be rapidly flushed out from the capillary inlet before the run. To avoid this problem, we recommend selecting an ESI-TOF–MS system of which electrospray probe is grounded. In this configuration, there is no potential difference between the capillary inlet and outlet, where the electrosprayer is connected, and therefore, no EOF is generated. If the previously mentioned conditions cannot be met, then no voltage should be applied to the MS detector until the sample has been completely injected.

4. To avoid a siphoning effect the CE inlet vial should be at the same height as the sprayer tip of the mass spectrometer.

5. We recommend avoiding capillary conditioning with sodium hydroxide because this degrades performance for this application.

6. The electrospray performance depends on the quality of the capillary cut. Jagged edges prevent the formation of a uniform spray and can also act as adsorption sites for sample components. We recommend using a diamond blade cutter (e.g., 5183-4670 Diamond blade replacement kit for CE cutter; Agilent).

7. When separation resolution deteriorates, the capillary should be replaced because the capillaries cannot be efficiently regenerated by washing, and so on.

8. If the sample contains proteins and the migration times increases from run to run, removal of proteins is recommended using centrifugal ultrafilters with a 5-kDa cutoff filter.

9. If the current suddenly drops or broadened peaks are observed, the sample should be diluted with Milli-Q water in order to reduce its conductivity (e.g., 1:10 or 1:50 dilution) and reanalyzed.

Acknowledgments

The author would like to thank to Dr. Martin Robert for critical reading of the manuscript.

References

1. Fiehn, O., Kopka, J., Dormann, P., Altmann, T., Trethewey, R. N., and Willmitzer, L. (2000) Metabolite profiling for plant functional genomics. *Nat. Biotechnol.* **18,** 1157–1161.

2. Wilson, I. D., Nicholson, J. K., Castro-Perez, J., et al. (2005) High resolution "Ultra performance" liquid chromatography coupled to a-TOF mass spectrometry as a tool for differential metabolic pathway profiling in functional genomic studies. *J. Proteome Res.* **4,** 591–598.

3. Griffin, J. L., Walker, L. A., Garrod, S., Holmes, E., Shore, R. F., and Nicholson, J. K. (2000) NMR spectroscopy based metabonomic studies on the comparative biochemistry of the kidney and urine of the bank vole (Clethrionomys glareolus), wood mouse (Apodemus sylvaticus), white toothed shrew (Crocidura suaveolens) and the laboratory rat. *Comp. Biochem. Physiol. Biochem. Mol. Biol.* **127,** 357–367.

4. Reo, N. V. (2002) NMR-based metabolomics. *Drug Chem. Toxicol.* **25,** 375–382.

5. Aharoni, A., Ric de Vos, C. H., Verhoeven, H. A., et al. (2002) Nontargeted metabolome analysis by use of fourier transform ion cyclotron mass spectrometry. *Omics* **6,** 217–234.

6. Soga, T., Ueno, Y., Naraoka, H., Ohashi, Y., Tomita, M., and Nishioka, T. (2002) Simultaneous determination of anionic intermediates for *Bacillus subtilis* metabolic pathways by capillary electrophoresis electrospray ionization mass spectrometry. *Anal. Chem.* **74,** 2233–2239.

7. Soga, T., Ohashi, Y., Ueno, Y., Naraoka, H., Tomita, M., and Nishioka, T. (2003) Quantitative metabolome analysis using capillary electrophoresis mass spectrometry. *J. Proteome Res.* **2,** 488–494.

8. Sato, S., Soga, T., Nishioka, T., and Tomita, M. (2004) Simultaneous determination of the main metabolites in rice leaves using capillary electrophoresis mass

spectrometry and capillary electrophoresis diode array detection. *Plant Journal* **40,** 151–163.

9. Soga, T. and Heiger, D. N. (2000) Amino acid analysis by capillary electrophoresis electrospray ionization mass spectrometry. *Anal. Chem.* **72,** 1236–1241.

10. Lukacs, K. D. and Jorgenson, J. W. (1985) Capillary zone electrophoresis: effect of physical parameters on separation efficiency and quantitation. *HRC CC J. High Resolut. Chromatogr. Chromatogr. Commun.* **8,** 407–411.

11. Katayama, H., Ishihama, Y., and Asakawa, N. (1998) Stable cationic capillary coating with successive multiple ionic polymer layers for capillary electrophoresis. *Anal. Chem.* **70,** 5272–5277.

12. Soga, T., Ueno, Y., Naraoka, H., Matsuda, K., Tomita, M., and Nishioka, T. (2002) Pressure-assisted capillary electrophoresis electrospray ionization mass spectrometry for analysis of multivalent anions. *Anal. Chem.* **74,** 6224–6229.

IV

Liquid Chromatography Coupled to Mass Spectrometry for Metabolomics and Structural Elucidation

9

Application of Liquid Chromatography–Mass Spectrometry Analysis in Metabolomics

Reversed-Phase Monolithic Capillary Chromatography and Hydrophilic Chromatography Coupled to Electrospray Ionization–Mass Spectrometry

Vladimir V. Tolstikov, Oliver Fiehn, and Nobuo Tanaka

Summary

Analysis of the entire metabolome as the sum of all detectable components in the sample rather than analysis of each individual metabolite is performed by the metabolomics approaches. To monitor in parallel hundreds or even thousands of metabolites, high-throughput techniques are required that enable screening for relative changes rather than absolute concentrations of compounds. Most analytical techniques for profiling small molecules consist of gas chromatography (GC) or high-performance liquid chromatography (HPLC) coupled to mass spectrometry. HPLC separations are better suited for the analysis of labile and high molecular weight compounds, and for the analysis of nonvolatile polar compounds in their natural form. Although GC- and HPLC-based profiling techniques are not truly quantitative, the compounds detecting and employing the acceptable standards may compare their relative amounts. We have demonstrated that reversed-phase monolithic capillary chromatography and hydrophilic chromatography can be successfully applied for sufficient plant crude extracts separations and metabolomics studies.

Key Words: Metabolome; HPLC; RP; HILIC; capillary; monolithic; hydrophilic; electrospray; mass spectrometry; ion trap; fragmentation.

1. Introduction

In accordance with the central doctrine of molecular biology, DNA is transcribed into RNA then translated to proteins, which then make small molecules.

From: *Methods in Molecular Biology, vol. 358: Metabolomics: Methods and Protocols*
Edited by: W. Weckwerth © Humana Press Inc., Totowa, NJ

However, often feedback loops and signaling circuits are overlooked, which may force the viewing of small molecules as actors and proteins (and DNA) as responding to alterations in metabolic levels. After all, the vision of complex regulatory networks will be closer to reality than a simplistic hierarchical paradigm. Although there may be over tens of thousands of genes, several hundred thousand transcripts, and up to 1 million proteins, it is estimated that there may be as few as 2000–3000 small molecules in the metabolome of higher organisms. The analysis of the metobolome looks very attractive from this point of view with fewer numbers of analytes to be identified and quantified. High chemical complexity, analytical and biological variance, and large dynamic range are quite challenging, even for the latest analytical methods. In most cases, analytical methods are based on chromatographic separation techniques like GC and high-performance liquid chromatography (HPLC), and in many cases comprise Fourier transform infrared spectroscopy, electron impact ionization–mass spectrometry (EI–MS), electrospray ionization–mass spectrometry (ESI–MS), and nuclear magnetic resonance (NMR) spectroscopy. Mass spectrometers are generally more sensitive and more selective than any other type of detector. Prior to MS detection, the metabolites have to be separated, and separated compounds must be ionized. Ionization techniques may vary, especially for GC–MS and LC–MS couplings. The high-throughput screening with GC– and LC–MS techniques generates large volumes of analytical data that require advanced software for data mining. Metabolomics studies and analysis of the tissue crude extracts cannot be accomplished with the use of a single separation/detection method owing to the high chemical diversity of the analyzed mixture. Hydrophobic components are nicely separated with the use of reversed-phase (RP) chromatography *(1–3)*, which is very popular and an appreciated method of separation. Hydrophilic and charged small molecules are well separated by the capillary electrophoresis. Hydrophilic and neutral compounds are best suited for hydrophilic (HILIC) separation *(4–6)*. We introduced HILIC-ESI–MS analysis for plant-derived samples and demonstrated feasibility of this approach, especially for analysis of the samples taken from hydrophilic compartments like the plant transport system *(7–11)*. Traditional particles packed columns as well as high-speed monolithic columns can be used for HPLC separations prior to MS detection. Because the metabolomic approach requires large batches of the samples to be analyzed in order to apply statistical methods of the data treatment, micro-HPLC and capillary columns should be mostly used in order to avoid a significant amount of organic solvent evaporated into the atmosphere during this process. Silica-based C18-modified capillary monolithic columns actually offer a new step in micro-HPLC RP chromatography providing up to hundreds of thousands of theoretical plates per column. Therefore, performance of these columns is expected to be superior to conventional ones at the same range of HPLC parameters applied. We introduced the utilization of these columns for metabolomics studies and demonstrated their suitability for very complex mixture separations.

2. Materials
2.1. Standards and Chemicals

1. Oligosaccharides kit, l-amino acids kit, and reserpine are purchased from SAF (Taufkirchen and Seelze, Germany).
2. Ammonium acetate and acetic acid: highest purity grade available from SAF.

2.2. Solvents and Standards (see Notes 1 and 2)

1. LC–MS-grade solvents are purchased from SAF.
2. Reserpine stock solution (0.2 mg/mL methanol).

2.3. Instrumentation

The LC–MS system consists of a Finnigan LCQ DECA mass spectrometer (ThermoFinnigan, San Jose, CA), a Rheos 2000 pump (Flux Instruments AB, Karlskoga, Sweden), and an HTS PAL auto sampler (CTC Analytics, Zwingen, Switzerland). The system was operated under the Xcalibur software (v1.3, ThermoFinnigan). Helium collision gas incoming pressure is kept at 2.6 bars, and the ion gauge pressure at 0.89×10^{-5}. Full-scan mass spectra are acquired from 150 to 2000 amu at unit mass resolution. For MS^n experiments, data-dependent scans are chosen with the wideband activation turned off. The normalized collision energy is set to 35%, and the activation Q is set to 0.250 with the source fragmentation turned off. Metal needle tips or online pico tips are from New Objective Inc., Woburn, MA. The mass spectrometer is tuned on sucrose solution (0.1 mg/mL) mixed with the acetonitrile/ammonium acetate buffer, pH 5.5 (1:1 [v/v]) prior to measurements.

2.3.1. HPLC–MS Setup
2.3.1.1. NORMAL FLOW SETUP

Normal flow HPLC operations with the use of conventional HPLC columns, having 4.6-mm I.D., require pneumatically assisted electrospray, and a postcolumn splitter that diverts in the range of 50 to 150 µL/min into the standard ESI ion source. Narrow bore columns do not require splitter. Nitrogen sheath gas pressure is set to six bars at the flow rate of 0.8 L/min. Spray voltage is set to 5 kV. The temperature of the heated transfer capillary is maintained at 250°C.

2.3.1.2. MICRO FLOW SETUP

Micro-HPLC utilizing capillary columns does not require sheath gas. Precolumn splitter (6) is used with the split ratio in the range of 1:10 to 1:1000.

Flow does not exceed 15 µL/min. Modified Protana nanospray source is used for column/tip assembly. A column is connected to a tip via a PEEK T-connector, with an inserted platinum wire in contact with the liquid. Voltage is applied through this wire. Spray voltage is set to 3 kV for positive and 2 kV for negative ionization modes. The temperature of the heated transfer capillary is maintained at 180°C.

2.4. Monolithic Silica-Based Capillary Columns (see Note 3)

RP C18 monolithic silica-based capillary columns are manufactured in the laboratory of Professor Nobuo Tanaka, Kyoto Institute of Technology, Kyoto, Japan. Columns with the dimensions of 0.2-mm I.D. and 600 mm in length are used for the separations *(10,11)*.

3. Methods

3.1. Sample Preparation for LC–MS Metabolomics Analysis

Sample preparation for LC–MS analysis is a very important part of the whole process. Live tissue or organ must be frozen prior to sampling because response to the sampling procedure quickly alters metabolism. Afterwards, extraction should be almost complete because an absence or insufficient amount of the component in the sample gives a zero detector response. This may not correspond to real tissue contents. Proteins should be precipitated and removed unless they are of particular interest. Concentration should be high enough to allow sufficient column loading with a low injection volume.

3.1.1. Leaf Harvest

1. Place a metal ball in each of the 2-mL sample tubes prior to harvest.
2. Submerge tubes into liquid nitrogen (N_2).
3. Harvest 150 ± 30 mg of fresh weight of the plant leaves (*Arabidopsis thaliana*, Columbia 24) in sample tubes. Keep it in there and proceed with extraction.
4. Alternatively, perform rapid lyophilization of your tissue to obtain approx 15 mg dry weight. Tissue stored at –80°C for longer than 4 wk should not be used, as it was observed that considerable metabolic changes occur after this time.

3.1.2. Leaf Tissue Extraction

1. Prechill Retsch ball-mill tube holders in liquid N_2. Put four samples into each of the ball-mill tube holders and homogenize the tissue for 1 min at 60% speed. Immediately put the tube holders and the samples back into liquid N_2.
2. Alternatively, grind the tissue in liquid N_2 using a mortar and pestle, and so on. Take out the sample tubes one-by-one and immediately add 1 mL of methanol in order to stop enzymatic activity. Vortex thoroughly. Add 50 µL of a reserpine stock solution (0.2 mg/mL methanol) as internal reference.

3. Add 50 μL of water and vortex. Shake the resulting suspension for 15 min at ambient temperature.
4. Centrifuge at 14,000g for 5 min. Carefully transfer the green supernatant into a sample glass vial that is equipped with a screw cap with Teflonized inlay.
5. Alternatively, acetonitrile or a mixture of isopropanol and acetone (1:1 [v/v]) can be used because rapid chlorophyll degradation occurs in methanol solutions during the storage.

3.1.3. Pumpkin Phloem Excudates

Pumpkin (giant pumpkin, *Cucurbitacea maxima*) phloem sampling should be done according to Richardson *(12)*. Phloem samples are acquired from the fully expanded, mature leaves that did not show any signs of senescence in 8-wk-old plants.

1. In order to preserve water-soluble components intact and simultaneously stop enzymatic activity, dilute 100 μL of the freshly collected phloem exudates in 300 μL of pure water, and add 300 μL of chloroform to precipitate proteins by vortexing.
2. Collect the water phase and do rapid lyophilization.
3. Redissolve the residue in 50 μL of water/acetonitrile (1:1 [v/v]) mixture.
4. Centrifuge at 14,000g for 5 min. Carefully transfer the clear supernatant into a sample glass vial that is equipped with a screw cap with Teflonized inlay.

3.2. HILIC ESI-LC–MS Analyses of Pumpkin Phloem Excudates

Analytical LC is performed using acetonitrile (A) and 6.5 m*M* ammonium acetate (pH 5.5, adjusted by acetic acid) (B) as the mobile phase at the flow rates of 0.2–0.1 mL/min at the ambient temperature. LC–MS analysis is performed on TSK Gel Amide 80 column, 250 × 2.0 mm, 5-μm particle size (TosoHaas, Montgomeryville, PA). After 5 min of isocratic run at 0% B, gradient to 15% B is concluded at 10 min, then gradient to 55% B is completed at 80 min.

1. Prepare standards mix using oligosaccharides and L-amino acid kits in a mixture of acetonitrile:water (1:1 [v/v]). All the standards presented in these kits can be used in a single mix. For a simple chromatogram one can use a small number of standards in a mix. Concentration should not exceed 1 mg/mL.
2. Equilibrate column with the starting buffer for at least 20 min. Inject 10 μL and acquire the data in the full-scan mode for the positive and negative ions in the range of 100 to 1500 amu.
3. After acquisition finishes, wash the column with buffer B for 5 min and equilibrate for 20 min with buffer A prior the next run.
4. α-Amino acids are mostly detected as [M+H]+ positive ions. Mono- and oligosaccharides are detected as ammonia adducts in the positive mode and as [M-H]– ions in the negative mode. Hydrophobic α-amino acids are eluted earlier than basic and acidic ones. Oligosaccharides are eluted in the order of increasing monomer units. Larger oligomers are eluted latest.

5. Use selected standards as internal or external ones for the instrument calibration by the serial dilutions. This procedure is essential for further semi-quantitative analysis.
6. Prepare the pumpkin phloem excudate sample in accordance with **Subheading 3.1.3.** Inject 10 μL and acquire the data in the full-scan mode for the positive and negative ions.
7. Introduce selected internal standards and repeat analysis.
8. Refer to **refs. 2–4** for peaks annotation.
9. Include MS/MS or MS^n experiments for both positive and negative modes in the analytical run in order to annotate peaks through the MS/MS libraries search and/ or collect fragmentation information for *de novo* identification.

A typical HILIC LC-ESI–MS chromatogram of the pumpkin phloem excudate (*C. maxima*) is shown in **Fig. 1**. Some structural annotations are illustrated. Structural elucidation for components shown in **Fig. 1** was accomplished by the comparison of the MS^n fragmentation patterns and spectral data for authentic compounds available commercially and/or received from research laboratories where these substances have been isolated, characterized, and this data published. Unknown compounds, including oligomers, have been successfully isolated by subsequent fractions collection. Off-line nano-ESI-MS^n, FT-ICRMS exact mass measurements, and two-dimensional NMR techniques have been applied to assign their chemical structures (*4,7,8*).

3.3. HILIC Capillary ESI-LC–MS Analyses of the Plant Leaf Extracts

Split analytical LC is performed with the same HPLC pump and injector as for convenient chromatography using acetonitrile (A) and 6.5 m*M* ammonium acetate (pH 5.5, adjusted by acetic acid) (B) as mobile phase at pump flow rates of 0.15–0.06 mL/min at ambient temperature. LC–MS analysis is performed on polyhydroxyethyl A column, 150 × 0.6 mm, 3-μm particle size (PolyLC, Inc., Columbia, MD). Split ratio is set to 1:10. After 5 min of isocratic run at 0% B, gradient to 8% B is concluded at 5 min, then gradient to 35% B is completed at 90 min.

1. Prepare the plant leaf extract sample in accordance with **Subheading 3.1.2.** Equilibrate column with the starting buffer for at least 20 min. Inject 3 μL and acquire the data in the full-scan mode for the positive and negative ions in the range of 100 to 1500 amu.
2. After acquisition finishes, wash the column with buffer B for 10 min and equilibrate for 20 min with buffer A prior to the next run.
3. Use selected standards as internal or external ones for the instrument calibration by serial dilutions. This procedure is essential for further semi-quantitative analysis.
4. Introduce selected internal standards and repeat analysis.
5. Refer to **Note 4** and publications (*5–9,12*) for peaks annotation.

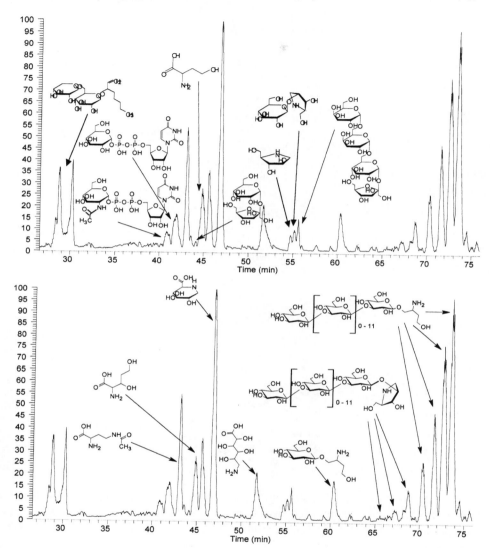

Fig. 1. Hydrophilic liquid chromatography-electrospray ionization–mass spectrometry chromatograms of the pumpkin pholoem excudate (*Cucurbitacea maxima*). Peak annotations are given by the chemical structures.

6. Include MS/MS or MS^n experiments for both positive and negative modes in the analytical run in order to annotate peaks through the MS/MS libraries search and/ or collect fragmentation information for *de novo* identification.

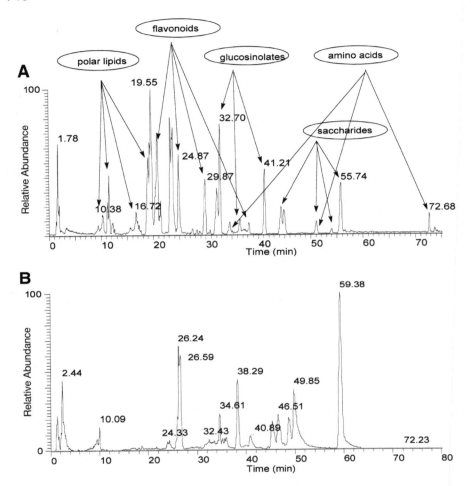

Fig. 2. Hydrophilic liquid chromatography-electrospray ionization–mass spectrometry chromatograms of the plant leaf extracts. (**A**) Chromatogram of *Arabidopsis thaliana* (Columbia 24) and (**B**) *Oriza sativa*. Peak annotations are given by the chemical classes.

Typical HILIC LC-ESI–MS chromatograms of plant leaf extracts (*A. thaliana*, Columbia 24, and *Oriza sativa*) are shown in **Fig. 2**.

3.4. RP C18 Capillary Monolithic ESI-LC–MS Analyses of Plant Leaf Extracts

Split analytical LC is performed using acetonitrile (B) and 6.5 m*M* ammonium acetate (pH 5.5, adjusted by acetic acid) (A) as the mobile phase at the

Table 1
Gradient Flow Table for HPLC

	Time (min)	%B	%A	HPLC flow rate (mL/min)
Startup	0.0	0	100	0.05
	5.0	0	100	0.05
Run	0.0	0	100	0.05
	2.0	0	100	0.05
	5.0	8	92	0.05
	25.0	30	70	0.07
	35.0	70	30	0.08
	50.0	99	1	0.10
	100.0	100	0	0.15
Shut-down	120.0	100	0	0.20
	125.0	0	100	0.07
	130.0	0	100	0.05
	150.0	0	100	0.05

pump flow rates of 0.05–0.2 mL/min at ambient temperature. LC–MS analysis is performed on a C18 monolithic silica-based column, 600 × 0.2 mm. Split ratio is set to 1:100. After 2 min of isocratic run at 0% B, gradient to 8% B is concluded at 5 min, then gradient to 30% B is completed at 25 min. Correspondingly, gradient to 70% B is completed at 35 min, then gradient to 99% B is completed at 50 min, and 99% B is run isocratically up to 100 min (*see* **Note 5**) (**Table 1**).

1. Prepare plant leaf extract sample in accordance with **Subheading 3.1.2.** Equilibrate column with the starting buffer for at least 15 min. Inject 3 μL and acquire data in the full-scan mode for the positive and negative ions in the range of 100 to 1500 amu.
2. After acquisition finishes, wash the column with buffer B for 10 min and equilibrate for 15 min with buffer A prior to the next run.
3. Use selected standards (i.e., reserpine) as internal or external ones for the instrument calibration by the serial dilutions. This procedure is essential for further semi-quantitative analysis.
4. Introduce selected internal standards and repeat analysis.
5. Refer to **Note 4** and **refs. 5–9,12** for peaks annotation.
6. Include MS/MS or MS^n experiments for both positive and negative modes in the analytical run in order to annotate peaks through the MS/MS libraries search and/or collect fragmentation information for *de novo* identification.

Typical RP C18 monolithic LC-ESI–MS chromatograms of plant leaf extracts (*A. thaliana*, Columbia 24, and *O. sativa*) are shown in **Fig. 3**.

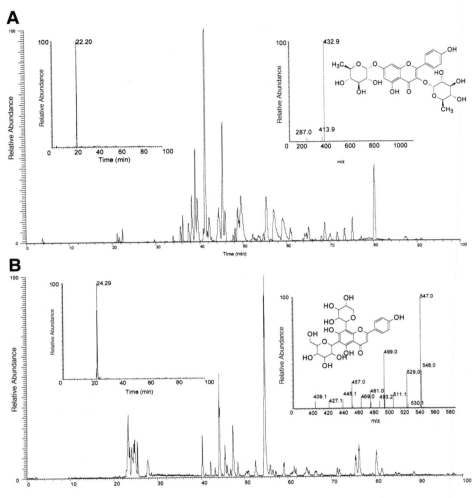

Fig. 3. Reversed-phase C18 monolithic liquid chromatography-electrospray ion-ization–mass spectrometry (MS) chromatograms of plant leaf extracts. (**A**) *Arabidopsis thaliana* leaf extract. (**B**) *Oriza sativa* leaf extract. Examples for specific extracted ion chromatograms are located in the upper left corners. Compound identifications by MS/MS spectra and corresponding structures are situated in the upper right corners.

4. Notes

1. Unless stated otherwise, water-based buffers for HPLC should be refreshed daily to avoid mold formation and possible contamination owing to bacteria growth.
2. Each lot of acetonitrile should be investigated on the presence of admixtures by infusion into the mass spectrometer. Manufacturers provide purity control only by GC–MS. Deionized water quality should be as high as possible.

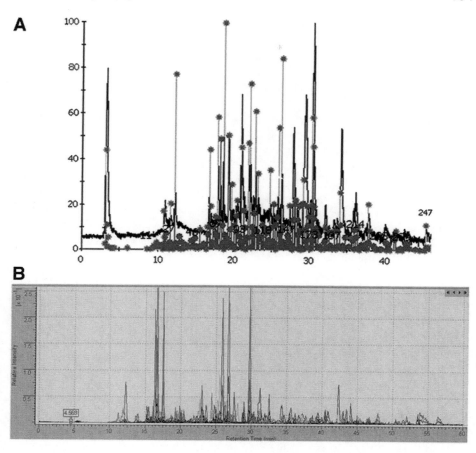

Fig. 4. Reversed-phase C18 monolithic liquid chromatography-electrospray ion-ization–mass spectrometry (MS) chromatograms of *Arabidopsis thaliana* leaf extract. **(A)** Components finding with the assistance of AnalyzerPro (Spectral Works) software. **(B)** Deconvoluted chromatogram with the ACS MS Manager suite (Advanced Chemistry Development).

3. Monolithic silica capillary columns commercially available from Merck KGaA (Darmstadt, Germany), are prepared from tetramethoxysilane and available with 0.1-mm I.D. and up to 150-mm length. Performance of monolithic silica capillary columns including the tetramethoxysilane type can be optimized by splitting injection (as well as on-column detection in the case of ultraviolet detection), as described in **refs.** *13* and *14*.
4. Peak finding and deconvolution, utilizing software designed to handle large files and large datasets, can unravel large numbers of components, illustrated in **Fig. 4**.

The number of components actually depends on the extraction protocol, which was recently demonstrated with the GC–MS and LC–MS methods (2). Structure elucidation and assignment, with the use of an ion trap mass spectrometer providing the fragmentation pathway, gets uncomplicated when the source of substance is known and fragments generated are in agreement with the predicted ones (Mass Frontier, HighChem), as illustrated in **Fig. 5**. Compound-specific fragmentation generating unique fragments actually provides a signature for this particular compound. Unfortunately it is problematic with the interpretation and in many cases requires strong evidence, like accurate masses and two-dimensional NMR data.

5. In gradient HPLC, increasing the stronger eluent (mobile phase B) can optimize separation by controlling a gradient range [ϕ_f (B% final)–ϕ_0 (B% initial)], gradient time (t_G), and flow rate (F), as well as column length. Three parameters, N (a number of theoretical plates of a column), α (a separation factor between peaks), and k (a retention factor of a solute) should be considered as in isocratic HPLC, particularly the average retention factor k^* (**Eq. 1**, the retention factor at the middle of a column) for gradient elution (*13–17*). The k^* is a function of S (the slope of the plot of log k against the content of solvent B in the mobile phase, $S = 4\sim10$ for small molecules less than 1000 molecular weight (MW), $S = $ ca. 30 for molecules with 10,000 MW, and $S = $ ca. 100 for macromolecules with 100,000 MW, V_m (mobile phase volume in a column is given in μL), $\Delta\phi$ (change in B solvent content in mobile phase from ϕ_0 to ϕ_f: $\Delta\phi = 1.0$ for gradient from 0 to 100% B), F (μL/min), and t_G (min) (*13–17*).

$$k^* = Ft_G/1.15V_m\Delta\phi S$$

as illustrated in **Fig. 6**.

In the case of the linear gradient of acetonitrile from 0 to 100%, k^* is estimated to be ca. 5 for monolithic silica capillary columns of 60-cm lengths, 200-μm I.D. with $t_G = 100$ min, and $F = 4$ μL/min. With fixed t_G and F, the shorter column provides the greater k^*. In the case of gradient elution of a macromolecule, a large S value results in a small k^* value. As a consequence, a short column becomes advantageous. Because a greater flow rate will reduce the number of theoretical plates, it generally leads to the decrease in resolution.

When one optimizes the separation conditions, (1) k^* should be kept around 5, and (2) a gradient range, $\Delta\phi$, should be minimized judging from the elution range of solutes in a given chromatogram, followed by (3) tuning of t_G, F, and column lengths, if possible. Longer t_G and a longer column lead to better resolution, whereas smaller k^* and shorter t_G lead to less resolution and better detection sensitivity, and smaller F results in better detection sensitivity. A good compromise between an efficient separation and good detection sensitivity can be obtained at $k^* = 5\sim10$ (*13–17*).

A certain level of a flow rate is required in order to provide a smooth gradient of the mobile phase. However, the higher flow rate leads to the greater dilution of solute bands, which will result in the decrease in detection sensitivity. Although the use of a longer column (increase in V_m) keeping k^* and F values constant may lead to the increase in separation time and peak widths, improvement of separa-

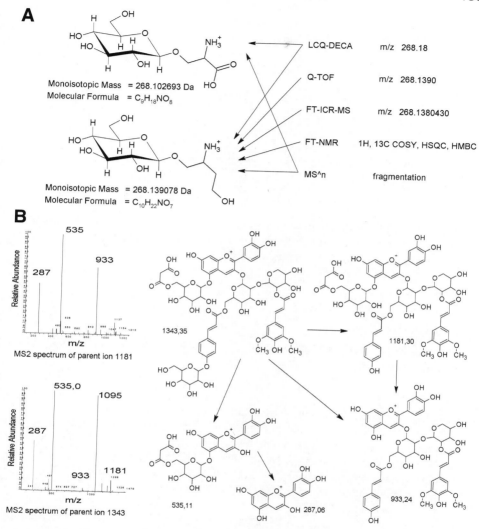

Fig. 5. (**A**) Structural assignment of the monomer. (**B**) Fragmentation pathways generated with the use Mass Frontier and MS2 spectra of two substances having different retention times.

tion efficiencies owing to the increase in the number of theoretical plates, and decrease in ion suppression, are expected (*1*). Because solutes are eluted with similar peak widths in linear gradient elution ($\Delta\phi/t_G$ = constant), it will be easy to optimize peak width for MS analysis by changing t_G and column lengths.

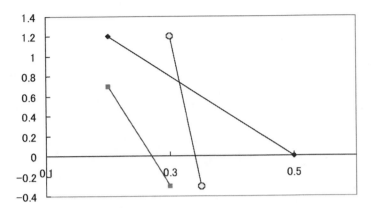

Fig. 6. Dependence of *S* value on the molecular weight of a solute. *S* value is a slope of the plots of log *k* values (retention factors of solutes) against φ (volume fraction of solvent B in mobile phase in isocratic elution).

Acknowledgments

The authors would like to thank the Max Planck Society, Munich, Germany, for funding the work.

References

1. Tolstikov, V. V., Lommen, A., Nakanishi, K., Tanaka, N., and Fiehn O. (2003) Monolithic silica-based capillary reversed phase liquid chromatography/electrospray mass spectrometry for plant metabolomics. *Anal. Chem.* **75**, 6737–6740.
2. Tolstikov, V. V., Fiehn, O., and Shulaev, V. (2005) The influence of the extraction methodology on global LC-MS and GC-MS metabolite profiling of arabidopsis thaliana leaf tissues. 53rd ASMS Conference, San Antonio, TX, June 5–9, 2005.
3. Tolstikov, V. V., Lorence, A., Cortes, D. F., et al. (2005) Use of capillary monolithic columns for untargeted metabolite profiling of the mutant lines overexpressing Miox4, the gene involved in L-ascorbic acid biosynthesis in arabidopsis. 28th International Symposium On Capillary Chromatography and Electrophoresis. Las Vegas, NV, May 22–25, 2005.
4. Tolstikov, V. V. and Fiehn, O. (2002) Analysis of highly polar compounds of plant origin: combination of hydrophilic interaction chromatography and electrospray ion trap mass spectrometry. *Anal. Biochem.* **301**, 298–307.
5. Tolstikov, V. V., Tanaka, N., and Fiehn O. (2003) Comprehensive metabolome analysis of crude *Arabidopsis thaliana* leaf extracts by LC/ESI-MS^n/UV coupling. 2nd Plant Metabolomics Conference, Potsdam, Germany, April 25–28, 2003.

6. Tolstikov, V. V., Tanaka, N., and Fiehn, O. (2003) Metabolomics: LC-MS analysis development. Joint BTS/Cereal Chemistry Symposium, Adelaide, Australia, September 8–10, 2003.
7. Tolstikov, V. V., Zhang, B., Weckwerth, W., and Fiehn O. (2001) Structural investigation of O-glycans derived from plant material by the use of the HILIC HPLC separation and ESI-mass spectrometry. 49th ASMS conference on Mass Spectrometry and Allied Topics, Chicago, IL, May 27–31, 2001.
8. Tolstikov, V. V., Costisella, B., Weckwerth W., Zhang B., and Fiehn O. (2002) Accurate QTOF and MS^n Ion trap measurements require additional NMR data for plant metabolites de-novo identification. 50th ASMS Conference on Mass Spectrometry and Allied Topics, Orlando, FL, June 2–7, 2002.
9. Tolstikov, V. V., Tanaka, N., and Fiehn, O. (2003) LC/MS analysis and development for plant metabolomic studies. 2003 LCMS Montreux Symposium. Savannah, GA, October 15–17, 2003.
10. Tanaka, N., Tolstikov, V., Weckwerth, W., Fiehn, O., and Fukusaki, H., (2003) Micro HPLC for metabolomics. In: *Frontier of Metabolomic Research*, Springer-Verlag, Tokyo, Japan, pp. 85–100.
11. Ikegami, T., Kobayashi, H., Kimura, H., Tolstikov, V., Fiehn, O., and Tanaka, N. (2005) HPLC for metabolomics: high efficiency separations utilizing monolithic silica columns. In: *Metabolomics. The Frontiers of Systems Biology,* Springer Verlag, Tokyo, Japan, pp. 107–126.
12. Nikiforova, V., Kopka, J., Tolstikov, V., Fiehn, O., Hesse, H., and Hoefgen, R. (2005) Systems rebalancing of metabolism in response to sulfur deprivation, as revealed by metabolome analysis of arabidopsis plants. *Plant Physiology* **138,** 304–318.
13. Kobayashi, H., Kajiwara, W., Inui, Y., et al. (2004) Chromatographic properties of monolithic silica capillary columns for polar and nonpolar compounds in reversed-phase HPLC. *Chromatographia* **60,** S19–S25.
14. Ikegami, T., Dicks, E., Kobayashi, H., et al. (2004) How to utilize true performance of monolithic silica columns? *J. Sep. Sci.* **27,** 1292–1302.
15. Richardson, P. T. and Baker, D. A. (1982) The chemical composition of cucurbit vascular exudates. *J. Exp. Bot.* **33,** 1239–1247.
16. Snyder, L. R., Glajch, J. L., and Kirkland, J. J. (1988) Non-ionic samples: reversed- and normal-phase HPLC. In: *Practical HPLC Method Development.* Wiley, New York, NY, pp. 233–291.
17. Snyder, L. R., Stadalius, M., and Quarry, M. A. (1983) Gradient elution in reversed-phase HPLC separation of macromolecules. *Anal. Chem.* **55,** 1412A–1430A.

V

Electrochemical Detection
of Metabolites

10

High-Performance Liquid Chromatography Separations Coupled With Coulometric Electrode Array Detectors

A Unique Approach to Metabolomics

Bruce S. Kristal, Yevgeniya I. Shurubor, Rima Kaddurah-Daouk, and Wayne R. Matson

Summary

Metabolomics is the systematic and theoretically comprehensive study of the small molecules that comprise a biological sample, e.g., sera or plasma. The primary analytical tools used in metabolomics are nuclear magnetic resonance and mass spectroscopy. We here address a different tool, high-performance liquid chromatography (HPLC) separations coupled with coulometric electrode array detection. This system has unique advantages, notably sensitivity and high quantitative precision, but also has unique limitations, such as obtaining little structural information on the metabolites of interest and limited scale-up capacity. The system also only detects redox-active compounds, which can be either a benefit or a detriment, depending on the experimental goals and design. Here, we discuss the characteristics of this HPLC/coulometric electrode array system in the context of metabolomics, and then present the method as practiced in our groups.

Key Words: HPLC; coulometric array; response ratio; electrochemical detection; metabolomics.

1. Introduction

Modern metabolomics studies are dominated by two general classes of instrumentation *(1,2)*, those whose primary detection is based on nuclear magnetic resonance (NMR) *(3–6)*, and those whose primary detection is based on mass spectrometry (MS) usually coupled with a prior integrated liquid chromatography (LC) *(7–10)* or gas chromatography (GC) *(11,12)* separation. Each of these instrumentation platforms offers different advantages for the profiling of the metabolome. NMR-based approaches allow high throughput and near invari-

From: *Methods in Molecular Biology, vol. 358: Metabolomics: Methods and Protocols*
Edited by: W. Weckwerth © Humana Press Inc., Totowa, NJ

ability in mapping signals to specific molecules among instruments. NMR-based approaches are also uniquely able to measure metabolites inside intact tissues and living cells. Such NMR-based approaches seem to have been particularly applicable in toxicology studies, where Nicholson et al. have published a broad series of papers in this area that, in many ways, helped to create the current interest in that aspect of the metabolomics field *(3–6)*. MS offers significantly greater sensitivity than NMR (the ability to detect nanomolar concentrations in the sample as opposed to micromolar). MS provides a high degree of qualitative certainty and in principle is capable of yielding information leading to structural analysis and identification of unknown compounds. MS also has a moderately high throughput and, given sufficiently high-quality instrumentation, a relatively invariate signal among instruments. Both NMR and MS, however, also have substantial weaknesses. For NMR, the major weakness lies in sensitivity. In practice, NMR is limited to micromolar concentrations in the sample. LC–MS is highly precise for targeted assays. However, for global metabolic profiling with LC–MS, a major weakness lies in compound-specific variable ionization efficiency and ion suppression effects. Variable ionization efficiency causes a situation where for a given concentration of different compounds the actual MS response can vary by a factor of 100. Variation in ion suppression effects, particularly in long assay sequences for unknown compounds identified by their retention time and mass, leads to a situation where the relative standard deviation (rsd) of many signals is greater than the rsd of biological variability. The utility of both approaches also suffers from the high initial cost of the instrumentation, which limits access to high-quality instrumentation, particularly for academic researchers.

We have been studying components of selected metabolic pathways (particularly purines, tyrosine, and tryptophan metabolites) for approx 15 yr with LC separations coupled with electrochemical array (ECA) detection. The LC-ECA system currently in use is a CoulArray detector (ESA, Inc., Chelmsford, MA; please *see* disclosure in Acknowledgments) *(13–22)*. The heart of the CoulArray system is a series of porous graphite electrodes that exhibit close to 100% coulometric efficiency for oxidation or reduction of electroactive species. These can be poised at a series of incremented voltages, which because of the 100% efficiency allows the separation of coeluting compounds as a function of their oxidation potential. The separation in the time and potential dimensions gives characteristic patterns from biological samples representing on the order of 2000–2500 distinct species. In our laboratories, the potentials are arranged in an array from 0 to 900 mV using 16 coulometric electrodes in series (16 channels). The principle disadvantage of LC-ECA is that it is responsive only to those compounds that can be oxidized or reduced electrochemically. A reasonable level of qualitative certainty is provided by the response characteristics of a compound on different channels in the array but this is not as absolute as a mass peak. The principle advantages of the LC-ECA are: for electroactive compounds the sensitivity is ca. 10–50 times greater than MS (low nanomolar-to-picomolar concentrations in the sample); the response factors are equivalent within a factor of two to three for estimating concentrations of unknown compounds; and the system is relatively invariant in response over long 500–1000 sample assay sequences. Because most of the compounds in the tyrosine, tryptophan, and purine pathways, most vitamins, neuromodulating drugs, and markers of oxidative stress are electroactive, and much work with the LC-ECA has focused on these classes of compounds.

The initial studies based on this technology were published in the mid-1980s *(23)*, and used the ability of this instrumentation to focus on pathways of interest, particularly the kynurenine pathway in Huntington's and Parkinson's disease *(24–28)* and the serotonin pathway in Alzheimer's disease *(29)*. An early focus was on the problems associated with creating reliable databases in brain tissue. Additional disease-oriented work has been undertaken on mitochondrial changes in diabetes *(30)*, DNA damage markers in urine *(31,32)*, and serum changes associated with amyotrophic lateral sclerosis *(33)*. Other profiling has focused on identification of bio-markers for nutrition, particularly caloric intake *(13–18)*. A series of basic papers describing both the basic technology and approaches, as well as a series of more specific papers dealing with technical aspects of mitochondrial and serum metabolomics, have also been published *(19–22)*.

1.1. Advantages and Disadvantages

The CoulArray has four primary disadvantages relative to other metabolomics platforms:

1. The instrument gives either indirect or no structural information about individual metabolites, often leading to the determination that certain peaks are important, but requiring subsequent work for identification. We and others are working on addressing this problem by coupling the instrument with a mass spectrometer, thus obtaining most of the benefits of both systems.
2. The instrument has limited throughput. Our primary chromatographic profile, for example, requires a run length of over 2 h, which means that only approx 10 samples/day can be analyzed given standard control series. This renders certain types of experiments unfeasible, but relatively few experiments in metabolomics to date have been limited by sample throughput.
3. The chromatographic drift that occurs over time can complicate analysis. In practice, we have controlled this problem by using algorithms that mathematically "stretch" the chromatogram to simplify analysis.
4. The CoulArray can only detect redox-active compounds, so components of interest may be missed. Measurements of inactive compounds require an additional pretreatment (like derivatization before analysis).

The CoulArray also has many advantages as either a primary or an adjunct profiling instrument relative to other instruments, such as NMR and MS:

1. The CoulArray is a highly sensitive instrument, with the ability to detect approx 1–10 pg of a given compound on the column.
2. The coulometric array detectors offer great specificity and selectivity for redox-active compounds, and generally makes contaminants/coelutions readily apparent.
3. The CoulArray detects most members of many major biochemical pathways, but does not detect less reactive compounds. This often enables one to focus on the more reactive compounds with a greater signal to noise than with other approaches (note: we are defining signal to noise here as pathways relevant to the situation of interest vs inert compounds).
4. The system has high quantitative precision; one of our studies, for example, in which we measured approx 60 metabolites from each of 30 samples, resulted in an approx 9% median coefficients of variance (CVs).
5. The CoulArray is expensive (approx $80,000), but it is less than 25% the cost of the typical mass spectrometer used in metabolomics studies, and even less expensive relative to an NMR machine.

The brevity of this chapter's introduction, and the focus of this series on techniques, prevents any broader or more in-depth description of the technologies and approaches being used in the field. Additional background may be found in the two seminal books in the field (*1,2*), and a series of useful links may be found on the Metabolomics Society website (http://www.metabolomics society.org).

The remainder of this chapter will deal with presenting our primary method. This method has changed slightly (**Subheadings 3.1.** and **3.2.1.**, **Figs. 2** and **3**, and minor readability changes) since it was published earlier in this series, and is otherwise reprinted essentially as previously presented in an earlier book (*34*) and in another concurrent in this series (Tollefsbol, in preparation).

2. Materials

2.1. Equipment and Supplies (see also *Note 1*)

1. CoulArray System (ESA, Inc.): the CoulArray system used includes two model 580 pumps, one gradient mixer/pulse damper, one PEEK pulse damper, a model 540 autoinjector, column heater, and a CoulArray detection system with four coulometric electrode detector cell modules (16 total channels).
2. Two TosoHaas TSK-GEL ODS-80™ columns in series (4.6 × 250 mm, 5μ C18) (*see also* **Note 2**).
3. A computer and color ink jet printer.
4. 1-mL and 200-μL adjustable pipets.
5. 250 μL Polypropylene autosampler vials and caps.
6. 1.5 mL Glass autosampler vials and caps.
7. Crimper for HPLC sample tube.

8. Vial trays.
9. Microcentrifuge evaporator with cold trap.
10. High-speed centrifuge.
11. Fume hood.

2.2. Reagents

1. 0.4% Acetic acid in acetonitrile.
2. Methanol.
3. Isopropanol.
4. Acetonitrile.
5. Lithium acetate.
6. Glacial acetic acid.
7. Pentane sulfonic acid.
8. 0.85% Saline solution.
9. Distilled, deionized water.

3. Methods

3.1. Sample Processing

3.1.1. Plasma or Serum

1. Plasma or sera samples (250 µL) are mixed with 1 mL of precooled 0.4% acetic acid in acetonitrile in a 1.5-mL microcentrifuge tube. The samples are vortexed for 20 s at top speed, and then centrifuged for 15 min at 12,000 rpm (11,000g) (–4°C). 1 mL of supernatant is transferred to a polypropylene autosampler vial and evaporated to dryness in a microcentrifuge evaporator. The initial extraction step is carried out below –10°C. The vacuum on the microcentrifuge evaporator must be sufficient to freeze the sample being evaporated. The dried residue is dissolved in 200 µL of mobile phase A (*see* **Subheading 3.2.1.**). Aliquots of 50 µL are injected into the CoulArray system. This protocol conserves reactive species such as ascorbate, homogentisic acid, and 6-OH dopamine at 1 ng/mL concentrations.
2. Several approaches to serum or plasma collection may be used depending on the resources of the study group for animal work or the clinical situation for human studies. The protocol currently used by one of the groups (WRM) follows (the BSK lab follows a highly similar protocol). For serum in animal studies, blood is typically taken at sacrifice into a polypropylene tube, chilled to 0°C on ice, and centrifuged at 3000g at 4°C for 15 min. Serum is carefully aspirated to avoid the buffy coat because platelets and leukocytes carried down in the fibrinogen clot can affect results for certain pathways, e.g., serotonin and its metabolites.
   Plasma is typically obtained from blood drawn into a Vacutainer™ with various anticoagulants. If the clinical site is adjacent to facilities with adequate centrifuge capabilities and technical support the following protocol is used. Blood is immediately chilled on ice. The Vacutainer is centrifuged at 1500g 0–2°C for 15 min. The plasma containing the leukocytes and platelets is transferred to a 15-mL polypropylene tube and centrifuged at 15,000g 0–2°C for 15 min. The

plasma is then aspirated from the platelet leukocyte pellet, subaliquoted, and archived at −80°C until use. The pellet is washed once with 0.5 mL of normal saline and archived at −80°C. For diverse clinical sites without technical support, the sample is drawn into a plastic Vacutainer chilled on ice, and centrifuged at 8000–9000g 0–2°C for 20 min. The sample is then frozen immediately on dry ice and subsequently archived at −80°C. On receipt of the sample the laboratory expels the frozen column from the Vacutainer and dissects out and subaliquots the plasma, buffy coat, and packed red blood cells on a cold plate maintained at −80°C.

The choice of anticoagulant involves several factors. The use of EDTA as anticoagulant will lead to highly unstable ascorbic acid values unless the samples are processed relatively rapidly. Noticeable decay in ascorbate values and formation of hemihydroascorbate begins after ca. 60 min holding the sample at ice temperature. Centrifugation, removing the red blood cells from intimate contact with the plasma, slows the process of ascorbate decay. Heparin provides better ascorbate stability but in long assay sequences has an effect of shifting the relative chromatographic retention of indoles in the later times of the gradient assay. Heparin also gives lower precision for glutathione, serotonin, and its metabolites and precursors. Oxalate gives good precision for glutathione but contains peaks that can interfere with MHPG (3-methoxy-4-hydroxy phenyl glycol) and other peaks in the same time domain.

3. Serum values for serotonergic metabolites are less consistent than plasma values in the presence of EDTA or heparin. Essentially any collection protocol must be evaluated for its specific effects and possible artifacts on the patterns as a whole. Since publication of this method (*34*), we have published several reports addressing optimizing serum metabolomics work (*19–22*).

3.1.2. Mitochondria

1. Mitochondria are isolated by standard differential centrifugation techniques. Following isolation (*30,34*), mitochondrial samples are pelleted in a microcentrifuge and the supernatant is removed. As described (*34*), we have found that washing the mitochondria in 160 mM KCl removes most of the organic buffers usually used in the isolation procedure. In most cases, this wash step is recommended, as the buffers used (e.g., HEPES) are highly electrochemically active and otherwise obscure portions of the chromatogram.

2. For analysis, mitochondrial pellets (typically containing ~2–10 mg protein) are suspended in 100 µL of ddH$_2$O in their original tube. The samples are vortexed for 20 s at top speed. 1 mL of 0.4% acetic acid in acetonitrile is added and the samples vortexed for another 20 s at top speed. The samples are placed in a cold pack (MeOH-containing tray prechilled at −80°C) and sonicated for 10 s at a setting of 4 (sonicator/cell disrupter, Model W-220F, Misonix, Farmingdale, NY). The samples are then centrifuged for 15 min at 12,000 rpm (11,000g). 1 mL of supernatant is taken off to a polypropylene autosampler vial and evaporated to dryness in a microcentrifuge evaporator. The dried residue is dissolved in 200 µL of mobile phase A (*see* **Subheading 3.2.1.**). An aliquot of 50 µL is injected into the CoulArray system.

3.1.3. Cerebral Spinal Fluid

Samples are centrifuged for 5 min at 12,000 rpm (11,000g). A 50-µL aliquot of the supernatant is injected into the CoulArray system.

3.1.4. Urine

Urine samples are diluted 1:10 with ddH$_2$O, and 50-µL aliquots of the diluted specimen are then injected directly into the array.

3.2. HPLC Mobile Phases

3.2.1. Mobile Phase A

1. Mobile phase A stock preparation: weigh out 399.98 g of pentane sulfonic acid. Add 1300 mL of ddH$_2$O and filter through GF/F Whatman filter paper. Filter through 0.2-µM nylon filter. Add 200 mL glacial acetic acid. Bring to 2 L with ddH$_2$O. The concentrated sulfonic acid stock solution, which is inherently contaminated, is cleaned by electrolyzing the final preparation over pyrolytic graphite at 1000 mV vs (αPd[H]) for 12–24 h with nitrogen deaeration. Subsequent to the cleaning step, the potential of the electrolysis is moved to –50 mV for 1–2 h to poise the oxidation potential (pE) of the concentrated buffer to a negative level. Poising the pE of the buffer gives greater stability to the response of easily oxidized compounds, such as homogentisic acid
2. Working mobile pA preparation: dilute 50 mL mobile phase A stock to a final volume of 1 L. Add 1 mg/L citric acid. Filter through 0.2-µm nylon filter. The pH of the final mobile phase is 3.02.

3.2.2. Mobile Phase B

1. Working mobile phase B preparation: mix 8 L methanol, 1 L isopropanol, 1 L acetonitrile, 100 mL 4 M lithium acetate, pH 4.1 (*see* **Subheading 3.2.2.**, **step 2**), 200 mL glacial acetic acid, and 10 mg citric acid/L. Filter through 0.2-µm nylon filter.
2. 4 M Lithium acetate: add 672 g of lithium hydroxide to 1760 mL of glacial acetic acid, mixing well over an ice bath. Add 880 mL of glacial acetic acid. Add 400 mL of ddH$_2$O. Adjust the pH with glacial acidic acid or 2 M LiOH such that the pH of a 1:20 dilution with ddH$_2$O is 4.10 (typically 200 µL acetic acid or 1 mL 2 M LiOH/0.05 pH units). Bring to a total volume of 4 L with ddH$_2$O. Filter with GF/F Whatman filter paper.

3.3. HPLC Standards

3.3.1. Preparation and Storage

1. In practice, we use different sets of standards (~40–80 compounds each) *(35,36)* for different experiments. For example, one set of standards might be useful for measurements related to oxidative stress, and might include markers such as *o*-, *m*-, *p*-, and *N*-tyrosine, glutathione, and glutathione disulfide, whereas markers for neurological studies might include dopamine, kynurenine, kynurenic acid, and

homovanillic acid. These different standard sets can be used either alone or in combination, as appropriate. Under optimized conditions the CoulArray can resolve all 40–80 compounds in any given standard in a single chromatographic run.

2. Individual stock standards are currently prepared as follows: 10–100 mg of each standard is placed into an appropriately labeled 100-mL amber bottle with a Teflon-lined cap (Wheaton, Millville, NJ). Each standard is dissolved in 100 mL of either 20% MeOH solution or 0.85% saline solution, depending on the solubility of the standard being used. Appropriate dilutions of these standards (based on the samples to be analyzed) are then made into a final volume of 1 L using 0.85% saline as a diluent. We generally use between 20 µL and 1 mL of each stock standard. Individual standards and aliquots of mixed standards are stored in autosampler vials at –80°C. Standards appear stable under these conditions for longer than 7 yr. Vials of mixed standards are thawed to 4°C and mixed thoroughly before using.

3.3.2. HPLC Separations and Coulometric Array Analysis

1. The CoulArray system allows analysis under either isocratic or gradient conditions. The basic gradient method that we use has been published (30,34–36). Briefly, samples are sequentially eluted over 120 min as the proportion of mobile phase B in the gradient is increased from 0 to 100%. The last approx 10 min incorporate a high-potential cell cleaning step and restore the column condition to 100% mobile phase A. The detergent action of the sulfonic acids in the A mobile phase and the high organic solvent levels in the B mobile phase keep the column free of residual proteins and lipids from the preparative protocols. The mobile phase selection and repetitive cell cleaning enables continuous stable operation over 3–6 mo periods. Flow rates are adjusted to compensate for azeotropic viscosity. Analyte detection is accomplished using a 16-channel coulometric array detector as previously described and in the legend to **Fig. 1**, which shows chromatograms generated from studies of rat sera and rat liver mitochondria.

2. An important capability in generating multicomponent patterns is that chromatographic profiles can be easily modified to suit a specific individual application. Such modifications might include shortening the gradient profile (to reduce run time) when the analytes of interest are more hydrophilic, or lengthening portions to separate peaks that coelute. For example, we have observed coelutions of methionine and guanosine in some samples. If these peaks were important for a specific study, the chromatographic profile would be altered to accommodate these desired changes.

3.3.3. Data Analysis

1. HPLC analysis on the coulometric array can be used to generate databases of all of the redox-active compounds in a sample. In the case of the chromatographic parameters presented here, all redox-active molecules with hydrophi-

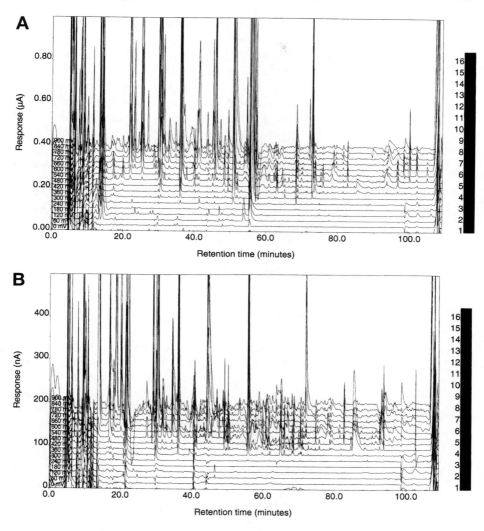

Fig. 1. Sample chromatograms. Analysis of sera collected from a 6-mo-old male Fischer x Brown Norway F1 rat (**A**). Analysis of a liver mitochondrial sample collected from a 4-mo-old male Fischer 344 rat (**B**). The specific mitochondrial sample shown was isolated by differential centrifugation using sucrose mannitol-based buffers. The mitochondria were processed as described in the text, including the 160-mM KCl wash. Full scale on the top and bottom chromatograms is 1 µA and 500 nA, respectively. In each case the chromatographic profile was obtained at 120 min.

licities between those of ascorbate and tocopherol and redox potentials from 0 to 900 mV (αPd[H]) can be readily detected. Databases can be analyzed either for specific compounds of interest (e.g., dopamine), related compounds (e.g., the lipoates, hydroxylated phenylalanine byproducts), entire pathways (e.g., purine catabolites [uric acid, xanthine, hypoxanthine, xanthosine, guanosine, and guanine]), or combinations of these. Alternatively, metabolic patterns can be addressed using multivariate analysis techniques (e.g., cluster analysis, pattern recognition, and others). Initial analyses in all cases are conducted using software supplied as a component of the CoulArray package.

2. The basic CoulArray for Windows 32 package (ESA, Inc.) is capable of carrying out all of the analysis described in **step 1**. This includes the qualitative analysis of peak identity as well as the quantitation of the peaks relative to either absolute or reference standards. Proprietary algorithms within the software automatically subtract backgrounds resulting from gradient drift. The software includes wizards designed to help individuals through most basic analyses.

3. The dynamic range enables analysis of analytes with concentrations ranging over five or more orders of magnitude (from approx 1–10 pg to approx 1–3 μg on column). In practice, compounds at the upper limits of detection may display altered chromatographic behavior and/or electrochemical response on the sensors. Typically at very high concentrations there is "spill over" to following sensors and a resultant change in the response ratios. These changes may be controlled by the selection of appropriate concentrations of the control standards and are typically less of a factor in the control of precision than are recoveries during preparative procedures (for samples requiring such procedures).

4. Analysis of a series of analytes in a complex mixture is automated by first generating a compound table from a standard or from a pooled sample comprised of aliquots from most or all of the members that comprise the sample and others.

5. In practice, initial quantitation requires manual oversight to confirm that the software has correctly identified peaks of interest. An earlier version of the software was, however, capable of greater than 95% success rate in peak analysis after three training runs (we have not yet tested the Windows version under equivalent conditions). Peak values can be directly transferred to Windows applications (e.g., Lotus, Excel).

3.3.4. Qualitative Analysis

Basic qualitative analyses of data generated using coulometric arrays are generally carried out on the basis of three criteria: retention time, dominant channel, and the ratio of reactivity on the dominant channel to reactivity on subdominant channels, as has been explained previously *(23,35–39)*. The majority of these analyses are handled automatically by the CoulArray software, but the user can alter the parameters as appropriate, for example to relax or tighten standards to resolve potential conflicts. Comparisons are made to standards run in parallel or to appropriate peaks in the pool. Peak identity can be further investigated by spiking the sample(s) with the analytes of interest.

3.3.5. Quantitative Analysis

1. Quantitative analysis can be carried out in either of two ways. Absolute quantitation of specific, known analytes of interest can be carried out by direct comparison to an analytical standard of known analyte(s) of known concentration(s). The analytical standard can be run alone, or if desired, spiked into a duplicate sample.
2. Alternatively, currently unidentified peaks can be quantitated relative to a standard pooled sample. In this case, all analytes in the pool are assigned a specific arbitrary value (e.g., 100). Peaks in individual samples are then quantitated relative to this standard.

3.4. Results

1. Sera: analyses of sera carried out at ESA, Inc. suggest that chromatographic retention times, monitored using authentic standards, do not vary by more than approx 1% over a 30-d period. Absolute qualitative channel ratio responses do not vary more than ± 20% and are controlled for by inclusion of authentic standards to within ± 5%.
2. Mitochondria: chromatographic parameters for mitochondria have been published *(30,34)* and variability observed was only slightly worse than those observed using sera samples. For our initial mitochondrial study, which was performed on a CEAS (an earlier generation of the CoulArray), criteria for qualitative acceptance of peaks was set at a retention time match of ±1.2% and a ratio accuracy of ±16% vs authentic standards. In this study, over a 1-mo time period, retention time of standards was held to within 1.7% based on raw data and to 1.1% when referenced to a tyrosine standard. Mean CV% of retention times of analytes measured was 0.35%, mean CV% of the ratio of the dominant to the subdominant reactivity was approx 11%. Note that, as described, some compounds are not included in this analysis.
3. Examples of the application of this chromatographic approach to sera and to mitochondria are shown in **Fig. 1**. The effectiveness of the combination of careful control of all chromatographic and reagent parameters on the stability of the system is shown for two pools run 3 mo apart and duplicate samples run 4 mo apart is shown in **Fig. 2**. The use of markers that are unique to the platelet leukocyte fraction of a blood sample to allow the determination that a particular sample has been compromised in the acquisition process is shown in **Fig. 3**.

   In many cases, peaks having maximum amplitudes of 1 nA can be successfully visualized and examined. Thus peaks having amplitudes of approx 0.1–0.2% of the full scale shown can generally be studied.

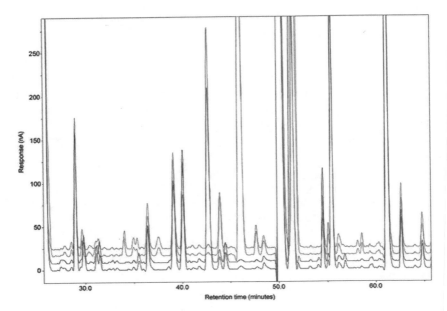

Fig. 2. Time normalization. This figure shows system stability using stretching software as needed. Bottom two traces: plasma samples from a Parkinson's disease patient run 4 mo apart. Top two traces: pooled sera samples run 3 mo apart.

In both panels, the array was set from 0 to 900 mV in even increments of 60 mV. The temperature of cells and columns was maintained at 35°C. The exact chromatographic method used in the two chromatograms shown was as follows:

Step	Time	Comment	Percent mobile phase B	Flow rate
01	0.00	Flow	0%	1.00 mL/min
02	0.10	Autozero on		
03	0.56	Autosampler inject (1 s)		
04	1.00	File Start		
05	30.00	Flow	12%	1.00 mL/min
06	35.00	Flow	20%	1.00 mL/min
07	55.00	Flow	48%	0.70 mL/min
08	90.00	Flow	100%	0.99 mL/min
09	95.00	Flow	100%	1.20 mL/min
10	100.00	Flow	100%	1.20 mL/min
11	100.10	Flow	0%	1.20 mL/min
12	104.00	Flow	0%	1.20 mL/min
13	107.00	Flow	0%	1.00 mL/min
14	110.00	File stop		
15	110.00	Clean cell on		
16	114.00	Flow	0%	1.00 mL/min
17	114.50	Clean cell off		
18	120.00	Flow	0%	1.00 mL/min

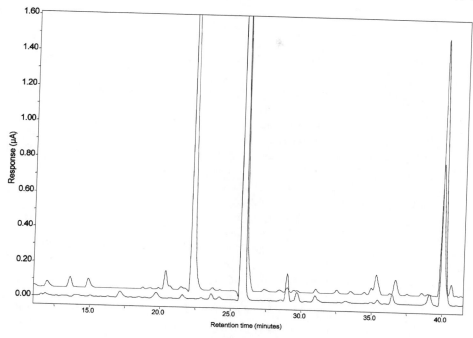

Fig. 3. Markers of platelet contamination. This figure shows one of the five markers that we have used to determine if samples are contaminated with platelets. If all five markers are present in a sample then that sample is removed from the study. The top trace shows a platelet containing sample; the bottom a clear plasma sample. The biochemical identity of these markers remains currently unknown.

4. Notes

1. Other necessary equipment/supplies includes standard lab safety equipment (gloves, eye protection, lab coat), glassware (including funnels), microcentrifuge, and 10-mL polypropylene tubes. Also, –80°C or liquid nitrogen storage will be required if the samples are not processed and run immediately.
2. Other columns have been successfully used in prior work (e.g., META 250, 4.6 × 250 mm, 5μ C18; 2 series MCM, 4.6 × 250 mm, 5μ C18).

Acknowledgments

This research was supported by NIA R21AG024232 (BSK). BSK has a non-financial consulting/collaborative arrangement with ESA, Inc. WRM was the founder and former technical director of ESA Inc., and consults on an NIH Metabolomics Roadmap Grant "Integrating LCEC/LC–MS in a Single Metabolomics Platform."

References

1. Harrigan, G. G. and Goodacre, R. (2003) *Metabolic Profiling: Its Role in Biomarker Discovery and Gene Function Analysis,* Kluwer, Boston/Dordrecht/London.
2. Vaidyanathan, S., Harrigan, G. G., and Goodacre, R. (2005) *Metabolome Analysis: Strategies for Systems Biology,* Springer, New York, NY.
3. Reo, N. V. (2002) NMR-based metabolomics. *Drug Chem. Toxicol.* **25,** 375–382.
4. Lenz, E. M., Bright, J., Wilson, I. D., Morgan, S. R., and Nash, A. F. (2003) A ¹H NMR-based metabonomic study of urine and plasma samples obtained from healthy human subjects. *J. Pharm. Biomed. Anal.* **33,** 1103–1115.
5. Brindle, J. T., Nicholson, J. K., Schofield, P. M., Grainger, D. J., and Holmes, E. (2003) Application of chemometrics to ¹H NMR spectroscopic data to investigate a relationship between human serum metabolic profiles and hypertension. *Analyst* **128,** 32–36.
6. Lindon, J. C., Nicholson, J. K., and Wilson, I. D. (2000) Directly coupled HPLC-NMR and HPLC-NMR-MS in pharmaceutical research and development. *J. Chromatogr. B. Biomed. Sci. Appl.* **748,** 233–258.
7. Plumb, R. S., Stumpf, C. L., Gorenstein, M. V., et al. (2002) Metabonomics: the use of electrospray mass spectrometry coupled to reversed-phase liquid chromatography shows potential for the screening of rat urine in drug development. *Rapid Commun. Mass Spectrom.* **16,** 1991–1996.
8. Plumb, R. S., Stumpf, C. L., Granger, J. H., Castro-Perez, J., Haselden, J. N., and Dear, G. J. (2003) Use of liquid chromatography/time-of-flight mass spectrometry and multivariate statistical analysis shows promise for the detection of drug metabolites in biological fluids. *Rapid Commun. Mass Spectrom.* **17,** 2632–2638.
9. Beaudry, F., Yves Le Blanc, J. C., Coutu, M., Ramier, I., Moreau, J. P., and Brown, N. K. (1999) Metabolite profiling study of propranolol in rat using LC/MS/MS analysis. *Biomed. Chromatogr.* **13,** 363–369.
10. Henion, J., Skrabalak, D., Dewey, E., and Maylin, G. (1983) Micro LC/MS in drug analysis and metabolism studies. *Drug Metab. Rev.* **14,** 961–1003.
11. Kimura, M., Yamamoto, T., and Yamaguchi, S. (1999) Automated metabolic profiling and interpretation of GC/MS data for organic acidemia screening: a personal computer-based system. *Tohoku J. Exp. Med.* **188,** 317–334.
12. Yamada, S. (1979) Metabolic profiling of rat brain homogenate and its developmental study using gas chromatography-mass spectrometry (GC/MS). *Kurume Med. J.* **26,** 319–320.
13. Vigneau-Callahan, K. E., Shestopalov, A. I., Milbury, P. E., Matson, W. R., and Kristal, B. S. (2001) Characterization of diet-dependent metabolic serotypes: analytical and biological variability issues in rats. *J. Nutr.* **131,** 924S–932S.
14. Shi, H., Vigneau-Callahan, K. E., Shestopalov, A. I., Milbury, P. E., Matson, W. R., and Kristal, B. S. (2002) Characterization of diet-dependent metabolic serotypes: proof of principle in female and male rats. *J. Nutr.* **132,** 1031–1038.

15. Shi, H., Vigneau-Callahan, K. E., Shestopalov, A. I., Milbury, P. E., Matson, W. R., and Kristal, B. S. (2002) Characterization of diet-dependent metabolic serotypes: primary validation of male and female serotypes in independent cohorts of rats. *J. Nutr.* **132**, 1039–1046.

16. Paolucci, U., Vigneau-Callahan, K. E., Shi, H., Matson, W. R., and Kristal, B. S. (2004) Development of biomarkers based on diet-dependent metabolic serotypes: characteristics of component-based models of metabolic serotypes. *OMICS* **8**, 221–238.

17. Paolucci, U., Vigneau-Callahan, K. E., Shi, H., Matson, W. R., and Kristal, B. S. (2004) Development of biomarkers based on diet-dependent metabolic serotypes: concerns and approaches for cohort and gender issues in serum metabolome studies. *OMICS* **8**, 209–220.

18. Shi, H., Paolucci, U., Vigneau-Callahan, K. E., Milbury, P. E., Matson, W. R., and Kristal, B. S. (2004) Development of biomarkers based on diet-dependent metabolic serotypes: practical issues in development of expert system-based classification models in metabolomic studies. *OMICS* **8**, 197–208.

19. Shurubor, Y., Matson, W. R., Martin, R. J., and Kristal, B. S. (2005) Relative contribution of specific sources of systematic errors and analytical imprecision to metabolite analysis by HPLC-ECD. *Metabolomics* **1**, 159–168.

20. Shurubor, Y. I., Paolucci, U., Krasnikov, B. F., Matson, W. R., and Kristal, B. S. (2005) Analytical precision, biological variation, and mathematical normalization in high data density *Metabolomics*. *Metabolomics* **1**, 75–85.

21. Shi, H., Vigneau-Callahan, K. E., Matson, W. R., and Kristal, B. S. (2002) Attention to relative response across sequential electrodes improves quantitation of coulometric array. *Anal. Biochem.* **302**, 239–245.

22. Kristal, B. S., Shurubor, Y., Paolucci, U., and Matson, W. R. (2005) Methodological issues and experimental design considerations to facilitate development of robust, metabolic profile-based classification. In: *Metabolic Profiling: Its Role in Drug Discovery and Integration with Genomics and Proteomics*, (Harrigan, G., Goodacre, R., and Vaidyanathan, S., eds.), Springer, New York, NY.

23. Matson, W. R., Langials, P., Volicer, L., Gamache, P. H., Bird, E. D., and Mark, K. A. (1984) N-electrode three dimensional liquid chromatography with electrochemical detection for determination of neurotransmitters. *Clinical Chem.* **30**, 1477–1488.

24. Beal, M. F., Matson, W. R., Swartz, K. J., Gamache, P. H., and Bird, E. D. (1990) Kynurenine pathway measurements in Huntington's disease striatum: evidence for reduced formation of kynurenic acid. *J. Neurochem.* **55**, 1327–1339.

25. Matson, W. R., Gamache, P. H., Beal, M. F., and Bird, E. D. (1987) EC array sensor concepts and data. *Life Sci.* **41**, 905–908.

26. Matson, W. R., Bouckoms, A., Svendson, C., Beal, M. F., and Bird, E. D. (1990) Generating and controlling multiparameter databases for biochemical correlates of disorders. In: *Basic, Clinical and Therapeutic Aspects of Alzheimer's and Parkinson's Diseases,* (Nagatsu, T., Fisher, A., and Yoshida, M., eds.), Plenum, New York, pp. 513–516.

27. Ogawa, T., Matson, W. R., Beal, M. F., et al. (1992) Kynurenine pathway abnormalities in Parkinson's disease. *Neurology* **42,** 1702–1706.

28. Beal, M. F., Matson, W. R., Storey, E., et al. (1992) Kynurenic acid concentrations are reduced in Huntington's disease cerebral cortex. *J. Neurol. Sci.* **108,** 80–87.

29. Volicer, L., Langlais, P. J., Matson, W. R., Mark, K. A., and Gamache, P. H. (1985) Serotoninergic system in dementia of the Alzheimer type. Abnormal forms of 5-hydroxytryptophan and serotonin in cerebrospinal fluid. *Arch. Neurol.* **42,** 1158–1161.

30. Kristal, B. S., Vigneau-Callahan, K. E., and Matson, W. R. (1999) Purine catabolism: links to mitochondrial respiration and antioxidant defenses? *Arch. Biochem. Biophys.* **370,** 22–33.

31. Bogdanov, M., Brown, R. H., Matson, W., et al. (2000) Increased oxidative damage to DNA in ALS patients. *Free Radic. Biol. Med.* **29,** 652–658.

32. Bogdanov, M. B., Beal, M. F., McCabe, D. R., Griffin, R. M., and Matson, W. R. (1999) A carbon column-based liquid chromatography electrochemical approach to routine 8-hydroxy-2'-deoxyguanosine measurements in urine and other biologic matrices: a one-year evaluation of methods. *Free Radic. Biol. Med.* **27,** 647–666.

33. Rozen, S, Cudkowicz, M. E., Bogdanov, M., et al. (2005) Metabolomic analysis and signatures in motor neuron disease. *Metabolomics* **1,** 101–108.

34. Kristal, B. S., Vigneau-Callahan, K. E., and Matson, W. R. (2002) Simultaneous analysis of multiple redox-active metabolites from biological matrices. In: *Oxidative Stress Biomarkers and Antioxidant Protocols,* (Armstrong, D., ed.), Humana Press, Totowa, NJ, pp. 185–194.

35. Milbury, P. E., Vaughan, M. R., Farley, S., Matula, G. J., Jr., Convertino, V. A., and Matson, W. R. (1998) A comparative bear model for immobility-induced osteopenia. *Ursus.* **10,** 507–520.

36. Milbury, P. E. (1997) CEAS generation of large multiparameter databases for determining categorical process involvement of biomolecules. In: *Coulometric Array Detectors for HPLC,* (Acworth, I. N., Naoi, M., Parvez, S., and Parvez, H., eds.), VSP Publications, Utrecht, The Netherlands, pp. 125–141.

37. Acworth, I. N., Naoi, M., Parvez, H., and Parvez, S. (1997) *Coulometric Electrode Array Detectors for the HPLC,* VSP International Science Publication, Utrecht, The Netherlands.

38. Svendsen, C. N. (1993) Multi-electrode detectors in high performance liquid chromatography: a new dimension in electrochemical analysis. *Analyst* **118,** 123–129.

39. Acworth, I. N. and Gamache, P. H. (1996) The coulometric electrode array for use in HPLC analysis, part 1: theory. *Amer. Lab. May.* **5,** 33–37.

VI

METABOLIC FLUXES

11

Determination of Metabolic Flux Ratios From ^{13}C-Experiments and Gas Chromatography–Mass Spectrometry Data

Protocol and Principles

Annik Nanchen, Tobias Fuhrer, and Uwe Sauer

Summary

Network topology is a necessary fundament to understand function and properties of microbial reaction networks. A valuable method for experimental elucidation of metabolic network topology is metabolic flux ratio analysis, which quantifies the relative contribution of two or more converging pathways to a given metabolite. It is based on ^{13}C-labeling experiments, gas chromatography–mass spectrometry analysis, and probabilistic equations that relate mass distributions in proteinogenic amino acids to pathway activity. Here, we describe the protocol for sample generation and illustrate the principles underlying the calculation of metabolic flux ratios with three examples. These principles are also implemented in the publicly available software FiatFlux, which directly calculates flux ratios from the mass spectra of amino acids.

Key Words: METAFoR; metabolic flux analysis; carbon flux; central metabolism; mass isotopes.

1. Introduction

Metabolic flux analysis is an integrated experimental/computational approach for comprehensive and quantitative understanding of biochemical reaction networks with a particular relevance in metabolic engineering and systems biology *(1)*. In its simplest form, metabolic flux analysis is solely based on a stoichiometric reaction model and extracellular consumption and secretion rates (*see also* Chapter 12). More elaborate methods are based on ^{13}C-labeling experiments. A particular example is metabolic flux ratio (METAFoR) analysis, which relies on probabilistic equations that relate ^{13}C-NMR multiplets *(2,3)* or gas chromatogra-

From: *Methods in Molecular Biology, vol. 358: Metabolomics: Methods and Protocols*
Edited by: W. Weckwerth © Humana Press Inc., Totowa, NJ

phy–mass spectrometry (GC–MS)-derived mass distributions *(4)* in proteino-genic amino acids to in vivo enzyme activity. For an experiment, ^{13}C-labeled substrates are administrated and protein hydrolyzates are subjected to nuclear magnetic resonance (NMR) or GC–MS analysis, which then provides labeling patterns of the amino acids. These labeling patterns can then be related to their precursor molecules that are key components of central metabolism. This method provides a comprehensive perspective on central carbon metabolism by quanti-fying 12 independent ratios of converging pathway and reaction fluxes from [1-^{13}C] and [U-^{13}C]glucose experiments *(4)*. METAFoR analysis has proven to be a valuable tool to characterize various organisms and knockout mutants to answer biologically important questions *(4–6)*.

These metabolic flux ratios can also be used as constraints in a stoichiometric reaction model for the estimation of intracellular carbon fluxes *(7)*. Although this goes beyond the scope of this chapter, the publicly available software tool FiatFlux *(8)* was developed to determine both metabolic flux ratios and intracel-lular net fluxes from ^{13}C-labeling experiments. In this chapter, we focus on the different steps necessary to determine metabolic flux ratios and use three exam-ples to illustrate key aspects of this methodology. Although explained for data generation from shake flask experiments, the approach is generic and can easily be adapted to microtiter plates, reactors, or chemostats. In FiatFlux *(8)*, all the steps described here for metabolic flux ratio calculation are implemented and the software directly calculates metabolic flux ratios from GC–MS raw data.

2. Materials

1. M9 minimal medium for cell growth (per liter of final medium): 7.52 g $Na_2HPO_4 \cdot 2H_2O$, 3.0 g KH_2PO_4, 0.5 g NaCl, and 0.8 g NH_4Cl (M9 salts). The following components are sterilized separately and then added (per liter of final medium): 1 mL 0.1 M $CaCl_2$, 2 mL 1 M $MgSO_4$, 0.6 mL 100 mM $FeCl_3$, 0.3 mL of 1 mM filter-sterilized thiamine HCl, and 10 mL M9 trace salts solution. The M9 trace salts solution contains (per liter): 0.18 g $ZnSO_4 \cdot 7H_2O$, 0.12 g $CuCl_2 \cdot 2H_2O$, 0.12 g $MnSO_4 \cdot H_2O$, and 0.18 g $CoCl_2 \cdot 6H_2O$. For two independent experiments, glucose is added either entirely as the [1-^{13}C]-labeled isotope iso-mer (99%; Cambridge Isotope Laboratories Inc., Andover, MA) or as a mixture of 20% (w/w) [U-^{13}C] (99%; Cambridge Isotope Laboratories Inc.) and 80% (w/w) natural glucose (*see* **Note 1**).

2. *N,N*-Dimethylformamide (>99.8% pure, Fluka AG, Buchs, Switzerland), *N*-tert-butyldimethylsilyl-*N*-methyltrifluoroacetamide (TBDMS) with 1% tert-butyl-dimethylchlorosilane (Fluka AG).

3. Methods

3.1. Cell Cultivation

1. *Escherichia coli* or *Bacillus subtilis* precultures are grown overnight in 5 mL M9 minimal medium supplemented with 5 g/L natural glucose.

2. Aerobic batch cultures are grown at 37°C in 500-mL baffled shake flasks with 30 mL of M9 minimal medium supplemented with 3 g/L of the appropriate mixture of ^{13}C-labeled glucose on a gyratory shaker at 250 rpm (*see* **Note 2**).
3. Cells are harvested at mid-exponential growth phase (at an OD_{600} of about 50% of the maximal value) by centrifugation at 1200g and 4°C for 10 min (*see* **Note 3**).

3.2. Protein Hydrolysis, Derivatization, and GC–MS Analysis

1. Cell pellets are washed twice by resuspension in 1 mL 0.9% NaCl, transferred into a 2-mL Eppendorf tube, and centrifuged in a table-top Eppendorf centrifuge at 15,800g and room temperature for 4 min.
2. The washed pellet is resupended in 1.5 mL of 6 M HCl, and hydrolyzed for 24 h at 110°C in a well-sealed tube to prevent evaporation (*see* **Note 4**).
3. The hydrolyzate is dried overnight in a heating block at around 60°C and under a constant air stream in a fume hood.
4. The hydrolyzate is dissolved in 30 μL dimethylformamide and transferred into a new 2-mL Eppendorf cup within a few seconds (*see* **Note 5**). For derivatization, 30 μL *N*-tert-butyldimethylsilyl-*N*-methyltrifluoroacetamide with 1% tert-buthyldimethylchlorosilane are added, which readily silylates hydroxyl groups, thiols, primary and secondary amines, amides, and carboxyl groups. The mixture is incubated at 85°C under slight shaking for 60 min (*see* **Note 6**).
5. The derivatized sample is then immediately transferred into an amber crimp vial and sealed with a cap (*see* **Note 7**).
6. 1-μL Derivatized sample is injected into a Series 8000 GC combined with a MD800 quadrupole mass spectrometer (Fisons Instruments, Beverly, MA), on a fused-silica capillary column (model SPB-1, 30 m × 0.32 mm × 0.25 μm; Sigma-Aldrich, St. Louis, MO) with a split injection of 1:20. GC conditions are as follows: carrier gas (helium, ≥99.996 (v/v) purity; PanGas, Dagmersellen, Switzerland) flow rate: 2 mL per min; injector temperature: 200°C; oven temperature profile: 150°C for 2 min, then increase at a rate of 10°C per minute to 280°C, and, finally, 3 min at 280°C; GC–MS interface temperature at 280°C. Electron impact (EI) spectra were obtained at –70 eV with a full scan ranging from 70 to 560 m/z and a solvent delay of 4 min. The source temperature was set at 200°C. GC–MS raw data are analyzed using the software package MassLab (Fisons). The obtained mass spectra are checked for detector overload and if it occurred, diluted and remeasured (*9*) (*see* **Note 8**).

3.3. Experimental Analysis: Mass Distribution Vectors for the Amino Acids MDV$_{AA}$ (Implemented in the Analysis Software FiatFlux)

1. For each chromatographic peak, the EI mass spectral data are analyzed (**Fig. 1**). During GC separation, undesired isotope fractionation of the derivatized amino acids can be observed (*9*). Therefore, the mass spectra considered for each amino acid is the sum of all scans for one chromatographic peak (**Fig. 1**).
2. The obtained EI mass spectral data are sets of ion clusters, each representing the mass isotopomer distribution of a given amino acid fragment (a mass isotopomer

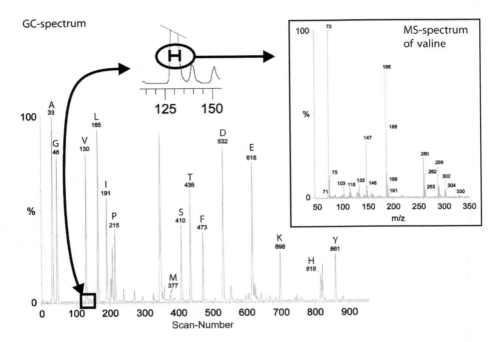

Fig. 1. Gas chromatogram of hydrolyzed, TBDMS-derivatized biomass. Detected amino acids are denoted with their one-letter symbol. The inset represents the integrated mass spectrum for valine.

is a family of isotope isomers with the same mass). The prominent detected fragments of TBDMS-derivatized amino acids are shown schematically in **Fig. 2**. Cracking leads to $(M-15)^+$, $(M-57)^+$, $(M-85)^+$, $(M-159)^+$ fragments as well as an $(f302)^+$ fragment, which is the double-silylated C_1-C_2 fragment of the amino acid. The mass of the lightest isotopomer (m_0) for each considered fragment and amino acid is given in **Table 1**.

3. For each fragment α, a mass isotopomer distribution vector MDV is assigned:

$$MDV_\alpha = \begin{bmatrix} (m_0) \\ (m_1) \\ \vdots \\ (m_n) \end{bmatrix} \text{ with } \sum_{i=0}^{n} m_i = 1 \tag{1}$$

where m_0 is the fractional abundance of fragments with the lowest mass and $m_i > 0$ the abundance of molecules with higher masses (**Subheading 3.7., step 1**). For each fragment, n has to be larger or equal to the number of amino acid C atoms present in the fragment (**Table 1**) (*see* **Note 9**).

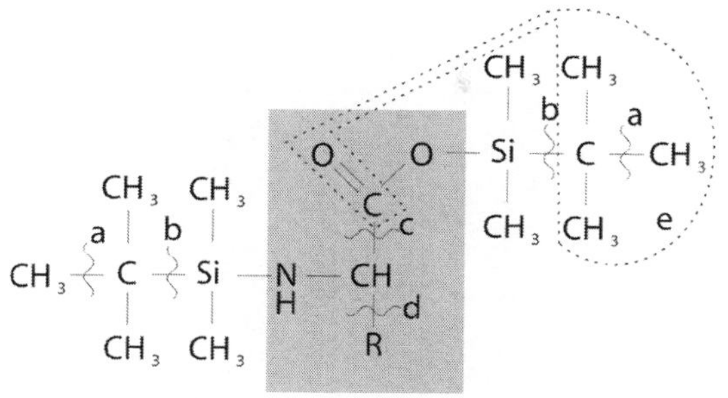

Fig. 2. The most prominent detected fragments of TBDMS-derivatized amino acids. The amino acid with its specific side chain (R) is in gray. Cracking at the denoted positions leads to the following fragments: (**A**) (M-15)⁺ and methyl group; (**B**) (M-57)⁺ and tert-butyl group; (**C**) (M-159)⁺ and C(O)O-TBDMS ion; (**D**) (f302)⁺ (the double silylated fragment) and the side chain (sc)⁺, consisting of R and possibly further TBDMS groups; (**E**) (M-85) ⁺ and the CO of the amino acid and a tert-butyl group (grouped within the dashed line).

Table 1
Mass of the Lightest Isotopomer
for Considered Amino Acid Fragments [a]

Amino acid	(M-15)⁺	(M-57)⁺	(M-85)⁺	(M-159)⁺	(f302)⁺
Alanine		260 (3)	232 (2)		
Glycine	288 (2)	246 (2)	218 (1)	144(1)	
Valine		288 (5)	260 (4)		302 (2)
Leucine	344 (6)		274 (5)	200 (5)	
Isoleucine	344 (6)		274 (5)	200 (5)	
Proline	328 (5)	286 (5)	258 (4)	184 (4)	
Methionine		320 (5)	292 (4)	218 (4)	
Serine	432 (3)	390 (3)	362 (2)	288 (2)	302 (2)
Threonine	446 (4)	404 (4)	376 (3)		
Phenylalanine		336 (9)	308 (8)	234 (8)	302 (2)
Aspartate	460 (4)	418 (4)	390 (3)	316 (3)	302 (2)
Glutamate	474 (5)	432 (5)	404 (4)	330 (4)	302 (2)
Lysine		431 (6)		329 (5)	
Histidine	482 (6)	440 (6)	412 (5)	338 (5)	302 (2)
Tyrosine	508 (9)	466 (9)	438 (8)	364 (8)	302 (2)

[a] The number in parenthesis represents the number of amino acid C atoms.

4. The higher masses from a mass cluster result from isotope signals that originate from (1) natural abundance in non-C atoms, (2) natural abundance of ¹³C in the derivatization reagent, and (3) ¹³C in the carbon skeleton of the amino acid fragment that were incorporated from naturally or artificially ¹³C-labeled substrates.

Table 2
Abundance of Natural Stable Isotopes for Biologically Relevant Elements[a]

Element	Mostly occurring mass (m_0)	Abundance of m_0	Abundance of m_1	Abundance of m_2
H	1	0.999885	0.000115	
C	12	0.9893	0.0107	
N	14	0.99632	0.00368	
O	16	0.99757	0.00038	0.00205
Si	28	0.922297	0.046832	0.030872

[a] *See* **ref. 12**.

To obtain the exclusive mass isotope distribution of the carbon skeleton MDV_α^*, MDV_α are corrected for the natural isotope abundance of O, N, H, Si, S, and C in the derivatization chains and for natural isotope abundance of O, N, H, Si, and S in the amino acid using a correction matrix (**Eq. 2**) *(10)*. The natural abundances of stable isotopes found in amino acids are summarized in **Table 2**.

$$MDV_\alpha^* = C_{corr,CONHSiS}^{-1} \cdot MDV_\alpha \qquad (2)$$

The correction matrix is squared and its dimension is defined by the size of the vectors MDV_α and MDV_α^*, which corresponds to $n + 1$ (*see* **step 3**). The correction matrix is the product of the correction matrices for all different atom species (**Eq. 3**).

$$C_{corr,\,CONHSiS} = C_{corr,\,C} \cdot C_{corr,\,O} \cdot C_{corr,\,N} \cdot C_{corr,\,H} \cdot C_{corr,\,Si} \cdot C_{corr,\,S} \qquad (3)$$

To determine these matrices, first the number of each atom species has to be determined for all fragment α (derivatization chain and amino acid, without the amino acid C atoms) (**Subheading 3.7., step 2**).

Second, correction matrices (a_{ij}) for individual atom species are set up. Position a_{11} represents all possibilities for the mass isotopomer m_0, a_{21} for m_1, a_{31}, for m_2... Position a_{i1} is equal to zero if no m_{i-1} mass isotopomer exists. For all other positions ($j > 1$), if $i < j$ a_{ij} is equal to zero and if $i \geq j$ a_{ij} is equal to $a_{(i-j+1)1}$ (**Subheading 3.7., step 3**). The chemical formulas of all these isotopologs (molecular species with identical elemental and chemical compositions but different isotopic contents *[11]*) in the correction matrices represent their respective abundances, which can be calculated according to **Eq. 4** (*see* **Note 10**) *(10)*.

$$\text{abundance} = \left(\sum_{k=1}^{N} \left\{ \nu\,[I(k)] \right\} \right)! \cdot \prod_{k=1}^{N} \left(\frac{c\,[I(k)]^{\nu\,[I(k)]}}{\nu\,[I(k)]!} \right) \qquad (4)$$

where the atom species of the considered elemental isotopolog has N naturally occurring isotopes $I(1), \ldots, I(N)$ with natural abundance $c[I(1)], \ldots, c[I(N)]$ and arising $\nu[I(1)], \ldots, \nu[I(N)]$ times within the isotopolog (**Subheading 3.7., step 4**) (*see* **Note 11**).

Third, having determined the individual correction matrices, the correction matrix $C_{corr, CONHSIS}$ (**Eq. 3**) and MDV_α^* (**Eq. 2**) can be calculated (**Subheading 3.7., step 5** and **step 6**, respectively). It has to be noted that the sum of the elements of MDV_α^* has to be equal to one. Therefore, after applying, **Eq. 2**, MDV_α^* has to be recalculated to fulfill this condition (**Subheading 3.7., step 6**).

5. To obtain the exclusive mass isotope distribution resulting from the incorporation of artificially ^{13}C-labeled substrates, the contribution of ^{13}C from unlabeled biomass (resulting for example from the inoculum [*see* **Note 12**]) was subtracted from MDV_α^* yielding MDV_{AA} according to **Eq. 5**.

$$MDV_{AA} = \frac{MDV_\alpha^* - f_{unlabeled} \cdot MDV_{unlabeled,\, n}}{1 - f_{unlabeled}} \tag{5}$$

where $f_{unlabeled}$ is the fraction of unlabeled biomass and $MDV_{unlabeled,n}$ is the mass distribution of an unlabeled fragment with n C atoms. $MDV_{unlabeled,n}$ can be determined according to **Eq. 4** (**Subheading 3.7., step 7**).

6. For [U-^{13}C]glucose experiments, the fractional labeling (FL) of the different amino fragments should be equal to the labeling content of the input substrate (i.e., when 20% [U-^{13}C]glucose is used, the FL should be 20% for all fragments) (*see* **Note 13**). Fractional labeling is calculated according to **Eq. 6**:

$$FL = \frac{\sum\limits_{i=0}^{n} i \cdot m_i}{n \cdot \sum\limits_{i=0}^{n} m_i} \tag{6}$$

where n represents the number of amino acid C atoms in the considered fragment and i the different mass isotopomers (**Subheading 3.7., step 8**).

3.4. Experimental Analysis: Mass Distribution Vectors of the Metabolites (Implemented in the Analysis Software FiatFlux)

The main pathways that synthesize the precursor metabolites for *E. coli* amino acids from glucose are shown in **Fig. 3**. Mass distribution vectors of the precursor metabolites (MDV_M) (or their fragments) can easily be derived from the MDV_{AA}.

1. Several amino acid carbon backbones are derived directly from one metabolite, e.g., alanine from pyruvate (**Fig. 4**). For these metabolites, the MDV_M are equal to the MDV_{AA}.
2. The carbon skeletons of other amino acids originate from two or more metabolites or fragments of metabolites. If we assume that the carbon backbone of one amino acid originates from the metabolites M1 and M2, then the mass distri-

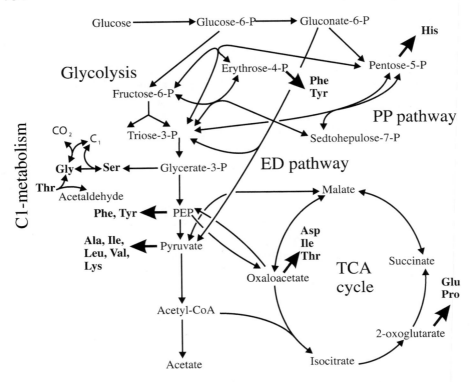

Fig. 3. Bioreaction network of *Escherichia coli* central carbon metabolism. Arrows indicate the assumed reaction reversibility. Solid arrows indicate precursor withdrawal for the amino acids analyzed by GC–MS. Abbreviations: ED pathway, Entner–Doudoroff pathway; PP pathway, pentose–phosphate pathway.

bution vector MDV_{AA} is a combination of the mass distributions MDV_{M1} and MDV_{M2} and can be derived according to **Eq. 7 (Subheading 3.8.)** (*see* **Note 14**).

$$MDV_{AA}(i) = \sum_{j=0}^{j=1} MDV_{M1}(i-j) \cdot MDV_{M2}(j) \qquad (7)$$

3. To determine all MDV_M, the contribution of a single metabolite to the synthesis of different amino acids (or fragments of amino acids) has to be considered. Therefore, MDV_M are given arbitrary starting values, using as a constraint that the sum of their elements equals 1, and all MDV_{AA} are calculated from the different MDV_M. The calculated MDV_{AA} are then compared to the measured MDV_{AA}. Using a least squares fit between measured MDV_{AA} and calculated MDV_{AA}, the MDV_M are determined (*see* **Note 15**). **Table 3** summarizes all MDV_M that can be determined from the amino acid fragments. The number in subscript indicates the C atoms included in each considered fragment.

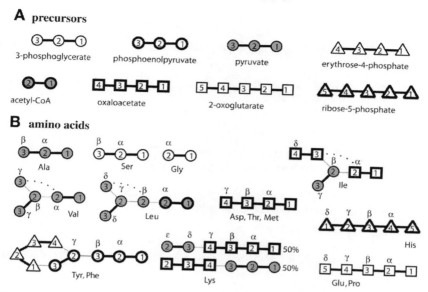

Fig. 4. Metabolic origin of the amino acid backbone. (**A**) Representation of the carbon skeleton of the intermediates of (○) glycolysis, (□) TCA cycle, and (△) pentose–phosphate pathway. (**B**) Representation of the carbon skeleton of the 14 used amino acids and the origin of their carbon atoms with respect to the metabolic intermediates displayed in **A**. Thin lines denote carbon bonds that are formed between fragments arising from different intermediate molecules, thick lines indicate carbon–carbon connectivities in intact fragments originating from a single intermediate metabolite. Dashed lines connect fragments arising from the same intermediate molecule that are not directly attached in the amino acid carbon skeleton. The representation was inspired by **ref. 3**.

Table 3
Metabolite Mass Distribution Vectors (MDV_M) Determined From the MDV_{AA}

Metabolite	MDV[a]		
Acetyl-CoA	$AcCoA_{(1-2)}$	$AcCoA_{(2)}$	
Erythrose-4-P	$E4P_{(1-4)}$		
Glycine	$Gly_{(1-2)}$	$Gly_{(2)}$	
Oxaloacetate	$OAA_{(1-4)}$	$OAA_{(2-4)}$	$OAA_{(1-2)}$
2-Oxoglutarate	$OGA_{(1-5)}$	$OGA_{(2-5)}$	$OGA_{(1-2)}$
Pentose-5-P	$PEN_{(1-5)}$	$PEN_{(2-5)}$	$PEN_{(1-2)}$
Phosphoenolpyruvate	$PEP_{(1-3)}$	$PEP_{(2-3)}$	$PEP_{(1-2)}$
Pyruvate	$PYR_{(1-3)}$	$PYR_{(2-3)}$	$PYR_{(1-2)}$
Serine	$SER_{(1-3)}$	$SER_{(2-3)}$	$SER_{(1-2)}$

[a] The carbon atoms included in each considered fragment are specified for each MDV in subscript.

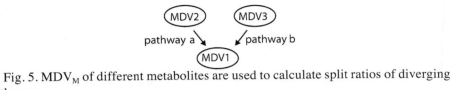

Fig. 5. MDV_M of different metabolites are used to calculate split ratios of diverging pathways.

3.5. Experimental Analysis: Calculation of Metabolic Flux Ratios (Implemented in the Analysis Software FiatFlux)

The intracellular pool of a given metabolite can be derived from other metabolite pools through biochemical pathways.

1. If a metabolite 1 (MDV1) can be derived through two alternative pathways, from metabolite 2 (MDV2) using pathway a or through metabolite 3 (MDV3) using an alternative pathway b, the contribution of each pathway can be determined (**Fig. 5**):

$$MDV1^T = f \cdot MDV2^T + (1 - f) \cdot MDV3^T \qquad (8)$$

where f is the fractional contribution of pathway a and $1-f$ is the contribution of the alternative pathway b (*see* **Note 16**). Because MDV are vectors and not single data points, **Eq. 8** represents a linear system of algebraic equations and is usually overdetermined. Rearrangement of **Eq. 8** leads to

$$f = \frac{MDV1^T - MDV3^T}{MDV2^T - MDV3^T} \qquad (9)$$

where f represents the least squares solution to **Eq. 9** and the division is a right-hand matrix division (**Subheading 3.9.**).

2. Accordingly, using MDV with $n+1$ elements (m_0 to m_n) up to $n+1$ alternative pathways can be distinguished. For three alternative pathways:

$$MDV1^T = f_1 \cdot MDV2^T + f_2 \cdot MDV3^T + (1 - f_1 - f_2) \cdot MDV4^T \qquad (10)$$

Solving **Eq. 10** for f_1 and f_2 leads to

$$[f_1 \ f_2] = \frac{\left(MDV1^T - MDV4^T\right)}{\left(\begin{array}{c} MDV2^T - MDV4^T \\ MDV3^T - MDV4^T \end{array}\right)} \qquad (11)$$

where f_1 and f_2 represent the least squares solutions to **Eq. 11** and the division is a right hand matrix division.

Table 4 summarizes the calculable ratios and gives the type of ^{13}C-labeling experiment needed to calculate them. For explanations on the different ratios please refer to **ref. 4**.

Table 4
Calculable Ratios and Type of ^{13}C-Labeling
Experiment Needed to Determine Them [a]

Ratio	Experiment [b]
PEP from PP pathway (ub)	U
PEP from transketolase	U
OAA from PEP	U
OAA from glyoxylate shunt	U
Pyruvate from malate (ub) [c]	U
Pyruvate from malate (lb) [c]	U
PEP from OAA	U
Serine from glycine	U
Glycine from serine	U
Erythrose-4-P from pentose-5-P	U
Pentose-5-P from glucose-6-P (lb) [c]	U
Pentose-5-P from erythrose-4-P	U
Serine through glycolysis	1
Pyruvate through ED pathway	1

[a] See **ref. 4**.
[b] U, 20% [U-^{13}C] and 80% unlabeled glucose experiment;
1, 100%[1-^{13}C]glucose experiment.
[c] ub, upper bound; lb, lower bound.

Error calculations are not considered here but are implemented in the publicly available software FiatFlux (*8*). The experimental error is determined from standard deviation of redundant data. Applying the law of error propagation using jacobian and covariance matrices, the standard deviations of the calculated ratio are determined (*4*).

3.6. Experimental Analysis: Mass Distribution Vectors of Substrate Fragments (Implemented in the Analysis Software FiatFlux)

The determination of several metabolic flux ratios requires the determination of mass distribution vectors for fragments of the input substrate. For a fragment with n carbon atoms of a mixture of uniformly and naturally ^{13}C-labeled substrate, as well as fragments with ^{13}C-labeling in one specific position, the mass distribution is

For $i=0$

$$MDV_{S,n_u,n_1}\left(m_1\right) = \left[1-\left(d_1 \cdot p_1\right)-d_u\right] \,^{12}C^{(n-i)} .$$

$$^{13}C^i\binom{n}{i} + d_u\left(1-p_u\right)^{(n-i)} p_u^i\binom{n}{i} \tag{12}$$

For $i \geq 1$
$$\mathrm{MDV}_{S,n_u,n_1}(m_1) = \left[1 - (d_1 \cdot p_1) - d_u\right] {}^{12}C^{(n-i)}$$
$$\cdot {}^{13}C^i \binom{n}{i} + d_u (1 - p_u)^{(n-i)} p_u^i \binom{n}{i} \tag{13}$$
$$+ d_1 \cdot p_1 \, {}^{12}C^{(n-i)} \cdot {}^{13}C^{i-1} \binom{n-1}{i-1}$$

where $\mathrm{MDV}_{S,n_u,n_1}(m_i)$ represents the abundance of the mass isotopomer m_i, ^{12}C and ^{13}C represent the abundance of ^{12}C and ^{13}C respectively, d_u is the labeled fraction of the uniformly labeled substrate, d_1 the labeled fraction of the specifically labeled substrate, p_u the purity of the uniformly labeled substrate, p_1 the purity of the specifically labeled substrate and

$$\binom{n}{i} \text{ and } \binom{n-1}{i-1}$$

are binomial numbers; i ranges from 0 to n.

3.7. Example 1:
Determination of MDV$_{AA}$ for the Alanine (M-57)$^+$ Fragment

1. Extraction of the data from the mass spectrum of a 20% [U-^{13}C]glucose experiment. The fragment alanine (M-57)$^+$ contains three amino acid C atoms, therefore n has to be greater or equal to three. Intensities extracted from the mass spectrum are:

	m_0	m_1	m_2	m_3
Intensities (ion count)	737,537	179,694	88,657	178,433

The corresponding mass distribution vector is:

$$\mathrm{MDV}_\alpha = \begin{pmatrix} 0.6228 \\ 0.1517 \\ 0.0749 \\ 0.1507 \end{pmatrix}$$

2. Characterization of the investigated fragment. The number of the specified atom in the fragment (without the amino acid C atoms) is determined. The fragment is an alanine (M-57)$^+$, which hence has lost a tert-butyl group (**Fig. 2**):

C	O	N	H	Si	S
8	2	1	26	2	0

3. Build up of individual correction matrices.

$$C_{\mathrm{corr,C}} = \begin{pmatrix} {}^{12}C_8 & 0 & 0 & 0 \\ {}^{12}C_7{}^{13}C & {}^{12}C_8 & 0 & 0 \\ {}^{12}C_6{}^{13}C_2 & {}^{12}C_7{}^{13}C & {}^{12}C_8 & 0 \\ {}^{12}C_5{}^{13}C_3 & {}^{12}C_6{}^{13}C_2 & {}^{12}C_7{}^{13}C & {}^{12}C_8 \end{pmatrix}$$

$$C_{corr,O} = \begin{pmatrix} {}^{16}O_2 & 0 & 0 & 0 \\ {}^{16}O{}^{17}O & {}^{16}O_2 & 0 & 0 \\ {}^{17}O_2 + {}^{16}O{}^{18}O & {}^{16}O{}^{17}O & {}^{16}O_2 & 0 \\ {}^{17}O{}^{18}O & {}^{17}O_2 + {}^{16}O{}^{18}O & {}^{16}O{}^{17}O & {}^{16}O_2 \end{pmatrix}$$

$$C_{corr,N} = \begin{pmatrix} {}^{14}N & 0 & 0 & 0 \\ {}^{15}N & {}^{14}N & 0 & 0 \\ 0 & {}^{15}N & {}^{14}N & 0 \\ 0 & 0 & {}^{15}N & {}^{14}N \end{pmatrix}$$

$$C_{corr,H} = \begin{pmatrix} {}^{1}H_{26} & 0 & 0 & 0 \\ {}^{1}H_{25}{}^{2}H & {}^{1}H_{26} & 0 & 0 \\ {}^{1}H_{24}{}^{2}H_2 & {}^{1}H_{25}{}^{2}H & {}^{1}H_{26} & 0 \\ {}^{1}H_{23}{}^{2}H_3 & {}^{1}H_{24}{}^{2}H_2 & {}^{1}H_{25}{}^{2}H & {}^{1}H_{26} \end{pmatrix}$$

$$C_{corr,Si} = \begin{pmatrix} {}^{28}Si_2 & 0 & 0 & 0 \\ {}^{28}Si{}^{29}Si & {}^{28}Si_2 & 0 & 0 \\ {}^{29}Si_2 + {}^{28}Si{}^{30}Si & {}^{28}Si{}^{29}Si & {}^{28}Si_2 & 0 \\ {}^{29}Si{}^{30}Si & {}^{29}Si_2 + {}^{28}Si{}^{30}Si & {}^{28}Si{}^{29}Si & {}^{28}Si_2 \end{pmatrix}$$

$$C_{corr,S} = \begin{pmatrix} 1 & 0 & 0 & 0 \\ 0 & 1 & 0 & 0 \\ 0 & 0 & 1 & 0 \\ 0 & 0 & 0 & 1 \end{pmatrix}$$

4. Calculation of the abundances in individual correction matrices. Using **Eq. 4**, $C_{corr,C}$ can be determined.

$$C_{corr,C} = \begin{pmatrix} 0.9175 & 0 & 0 & 0 \\ 0.0794 & 0.9175 & 0 & 0 \\ 0.0030 & 0.0794 & 0.9175 & 0 \\ 0.0000 & 0.0030 & 0.0794 & 0.9175 \end{pmatrix}$$

5. Determination of the overall correction matrix. According to **Eq. 3**, the overall correction matrix becomes:

$$C_{corr,CONHSiS} = \begin{pmatrix} 0.7715 & 0 & 0 & 0 \\ 0.1509 & 0.7715 & 0 & 0 \\ 0.0672 & 0.1509 & 0.7715 & 0 \\ 0.0087 & 0.0672 & 0.1509 & 0.7715 \end{pmatrix}$$

6. Calculation of MDV_α^*

$$MDV_\alpha^* = C_{corr,CONHSiS}^{-1} \cdot MDV_\alpha$$

$$= \begin{pmatrix} 0.7715 & 0 & 0 & 0 \\ 0.1509 & 0.7715 & 0 & 0 \\ 0.0672 & 0.1509 & 0.7715 & 0 \\ 0.0087 & 0.0672 & 0.1509 & 0.7715 \end{pmatrix}^{-1} \cdot \begin{pmatrix} 0.6228 \\ 0.1517 \\ 0.0749 \\ 0.1507 \end{pmatrix}$$

$$= \begin{pmatrix} 0.8072 \\ 0.0388 \\ 0.0191 \\ 0.1791 \end{pmatrix}$$

The sum of the elements of MDV_α^* is not equal to one (it is equal to 1.04). Therefore, the correct MDV_α^* is

$$MDV_\alpha^* = \begin{pmatrix} 0.7730 \\ 0.0372 \\ 0.0183 \\ 0.1715 \end{pmatrix} \text{ with } \sum_{i=0}^{3} m_i = 1$$

7. Correction for unlabeled biomass and determination of MDV_{AA}. To account for the contribution of 1% unlabeled biomass ($f_{unlabeled} = 0.01$) owing to the inoculum, **Eq. 5** is used:

$$MDV_{AA} = \frac{MDV_\alpha^* - f_{unlabeled} \cdot MDV_{unlabeled,\,n}}{1 - f_{unlabeled}}$$

$$= \frac{\begin{pmatrix} 0.7730 \\ 0.0372 \\ 0.0183 \\ 0.1715 \end{pmatrix} - 0.01 \cdot \begin{pmatrix} 0.9682 \\ 0.0314 \\ 0.0003 \\ 0.0000 \end{pmatrix}}{1 - 0.01} = \begin{pmatrix} 0.7710 \\ 0.0373 \\ 0.0185 \\ 0.1732 \end{pmatrix}$$

$MDV_{unlabeled,n}$ was determined according to **Eq. 4** with

$$MDV_{unlabeled,\,3} = \begin{pmatrix} m_0 \\ m_1 \\ m_2 \\ m_3 \end{pmatrix} = \begin{pmatrix} {}^{12}C_3 \\ {}^{12}C_2\,{}^{13}C \\ {}^{12}C\,{}^{13}C_2 \\ {}^{13}C_3 \end{pmatrix} = \begin{pmatrix} 0.9682 \\ 0.0314 \\ 0.0003 \\ 0.0000 \end{pmatrix}$$

8. Calculation of the fractional labeling FL.To check whether the MDV_{AA} of alanine $(M-57)^+$ can be further considered, the fractional labeling is determined according to **Eq. 6**.

$$FL = \frac{0 \cdot 0.7710 + 1 \cdot 0.0373 + 2 \cdot 0.0185 + 3 \cdot 0.1732}{3 \cdot (0.7711 + 0.0372 + 0.0185 + 0.1733)} = 0.20$$

Because the fractional labeling is equal to the fractional labeling of the input substrate (20% [U-^{13}C]glucose) the fragment can be considered for further analysis.

3.8. Example 2: Determination of MDV$_M$

From the measured MDV_{AA} of the $(M-15)^+$ fragment of isoleucine, the MDV_M of oxaloacetate $(OAA)_{1-4}$ and Pyr_{2-3} can be determined (**Fig. 4**). The MDV_{AA} of isoleucine is known, while the MDV_M of OAA_{1-4} and Pyr_{2-3} are unknown.

$$MDV_{AA,ILE} = \begin{pmatrix} 0.501 \\ 0.121 \\ 0.192 \\ 0.121 \\ 0.038 \\ 0.023 \\ 0.004 \end{pmatrix} \quad MDV_{M,OAA1-4} = \begin{pmatrix} O_0 \\ O_1 \\ O_2 \\ O_3 \\ O_4 \end{pmatrix} \quad MDV_{M,Pyr2-3} = \begin{pmatrix} P_0 \\ P_1 \\ P_2 \end{pmatrix}$$

The mass distribution vector MDV_{AA} can be written as a function of the MDV_M of OAA_{1-4} and Pyr_{2-3} according to **Eq. 7**:

$$MDV_{AA,ILE,calc} = \begin{pmatrix} O_0 P_0 \\ O_0 P_1 + O_1 P_0 \\ O_0 P_2 + O_1 P_1 + O_2 P_0 \\ O_1 P_2 + O_2 P_1 + O_3 P_0 \\ O_2 P_2 + O_3 P_1 + O_4 P_0 \\ O_3 P_2 + O_4 P_1 \\ O_4 P_2 \end{pmatrix}$$

Because the number of unknowns equals the number of independent equations, the MDV_M of OAA_{1-4} and Pyr_{2-3} can now be obtained by solving the resulting equations for the MDV_{AA} of isoleucine with the constraint that the sum of the elements of the two MDV_M is equal to one.

$$MDV_{M,OAA14} = \begin{pmatrix} 0.635 \\ 0.132 \\ 0.090 \\ 0.120 \\ 0.023 \end{pmatrix} \quad MDV_{M,Pyr23} = \begin{pmatrix} 0.789 \\ 0.026 \\ 0.185 \end{pmatrix}$$

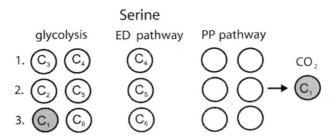

Fig. 6. Positional labeling in serine using 100% [1-^{13}C]glucose. The circles represent C atoms. Numbering in the circles represent the original numbering in the glucose molecule, while numbering next to the circles represents serine C atoms. The gray circles represent the ^{13}C-labeled C atoms. Abbreviations: ED pathway, Entner–Doudoroff pathway; PP pathway, pentose–phosphate pathway.

If the number of equations is larger than the number of unknowns, the solution is obtained by doing a least squares fit between the calculated MDV_{AA} and the measured MDV_{AA} with the additional constraint that the sum of the elements of the two MDV_M is equal to 1. Random starting values are then chosen for the MDV_M of the metabolites.

One metabolite will contribute to the synthesis of several amino acids (**Fig. 4**). Furthermore, different fragments of amino acids will yield redundant information. Thus, in reality, a least squares fit will be done for all metabolites simultaneously.

3.9. Example 3: Determination of Two Flux Ratios

3.9.1. Serine Derived Through Glycolysis

This ratio quantifies the fraction of serine (triose-3P) derived through glycolysis vs the fraction of serine (triose-3P) derived through the pentose–phosphate (PP) pathway or Entner–Doudoroff pathway (ED) pathways (**Fig. 3**). This ratio can be quantified from positional labeling using cells grown exclusively on [1-^{13}C]glucose. Indeed, if the serine molecules originate through glycolysis, half of the serine molecules will be labeled at position 3 of serine while the other half will be unlabeled (**Fig. 6**). If the serine molecules originate from the oxidative PP pathway, none of the molecules will be labeled because the ^{13}C-labeled carbon at position one was lost as CO_2 in the oxidative part of the PP pathway (**Fig. 6**). The serine molecules derived through the ED pathway also yield unlabeled triose-3P molecules (**Fig. 6**). The exchange flux with glycine does not change the label content in serine, unless substantial fractions of glycine or the one carbon unit are produced from other sources than serine (**Fig. 3**).

This ratio is calculated from **Eq. 9**, with (1) MDV1 being the MDV_{AA} of serine$_{1-3}$, (2) MDV2 being a mixture of 50% three carbon molecules with one ^{13}C-labeled atom and 50% unlabeled three carbon atom molecules (contribution of glycolysis to serine pool) and (3) MDV3 being unlabeled three carbon atom molecules (contribution of PP and ED pathways).

MDV1 is equal to the determined MDV_{AA} of serine$_{1-3}$:

$$MDV1 = \begin{pmatrix} 0.612 \\ 0.381 \\ 0.007 \\ 0.000 \end{pmatrix}$$

To determine MDV2, the MDV of a three-carbon atom fragment of the substrate with one ^{13}C can be calculated based on **Eqs. 12** and **13**. Here we assume that the purity p_1 of the substrate is 0.99 and that only 1-^{13}C-labeled substrate is used ($d_1=1$).

$$MDV_{S,3_1} = \begin{pmatrix} 0.010 \\ 0.969 \\ 0.021 \\ 0.000 \end{pmatrix}$$

The MDV of an unlabeled three carbon fragment can be calculated from **Eq. 4**.

$$MDV_{unlabeled,3} = \begin{pmatrix} 0.968 \\ 0.031 \\ 0.000 \\ 0.000 \end{pmatrix}$$

MDV2 is a 50–50% mixture of $MDV_{S,31}$ and $MDV_{unlabeled,3}$:

$$MDV2 = \begin{pmatrix} 0.489 \\ 0.500 \\ 0.011 \\ 0.000 \end{pmatrix}$$

MDV3 is equal to $MDV_{unlabeled,3}$:

$$MDV3 = \begin{pmatrix} 0.968 \\ 0.031 \\ 0.000 \\ 0.000 \end{pmatrix}$$

Applying **Eq. 9**, the fraction of serine derived through glycolysis can be calculated. The ratio represents the least squares solution to the equation

$$f = \frac{\text{MDV1}^T - \text{MDV3}^T}{\text{MDV2}^T - \text{MDV3}^T} = \text{serine through glycolysis} =$$

$$\frac{(0.612 \quad 0.381 \quad 0.007 \quad 0.000) - (0.968 \quad 0.031 \quad 0.000 \quad 0.000)}{(0.489 \quad 0.500 \quad 0.011 \quad 0.000) - (0.968 \quad 0.031 \quad 0.000 \quad 0.000)} = 0.74$$

where the division is a right hand matrix division.

3.9.2. OAA Originating From Phosphoenolpyruvate

This ratio quantifies the fraction of OAA originating from phosphoenolpyruvate (PEP) through the anaplerotic reaction catalyzed by PEP carboxylase vs the fraction of OAA derived through the TCA cycle. This ratio is determined using [U-^{13}C]glucose experiments. For this ratio, the MDV_M of OAA_{1-4}, PEP_{1-3}, CO_2 (anaplerosis), and OGA_{2-5} (TCA cycle) are necessary *(4)*. As the fractional labeling of CO_2 is unknown in batch cultures and may be lower than the fractional enrichment of the input substrate, it has to be considered as an additional unknown.

Equation 8 then becomes

$$\text{OAA}_{14}{}^T = f(\text{PEP}_{1-3} \times CO_2)^T + (1 - f)\,\text{OGA}_{2-5}^T$$

PEP × CO_2 represents the combination of two metabolites as calculated from **Eq. 7**. However, the MDV of CO_2 is unknown and depends upon the labeling content of CO_2 (d_{CO2}):

$$\text{MDV}_{CO2} = \begin{pmatrix} 1 - d_{CO2} \\ d_{CO2} \end{pmatrix}$$

If one writes the former equation explicitly for m_0 and m_1 of OAA_{1-4}:

$$\text{OAA}_{1-4}(0) = \text{PEP}_{1-3}(0) \cdot (1 - d_{CO2}) \cdot f + (1 - f) \cdot \text{OGA}_{2-5}(0)$$

$$\text{OAA}_{1-4}(1) = \left[\text{PEP}_{1-3}(1) \cdot (1 - d_{CO2}) + \text{PEP}_{1-3}(0) \cdot d_{CO2}\right] \cdot f + (1 - f) \cdot \text{OGA}_{2-5}(1)$$

Rearranging,

$$\text{OAA}_{1-4}(0) - \text{OGA}_{2-5}(0) = f\left[\text{PEP}_{1-3}(0) - \text{OGA}_{2-5}(0)\right] - f \cdot d_{CO2}\text{PEP}_{1-3}(0)$$

$$\text{OAA}_{1-4}(1) - \text{OGA}_{2-5}(1) = f\left[\text{PEP}_{1-3}(1) - \text{OGA}_{2-5}(1)\right] + f \cdot d_{CO2}\left[\text{PEP}_{1-3}(0) - \text{PEP}_{1-3}(1)\right]$$

Solving for the two unknowns f and d_{CO2}, from the previous two equations it becomes clear that the general solution (for m_0 to m_4) is

$$\begin{bmatrix} f & f \cdot d_{CO2} \end{bmatrix} = \frac{(OAA_{14}^T - OGA_{25}^T)}{\begin{bmatrix} \left(PEP_{13}^T \quad 0 \right) - OGA_{25}^T \\ \left(0 \quad PEP_{13}^T \right) - \left(PEP_{13}^T \quad 0 \right) \end{bmatrix}}$$

where the division is a right-hand matrix division.

Numerically for,

$$OAA_{1-4} = \begin{pmatrix} 0.630 \\ 0.129 \\ 0.089 \\ 0.134 \\ 0.018 \end{pmatrix} \quad PEP_{1-3} = \begin{pmatrix} 0.795 \\ 0.011 \\ 0.001 \\ 0.193 \end{pmatrix} \quad OGA_{2-5} = \begin{pmatrix} 0.583 \\ 0.110 \\ 0.260 \\ 0.022 \\ 0.025 \end{pmatrix}$$

the least squares fit solution is

$$\begin{pmatrix} f & f \cdot d_{CO2} \end{pmatrix} = \begin{pmatrix} 0.686 & 0.113 \end{pmatrix}$$

therefore, d_{CO2} is equal to 0.17 and the fraction of OAA originating from PEP is 0.69.

4. Notes

1. The indicated M9 minimal medium is intended for the cultivation of *E. coli* or *B. subtilis* and should be prepared fresh from stock solutions because precipitation occurs after the addition of $FeCl_3$ or $CaCl_2$. Thiamine has to be stored at 4°C and the $FeCl_3$ solution has to be protected from light. Any other medium may be suitable as long as glucose is the sole carbon source. The two different mixtures of labeled and natural glucose, as well as the choice of the glucose isotope isomers themselves, are recommended for the METAFoR analysis described later (*see* **Subheadings 3.3.–3.6.**).
2. For later analysis it is advantageous to inoculate the 30-mL growth cultures with as little preculture as possible to obtain a percentage fraction of unlabeled biomass of 3% or less.
3. The minimum amount of labeled biomass is in the range of 1 mg of cell dry weight. Because the efficiency of hydrolysis, derivatization, and the sensitivity of GC–MS can vary, we recommend taking aliquots of 5 mg cell dry weight when working with shake flask cultures.

    If the biomass pellets are not immediately processed, they can be stored for several weeks at –30°C. Storage is not recommended at later stages of sample processing.

4. *Caution:* strong acid under overpressure. We recommend to mechanically seal the Eppendorf tubes during hydrolization to prevent evaporation of HCl. We use a homemade metal rack for Eppendorf tubes with a tightly screwed cover plate.
5. Not the whole pellet is dissolved. It is enough to obtain a brown color.
6. Derivatization is impaired by the presence of water. Therefore dryness of the hydrolizate and the use of pure, water-free dimethylformamide and derivatization agent is crucial.
7. If cell debris is present in the derivatized sample, centrifuge shortly to avoid transfer of any particles into the amber crimp vials. The samples should be analyzed soon, as degradation occurs within a few days.
8. In our case, the detector is overloaded if the intensity rises over 1.5 million counts for a single scan and mass.
9. To simplify data treatment, n can be chosen to have the same value for all amino acid fragments. In our case we chose n to be equal to nine because tyrosine and phenylalanine contain nine carbon atoms.
10. In **Eq. 4,** the first term:

$$\left(\sum_{i=1}^{N} \left\{ v\left[I\left(k\right) \right] \right\} \right)$$

is equal to the number of atoms in the isotopolog.
11. If an atom species is not present, the correction matrix for this species is an identity matrix (**Subheading 3.7., step 3**).
12. In a chemostat, where the labeled substrate is only used for a defined amount of time, the fraction of unlabeled biomass $f_{unlabeled}$ is determined using first-order kinetics:

$$f_{unlabeled} = e^{-D \cdot t}$$

where D is the dilution rate and t the time of labeled substrate feeding.
13. If the fractional labeling of a fragment has more than 10% variation from the input substrate, the fragment is not considered for further analysis. This lower fractional labeling most of the time results from bad mass spectra (interference, bad calibration, or too little biomass) but could also result from the incorporation of unlabeled carbon atoms (storage material, CO_2...) that would have to be further investigated.
14. If an amino acid originates from more than two metabolites or fragments of metabolites, first the combination for two metabolites is determined, which, in turn, is then combined to the third metabolite and so on.
15. We perform the least squares fit using the MATLAB® function lsqnonlin.
16. A^T is the matrix transpose of A and is obtained by exchanging A's rows with A's columns.

Acknowledgments

The authors would like to thank Eliane Fischer and Simon Tännler for their advice and valuable comments on the manuscript.

References

1. Sauer, U. (2004) High-throughput phenomics: experimental methods for mapping fluxomes. *Curr. Opin. Biotechnol.* **15**, 58–63.
2. Szyperski, T., Glaser, R. W., Hochuli, M., et al. (1999) Bioreaction network topology and metabolic flux ratio analysis by biosynthetic fractional ¹³C labeling and two-dimensional NMR spectroscopy. *Metab. Eng.* **1**, 189–197.
3. Szyperski, T. (1995) Biosynthetically directed fractional ¹³C-labeling of proteinogenic amino acids. An efficient analytical tool to investigate intermediary metabolism. *Eur. J. Biochem.* **232**, 433–448.
4. Fischer, E. and Sauer, U. (2003) Metabolic flux profiling of *Escherichia coli* mutants in central carbon metabolism using GC-MS. *Eur. J. Biochem.* **270**, 880–891.
5. Sauer, U., Lasko, D. R., Fiaux, J., et al. (1999) Metabolic flux ratio analysis of genetic and environmental modulations of *Escherichia coli* central carbon metabolism. *J. Bacteriol.* **181**, 6679–6688.
6. Fuhrer, T., Fischer, E., and Sauer, U. (2005) Experimental identification and quantification of glucose metabolism in seven bacterial species. *J. Bacteriol.* **187**, 1581–1590.
7. Fischer, E., Zamboni, N., and Sauer, U. (2004) High-throughput metabolic flux analysis based on gas chromatography-mass spectrometry derived ¹³C constraints. *Anal. Biochem.* **325**, 308–316.
8. Zamboni, N., Fischer, E., and Sauer, U. (2005) Fiat Flux: a software for metabolic flux analysis from ¹³C-glucose experiments. *BMC Bioinformatics* **6**, 209.
9. Dauner, M. and Sauer, U. (2000) GC-MS analysis of amino acids rapidly provides rich information for isotopomer balancing. *Biotechnol. Prog.* **16**, 642–649.
10. Van Winden, W. A., Wittmann, C., Heinzle, E., and Heijnen, J. J. (2002) Correcting mass isotopomer distributions for naturally occurring isotopes. *Biotechnol. Bioeng.* **80**, 477–479.
11. Hellerstein, M. K. and Neese, R. A. (1999) Mass isotopomer distribution analysis at eight years: theoretical, analytic, and experimental considerations. *Am. J. Physiol.* **276**, E1146–E1170.
12. Rosman, K. J. R. and Taylor, P. D. P. (1998) Isotopic compositions of the elements 1997. *Pure Appl. Chem.* **70**, 217–235.

12

Understanding the Roadmap
of Metabolism by Pathway Analysis

Stefan Schuster, Axel von Kamp, and Mikhail Pachkov

Summary

The theoretical investigation of the structure of metabolic systems has recently attracted increasing interest. In this chapter, the basic concepts of metabolic pathway analysis are described and various applications are outlined. In particular, the concepts of nullspace and elementary flux modes are explained. The presentation is illustrated by a simple example from tyrosine metabolism and a system describing lysine production in *Corynebacterium glutamicum*. The latter system gives rise to 37 elementary modes, 36 of which produce lysine with different molar yields. The examples illustrate that metabolic pathway analysis is a useful tool for better understanding the complex architecture of intracellular metabolism, for determining the pathways on which the molar conversion yield of a substrate–product pair under study is maximal, and for assigning functions to orphan genes (functional genomics). Moreover, problems emerging in the modeling of large networks are discussed. An outlook on current trends in the field concludes the chapter.

Key Words: Elementary flux modes; extreme pathways; lysine synthesis; metabolic networks; metabolic pathway analysis; stoichiometry matrix.

1. Introduction

The complete sequencing of a large number of genomes has resulted in a drastic increase of available data, which should be interpreted in terms of the cellular machinery. For the prediction of functions to newly sequenced genes, it is promising to go beyond the purely genetic approach and consider the relations between genes at a higher level, for example, from the viewpoint of metabolic networks. Whereas efficient tools for comparing gene sequences are used extensively nowadays, tools for testing the feasibility of pathways in

From: *Methods in Molecular Biology, vol. 358: Metabolomics: Methods and Protocols*
Edited by: W. Weckwerth © Humana Press Inc., Totowa, NJ

the deduced metabolic network are not yet common, although there has been a rapid development in that direction during the last decade (1–5).

Various approaches to metabolic network analysis have been proposed (6–11). All of these focus on the properties of metabolic networks at steady state imposed by their stoichiometric structure rather than on their dynamic properties. The main underlying idea is to detect all the simplest stoichiometrically feasible pathways. The term metabolic pathway analysis (MPA) is now finding increasingly wide acceptance for this field of research. Another, more general term, is "constraint-based analysis" (because constraints such as the steady-state equation are included), which also involves optimization approaches.

This chapter is concentrated on MPA, that is, on the structural analysis of metabolic networks. Methods discussed here only use stoichiometric and, to some extent, thermodynamic information to infer properties of reaction networks. This implies advantages in comparison with dynamic modeling because stoichiometric parameters are well known, whereas kinetic constants (such as maximal enzyme velocities) are frequently unavailable and difficult to measure. Note, however, that structural analysis provides less output information than dynamic modeling. As will become clear next, the information is nevertheless interesting and of practical importance.

The first effort to a systematic computation of biochemical pathways was made by Seressiotis and Bailey (10). They presented an approach for finding pathways leading from a given substrate to a desired product in a given reaction system. That approach starts by selecting all reactions that consume the substrate of interest. Each of these reactions produces certain products. The next step is adding to the model those reactions that consume these intermediate products, and so on. Pathways are, thus, constructed in a stepwise manner, moving from a substrate toward all possible products.

Mavrovouniotis et al. (6) introduced a refined algorithm for computing all possible pathways. The algorithm is based on the iterative satisfaction of constraints and the stepwise transformation of the initial set of reactions into the final set of pathways satisfying all imposed constraints. Mavrovouniotis et al. (6) made a distinction between necessary substrates, possible (co)substrates, intermediates, necessary products, and possible (by)products. They applied the approach to the problem of lysine synthesis from glucose and ammonia. In addition to the established synthesis routes, they have found several alternative pathways bypassing several key enzymes (see also **Subheading 4.**). Apart from the construction of biochemical pathways, they demonstrated that a stoichiometry-based approach can reveal fundamental constraints in a reaction system. For example, in the case of lysine biosynthesis, the algorithm revealed that oxaloacetate (OAA) is a necessary intermediate in all pathways from glucose to lysine, and that the yield of lysine over glucose cannot exceed 67% in the absence of enzymatic recovery of carbon dioxide.

Modern approaches in the structural analysis of metabolic networks make use of the algebraic properties of the steady-state equation, an approach pioneered in chemistry by B. Clarke *(12)*. These are elementary-mode analysis *(7,13,14)* and the extreme pathways *(11)*. In these approaches, the stoichiometric matrix is analyzed and use is made of a field in mathematics called convex analysis, as outlined in the following sections.

Often, metabolic networks are represented as graphs involving vertices and edges *(15,16)*. However, determining the metabolic route that leads from a particular initial substrate to a desired product is usually a difficult task, all the more as many enzymatic reactions are bimolecular so that byproducts are formed which need to be processed further to avoid their accumulation, and cosubstrates are required that need to be supplied either by uptake from the outside or by formation from other substances. Thus, the presence of bimolecular reactions implies that metabolism is more complex than a simple graph in the sense of graph theory. Therefore, the term "roadmap" used in the title of this chapter should be regarded as a metaphor rather than a technical term, because metabolism is more complex than a network of roads. A possible approach is to consider graphs with two types of nodes corresponding to metabolites and reactions, called Petri nets *(17–19)* or P-graphs *(20)*. Most approaches in MPA, however, are based on algebraic methods because often a treatment by computer requires a translation into algebraic terms (such as matrices).

The most promising field of application for MPA is bioengineering. Modern genetic techniques allow one to insert, upregulate, or downregulate genes in micro-organisms. This is an effective way of increasing the rate and yield of product synthesis or suppressing the synthesis of undesired products. It is not, however, an easy task to predict the outcome of such genetic manipulations because the genetic, metabolic, and regulatory networks in living cells are extremely complex and cannot be understood intuitively. Therefore, theoretical methods such as mathematical modeling are needed *(13,21–24)*.

Although pathway analysis was first developed as a tool for bioengineering, it has a wide range of application. It has been successfully applied for analyzing the metabolic capabilities of several subsystems in bacteria *(2,4,25)*, yeast *(3,26,27)*, and higher organisms *(28,29)*. It has been employed to determine the maximum molar yield of biotransformations *(4,26,30,31)*, to analyze futile cycling in metabolism *(4,32)*, to examine structural robustness of biochemical networks *(33)*, and it has been used as a guideline for reconstructing metabolic networks in functional genomics *(1,3,4)*. The elementary-mode approach has been shown to be a very useful tool for predicting functional properties of metabolic genes, such as lethality of knockouts *(34)*.

In this chapter, the basic concepts of MPA are explained and various applications are reviewed. Special focus is laid on the calculation of maximum molar yields, and problems arising with large networks are discussed. The presentation is illustrated by several examples.

2. Methods

2.1. Theoretical Background

In the modeling of biochemical systems, usually two different types of metabolites are distinguished—internal and external metabolites *(13,21,35)*. Internal metabolites only participate in reactions included in the reaction scheme under consideration. They are the intermediates in biochemical conversion routes. In contrast, external metabolites (sometimes called source and sink metabolites) take part not only in the reaction set under consideration but also in reactions external to the model. They constitute the model boundary. Frequently, their concentrations are assumed to be virtually constant even in time-dependent, dynamical regimes. This may be owing to availability in large excess, regulated supply, or saturation of an enzyme with its substrate. End products can frequently be regarded to be external as well, notably when they are permanently removed from the system or are formed in perfectly irreversible reactions.

Whenever the metabolites are homogeneously distributed in the cell and the system's inputs are time-independent, the time course of metabolite levels can be described by the differential equation (cf. **ref. 22**)

$$\frac{dS}{dt} = NV(S,p) - \mu S \tag{1}$$

where, $S = (S_1, S_2,...,S_n)^T$, V, and p are the vectors of the concentrations of internal metabolites, net reaction velocities, and parameters, respectively. T denotes the transposition of vectors or matrices. The stoichiometry matrix, N, includes the stoichiometric coefficients of reactions. For a dimerization reaction, $2A \rightarrow A_2$, for example, the column in N reads $(-2\ 1)^T$. Note that the external metabolites should not be included in matrix N because **Eq. 1** does not apply to these. The symbol μ denotes the rate of cell growth, which implies a dilution effect for metabolites.

In many cases, the growth rate is negligible in comparison to the turnover of metabolites by enzymatic reactions *(22,36)*. One reason for that approximation is that, during cell growth, enzymes and metabolites are permanently replenished. Moreover, the concentrations S_i are often so small that the growth term in **Eq. 1** can be neglected. Alternatively, the dilution effect can formally be treated in the form of additional withdrawal reactions.

In MPA, usually stationary states (or stationary oscillations) are considered *(6,7,22)*. Thus, for any internal metabolite, total production is equal to total consumption (at least, averaged over time). This implies that the differential **Eq. 1** can be simplified into an algebraic equation,

$$NV(S,p) = 0 \tag{2}$$

One possible, relatively simple approach to determining metabolic pathways mathematically is by computing the nullspace (kernel) to the stoichiometry matrix N *(37,38)*. The nullspace to a matrix, N, is the Euclidean subspace of all vectors V fulfilling **Eq. 2**. By the Gaussian elimination method (cf. **ref. *39***), a set of basis vectors to this nullspace can be calculated. These vectors may be interpreted as pathways provided that they are relatively simple. "Simple" is meant to imply that the vectors include as many zeroes as possible, so that the pathway includes a minimum number of enzymes. The Gaussian elimination method indeed produces such vectors. As biochemically relevant examples, futile cycles *(37)*, and independent pathways in the aromatic amino acid biosynthetic network *(22,38)* have been determined. Moreover, the nullspace can be used to calculate "enzyme subsets," that is, sets of enzymes that always operate together, in fixed flux proportions *(40,41)*.

Using basis vectors of the nullspace has, however, a number of drawbacks. First, these vectors are not uniquely determined (cf. **ref. *39***). Depending on the calculation procedure one may receive different sets of nullspace basis vectors. Second, basis vectors need not comply with the sign constraints for the fluxes of irreversible reactions. For many biochemical reactions it is known whether they are reversible or irreversible. Irreversibility is not meant to imply that there would be no backward step; rather, the backward step must always have a lower velocity than the forward step. For example, most phosphatases (EC 3.1.3.z) and deaminases (EC 3.5.4.z) are irreversible while all isomerase (EC numbers 5.x.y.z) and aminotransferase reactions (EC 2.6.1.z) are reversible. The information about irreversibility is available much more frequently than the values of kinetic parameters. It can be extracted from common on-line pathway databases, such as EMP (http://www.empproject.com/) and KEGG (http://www.genome.ad.jp/kegg/). The third disadvantage of the nullspace approach is that often not all biochemical meaningful pathways are detected. Because the basis vectors of the nullspace are linearly independent, their linear combinations representing pathways are not immediately considered. This implies the fourth drawback of the nullspace: gene knockouts and enzyme deficiencies cannot be described properly because the basis does not include all meaningful pathways. Thus, deletion of an enzyme may block all pathways corresponding to the chosen basis vectors, although there do remain pathways operating in the system. The disadvantages of the nullspace over the elementary-mode approach are illustrated in **Subheading 2.2.**

To eliminate the drawbacks of the nullspace approach, a different, yet somewhat related approach was proposed, elaborating on the concept of "extreme currents" developed by Clarke *(12)*. Clarke only considered irreversible reactions; reversible reactions were decomposed into forward and reverse steps. In a more flexible approach, this decomposition is not necessary. Then, only a subvector (corresponding to the irreversible reactions) of the flux vector V is constrained,

$$V^{irr} \geq 0 \tag{3}$$

Equations 2 and **3** constitute a linear system of equations and inequalities. The solutions V are indeterminate with respect to scaling. Thus, it is sensible to consider relative flux distributions, often called flux modes. Each flux mode can be described by one representative flux vector, V^*, (unequal to the null vector) fulfilling the conditions of **Eqs. 2** and **3**. All vectors generated from V^* by scaling, $V = \lambda V^*$, $\lambda > 0$, correspond to the same flux mode.

Often, one is interested in seeking a *simple* flux distribution rather than an arbitrary distribution fulfilling relations **Eqs. 2** and **3**. This is motivated by the general scientific paradigm of decomposing the system under study into its simplest functional components. Examples of this paradigm are the widely used Fourier analysis and the decomposition of luminance into multiple layers in visual perception (*42*). In bioinformatics, related approaches are aimed at the decomposition of gene expression patterns into principal components (*43*) or independent components (*44*) (*see also* Chapters 4 and 6 for the application of independent components analysis to metabolomic data). To deal with enzyme sets involving only a few enzymes, that is, simple conversion routes, is particularly interesting in functional genomics, because the set of identified metabolic genes is often incomplete, so that it is of interest to test whether at least one functional route is feasible in this set (*1*).

To give a theoretically sound definition to the ideas of "simple flux distribution" and "biochemical pathway," the concept of "elementary flux mode" was introduced (*7,14,45*). An elementary flux mode is a flux mode, V^*, as previously defined for which there is no other flux mode involving only a subset of the enzymes involved in V^* (nondecomposibility condition). In mathematical terms, this means that there is no flux vector, V', satisfying **Eqs. 2** and **3**, including zero elements wherever V^* does, and involving at least one additional zero component. For checking whether a vector V^* is elementary, the test vector V' need not have the same values of the nonzero components as V^* (*46*).

The admissible region of flux vectors given by **Eqs. 2** and **3** is a convex polyhedral cone (in everyday language, this is a pyramid with infinitely long edges). All edges (generating vectors) of this cone correspond to elementary modes. When the system involves reversible reactions, there may be additional elementary modes corresponding to vectors inside the cone. For a geometric interpretation of elementary modes in flux space, *see also* Pfeiffer et al. (*40*). In contrast to the basis vectors of the nullspace, the elementary modes are uniquely determined up to scaling. Furthermore, each flux mode admissible in the living cell can be written as a linear combination of basis vectors or as a non-negative linear combination of elementary flux modes (*46*),

$$V = \sum_k \lambda_k e^{(k)} \, , \, \lambda_k \geq 0$$

(4)

The coefficients in the combination of elementary modes should be non-negative in order not to violate the irreversibility constraint.

In contrast to earlier approaches (6,10), in elementary-mode analysis, a distinction is made only between internal and external metabolites. This is meaningful because some substances can be a substrate or a product depending on conditions, e.g., ethanol in the case of *Saccharomyces cerevisiae*.

Schilling et al. (11) introduced the concept of extreme pathways. In that approach, all source and sink metabolites are treated as internal and exchange reactions are added so as to supply or remove those metabolites. All internal reactions are considered irreversible. If reversible internal reactions occur, they are split into forward and reverse steps. The pathways corresponding to cycles within such reactions need to be eliminated. Extreme pathways are then defined to be flux vectors that span the admissible flux region (11). This region is again a cone, which has, however, a higher dimension owing to the decomposition of reversible internal reactions. The extreme pathways are the edges of that cone.

2.2. A Simple Example

Here, we consider a simple system to illustrate application of elementary modes analysis and the advantages of the approach over describing a system by nullspace vectors. The example (**Fig. 1**) represents part of tyrosine metabolism in chromaffin cells (47) and has been briefly discussed earlier (45). The system consists of three reactions. Only tyrosine is considered internal. The stoichiometric matrix is very simple: $N = (1 \; -1 \; -1)$. The columns correspond to phenylalanine 4-mono-oxygenase (Ph4H), tyrosine aminotransferase (AttY), and tyrosine 3-mono-oxygenase (Ty3H), respectively. Ph4H and Ty3H can be considered irreversible (*see* KEGG [http://www.genome.ad.jp/kegg/]), whereas AttY, like all aminotransferases, is reversible. The reaction system gives rise to three elementary modes and only two nullspace vectors.

The vector $V^{(1)} = (1 \; 1 \; 0)$ represents an elementary mode. Note that multiplication of the vector $V^{(1)}$ by any positive number gives the same elementary mode. If it is multiplied by a negative value (e.g., -1), the resulting vector is not an elementary mode because it violates the irreversibility condition for the reaction Ph4H. Nevertheless, this vector could be a basis vector of the nullspace. The two other elementary modes are $V^{(2)} = (1 \; 0 \; 1)$ and $V^{(3)} = (0 \; -1 \; 1)$. Although vector $V^{(2)}$ is the sum of $V^{(1)}$ and $V^{(3)}$, it fulfils the nondecomposability condition because its decomposition into these vectors requires an additional enzyme (tyrosine aminotransferase). The sum of $V^{(1)}$

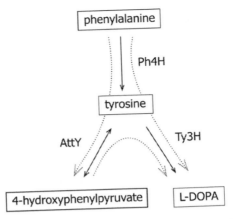

Fig. 1. Reaction scheme representing part of tyrosine metabolism in chromaffin cells. Tyrosine is considered to be an internal metabolite and all others are considered to be external metabolites. Abbreviations: AttY, tyrosine aminotransferase; L-DOPA, L-dihydroxyphenylalanine; Ph4H, phenylalanine 4-mono-oxygenase; Ty3H, tyrosine 3-mono-oxygenase. Dotted arrows depict elementary modes.

and $V^{(2)}$ is not elementary because it can be decomposed into elementary modes with no additional enzymes.

Even this simple system shows the incompleteness of the nullspace approach to exploring metabolic systems. The nullspace of this network can be given, for example, by the basis vectors $V^{(1)} = (1\ \ 1\ \ 0)$ and $V^{(3)} = (0\ \ -1\ \ 1)$. Such a representation does not contain all possible pathways. The vector $V^{(2)}$ is not included because it is the sum of the two basis vectors. If the system is deficient in AttY, then both pathways corresponding to the nullspace vectors drop out. However, the mode $V^{(2)} = (1\ \ 0\ \ 1)$ would still operate in the system, although it is not in the basis. This has the biochemical consequence that the synthesis of L-dihydroxyphenylalanine (L-DOPA) (a precursor of the neurotransmitter dopamine) from phenylalanine nevertheless continues.

2.3. Biochemical Interpretation

Knowledge of the elementary modes allows one to determine the full set of metabolic capabilities of a metabolic network, which are often much more varied than the pathways known from biochemistry textbooks. An example is provided by a pathway discovered experimentally in glucose-limited *Escherichia coli* by **ref. 48**. It involves part of the tricarboxylic acid (TCA) cycle, the glyoxylate shunt, and phosphoenolpyruvate carboxykinase. It had been predicted earlier by elementary-mode analysis in Schuster et al. (**14**).

The set of elementary modes remaining after deletion of an enzyme is given by the subset of all elementary modes not involving this enzyme. Thus, elementary modes are well suited to describe enzyme deficiencies and knockout mutations, in contrast to the basis vectors of the nullspace. Furthermore, elementary-mode analysis enables one to detect all futile cycles in a biochemical system. This requires that the currency metabolites driving these cycles, such as ATP, are considered external. Rohwer and Botha *(32)* studied a system involving hexoses, hexose phosphates, sucrose, and sucrose phosphate and found 14 elementary modes. Five of these correspond to futile cycles. Detecting such cycles is of importance when studying the fraction of ATP production lost by futile cycling *(37,49)*. The approach is also relevant in determining molar conversion yields, *see* **Subheading 3.**

MPA is particularly helpful when the system under study involves many bimolecular reactions. These render the network very interwoven and entangled, so that molecular moieties are exchanged among various metabolites. The network is then more complex than a usual graph in the sense of graph theory so that it is very difficult to see the routes in the system by inspection. For instance, in tryptophan synthesis, phosphoenolpyruvate (PEP) reacts with erythrose-4-phosphate to form one building block of tryptophan and, downstream in the synthesis route, another molecule of PEP reacts with shikimate 3-phosphate. In lysine synthesis (*see* **Subheading 4.**), pyruvate enters the synthesis route twice, and succinate enters it in one reaction and is released in another.

2.4. Algorithms and Software

Even for metabolic networks of moderate complexity, it is infeasible to detect the elementary modes by inspection of the reaction scheme. Therefore, an algorithm for computing them has been developed *(45)* based on an algorithm for computing the generating vectors of convex cones *(50)*. It is performed by the C program METATOOL *(40)*. The program has been extended and refined since then and is available from http://pinguin.biologie.uni-jena.de/bioinformatik/. Using METATOOL, other structural characteristics of metabolic networks can be determined as well, such as conservation relations (cf. **ref. 13**), enzyme subsets *(40,41)*, and the nullspace to the stoichiometry matrix, and fits a power law to the distribution of metabolite connectivities, that is, the numbers of reactions in which metabolites participate *(15)*. Elementary modes can also be computed by the software packages GEPASI *(51)* (http://www.gepasi.org/), JARNAC (http://www.sys-bio.org), and FluxAnalyzer *(52)*.

Recently, a new method for calculating elementary modes has been proposed *(53)*. In that approach, first the basis vectors of the nullspace are computed (this can be done fast) and then the elementary modes are computed by iterative, pairwise combination of the basis vectors. The algorithm exploits the facts that the nullspace matrix can be chosen so as to involve an identity matrix as a submatrix and that elementary modes consist of a minimal set of flows. The advantage of the algorithm is a reduction of computational costs by diminishing the combinatorial possibilities to design elementary modes. The new method has been implemented in the recent releases (v4.9; v5.0) of META TOOL. Another feature of v5.0 is a much faster test for non-decomposability when dealing with systems that have a large number of elementary modes. Whether or not the vector $V*$ fulfils the non-decomposibility condition can directly be tested with a rank criterion so that it is not necessary to compare $V*$ with other vectors V' (*54,55*). For this test, a submatrix of N is formed by selecting those columns that correspond to the reactions that participate in $V*$. If the rank (number of linearly independent columns) of this submatrix equals $m-1$ (m being the number of its columns), then V' is elementary. A further feature of METATOOL 5.0 is its integration into the GNU Octave and MATLAB® environments. This allows for interactive usage of the algorithms and easy postprocessing of the results.

3. Application to Biotechnology

An important goal in bioengineering is to increase the yield of biotransformations, that is, the molar product:substrate ratio. Some desired product can often be synthesized on more than one route, as in lysine synthesis (*see* **Subheading 4.**) or tryptophan synthesis (cf. **ref. *14***). After detecting that route on which the product:substrate ratio is maximal, one may try to overexpress the enzymes along that route and possibly suppress other enzymes. A flux mode using only the optimal route is certainly not feasible alone because other products (e.g., other amino acids) must also be produced. Nevertheless, it is of interest to compute upper bounds on the molar yield, to know what can at best be expected.

The molar yield of a biotransformation can be written as

$$\eta = \frac{\text{rate of product synthesis}}{\text{rate of substrate consumption}} \tag{5}$$

Let S and P denote the substrate and product under study, respectively. Let their stoichiometric coefficients (which are not included in the stoichiometry matrix N according to the above convention) be denoted by m_{Sk} and m_{Pk}, respectively, where k is the reaction index. Then the optimization principle can be written as

$$\text{maximize } \eta = -\frac{\sum_k m_{Pk} v_k}{\sum_k m_{Sk} v_k} \tag{6}$$

where a minus sign has been included because the coefficients m_{Sk} are negative. The variables of the optimization problem, **Eq. 6**, are the fluxes v_k. Note that the objective function is nonlinear. As **Eq. 6** is invariant to a scaling of the fluxes v_k by a common factor and the side constraints of **Eqs. 2** and **3** are linear and homogeneous, the solution to the optimization problem is indeterminate with respect to such a scaling. Thus, it is suitable to normalize the substrate consumption rate:

$$-\sum_k m_{1k} v_k = 1 \tag{7}$$

Combining this with **Eq. 6** yields a linear objective function. Sometimes, **Eq. 7** is written as an inequality imposing an upper bound on the input rate. However, in most cases, maximization of yields implies that the upper bound is attained, so that such a side constraint is equivalent with **Eq. 7**.

Because any flux mode is a superposition of elementary modes with non-negative coefficients (*see* **Eq. 4**), the molar product/substrate yield of a flux pattern is a weighted average of the yields of the elementary modes involved,

$$\eta = \frac{\sum_k \lambda_k \eta_k}{\sum_k \lambda_k} \tag{8}$$

where the λ_k are the weighting coefficients as used in **Eq. 4**. Thus, η cannot be greater than the maximum of all η_k. Therefore, the optimal flux distribution with respect to maximizing the molar yield always coincides with an elementary mode. In the case where two or more elementary modes achieve the same maximum yield, any linear combination of these realizes the maximum yield. The previously mentioned subject will be illustrated by the example of lysine production in **Subheading 4.** MPA was also successfully applied by Liao et al. *(30)* to the prediction of maximum yields in the production of precursors for aromatic amino acids in *E. coli* and by several other research groups (*see also* **Subheading 5.**).

Because the objective function of maximizing molar yields and the side constraints (relations **Eqs. 2** and **3**) are linear, the optimization problem can alternatively be solved by linear programming *(56–59)*. This method detects the pathway with the highest yield. In case there are multiple equivalent solutions, special care has to be taken that all of them are obtained *(60)*. By contrast, elementary-mode analysis yields a set of candidate solutions, from which the best for a particular substrate–product pair can easily be selected. This enables one to find not only optimal but also suboptimal situations. These may sometimes be more readily realized (at least approximately) in biotechnological applications than the optimal situation. Moreover, from the elementary modes, the optimal and suboptimal modes with respect to different substrate–product pairs can be selected consecutively. To sum up, elementary-mode analysis yields more output information than linear programming (*see also* **Subheading 6.**).

It is worth noting that the normalization described by **Eq. 7** is only feasible if the rate of substrate consumption is nonzero. This precondition may not be satisfied when alternative substrates are available. Consider, for example, the system depicted in **Fig. 1**. If the yield of L-DOPA over tyrosine is to be maximized, the optimization principle **Eq. 6** will give the result that the yield can tend to infinity, notably if L-DOPA is synthesized from the alternative substrate 4-hydroxyphenylpyruvate rather than from tyrosine. In such a case, linear programming cannot easily be applied. One consequence of this fact is that the flux distribution giving the highest yield need not be situated on the boundary of the flux cone, but corresponds to an elementary mode inside the cone *(31)*. In the L-DOPA example, the best pathway is the elementary mode $V^{(2)}$, which lies inside the cone because it is the sum of $V^{(1)}$ and $V^{(3)}$. Therefore, by determining the "extreme pathways," one may miss optimal solutions *(61)*. This is because the optimality criterion *(6)* is actually nonlinear. Moreover, multiple solutions to the linear programming problem may occur when the system involves internal cycles that do not affect substrate consumption or product formation. In this case, the biochemically meaningful, "pure" solution not involving the cycle(s) is achieved by an elementary mode *(31)*.

4. Example: Lysine Biosynthesis

As an illustrative example, we consider the synthesis of lysine from glucose and/or acetate in *C. glutamicum*, for which ammonia serves as a nitrogen source. The essential amino acid lysine is of great economic relevance *(62,63)*. Industrially, it is produced mainly by *Corynebacterium* and *Brevibacterium* species. The set of enzyme reactions considered here is listed in **Table 1**. It is similar to the condensed reaction network used by de Graaf *(62)*, which comprises reactions from the central metabolism, oxidative phosphorylation, and lysine biosynthesis. A related scheme describing the synthesis of lysine in *E. coli* has been studied earlier *(64)*. The network considered here extends the earlier scheme by including the pentose–phosphate pathway, additional anaplerotic reactions, oxidative phosphorylation, and the upper part of glycolysis. Series of sequential reactions with no branching points in between and all sets of reactions with the same overall reaction equations have been lumped together in the condensed network *(62)*. Following de Graaf *(62)*, P/O ratios of 2 and 1 are assumed for "oxp1" and "oxp2" (oxidative phosphorylation), respectively. Further compression of the network into "enzyme subsets" is done automatically by METATOOL by combining those reactions whose flux in steady state is always in a fixed proportion. The result of this procedure is shown in **Fig. 2**. Already at this stage, it can be seen that OAA is a necessary intermediate for lysine synthesis, in agreement with results of Mavrovouniotis et al. *(6)*.

Table 1
Reactions of Condensed Lysine Network [a]

Reaction	Stoichiometry
upt	Glucose + PEP → G6P + Pyr
ace	Acetate + ATP + CoA → AcCoA + ADP
ppp1	G6P + 2 NADP → Rul5P + CO_2 + 2 NADPH
ppp2	Rul5P ↔ Xul5P
ppp3	Rul5P ↔ Rib5P
ppp4	Xul5P + Ery4P ↔ F6P + GAP
ppp5	Xul5P + Rib5P ↔ Sed7P + GAP
ppp6	Sed7P + GAP ↔ Ery4P + F6P
emp1	G6P ↔ F6P
emp2	F6P + ATP → F16BP + ADP
emp3	F16BP → 2 GAP
emp4	GAP + ADP + NAD ↔ PGA + ATP + NADH
emp5	PGA ↔ PEP
emp6	PEP + ADP → Pyr + ATP
ana1	PEP + CO_2 ↔ OAA
ana2	Pyr + CO_2 + NADPH ↔ Mal + NADP
ana3	Pyr + CO_2 + ATP ↔ OAA + ADP
tcc1	Pyr + CoA + NAD → AcCoA + CO_2 + NADH
tcc2	AcCoA + OAA → Icit + CoA
tcc3	Icit + NADP → AKG + CO_2 + NADPH
tcc4	AKG + NAD + ADP → Suc + CO_2 + NADH + ATP
tcc5	Suc + FAD → Mal + FADH
tcc6	Mal + NAD → OAA + NADH
gs1	Icit → Suc + GlyOx
gs2	GlyOx + AcCoA → Mal + CoA
lys	OAA + Pyr + ATP + 4 NADPH → Lysine + CO_2 + ADP + 4 NADP
oxp1	2 NADH + O_2 + 4 ADP → 2 NAD + 4 ATP
oxp2	2 FADH + O_2 + 2 ADP → 2 FAD + 2 ATP

[a] Reactions considered for the lysine production system in *Corynebacterium glutamicum* (de Graaf *[62]*). Note that some of the reactions comprise several enzymatic steps. For details *see* de Graaf *(62)*. AcCoA, acetyl-coenzyme A; AKG, 2-oxoglutarate; Ery4P, erythrose-4-phosphate; F16BP, fructose-1,6-bisphosphate; F6P, fructose-6-phosphate; G6P, glucose-6-phosphate; GAP, glyceraldehyde-3-phosphate; GlyOx, glyoxylate; Icit, isocitrate; Mal, malate; OAA, oxaloacetate; PEP, phosphoenolpyruvate; PGA, 2-phosphoglycerate; Pyr, pyruvate; Rib5P, ribose-5-phosphate; Rul5P, ribulose-5-phosphate; Sed7P, sedoheptulose-5-phosphate; Suc, succinate; Xul5P, xylulose-5-phosphate; ace, acetate uptake; ana, anabolism; emp, Embden–Meyerhof pathway; gs, glyoxylate shunt; lys, lysine synthesis; ppp, pentose–phosphate pathway; oxp, oxidative phosphorylation; tcc, tricarboxylic acid cycle; upt, glucose uptake.

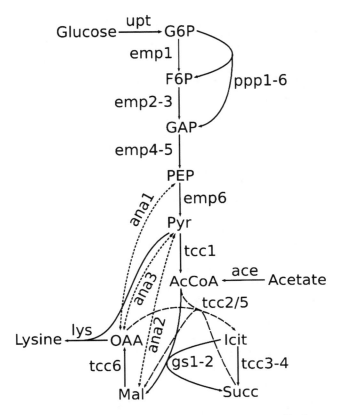

Fig. 2. Compressed reaction scheme of the lysine network. Each arrow represents one enzyme subset. Only the metabolites that are involved in the transformations of the carbon skeleton from glucose/acetate to lysine are shown. The reaction oxp1 is not included in the figure. Oxp2 is in the same subset as tcc2/5.

In the present model, the external metabolites are lysine, acetate, glucose, NAD/NADH, O_2, and CO_2. The cofactors ADP/ATP, NADP/NADPH, FAD/ FADH$_2$, and coenzyme A are set internal. Because fixation of NH$_3$ and trans- amination are not considered explicitly, the NADPH requirements for NH$_3$ fixa- tion are included in the lysine synthesis reaction.

Using the program METATOOL, we have obtained 37 elementary modes for this system; this result has been confirmed by using the program Flux- Analyzer developed by Klamt et al. *(52)*. One of the modes is a futile cycle which involves the decarboxylation of OAA and carboxylation of pyruvate, whereas the remaining 36 modes all produce lysine. The resource usage of these 36 modes differs: two modes only use glucose as a substrate, five modes only use acetate, and 29 use a combination of both. The elementary modes that only use glucose read as follows:

{4 upt, 6 ppp1, 4 ppp2, 2 ppp3, 2 ppp4, 2 ppp5, 2 ppp6, 2 emp1, 2 emp2, 2 emp3, 6 emp4, 6 emp5, 2 ana1, ana3, 3 lys},
{4 upt, 6 ppp1, 4 ppp2, 2 ppp3, 2 ppp4, 2 ppp5, 2 ppp6, 2 emp1, 2 emp2, 2emp3, 6 emp4, 6 emp5, 2 emp6, 3 ana3, 3 lys}.

Both of these have the overall stoichiometry

4 glucose + 6 NAD = 6 CO2 + 3 Lys + 6 NADH,

that is, they exhibit a yield of 3 M of lysine per 4 M of glucose. This coincides with the optimal molar conversion yield of 0.75 calculated for non-growing cells by de Graaf *(62)* with the help of metabolite balancing. Both modes bypass the TCA cycle. More exactly, it should be noted that, in *C. glutamicum*, the combined reaction "lys" involves two parallel routes with one of them using succinyl-CoA synthetase in direction of succinyl-CoA formation. Involvement of this enzyme is not seen in the computed elementary modes because it is hidden in the combined reaction "lys." The two optimal modes differ only in their usage of the anaplerotic reactions to regenerate OAA. Although one of these modes uses pyruvate carboxylase, the other uses this enzyme and phosphoenolpyruvate carboxylase. They also produce an excess of 1.5 M of NADH per mole of glucose and generate sufficient ATP for lysine production without using oxidative phosphorylation.

For the five modes that only use acetate as a substrate (not analyzed by de Graaf *[62]*), the conversion ratios range from 1 M of lysine per 4 M of acetate to 1 M of lysine per 10 M of acetate. All of these modes use reactions from various parts of the TCA cycle including the glyoxylate shunt, and use oxidative phosphorylation to regenerate ATP. The mode with the highest yield (0.25) is special in that it consumes external NADH to regenerate the necessary ATP. (All other modes that produce lysine produce NADH.) Moreover, it has the same molar yield in terms of C6 units as the glucose-consuming modes, notably 0.75. The other four modes produce NADH, but of course have reduced molar conversion yields (1 M of lysine per 7 or 10 M of acetate), because they need to break down some of the acetate for NADH synthesis.

If one wants to find flux distributions with optimal conversion yields when both glucose and acetate are used as substrates, then those distributions would be a combination of the two elementary modes that only consume glucose with the one elementary mode that has the highest yield when only consuming acetate. Because all three modes have a yield of 0.75 per C6 unit, any combination of them would have the same yield. However, the combinations would differ in their use of the anaplerotic reactions as well as in the production or consumption of NADH. If consumption of NADH is to be excluded, then at least 1 M of glucose per 2 M of acetate would have to be metabolized. A further increase of the glucose:acetate ratio would result in a production of NADH. It is also interesting to note that none of the combinations that have an optimal conversion yield uses any of the enzymes from tcc1, tcc3-4, and tcc6 (again except for the usage of succinyl-CoA synthetase). Moreover, if at least one enzyme from each of these subsets were knocked out, none of the lysine-producing modes with lower conversion yields would function anymore.

Earlier, we analyzed a scheme of lysine synthesis in *E. coli* in which all cofactors were considered to be external and 2-phosphoglycerate was the starting point, whereas glucose and acetate were not explicitly considered *(64)*. In that scheme, the optimal lysine/phosphoglycerate yield was one-half, which implies a lysine/glucose yield of unity. It is understandable that, when ATP is considered to be internal as is done here, a lower optimal yield is obtained because part of the carbon source is needed to regenerate ATP. In contrast to the earlier study on *E. coli* *(64)*, here we analyze *C. glutamicum* (which is of greater interest in biotechnology). This requires inclusion of the malic enzyme ("ana2") as well as the carboxylating and decarboxylating enzymes linking pyruvate with OAA ("ana3").

In an earlier modeling study, Mavrovouniotis et al. *(6)* analyzed lysine synthesis with all cofactors assumed to be external. They found the yield of lysine over glucose cannot exceed 67% in the absence of enzymatic recovery of carbon dioxide. From our present calculations, it follows that all modes using only glucose as a carbon source require anaplerotic reactions binding carbon dioxide if ATP and NADPH are to be balanced. If, on the other hand, glucose and acetate are used as substrates, lysine can be produced with a yield of 67% per C6 unit in the absence of CO_2 recovery.

Certain assertions about yields can by made by intuitive arguments. For example, by considering the carbon balance, one may guess that the optimal lysine/glucose yield in the case of NADPH excess is unity because both compounds involve six carbons. If NADPH needs to be balanced, the optimal yield is decreased to be three-fourths because 4 M of NADPH are necessary for 1 M of lysine and 12 M of NADPH can be produced per mole of glucose, in the oxidative pentose–phosphate pathway *(62)*. However, this intuitive reasoning has its limitations because it does not take into account the balance of all intermediates. Moreover, carboxylation and decarboxylation reactions may change the carbon balance. Therefore, it is preferable to perform an automated pathway analysis, e.g., by using elementary modes.

5. Large-Scale Metabolic Networks
5.1. Case Studies

The huge amount of data produced by the sequencing of complete genomes can, together with "classical" biochemical knowledge, be used for the reconstruction of metabolic networks. By sequence comparison methods and genome context methods *(65)*, for greater than half of the newly sequenced genes, the physiological functions can be predicted. With such information available, the idea has arisen to perform a pathway analysis at the scale of whole-cell models.

As it stands, the metabolism of those species for which the metabolic chart is well known, at least for central metabolism, such as humans, *E. coli*, and *S. cerevisiae*, is very complex. Intracellular parasites such as *Rickettsia* sp. or *Mycoplasma* sp. harbor a much simpler metabolism, which is, however, less well known because biochemical assays in parasites are difficult to conduct owing to interference with the host.

Elementary-mode analysis has been performed for systems of considerable complexity. Van Dien and Lidstrom *(4)* conducted a theoretical and experimental study on the facultative methylotroph bacterium, *Methylobacterium extorquens* AM1. In establishing the metabolic network comprising 67 reactions, available genome data was taken into account. The admissible flux region of the network was determined by computing and analyzing the elementary modes separately for three different substrates: methanol, pyruvate, and succinate. Growth on methanol is of particular biotechnological interest. For that substrate, 467 elementary modes were computed with several of these representing futile cycles. The optimal biosynthetic yield was computed to be 0.498 g biomass carbon per mole of methanol. Because this is close to the experimentally observed value (0.375–0.5), it is in support of the proposed network stoichiometry. Van Dien and Lidstrom *(4)* also analyzed mutants, both experimentally and theoretically, by determining which elementary modes remain after knockout of an enzyme.

Förster et al. *(3)* investigated a metabolic model of *S. cerevisiae* including 45 reactions and taking into account compartmentation. From the 89 elementary modes computed, 85 produce biomass. As some enzymes appear in all of these modes, they can be classified as essential. Förster et al. *(3)* also computed maximal yields and proposed to use pathway analysis in conjunction with the measurement of external metabolites in functional genomics (*see* **Subheading 5.2.**).

Carlson et al. *(26)* studied a metabolic reaction scheme of a *S. cerevisiae* strain that had been engineered genetically so as to synthesize poly-β-hydroxybutyrate (PHB). For the wild-type *S. cerevisiae* model involving 60 reactions, 241 elementary modes were computed. When the four reactions required for PHB synthesis were added and glucose was excluded as a substrate, leaving succinate, glycerol, acetate, and ethanol as substrates (and also as potential products), 20 modes were obtained. Seven of these produce PHB, with different yields. Adding the normally absent ATP citrate lyase to the network, 496 elementary modes were computed. The maximum theoretical PHB/carbon yield increased from 0.67 to 0.83.

Carlson and Srienc *(25)* studied pathways of energy and biomass production in *E. coli*. The model includes 44 reactions and results in 205 energy-generating modes and 862 biomass-producing modes. The authors found four most efficient pathways for biomass production from glucose and oxygen. Interestingly, all other modes used in the system in different oxygen sufficiency conditions are linear combinations of those four modes. Mode 1 utilizes the TCA cycle and PEP carboxylase to regenerate OAA. Mode 2 does not use the TCA cycle and all OAA required for biomass production comes from PEP carboxylase. Mode 3 is similar to mode 2 except that formate lyase is used instead of the pyruvate dehydrogenase complex. Mode 4 produces biomass anaerobically. An interesting finding is that each energy-producing mode has a counterpart for biomass production. The coexistence of the energy- and biomass-generating fluxes allows one to find the most efficient way to regulate them simultaneously. Five knockout mutations were predicted to generate a strain that supports growth using only the most efficient reaction sequence.

The concept of extreme pathways, which is related to that of elementary modes, has been applied to relatively large sections of metabolism. As shown by Klamt and Stelling *(61)*, the extreme pathways are identical to the elementary modes if all reactions connecting to external metabolites are irreversible. This is the case, for example, for the substrates and products of interest in the networks analyzed by Schilling and Palsson *(66)*, Papin et al. *(67)*, and Price et al. *(68)*. Schilling and Palsson *(66)* considered a network of 461 metabolic reactions of *Haemophilus influenzae*. The system was then dissected heuristically into biologically relevant subsystems (e.g., amino acid metabolism) and the extreme pathways were computed separately for each subsystem. The largest subnetwork (transport and energy/redox metabolism) includes 210 extreme pathways. For the same network, Papin et al. *(67)* used a different method for coping with the problem of combinatorial explosion. Rather than decomposing the reaction scheme, they studied the synthesis of each proteinogenic amino acid consecutively. A similar study was carried out for *Helicobacter pylori*, leading to the result that this bacterium has a lower pathway redundancy than *H. influenzae (68)*.

Vo et al. *(69)* have presented a reconstruction of human mitochondrial metabolism. Constraint-based analysis was used to determine optimal steady-state flux distributions. These distributions were calculated individually for three metabolic functions—ATP, heme, and phospholipid synthesis. The model includes 189 reactions and 230 metabolites, and incorporates the latest proteomic data. Vo et al. *(69)* determined the capabilities of the network and found that the overall ATP yield is 31.5 M per mole of glucose. The network turned out to have high flexibility for the biosynthesis of heme and phospholipids but modest flexibility for the maximal ATP production. A subset of all the optimal flux distributions, computed for three metabolic functions, is highly correlated suggesting that this set may contain physiologically meaningful pathways.

5.2. Functional Genomics

MPA is instrumental also in functional genomics *(3,5)*. To assign functions to ORFs for which sequence similarity search or other gene-based methods have not yet produced reliable results, it is promising to study the potential gene products in their functional context, for example, in the framework of metabolic pathways. In the reconstruction of metabolic networks, there are many gaps resulting from orphan genes. MPA can be used to check hypotheses about potential enzymes to fill these gaps *(14)*. However, pathway analysis cannot provide a unique answer because there are usually several candidate enzymes, which may use different cofactors. For example, both pyruvate kinase (Pyk) and phosphoenolpyruvate synthetase (Pps) interconvert pyruvate and phosphoenolpyruvate. Whereas Pyk depends on ATP and ADP, Pps converts ATP into AMP. Here, it would be useful to combine pathway analysis with metabolomics *(3)*.

A promising approach to the problem of the identification of putative enzymes *(70)* is to use MPA in conjunction with genome context analysis *(65,71)*. Elementary-mode analysis reveals gaps in the metabolic network and genomic context methods give plausible gene candidates, which can be associated with missing enzyme activities. The analysis of the genomic data (gene neighborhood, co-occurrence, fusion, and others) can find associations between genes that are closely related to the functional role of the corresponding proteins in cell processes *(65)*. The search for missing genes in metabolic pathways using genome context analysis methods was extensively reviewed by Osterman and Overbeek *(72)*. For example, genes of enzymes from the same pathway will be close to each other in the association network and a relation of an unannotated gene to such a cluster indicates with high probability that this gene encodes a protein taking part in a pathway, as an enzyme, regulatory factor, or the like. The combination of these two techniques was applied to the nucleotide metabolism of *Mycoplasma pneumoniae (70)*. The authors have found gaps in the pathways and suggested four enzymes necessary to fill them. The genomic context pointed out a few genes that can code some of the absent activities.

5.3. Decomposition of Networks

The number of elementary modes (or extreme pathways) can increase enormously when various substrates are available and various products can be synthesized. For instance, a model of central metabolism in *E. coli (34)* involving 89 internal metabolites and 110 reactions gives rise to 507,632 elementary modes when four substrates and five products are simultaneously taken into account.

These examples show that the number of pathways increases with increasing system size in such a way that the analysis of an entire micro-organism is hindered by the problem of combinatorial explosion. In large networks, "partial pathways" can combine to larger pathways in multiple ways. The worst case is that the number of pathways increases exponentially with the number of reactions *(6)*. Moreover, the weighting coefficients of the enzymes in the elementary modes can be very high owing to repeated multiplication of stoichiometric coefficients. Thus, sometimes computational problems resulting from memory overflow or integer precision overflow occur. As stoichiometric coefficients are integers in most cases (with some exceptions such as production of biomass and oxidative phosphorylation), it is reasonable to use integer variables in the program because otherwise, rounding problems may occur that may lead to nonelementary modes. Note that for testing the nondecomposibility of elementary modes it is crucial do distinguish zero from nonzero fluxes. The program METATOOL comes in two variants: the integer and the double-real version (*see* http://pinguin.biologie.uni-jena.de/bioinformatik/networks). The first avoids any rounding errors whereas the second can deal with larger systems as well as with floating-point coefficients, which occur, for example, in pseudo-reactions, which are used to represent cell growth. In recent implementations of METATOOL, the rank criterion is used in the test for nondecomposability (*see* **Subheading 2.4.**) because it significantly improves the performance in systems with a large number of elementary modes.

Even if computation of a huge number of elementary modes is feasible, the problem of how to interpret them arises. This problem is not a fault of MPA itself; it rather reflects the high flexibility of metabolic networks. A possible strategy is to extract, by computer, selected pathways of special interest. For example, one may be interested in all pathways producing a specific product or having the maximum yield or a certain length. Another option is to decompose large networks into smaller subsystems. In fact, biochemists usually discern distinct "metabolisms" such as lipid metabolism and nucleotide metabolism. As previously mentioned, heuristic biological criteria have been used to delimit suitable subnetworks *(45,66)*.

To avoid any bias in the decomposition, we have proposed an algorithmic method based on network topology *(2)*. Clearly, the number of elementary methods depends on the classification of external and internal metabolites. This dependence is not, however, straightforward. Changing the status of a given substance from internal to external may decrease or increase the number of pathways *(2)*. It is often reasonable to consider particular internal metabolites located at branch points operationally as external, because they are "articulation points" between subpathways. If this is done appropriately, the system disintegrates into subnetworks. A possible criterion for choosing these branch points is to select those metabolites that participate in a number of reactions greater than threshold. They can be considered to be buffered because they participate in many reactions. We found that an appropriate value for the threshold is four. Applying this method, which is supported by the theory of scale-free networks *(15)*, to a reaction scheme of the metabolism of *M. pneumoniae* and cancelling all subsystems that only involve external metabolites, 19 subsystems are derived *(2)*. Each of these involves less than 20 elementary modes. Interestingly, these subnetworks constitute coherent biochemical units, most of which are in agreement with biochemical practice, such as nucleotide metabolism, arginine degradation, and the tetrahydrofolate system. A more sophisticated procedure would consider the incoming and outgoing irreversible reactions for each metabolite separately. For example, two metabolites both participating in five reactions would be treated differently if one metabolite is produced by four irreversible reactions and consumed by one (then it would be considered internal because $4 + 1 > 4 * 1$) and the other metabolite is produced by three irreversible reactions and consumed by two (then it would be considered external because $3 + 2 < 3 * 2$).

The procedure of classifying metabolites as external and internal can be automated in such a way that the minimal number of elementary modes is produced *(73)*. That method is based on the idea that it is meaningful to find the simplest description of the system. As this combinatorial minimization problem is very complex, Dandekar et al. *(73)* chose the Metropolis algorithm. Other options would be, for instance, simulated annealing, evolutionary optimization, or other stochastic strategies. The method of finding the minimal number of elementary modes was illustrated by a system representing glutathione metabolism involving 79 metabolites and 59 reactions *(73)*.

6. Concluding Remarks

MPA is a framework of tools within the field of metabolic modeling. It is instrumental in finding biochemically meaningful pathways in large and complex metabolic networks. This approach does not require any kinetic parameters of the reactions involved in the system of interest, which significantly simplifies the modeling procedure. It needs only stoichiometric coefficients (molecularities) and information about reversibility of reactions. These data are usually available. The method has a wide range of application in biology, especially in bioengineering. A major advantage of MPA is that it is relatively easy to use and implement on the computer. A limitation is that MPA only allows conclusions on steady states of the reaction system and is not capable of predicting the system behavior in time or under gradually changing environmental conditions. The term "steady state" can, however, be interpreted in the widest sense. For example, MPA can even be applied when the metabolic system exhibits stationary self-sustained oscillations because the time average of fluxes then fulfils a balance condition as well.

MPA allows one to draw interesting and far-reaching conclusions with a very limited amount of input information. For example, because MPA allows one to determine the substrate requirements for the synthesis of desired products, optimization of growth media for micro-organisms is a promising field of application. Moreover, MPA allows one to find essential reactions, essential reaction pairs (synthetic lethal genes), and so on. Essential reactions can be considered to be bottlenecks of the system—all the flow toward a product of interest goes through these. A theoretically sound procedure for analyzing this was introduced by defining the concept of minimal cut sets (MCSs) *(74)*. MCSs can be considered as the smallest sets of reactions the deletion of which prevent a given output reaction from processing. A very similar definition exists for fault trees studied in reliability and risk assessment of industrial systems *(75)*. For example, "lys" is an MCS of size one in the system of lysine production (**Fig. 2**), whereas "upt" and "ace" make up an MCS of size two. (This example is used here for didactic purposes; normally, one would determine MCSs at the level of individual enzyme reactions rather than condensed reactions.) There are manifold possible applications for MCSs including target identification in metabolic engineering and drug discovery, network verification, structural fragility analysis, and so on. The computational algorithm operates on the elementary modes of the system. The algorithm has been implemented in the program FluxAnalyzer *(52)*.

Elementary modes represent potential capabilities of the system; whether they are realized cannot be decided by pathway analysis alone, it depends on the regulatory properties. A first attempt to include such properties by Boolean logic rules was made by Covert and Palsson *(76)*. The values of kinetic parameters become more and more available. This information is, in a sense, wasted in MPA. It is desirable to develop methods allowing inclusion of the available kinetic information, for instance, about enzyme regulation.

There is growing interest in applying MPA to signal transduction networks or combined systems including both signaling and metabolic processes. For signaling systems subject to mass balance, pathway analysis can be adapted relatively easily *(77)*. However, there are important differences between metabolism and most signal transduction systems. Although there is a conversion of substrates into products in metabolism and, hence, mass flow, signals are usually transferred without a mass flow from the starting point to the target. Some signaling pathways are well described in terms of chemical reactions like the B-cell antigen receptor signaling cascade *(78)*. The extreme pathway approach has been applied for the modeling of the JAK-STAT signaling network in the human B-cell *(79)*. A good example of signal transduction without mass transfer along a pathway is a change of catalytic properties of enzymes by their modification (phosphorylation, methylation, and so on). One mitogen-activated protein kinase (MAPK) molecule can catalyze the phosphorylation of several MAP molecules without being consumed at all (cf. **ref. 80**). When computing the elementary modes, one would obtain cyclic modes for each kinase/phosphatase cycle. This would be a trivial result not telling us anything about the flow of information. Another distinguishing feature is the temporal aspect. Metabolic systems often subsist in steady state, whereas signaling systems can be inherently dynamic or switch from one steady state to another. In the latter case, the amplification in signal transduction, which is in a sense incompatible with mass conservation, could be quantified by methods of metabolic control analysis *(81)*. Because of the previously mentioned arguments, mass balance at steady-state conditions (**Eq. 2**) is not normally applicable to signal transduction. Therefore, we cannot directly apply the elementary-mode approach for computing pathways in signal networks without mass transfer.

MPA is very helpful in determining maximal molar yields (*see* **Subheading 3.**). This feature has been used in manifold applications *(4,26,27,32,82)*. However, maximum yield is not the only criterion; synthesis rates are of course important as well, both in biological evolution and in biotechnological setups. For example, *S. cerevisiae* uses the respirofermentative pathways rather than pure respiration if sufficient glucose is available even under aerobic conditions. This is probably owing to the higher rate, which allows *S. cerevisiae* to outcompete other micro-organisms *(83)*. It is a limitation of pathway analysis proper that it does not deal with reaction rates. A combination with other approaches is desirable. First attempts have been made at combining pathway analysis with metabolic flux analysis *(52,84,85)* and with linear programming *(86)*. Another possible extension is to include maximal activities of enzymes owing to saturation.

Maximal conversion yields are frequently computed by linear programming *(56–59)*. This provides the best situation and has the advantage that computation time is relatively fast. As outlined in **Subheading 3.**, an advantage of elementary-mode analysis is that a more comprehensive picture of the system is provided because all extreme situations are obtained. From this, the best solutions with respect to different substrate–product pairs can be selected. Moreover, also the second-best, third-best solution, and so on can be selected, which might be easier to realize in the biotechnological setup. Furthermore, knockouts can be simulated more easily. One only needs to check which elementary mode involves the deleted enzymes (these modes then need to be deleted as well). In linear programming, a new simulation run is needed for each knockout.

A general result of applications of pathway analysis to metabolic systems is that the systems show significant redundancy, that is, end products can be synthesized in many different ways *(18,31,33,34,67,68)*. Redundancy makes living cells robust to perturbations, e.g., mutations. The number of elementary modes can be taken as a rough measure of metabolic richness *(7,26)* and structural robustness *(34)*. A more sophisticated measure of robustness (against single mutations) has been proposed by comparing the numbers of elementary modes in the intact and mutated systems *(33)*.

Acknowledgments

We would like to thank Drs. David Fell (Oxford), Steffen Klamt (Magdeburg), and Eric von Lieres (Jülich) for stimulating discussions.

References

1. Dandekar, T., Schuster, S., Snel, B., Huynen, M., and Bork, P. (1999) Pathway alignment: application to the comparative analysis of glycolytic enzymes. *Biochem. J.* **343**, 115–124.
2. Schuster, S., Pfeiffer, T., Moldenhauer, F., Koch, I., and Dandekar, T. (2002) Exploring the pathway structure of metabolism: decomposition into subnetworks and application to *Mycoplasma pneumoniae*. *Bioinformatics* **18**, 351–361.
3. Förster, J., Gombert, A. K., and Nielsen, J. (2002) A functional genomics approach using metabolomics and *in silico* pathway analysis. *Biotechnol. Bioeng.* **79**, 703–712.
4. Van Dien, S. J. and Lidstrom, M. E. (2002) Stoichiometric model for evaluating the metabolic capabilities of the facultative methylotroph *Methylobacterium extorquens* AM1, with application to reconstruction of C_3 and C_4 metabolism. *Biotechnol. Bioeng.* **78**, 296–312.
5. Romero, P., Wagg, J., Green, M. L., Kaiser, D., Krummenacker, M., and Karp, P. D. (2005) Computational prediction of human metabolic pathways from the complete human genome. *Genome Biol.* **6**, R2.1–R2.17.
6. Mavrovouniotis, M. L., Stephanopoulos, G., and Stephanopoulos, G. (1990) Computer-aided synthesis of biochemical pathways. *Biotechnol. Bioeng.* **36**, 1119–1132.
7. Schuster, S. and Hilgetag, C. (1994) On elementary flux modes in biochemical reaction systems at steady state. *J. Biol. Syst.* **2**, 165–182.
8. Alberty, R. A. (1996) Calculation of biochemical net reactions and pathways by using matrix operations. *Biophys. J.* **71**, 507–515.
9. Stephanopoulos, G. and Simpson, T. W. (1997) Flux amplification in complex metabolic networks. *Chem. Eng. Sci.* **52**, 2607–2627.
10. Seressiotis, A. and Bailey, J. E. (1988) MPS: an artificially intelligent software system for the analysis and synthesis of metabolic pathways. *Biotechnol. Bioeng.* **31**, 587–602.
11. Schilling, C. H., Letscher, D., and Palsson, B. O. (2000) Theory for the systemic definition of metabolic pathways and their use in interpreting metabolic function from a pathway-oriented perspective. *J. Theor. Biol.* **203**, 229–248.

12. Clarke, B. L. (1981) Complete set of steady states for the general stoichiometric dynamical system. *J. Chem. Phys.* **75**, 4970–4979.
13. Heinrich, R. and Schuster, S. (1996) *The Regulation of Cellular Systems,* Chapman and Hall, New York, NY.
14. Schuster, S., Dandekar, T., and Fell, D. A. (1999) Detection of elementary flux modes in biochemical networks: a promising tool for pathway analysis and metabolic engineering. *Trends Biotechnol.* **17**, 53–60.
15. Jeong, H., Tombor, B., Albert, R., Oltvai, Z. N., and Barabási, A. L. (2000) The large-scale organization of metabolic networks. *Nature* **407**, 651–654.
16. Ma, H. and Zeng, A. P. (2003) Reconstruction of metabolic networks from genome data and analysis of their global structure for various organisms. *Bioinformatics* **19**, 270–277.
17. Hofestädt, R. (1994) A petri net application to model metabolic processes. *Syst. Anal. Mod. Simul.* **16**, 113–122.
18. Küffner, R., Zimmer, R., and Lengauer, T. (2000) Pathway analysis in metabolic databases via differential metabolic display (DMD). *Bioinformatics* **16**, 825–836.
19. Zevedei-Oancea, I. and Schuster, S. (2003) Topological analysis of metabolic networks based on Petri net theory. *In Silico Biol.* **3**, 323–345.
20. Seo, H., Lee, D.-Y., Park, S., et al. (2001) Graph-theoretical identification of pathways for biochemical reactions. *Biotechnol. Lett.* **23**, 1551–1557.
21. Fell, D. A. (1992) Metabolic control analysis: a survey of its theoretical and experimental development. *Biochem. J.* **286**, 313–330.
22. Stephanopoulos, G. N., Aristidou, A. A., and Nielsen, J. (1998) *Metabolic Engineering: Principles and Methodologies,* Academic Press, San Diego, CA.
23. Wiechert, W. (2002) Modeling and simulation: tools for metabolic engineering. *J. Biotechn.* **94**, 37–63.
24. Palsson, B. O. (2004) In silico biotechnology. Era of reconstruction and interrogation. *Curr. Opin. Biotechnol.* **15**, 50–51.
25. Carlson, R. and Srienc, F. (2004) Fundamental *Escherichia coli* biochemical pathways for biomass and energy production: identification of reactions. *Biotechnol. Bioeng.* **85**, 1–19.
26. Carlson, R., Fell, D., and Srienc, F. (2002) Metabolic pathway analysis of a recombinant yeast for rational strain development. *Biotechnol. Bioeng.* **79**, 121–134.
27. Cakir, T., Kirdar, B., and Ulgen, K. O. (2004) Metabolic pathway analysis of yeast strengthens the bridge between transcriptomics and metabolic networks. *Biotechnol. Bioeng.* **86**, 251–260.
28. Poolman, M. G., Fell, D. A., and Raines, C. A. (2003) Elementary modes analysis of photosynthate metabolism in the chloroplast stroma. *Eur. J. Biochem.* **270**, 430–439.
29. Cakir, T., Tacer, C. S., and Ulgen, K. O. (2004) Metabolic pathway analysis of enzyme-deficient human red blood cells. *Biosystems* **78**, 49–67.
30. Liao, J. C., Hou, S. Y., and Chao, Y. P. (1996) Pathway analysis, engineering and physiological considerations for redirecting central metabolism. *Biotechnol. Bioeng.* **52**, 129–140.

31. Schuster, S., Dandekar, T., Mauch, K., Reuss, M., and Fell, D. (2000) Recent developments in metabolic pathway analysis and their potential implications for biotechnology and medicine. In: *Technological and Medical Implications of Metabolic Control Analysis,* (Cornish-Bowden, A. and Cárdenas, M. L., eds.), Kluwer, Dordrecht, The Netherlands, pp. 57–66.

32. Rohwer, J. M. and Botha, F. C. (2001) Analysis of sucrose accumulation in the sugar cane culm on the basis of in vitro kinetic data. *Biochem. J.* **358,** 437–445.

33. Wilhelm, T., Behre, J., and Schuster, S. (2004) Analysis of structural robustness of metabolic networks. *System Biology* **1,** 114–120.

34. Stelling, J., Klamt, S., Bettenbrock, K., Schuster, S., and Gilles, E. D. (2002) Metabolic network structure determines key aspects of functionality and regulation. *Nature* **420,** 190–193.

35. Heinrich, R., Rapoport, S. M., and Rapoport, T. A. (1977) Metabolic regulation and mathematical models. *Prog. Biophys. Mol. Biol.* **32,** 1–82.

36. Klamt, S., Schuster, S., and Gilles, E. D. (2002) Calculability analysis in underdetermined metabolic networks illustrated by a model of the central metabolism in purple nonsulfur bacteria. *Biotechnol. Bioeng.* **77,** 734–751.

37. Fell, D. A. (1990) Substrate cycles: theoretical aspects of their role in metabolism. *Comm. Theor. Biol.* **6,** 1–14.

38. Simpson, T. W., Follstad, B. D., and Stephanopoulos, G. (1999) Analysis of the pathway structure of metabolic networks. *J. Biotechnol.* **71,** 207–223.

39. Lay, D. C. (2002) *Linear Algebra and its Applications,* Addison-Wesley, Boston, MA.

40. Pfeiffer, T., Sanchez-Valdenebro, I., Nuno, J. C., Montero, F., and Schuster, S. (1999) METATOOL: for studying metabolic networks. *Bioinformatics* **15,** 251–257.

41. Schuster, S., Klamt, S., Weckwerth, W., Moldenhauer, F., and Pfeiffer, T. (2002) Use of network analysis of metabolic systems in bioengineering. *Bioprocesses Biosyst. Eng.* **24,** 363–372.

42. Anderson, B. L. and Winawer, J. (2005) Image segmentation and lightness perception. *Nature* **434,** 79–83.

43. Holter, N. S., Mitra, M., Maritan, A., Cieplak, M., Banavar, J. R., and Fedoroff, N. V. (2000) Fundamental patterns underlying gene expression profiles: simplicity from complexity. *Proc. Natl. Acad. Sci. USA* **97,** 8409–8414.

44. Liebermeister, W. (2002) Linear modes of gene expression determined by independent component analysis. *Bioinformatics* **18,** 51–60.

45. Schuster, S., Fell, D. A., and Dandekar, T. (2000) A general definition of metabolic pathways useful for systematic organization and analysis of complex metabolic networks. *Nat. Biotechnol.* **18,** 326–332.

46. Schuster, S., Hilgetag, C., Woods, J. H., and Fell, D. A. (2002) Reaction routes in biochemical reaction systems: algebraic properties, validated calculation procedure and example from nucleotide metabolism. *J. Math. Biol.* **45,** 153–181.

47. Nussey, S. and Whitehead, S. (2001) *Endocrinology. An Integrated Approach,* BIOS Scientific Publishers Ltd, Oxford, UK.

48. Fischer, E. and Sauer, U. (2003) A novel metabolic cycle catalyzes glucose oxidation and anaplerosis in hungry *Escherichia coli. J. Biol. Chem.* **278,** 46,446–46,551.

49. Hers, H., G., and Hue, L. (1983) Gluconeogenesis and related aspects of glycolysis. *Annu. Rev. Biochem.* **52,** 617–653.
50. Nozicka, F., Guddat, J., Hollatz, H., and Bank, B. (1974) *Theorie der Linearen Parametrischen Optimierung,* Akademie-Verlag, Berlin, Germany.
51. Mendes, P. (1997) Biochemistry by numbers: simulation of biochemical pathways with Gepasi 3. *Trends Biochem. Sci.* **22,** 361–363.
52. Klamt, S., Stelling, J., Ginkel, M., and Gilles, E. D. (2003) FluxAnalyzer: exploring structure, pathways, and flux distributions in metabolic networks on interactive flux maps. *Bioinformatics* **19,** 261–269.
53. Wagner, C. (2004) Nullspace approach to determine the elementary modes of chemical reaction systems. *J. Phys. Chem. B* **108,** 2425–2431.
54. Urbanczik, R. and Wagner, C. (2005) An improved algorithm for stoichiometric network analysis: theory and applications. *Bioinformatics* **21,** 1203–1210.
55. Gagneur, J. and Klamt, S. (2004) Computation of elementary modes: a unifying framework and the new binary approach. *BMC Bioinformatics* **5,** 175.
56. Fell, D. A. and Small, J. R. (1986) Fat synthesis in adipose tissue. An examination of stoichiometric constraints. *Biochem. J.* **238,** 781–786.
57. Watson, M. R. (1986) A discrete model of bacterial metabolism. *Comput. Appl. Biosci.* **2,** 23–27.
58. Varma, A. and Palsson, B. O. (1993) Metabolic capabilities of *Escherichia coli.* I. Synthesis of biosynthetic precursors and cofactors. *J. Theor. Biol.* **165,** 477–502.
59. Edwards, J. S., Ibarra, R. U., and Palsson, B. O. (2001) In silico predictions of *Escherichia coli* metabolic capabilities are consistent with experimental data. *Nat. Biotechnol.* **19,** 125–130.
60. Mahadevan, R. and Schilling, C. H. (2003) The effects of alternate optimal solutions in constraint-based genome-scale metabolic models. *Metab. Eng.* **5,** 264–276.
61. Klamt, S. and Stelling, J. (2003) Two approaches for metabolic pathway analysis? *Trends Biotechnol.* **21,** 64–69.
62. de Graaf, A. A. (2000) Metabolic flux analysis of *Corynebacterium glutamicum.* In: *Bioreaction Engineering, Modelling and Control,* (Schügerl, K. B. and Bellgardt, K. H., eds.), Springer, New York, NY, pp. 506–555.
63. Hermann, T. (2003) Industrial production of amino acids by coryneform bacteria. *J. Biotechnol.* **104,** 155–172.
64. Schuster, S. (2004) Metabolic pathway analysis in biotechnology. In: *Metabolic Engineering in the Post Genomic Era,* (Kholodenko, B. N. and Westerhoff, H. V., eds.), Horizon Bioscience, Wymondham, UK, pp. 181–208.
65. von Mering, C., Jensen, L. J., Snel, B., et al. (2005) STRING: known and predicted protein protein associations, integrated and transferred across organisms. *Nucleic Acids Res.* **33,** D433–D437.
66. Schilling, C. H. and Palsson, B. O. (2000) Assessment of the metabolic capabilities of *Haemophilus influenzae* Rd through a genome-scale pathway analysis. *J. Theor. Biol.* **203,** 249–283.
67. Papin, J. A., Price, N. D., Edwards, J. S., and Palsson, B. O. (2002) The genome-scale metabolic extreme pathway structure in *Haemophilus influenzae* shows significant network redundancy. *J. Theor. Biol.* **215,** 67–82.

68. Price, N. D., Papin, J. A., and Palsson, B. O. (2002) Determination of redundancy and systems properties of the metabolic network of *Helicobacter pylori* using genome-scale extreme pathway analysis. *Genome Res.* **12,** 760–769.

69. Vo, T. D., Greenberg, H. J., and Palsson, B. O. (2004) Reconstruction and functional characterization of the human mitochondrial metabolic network based on proteomic and biochemical data. *J. Biol. Chem.* **279,** 39,532–39,540.

70. Pachkov, M., Dandekar, T., Korbel, J., Bork, P., and Schuster, S. (2005) Pathway analysis of *Mycoplasma pneumoniae* nucleotide metabolism. *Gene*, in press.

71. Huynen, M. A., Snel, B., von Mering, C., and Bork, P. (2003) Functional prediction and protein networks. *Curr. Opin. Cell Biol.* **15,** 191–198.

72. Osterman, A. and Overbeek, R. (2003) Missing genes in metabolic pathways: a comparative genomics approach. *Curr. Opin. Chem. Biol.* **7,** 238–251.

73. Dandekar, T., Moldenhauer, F., Bulik, S., Bertram, H., and Schuster, S. (2003) A method for classifying metabolites in topological pathway analyses based on minimization of pathway number. *BioSystems* **70,** 255–270.

74. Klamt, S. and Gilles, E. D. (2004) Minimal cut sets in biochemical reaction networks. *Bioinformatics* **20,** 226–234.

75. Fard, N. S. (1997) Determination of minimal cut sets of a complex fault tree. *Comput. Ind. Eng.* **33,** 59–62.

76. Covert, M. and Palsson, B. (2003) Constraints-based models: regulation of gene expression reduces the steady-state solution space. *J. Theor. Biol.* **221,** 309–325.

77. Papin, J. A. and Palsson, B. O. (2004) Topological analysis of mass-balanced signaling networks: a framework to obtain network properties including crosstalk. *J. Theor. Biol.* **227,** 283–297.

78. Campbell, K. S. (1999) Signal transduction from the B cell antigen-receptor. *Curr. Opin. Immunol.* **11,** 256–264.

79. Papin, J. A. and Palsson, B. O. (2004) The JAK-STAT signaling network in the human B-cell: an extreme signaling pathway analysis. *Biophys. J.* **87,** 37–46.

80. Berg, J., Tymoczko, J., and Stryer, L. (2002) *Biochemistry,* Freeman, New York, NY.

81. Schuster, S., Kholodenko, B. N., and Westerhoff, H. V. (2000) Cellular information transfer regarded from stoichiometry and control analysis perspective. *Biosystems* **55,** 73–81.

82. Carlson, R. and Srienc, F. (2004) Fundamental *Escherichia coli* biochemical pathways for biomass and energy production: creation of overall flux states. *Biotechnol. Bioeng.* **86,** 149–162.

83. Pfeiffer, T., Schuster, S., and Bonhoeffer, T. (2001) Cooperation and competition in the evolution of ATP producing pathways. *Science* **292,** 504–507.

84. Schuster, R. and Schuster, S. (1993) Refined algorithm and computer program for calculating all non-negative fluxes admissible in steady states of biochemical reaction systems with or without some flux rates fixed. *Comp. Appl. Biosci.* **9,** 79–85.

85. Poolman, M., Venkatesh, K., Pidcock, M., and Fell, D. (2004) A method for the determination of flux in elementary modes, and its application to *Lactobacillus rhamnosus*. *Biotechnol. Bioeng.* **88,** 601–612.

86. Schilling, C. H., Edwards, J. S., Letscher, D., and Palsson, B. O. (2000) Combining pathway analysis with flux balance analysis for the comprehensive study of metabolic systems. *Biotechnol. Bioeng.* **71,** 286–306.

VII

NMR Metabolome Analysis

13

Revealing the Metabolome of Animal Tissues Using ¹H Nuclear Magnetic Resonance Spectroscopy

Mark R. Viant

Summary

The measurement of tissue-specific metabolic fingerprints can be of particular interest when investigating disease processes, mechanisms of toxicity, or when knowledge of the metabolic interactions between different organs is required. This chapter presents several optimized protocols for the extraction of metabolites from animal tissues, their analysis by ¹H nuclear magnetic resonance (NMR) spectroscopy, and the subsequent spectral preprocessing required for an NMR-based metabolomics experiment. First, the three critical steps in the preparation of tissue extracts for NMR analysis are described, including both a perchloric acid protocol for the extraction of polar metabolites, and a methanol:chloroform protocol for extraction of polar and lipophilic metabolites. Then a series of NMR experiments are described including a standard one-dimensional (1D) ¹H NMR study, a 1D ¹H Carr–Purcell–Meiboom–Gill spin-echo experiment, and a two-dimensional ¹H-¹H J-resolved NMR experiment. The advantages and limitations of each experiment for metabolomics research are discussed. Analysis of the resulting NMR datasets is typically conducted in two phases comprising "low level" spectral preprocessing and "high level" multivariate analysis. NMR spectral preprocessing is a critical step that converts raw NMR spectra into an appropriate data format for multivariate analysis. A detailed protocol for preprocessing NMR data, using ProMetab software, is presented. Because a plethora of algorithms exist for multivariate analyses, which can be used to construct classification models or for biomarker discovery, this is beyond the scope of the current chapter.

Key Words: NMR; metabolomics; metabonomics; tissue extract; perchloric acid; methanol chloroform; J-resolved; p-JRES; generalized log transformation; ProMetab.

1. Introduction

To date, the majority of metabolomics studies using ¹H nuclear magnetic resonance (NMR) spectroscopy have investigated the metabolic fingerprints of

From: *Methods in Molecular Biology, vol. 358: Metabolomics: Methods and Protocols*
Edited by: W. Weckwerth © Humana Press Inc., Totowa, NJ

animal biofluids, in particular, plasma and urine *(1,2)*. Biofluids are in general easier to collect than tissue samples or biopsies, and facilitate time-course studies of changes in metabolism within individual organisms. The metabolic information obtained from a biofluid such as plasma, however, is effectively an integration of the individual metabolic changes occurring within each of the animal's organs. In order to determine organ-specific metabolic fingerprints, which are of interest when investigating certain diseases *(3,4)* or sites of toxicity *(5)*, or when the metabolic interaction between different tissues is of interest *(1,6)*, metabolomic studies of tissues become highly desirable. Furthermore, this approach is particularly useful in cases where tissue samples are readily available, such as from the operating theatre or from environmental studies. In this chapter we present several optimized methods for extracting metabolites from animal tissues, their analysis by ¹H NMR spectroscopy, and the subsequent spectral preprocessing required for an NMR-based metabolomics experiment.

The preparation of tissue extracts, described in **Subheading 3.1.**, involves three critical steps. The first step is to rapidly collect and freeze the tissue sample, so as to immediately "quench" metabolism and preserve the metabolite concentrations. Samples can then be stored at –80°C to temporarily prevent any metabolic decay *(7)*. The second step involves mechanically disrupting the tissue to allow the extraction of the low molecular weight metabolites. The goals of this process are to deproteinize the sample in order to permanently halt metabolism, and to extract only those metabolites of interest (e.g., lipids, carbohydrates, amino acids, and other small metabolites) from the tissue while leaving other compounds in the tissue pellet (e.g., DNA, RNA, proteins). Unlike mass spectrometry (MS), NMR is moderately tolerant of salt within samples and, hence, its removal is not required. The final step for preparing tissue extracts is to optimize the solution for high-resolution NMR spectroscopy. This entails resuspending the metabolite extract in an appropriate deuterated solvent buffer and adding an NMR internal standard.

The two leading analytical platforms for metabolomics are ¹H NMR spectroscopy and MS *(1,8,9)*. In **Subheading 3.2.**, we focus on ¹H NMR-based methods that have several benefits for measuring metabolic fingerprints, including: (1) global observation of all high-abundance metabolites that contain nonexchangeable hydrogen atoms in a single "all-in-one" analysis; (2) potentially quantitative metabolite measurements with a high degree of reproducibility; (3) relatively high throughput and automated analyses (>100 samples/day); (4) robust and established NMR technology with minimal instrument downtime; and (5) inexpensive on a per-sample basis. Undoubtedly the largest disadvantage of NMR spectroscopy is its relatively poor sensitivity. This limits the observation, under standard conditions, to an estimated 100 metabolites per sample. MS is a significantly more sensitive analytical tool and can directly complement the use of NMR spectroscopy in metabolomics by facilitating the analysis of less abundant metabolites *(9)*. In summary, NMR-based meta-bolomics provides an unbiased top-down (or screening) approach that can provide insight into a broad array of metabolism in a rapid and cost-effective manner.

The analysis of NMR metabolomics datasets is typically conducted in two phases. The first comprises "low level" spectral preprocessing, which is then followed by "high level" multivariate analysis. A plethora of tools exist for multivariate analyses *(10–12)* including unsupervised (e.g., principal compo-nents analysis [PCA]) and supervised (e.g., partial least squares regression [PLS]) methods. Such multivariate analyses, which can be used to construct classification models or for biomarker discovery, are best conducted using one of the many user-friendly commercial software packages that are available. In contrast, extremely few commercial packages exist for the first phase of NMR spectral preprocessing, which is a critical step for converting raw NMR spectra into an appropriate format for multivariate analysis. In fact, spectral prepro-cessing is an active research area, and new algorithms are frequently reported in the literature. As such, we have developed our own software, "ProMetab – Processing Metabolite profiles derived from NMR spectra" *(13)*, which offers great flexibility in terms of its continued development and optimization as novel algorithms are reported. **Subheading 3.3.** describes a detailed protocol for spectral preprocessing NMR metabolomics data using ProMetab (release 1.1), which is freely available from the author to the scientific community.

2. Materials

2.1. Preparation of Tissue Extracts

2.1.1. Tissue Collection and Storage

1. Liquid nitrogen and a benchtop dewar. Insulated gloves are recommended when decanting liquid nitrogen into the dewar.

2.1.2. Extraction of Polar Metabolites Using Perchloric Acid

1. Perchloric acid ($HClO_4$; Fisher Scientific, Loughborough, UK): prepare 6% solu-tion in water, store at 4°C, and place on ice during the procedure.
2. Potassium carbonate (K_2CO_3; Fisher Scientific): prepare 2 M solution, store at 4°C, and place on ice during the procedure.

2.1.3. Combined Extraction of Polar and Lipophilic Metabolites Using Methanol:Chloroform

1. Straight-sided glass vials with aluminum-lined black urea screw caps, including both "large" (height $\times$ diameter of 46 $\times$ 12.5 mm) and "small" (36 $\times$ 11 mm) ones (Fisher Scientific).

2. Methanol (HPLC grade; Fisher Scientific): store at room temperature and place on ice during the procedure.
3. Chloroform (pesticide analysis grade; Fisher Scientific): store at room temperature and place on ice during the procedure.

2.1.4. Preparation of Polar Extracts for NMR Spectroscopy

1. NMR buffer: 100 mM sodium phosphate buffer (composed of NaH_2PO_4 and Na_2HPO_4 salts; Fisher Scientific), at pH 7.4, made up in D_2O (99.9% purity; Goss Scientific Instruments, Great Baddon, UK), containing 0.5 mM sodium 3-(trimethylsilyl)proprionate-2,2,3,3-d_4 (TMSP; 98% purity; Goss Scientific Instruments) as an internal chemical shift standard. Store at room temperature in a dessicator.
2. Norell NMR tubes and caps (5-mm diameter; Goss Scientific Instruments).

2.1.5. Preparation of Lipophilic Extracts for NMR Spectroscopy

1. Deuterated NMR solvent: 2:1 mixture of chloroform-d ($CDCl_3$; 99.8% purity; Goss Scientific Instruments) and methanol-d_4 (CD_3OD; 99.8% purity; Goss Scientific Instruments), containing 0.5 mM tetramethylsilane (TMS; 99.9% purity; Goss Scientific Instruments) as an internal chemical shift standard. Store at room temperature in a dessicator.
2. Norell NMR tubes and caps (5-mm diameter; Goss Scientific Instruments).

2.2. High-Resolution ¹H NMR Spectroscopy

1. 500 or 600 MHz NMR spectrometers are typically used for metabolomics.
2. A conventional NMR probe is acceptable, although the elevated sensitivity provided by an NMR cryo- or cold-probe is a definite advantage.

2.3. Data Management: Files, Filenames, and Software Compatibility

The following files are supplied with ProMetab (Release 1.1):

1. ProMetab user manual v1.1: software manual.
2. ProMetab_v1_1.m: main data processing script.
3. PM_input_parameters.m: file containing input parameters for ProMetab.
4. PM_read_1Ddata.m: function to read in Bruker NMR spectral data.
5. PM_read_procs.m: function to read in Bruker processing parameters.

3. Methods
3.1. Preparation of Tissue Extracts

When collecting tissues, as described in **Subheading 3.1.1.**, the ideal sample size is 100–150 mg (wet mass) although the methods presented in this chapter have successfully been applied to only 20 mg tissue. Several methods can be used to mechanically disrupt tissue, the choice of which will depend on whether the tissue is "hard" and fibrous (e.g., muscle) or "soft" (e.g., liver or brain).

Here, we describe a manual grinding method with a mortar and pestle, which is ideal for both tissue types. Furthermore, several extraction methods can be used, the choice of which depends on the polarity of the metabolites that are required. In **Subheading 3.1.2.**, we describe a method for the extraction of polar metabolites only, using perchloric acid. If both polar and lipophilic metabolites are desired, then we recommend the method in **Subheading 3.1.3.**, which uses a methanol:chloroform procedure to yield two separate fractions *(14)*. Prior to NMR analysis, all polar tissue extracts are prepared as described in **Subheading 3.1.4.**, which includes the buffering of sample pH (to minimize variation in the chemical shifts of the NMR resonances), the addition of D_2O (to provide a frequency lock for the NMR spectrometer and to minimize the concentration of H_2O in the aqueous sample), and the addition of an NMR chemical shift standard. For lipophilic metabolites, **Subheading 3.1.5.** describes the final steps in the preparation, including the addition of deuterated solvents for frequency lock, and addition of a chemical shift standard.

3.1.1. Tissue Collection and Storage

1. Rapidly dissect the tissue sample (ideally 100–150 mg) and then immediately freeze it in liquid nitrogen to quench metabolism and to prevent degradation. Transfer the sample to a labeled cryovial and return to liquid nitrogen or place in dry ice (*see* **Note 1**).
2. Samples should always be maintained at –80°C (or colder) either in liquid nitrogen, dry ice, or a freezer. Long-term storage in a –80°C freezer is typically most convenient (*see* **Note 2**).

3.1.2. Extraction of Polar Metabolites Using Perchloric Acid

1. Label three Eppendorf tubes (2-mL volume) for each tissue sample (*see* **Note 3**). Weigh one set of these tubes and then cool them on dry ice.
2. Precool a porcelain mortar (ca. 60-mm diameter) and pestle by decanting liquid nitrogen into the mortar. It is sufficiently cold when liquid nitrogen pools in the bottom of the mortar.
3. Precool a stainless steel spatula and stainless steel microspoon in liquid nitrogen using a small benchtop dewar.
4. Transfer the frozen tissue (ideally 100–150 mg) to the precooled mortar and carefully crush and then grind into a fine powder (*see* **Note 4**). When grinding is completed, add a small volume of liquid nitrogen to consolidate the frozen powder in the bottom of the mortar.
5. Using the precooled metal spoon, scrape up and collect the powder, and then transfer the still frozen powder to the V-shaped grove of the precooled metal spatula. Place the end of the spatula into the neck of an Eppendorf tube (sitting in dry ice) and tap the spatula with the spoon, transferring the frozen powder rapidly into the tube.
6. Repeat the process for all the tissue samples (*see* **Note 3**).

7. Reweigh all the Eppendorf tubes to calculate the wet tissue mass of each sample, making sure to keep all samples frozen on dry ice (*see* **Note 5**).

8. Add 5 mL/g (wet weight basis) of 6% ice-cold perchloric acid to the first two samples. Vortex these for 30 s at maximum power and then place on ice. Repeat this process for all the samples in a sequential order.

9. Incubate the samples on ice for an additional 10 min.

10. Centrifuge the samples at 12,000*g* for 10 min at 4°C.

11. Transfer a known volume (e.g., 500 μL) of supernatant from the first sample to an Eppendorf tube (*see* **Note 6**). Repeat for all samples using a sequential order, and place the samples on ice.

12. Neutralize the first sample to pH 7.4 with 2 *M* K$_2$CO$_3$ using a previously established ratio, typically 210 μL K$_2$CO$_3$ per milliliter supernatant (*see* **Note 7**). Do this slowly to avoid the solution bubbling out of the tube as CO$_2$ is produced. Repeat for all samples, and place them on ice with their lids open to allow CO$_2$ to escape.

13. Vortex each sample, and then open each Eppendorf lid to further release CO$_2$. Incubate on ice for 30 min to precipitate the potassium perchlorate salt (*see* **Note 8**).

14. Check that the pH of each sample is 7.4 (±0.2). This can conveniently be achieved by spotting 1–2 μL of solution onto pH paper (with pH range of 6.0 to 8.0). In the unlikely case that the sample pH is abnormal, adjust using small volumes of perchloric acid or K$_2$CO$_3$.

15. Centrifuge the samples at 12,000*g* for 10 min at 4°C.

16. Transfer a known volume (e.g., 500 μL) of supernatant to an Eppendorf tube and freeze in dry ice. Repeat for all samples.

17. Freeze-dry the tissue extracts overnight and then store at −80°C until required.

3.1.3. Combined Extraction of Polar and Lipophilic Metabolites Using Methanol:Chloroform

1. Label three glass vials (two small and one large) for each tissue sample. Weigh the large vials and then cool on dry ice.

2. Follow the same procedure as in **Subheading 3.1.2.**, **steps 2–7**, for grinding and weighing the frozen tissue samples, except collect the powdered samples in the large glass vials.

3. Add 4 mL/g (wet weight basis) methanol and 0.85 mL/g deionized water to the first frozen sample and vortex for 60 s.

4. Add 2 mL/g chloroform to the sample, vortex for an additional 60 s, and then place on ice. Repeat this process for all the samples.

5. Mix all the samples, on ice, using an orbital shaker at 300 rpm for 10 min. All solutions will be monophasic (*see* **Note 9**).

6. Add 2 mL/g chloroform and 2 mL/g deionized water to each sample (*see* **Notes 9 and 10**) and vortex for 60 s.

7. Centrifuge the samples at 1000*g* for 15 min at 4°C. The solutions will separate into an upper methanol:water phase (with polar metabolites) and a lower chloroform phase (with lipophilic compounds), separated by protein debris.

8. Using two glass Pasteur pipets or Hamilton syringes, transfer the upper and then lower layers of each sample into separate small glass vials (*see* **Note 11**).
9. Remove the solvents from all samples using a speed vacuum concentrator and then store at –80°C until required.

3.1.4. Preparation of Polar Extracts for NMR Spectroscopy

1. Resuspend the polar tissue extracts (either from the perchloric acid extraction or the dried methanol phase from the methanol:chloroform extraction) in 550 μL NMR buffer, and vortex for 10 s (*see* **Note 12**).
2. Centrifuge at 12,000*g* for 5 min at room temperature.
3. Transfer 520 μL into each labeled NMR tube.

3.1.5. Preparation of Lipophilic Extracts for NMR Spectroscopy

1. Resuspend the lipophilic tissue extracts (from the dried chloroform phase from the methanol:chloroform extraction) in 550 μL deuterated NMR solvent, and vortex for 10 s.
2. Centrifuge at 1000*g* for 5 min at room temperature.
3. Transfer 520 μL into each labeled NMR tube.

3.2. High-Resolution ^{1}H NMR Spectroscopy

NMR spectrometers are specialized analytical instruments and, hence, their operation requires some training. The methods described in this section assume a basic working knowledge of NMR spectroscopy. Although a number of companies supply NMR systems, including Bruker BioSpin, JEOL, and Varian, the methods described next have been optimized using Bruker spectrometers (for which the author has the most experience). These methods, however, are directly applicable to other NMR systems. **Subheading 3.2.** describes the general optimization required for a sample (*see* **Note 13**). **Subheadings 3.2.1.–3.2.3.** describe specific one-dimensional (1D) and two-dimensional (2D) NMR experiments for metabolomics including the advantages and limitations of each particular approach. Because NMR is nondestructive, immediately following analysis the samples can be returned to a –80°C freezer, or analyzed by an alternative method.

1. Load the NMR tube into the spectrometer.
2. Set the sample temperature to 295 K and allow the solution a few minutes to thermally equilibrate within the spectrometer (*see* **Note 13**).
3. Tune and match the NMR probe.
4. Lock the spectrometer frequency to the deuterium resonance arising from the NMR solvent (either D_2O or $CDCl_3$).
5. Shim the sample using either manual or automated methods (*see* **Note 14**).
6. Determine the pulse duration for a 360° tip angle of the residual water resonance, from which 60° and 90° tip angles can easily be calculated.

7. Determine the frequency of the water resonance and set the center of the spectrum to this frequency.

3.2.1. Standard 1D ¹H NMR Experiment

The 1D ¹H NMR with water presaturation is a standard pulse sequence used in the NMR metabolomics approach *(4)*. The primary advantages include a rapid and relatively sensitive acquisition of a metabolic fingerprint in typically 3–10 min per 100 mg sample, although samples of only 20 mg can be analyzed. The spectrum produced will often, however, be composed of highly overlapping peaks and the baseline may contain several broad resonances from high molecular weight compounds.

1. Acquisition parameters: pulse sequence comprising [relaxation delay–60°–acquire], where the pulse power is set to achieve a 60° tip angle; 7 kHz spectral width; water presaturation applied during 2.5-s relaxation delay; typically 40–160 transients are collected into 32k data points.
2. Processing parameters: zero-fill to 64k data points, apply exponential line broadening of 0.5 Hz, apply Fourier transformation, manually phase spectrum (zero and first order corrections), manually correct the baseline using a polynomial function, and calibrate the spectrum by setting TMSP or TMS peak to 0.0 ppm.
3. Record and process the spectrum as in **steps 1** and **2**. *See* example spectrum in **Fig. 1**.

3.2.2. 1D ¹H CPMG Spin-Echo NMR Experiment

The 1D ¹H Carr–Purcell–Meiboom–Gill (CPMG) spin-echo NMR sequence with water presaturation enables T_2-spectral editing *(4)*. This removes the broad resonances associated with high molecular weight macromolecules and motionally constrained compounds, facilitating observation of just the free, low molecular weight metabolites. The acquisition time is slightly longer than for the standard 1D NMR sequence (**Subheading 3.2.1.**), and the spectrum will often be composed of highly overlapping peaks.

1. Acquisition parameters: pulse sequence comprising (relaxation delay–90°–[τ–180°–τ]$_n$–acquire), where τ is the spin-echo delay (set the total spin–spin relaxation delay $2\tau n = 80$ ms) and n represents the number of loops (set $n = 100$); 7 kHz spectral width; water presaturation applied during 3.5-s relaxation delay; typically 40–160 transients are collected into 32k data points.
2. Processing parameters: as for 1D **Subheading 3.2.1.**, **step 2**.
3. Record and process the spectrum as in **steps 1** and **2**.

3.2.3. 2D ¹H-¹H J-Resolved NMR Experiment

The 2D ¹H-¹H J-resolved (JRES) NMR sequence with water presaturation can be used to generate a considerably less congested metabolic fingerprint, which is effectively a "proton broad-band decoupled" 1D ¹H NMR spectrum

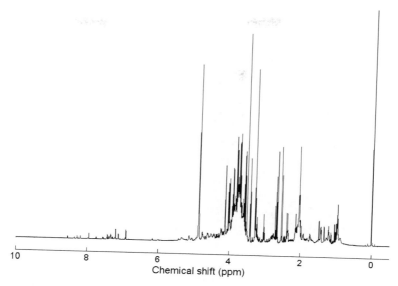

Fig. 1. Representative one-dimensional ¹H nuclear magnetic resonance spectrum of the polar metabolites from a perchloric acid extraction of medaka (*Oryzias latipes*) eggs. Note the intense sodium 3-(trimethylsilyl)proprionate-2,2,3,3-d_4 chemical shift standard at 0 ppm, the residual water resonance near 4.7 ppm, and the region of significantly overlapping peaks between 3 and 4.5 ppm.

(termed p-JRES) *(13)*. This is achieved by projecting the JRES spectrum, which itself is composed of chemical shift (F2) and spin–spin coupling (F1) axes, along the F1 axis as shown in **Fig. 2**. The reduced spectral congestion in the p-JRES spectrum increases the likelihood that a specific metabolite will appear as a well-resolved and identifiable peak, thereby maximizing the extraction of metabolic information from each spectrum. In addition, the p-JRES spectrum has a flat baseline and provides spin–spin coupling data that can aid metabolite identification. This approach is therefore the preferred method for NMR metabolomics *(13)*. However, it requires longer acquisition times of typically 10–20 min per 100 mg tissue sample, and cannot readily be used if considerably less tissue is available.

1. Acquisition parameters: pulse sequence comprising (relaxation delay–90°–[t_1/2]–180°–[t_1/2]–acquire), where t_1 is an incremented time delay; 7 kHz spectral width in F2 (chemical shift axis) and 50 Hz in F1 (spin–spin coupling constant axis); water presaturation applied during 3.5-s relaxation delay; typically eight transients per increment for 32 increments in total are collected into 8k data points.

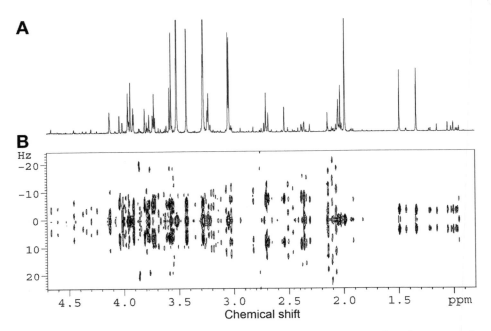

Fig. 2. Contour plot representation of a two-dimensional J-resolved nuclear magnetic resonance spectrum of the polar metabolites from a perchloric acid extraction of fish eggs, shown in (**B**), and immediately above is a skyline projection of the J-resolved spectrum yielding a one-dimensional p-JRES dataset (**A**).

2. Processing parameters: zero-fill to 128 points in F1; multiply both F1 and F2 dimensions by sine-bell window functions; apply Fourier transformation; tilt the spectrum by 45°; symmetrize; calibrate the spectrum by setting TMSP or TMS peak to 0.0 ppm.
3. Record and process the spectrum in **steps 1** and **2**. *See* example spectrum in **Fig. 2B**.
4. Calculate the 1D skyline projection of the 2D spectrum (**Fig. 2A**).

3.3. NMR Spectral Preprocessing

ProMetab software *(13)* is a metabolomics data processing tool that converts raw Bruker NMR spectra into a format for multivariate analysis. It is written in MATLAB™ (The MathWorks, Inc., Natick, MA), which provides a technical computing environment for high-performance numeric computation and visualization. Both 1D NMR spectra and projections of 2D JRES NMR spectra are compatible with ProMetab, which first segments the spectra into chemical shift bins of a user-defined width. Following removal of unwanted spectral features, such as the residual water resonance, specific groups of bins can be compressed into single segments to minimize the effects of pH-induced shifting of the NMR peaks. Various normalization strategies are available, as is the generalized log transformation *(15)*. Finally, multivariate analyses of the preprocessed data can be performed using a commercial software package, for example, to construct classification models or for biomarker discovery. Multivariate analyses are beyond the scope of the current chapter, but interested readers are advised to consult **refs. *11*** and ***12***.

3.3.1. Data Management: Files, Filenames, and Software Compatibility

1. After obtaining the ProMetab software (release 1.1) from the author, copy all the files to the MATLAB working directory. If a new working directory is created then point MATLAB to this location using the *File → Set Path* option.
2. Copy all the NMR spectra that require preprocessing to the MATLAB working directory, retaining the same file and directory structure as created by the Bruker XWINNMR software (*see* **Notes 15** and **16**).
3. Edit the M-file called *PM_input_parameters.m*, which contains many of the input parameters for ProMetab, from within the MATLAB command window by typing:

```
edit pm_input_parameters
```

(*See* **Note 17**.)

3.3.2. The Execution of ProMetab NMR Spectral Preprocessing Software

1. Run the ProMetab software from the MATLAB command window by typing:

```
Prometab_v1_1
```

2. Answer the following questions concerning the NMR spectra data files:

```
Process 1D or 2D spectra? [default = 1]:
Enter filename of NMR data:
How many spectra require processing?
Enter file number of first file [default = 1]:
```

The "**1D**" option is for spectra collected using **Subheadings 3.2.1.** and **3.2.2.**, and the "**2D**" option is for projections of the 2D JRES spectra collected using **Subheading 3.2.3.**

3. Answer the following questions concerning various "binning" options for the NMR spectra:

```
Enter start of binning [default = 10.0 ppm]:
Enter end of binning [default = 0.2 ppm]:
Enter bin stepsize [default = 0.005 ppm]:
```

4. Wait as ProMetab reads in the Bruker XWINNMR NMR spectra, which prints:

```
Reading Bruker file n
```

for each file *n*.

5. Reply to the prompt to print the raw un-normalized NMR data:

```
Display raw un-normalized 1D spectra (yes=1)? [default = no]::
```

The default option is "**no**" because viewing un-normalized data is often unnecessary.

6. If bin compression was requested in file *PM_input_parameters.m*, then the following message appears:

    `Compressing bins now...`

7. Answer the following question concerning normalization of the NMR spectra:

    `Enter normalization procedure?`
    `(1) TSA, (2) TMSP, (3) TMSP w/ sample scaling, (4) none [default = 1]:`

    These options include normalizing each spectrum to: (1) the total spectral area (TSA) of that binned spectrum, effectively yielding a total area of one; (2) the peak area of the TMSP chemical shift standard; (3) the area of the TMSP standard, and in additional multiplying by a unique sample scaling factor listed in file *P M_input_parameters.m*; and (4) apply no normalization. The results of the normalization will then be displayed as, for example:

Original TSA	TMSP area	Normalized TSA
3.4187e+010	2.1778e+009	1.0000e+003
3.1399e+010	2.0825e+009	1.0000e+003
3.0522e+010	2.1590e+009	1.0000e+003

    and others.

8. Reply to the prompts to print the raw normalized and the binned normalized NMR data:

    `Display raw normalized 1D spectra (yes=1)? [default = yes]:`
    `Display binned normalized 1D spectra (yes=1)? [default = yes]:`

    See an example binned normalized spectrum in **Fig. 3A**.

9. Answer the following question concerning transformation of the NMR spectra (if you select the generalized log transformation *[15]* then the transformation parameter, λ, is echoed to the screen; *see* **Note 18**):

    `Enter transformation procedure (1) generalized log, (2) none [default = 1]:`
    `lambda = 0.2`

10. Reply to the prompts to print the generalized log transformed, binned, normalized NMR data, and also to plot the relationship between the bin number (reordered according to the ranked means of the binned data) and standard deviation of the pre- and post-transformed data (which facilitates the optimization of λ):

    `Display transformed binned 1D spectra (yes=1)? [default = yes]:`
    `Display bin vs SD of pre- and post-transformed data (yes=1)? [default = no]:`

    The default option for the second plot is "**no**" because it is generally unnecessary to view this relationship. *See* an example generalized log transformed spectrum in **Fig. 3B**.

3.3.3. Multivariate Data Analysis

1. The preprocessed NMR data will now exist in the form of a matrix of size $r \times c$, comprising r samples (one per row) and c chemical shift "bins" (one per column), in a convenient format for multivariate analysis. This matrix is called

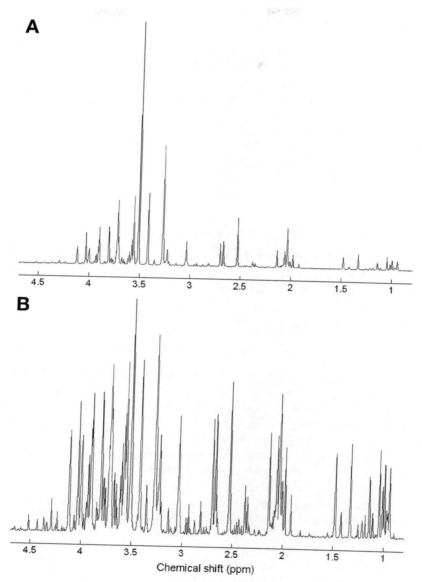

Fig. 3. (**A**) Representative binned, one-dimensional projection of a-¹H-¹H J-resolved nuclear magnetic resonance spectrum of the extracts of medaka eggs. (**B**) The same dataset as above after applying the generalized log transformation. The most striking beneficial effects of the transformation include an increased weighting of the less intense peaks.

spec_array_glognbin, for the generalized log transformed data, and *spec_array_nbin*, for untransformed data. Two options now exist for multivariate data analysis.

2. The most convenient strategy for multivariate analysis is to do this within MATLAB, for example using the *PLS_Toolbox* (Eigenvector Research). This software package contains many chemometric routines, including PCA (*see* **Note 19**) and PLS. Follow the instruction manuals provided with the *PLS_Toolbox* software.

3. Multivariate analysis of the preprocessed NMR data can alternatively be conducted outside of the MATLAB environment, following export of the data in ASCII format. To save the log-transformed, binned, normalized NMR data to the MATLAB working directory, type the following in the MATLAB Command Window:

`save <filename> spec_array_glognbin -ascii`

To save the data without log-transformation, type:

`save <filename> spec_array_nbin -ascii`

Then import and process this data in an alternative statistical analysis software package, following their instructions.

4. Finally, save the MATLAB workspace, including all the data matrices, using the *File → Save Workspace As...* option.

4. Notes

1. When dissecting many samples it is fastest to place the dissected tissue directly in a cryovial and then freeze that vial immediately in liquid nitrogen.

2. Samples can be stored for many months. For example, plasma samples that were snap-frozen and then maintained at $-80°C$ showed no significant metabolic changes after storage for up to 9 mo *(7)*.

3. To facilitate high-throughput analyses, several tissues can be prepared at the same time. It is recommended that the number of samples prepared is dictated by the size of the centrifuge rotor, often 18 samples per batch.

4. To avoid tissue fragments being lost during the initial crushing, a small plastic bag can be slotted over the handle of the pestle to serve as a "lid" for the mortar. Grinding should last 15–30 s per sample, depending on the nature of the tissue, with fibrous muscle tissue requiring the most time. It is imperative that the tissue is kept frozen at all times. Should the sample begin to thaw and exhibit a "wet" appearance, immediately add more liquid nitrogen to the mortar.

5. A small amount of condensation will form during the grinding process that can artificially elevate the sample mass. For highly accurate quantitative measurements it is suggested that the ground samples are freeze-dried prior to weighing to eliminate this potential source of error.

6. Ideally, the same volume of supernatant is removed from every sample as this will facilitate subsequent steps and improve the consistency of the extraction.

This often necessitates discarding excess supernatant from several samples. However, should a few samples contain significantly smaller supernatant volumes compared with the other samples, then remove as much supernatant as possible from those and record the volume transferred.

7. The ratio of 210 μL K_2CO_3 per milliliter supernatant was determined empirically by repeatedly adding small volumes of K_2CO_3 to the supernatant and checking the pH after each addition. It is recommended that this ratio is used as a guide, and that this step is optimized for each new tissue type and when using new solutions of acids and bases.

8. It is important to neutralize the perchloric acid using K_2CO_3 because the product, potassium perchlorate, is relatively insoluble in cold aqueous solution and, therefore, precipitates. Sodium perchlorate, however, is considerably more soluble and so would leave a higher concentration of residual salt in solution, which can be detrimental for NMR spectroscopy.

9. Bligh and Dyer *(16)* determined that the volumes of solutions should have the following ratios: monophasic solution for metabolite extraction, 2:1:0.8 methanol:chloroform:water, and the biphasic solution for separating the fractions, 2:2:1.8 methanol:chloroform:water. The total volume of water includes both the water already present in the tissue plus the added deionized water.

10. To better partition the polar (phospho)lipids into the chloroform layer, the polarity of the methanol phase can be increased by replacing the water with 0.8% KCl aqueous solution.

11. All sample handling and storage must be conducted in glass because chloroform can leach compounds from plastic tubes and pipet tips, which can contaminate the NMR spectra.

12. For the extracts derived from the methanol:chloroform extraction, only after vortexing transfer the sample from the glass vial to an Eppendorf tube.

13. Ideally, within a particular metabolomics study, all the samples should be consistent in terms of the approximate amounts of tissue extracted, the extraction method, the NMR buffer, and the volume of solution in the NMR tube. In this case, minimal optimization of each sample in the NMR spectrometer is required. Specifically, only **steps 1, 2, 4**, and **5** in **Subheading 3.2.** are required, and the quality of optimization can be checked using the criteria in **Note 14**.

14. The quality of shimming, as measured using the full-width at half-maximum of the TMSP or TMS peak, should be less than 2.5 Hz (prior to any line broadening induced by apodization).

15. ProMetab (release 1.1) *(13)* is only compatible with NMR spectra recorded on a Bruker spectrometer using Bruker XWINNMR software (or be in the same format as used by XWINNMR software). ProMetab is compatible with data collected on both UNIX and Windows systems.

16. All NMR spectra to be analyzed must have the same file name and must be numbered sequentially, although this numbering can start at any value.

17. Once optimized, many of the input parameters for ProMetab remain fixed for a given analysis. To avoid re-entering these parameters for each analysis, they

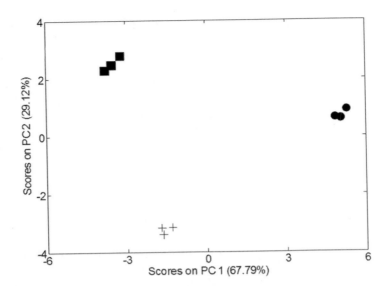

Fig. 4. Scores plot from a principal components analysis of one-dimensional ¹H nuclear magnetic resonance spectra. Polar metabolites were extracted from one liver tissue using three different methods, perchloric acid (■), methanol:chloroform (+), and acetonitrile:water (●), each in triplicate. The clustering of the three replicates in each method confirms the reproducibilities of these methods. In addition, different methods clearly extract different types of metabolites, with the acetonitrile:water extraction separating from both other methods along PC1, and the perchloric acid and methanol:chloroform methods separating along PC2.

should be saved in an M-file called *PM_input_parameters.m*, which is automatically read each time ProMetab is executed. The file is heavily commented in order to explain the use of each of the parameters. The parameters should initially be set to their default values and then as the analysis proceeds, and the various parameters are optimized by the user, the *PM_input_parameters.m* file will require updating.

18. Optimization of the transformation parameter, λ, is described in the file *PM_input_parameters.m*.

19. The results of an example PCA are illustrated in **Fig. 4**. In this study, fish liver tissue was ground in a mortar and then the polar metabolites were extracted using perchloric acid (**Subheading 3.1.2.**), methanol:chloroform (**Subheading 3.1.3.**), and acetonitrile:water (method not described here), each in triplicate. Following final preparation of the samples for NMR (**Subheading 3.1.4.**), 1D ¹H NMR spectra were measured (**Subheading 3.2.1.**) and then preprocessed (**Subheading 3.3.2.**), prior to multivariate analysis.

Acknowledgments

The author would foremost like to thank the Natural Environment Research Council, UK, for an Advanced Fellowship in metabolomics (NER/J/S/2002/00618). The methods presented here have been optimized in conjunction with several postdoctoral researchers and graduate students whom the author would also like to thank, in particular Dr. Jake Bundy, Dr. Ching-Yu Lin, Dr. Eric Rosenblum, Mr. Andrew Southam, and Mr. Adam Hines.

References

1. Nicholson, J. K., Connelly, J., Lindon, J. C., and Holmes, E. (2002) Metabonomics: a platform for studying drug toxicity and gene function. *Nat. Rev. Drug Discov.* **1,** 153–161.
2. Brindle, J. T., Antti, H., Holmes, E., et al. (2002) Rapid and noninvasive diagnosis of the presence and severity of coronary heart disease using H-1 NMR-based metabonomics. *Nat. Med.* **8,** 1439–1444.
3. Griffin, J. L., Williams, H. J., Sang, E., Clarke, K., Rae, C., and Nicholson, J. K. (2001) Metabolic profiling of genetic disorders: a multi-tissue H-1 nuclear magnetic resonance spectroscopic and pattern recognition study into dystrophic tissue. *Anal. Biochem.* **293,** 16–21.
4. Viant, M. R., Rosenblum, E. S., and Tjeerdema, R. S. (2003) NMR-based metabolomics: A powerful approach for characterizing the effects of environmental stressors on organism health. *Environ. Sci. Technol.* **37,** 4982–4289.
5. Waters, N. J., Holmes, E., Waterfield, C. J., Farrant, R. D., and Nicholson, J. K. (2002) NMR and pattern recognition studies on liver extracts and intact livers from rats treated with alpha- naphthylisothiocyanate. *Biochem. Pharmacol.* **64,** 67–77.
6. Viant, M. R., Werner, I., Rosenblum, E. S., Gantner, A. S., Tjeerdema, R. S., and Johnson, M. L. (2003) Correlation between heat-shock protein induction and reduced metabolic condition in juvenile steelhead trout (*Oncorhynchus mykiss*) chronically exposed to elevated temperature. *Fish Physiol. Biochem.* **29,** 159–171.
7. Deprez, S., Sweatman, B. C., Connor, S. C., Haselden, J. N., and Waterfield, C. J. (2002) Optimisation of collection, storage and preparation of rat plasma for H-1 NMR spectroscopic analysis in toxicology studies to determine inherent variation in biochemical profiles. *J. Pharmaceut. Biomed.* **30,** 1297–1310.
8. Griffin, J. L. (2003) Metabonomics: NMR spectroscopy and pattern recognition analysis of body fluids and tissues for characterisation of xenobiotic toxicity and disease diagnosis. *Curr. Opin. Chem. Biol.* **7,** 648–654.
9. Kell, D. B. (2004) Metabolomics and systems biology: making sense of the soup. *Curr. Opin. Microbiol.* **7,** 296–307.
10. Lindon, J. C., Holmes, E., and Nicholson, J. K. (2001) Pattern recognition methods and applications in biomedical magnetic resonance. *Prog. Nucl. Magn. Reson. Spec.* **39,** 1–40.

11. Eriksson, L., Johansson, E., Kettaneh-Wold, N., and Wold, S. (2001) *Multi- and Megavariate Data Analysis: Principles and Applications,* Umetrics, Umea, Sweden.

12. Wise, B. M., Gallagher, N. B., Bro, R., Shaver, J. M., Windig, W., and Koch, R. S. (2004) *PLS_Toolbox Version 3.5 Manual.* Eigenvector Research, Manson, WA.

13. Viant, M. R. (2003) Improved methods for the acquisition and interpretation of NMR metabolomic data. *Biochem. Biophys. Res. Comm.* **310,** 943–948.

14. Weckwerth, W., Wenzel, K., and Fiehn, O. (2004) Process for the integrated extraction identification, and quantification of metabolites, proteins and RNA to reveal their co-regulation in biochemical networks. *Proteomics* **4,** 78–83.

15. Purohit, P. V., Rocke, D. M., Viant, M. R., and Woodruff, D. L. (2004) Discrimination models using variance stabilizing transformation of metabolomic NMR data. *OMICS* **8,** 118–130.

16. Bligh, E. G. and Dyer, W. J. (1959) A rapid method of total lipid extraction and purification. *Can. J. Biochem. Physiol.* **37,** 911–917.

14

Nuclear Magnetic Resonance Metabonomics

Methods for Drug Discovery and Development

Karl-Heinz Ott and Nelly Aranibar

Summary

Nuclear magnetic resonance (NMR)-based metabonomics is gaining popularity in drug discovery and development and in academia in a variety of settings, ranging from toxicology, preclinical, and clinical approaches to nutrition research, studies on microorganisms, and research on plants. This chapter focuses on the basic steps in a metabonomics study and emphasizes experience and lessons learned in our lab where we focused on metabonomic analyses of plant extracts, cell lines, and a variety of animal tissues and biofluids.

We emphasize that a comprehensive and suitable study design is pivotal for a correct biological interpretation of the results, as well as highly controlled experimental conditions. Sample preparation and NMR protocols are detailed for a wide range of sample types. We discuss alternative data processing strategies and considerations for a general data analysis approach, paying particular attention to the statistical interpretation and validation of the results while also highlighting approaches to avoid possible pitfalls resulting from systematic and random errors.

A tutorial written for the R statistical package and other small utilities are available from the authors upon request.

Key Words: Metabolomics; metabonomics; ^{1}H-NMR; sample preparation; data preprocessing; quality control; univariate analysis; multivariate analysis; data visualization; data management; ANOVA; PCA; PLS; discriminant analysis.

1. Introduction

Metabonomics is increasingly utilized in a variety of research and industrial applications. In the drug discovery and development processes, metabonomics has become a technology for exploring the response of animals to different treatments *(1,2)*. This research has often been driven by the need to address

From: *Methods in Molecular Biology, vol. 358: Metabolomics: Methods and Protocols*
Edited by: W. Weckwerth © Humana Press Inc., Totowa, NJ

questions of toxicological origin, and has largely utilized nuclear magnetic resonance (NMR)-spectroscopic analyses of urine samples from rodents. There is a large body of literature references that describe this approach to NMR-based metabonomics analysis *(3,4)*. Earlier biomedical approaches of NMR-based metabonomics were pioneered for early detection and classification of certain cancers *(5–7)*. A few approaches have been developed for a clinical setting *(8–12)*. In addition, there are metabonomics and analog, traditional chemometric approaches utilized in the food industry *(13)* and in industrial process controls. Also, metabonomics has become a well-established tool to study micro-organisms *(14)*, cell lines, and plants *(15,16)*. Although the examples and language used in this chapter refer to the use of metabonomics in drug toxicology studies, most of these methods will be valid to a wide range of applications.

Patterns of variation of the composition of endogenous metabolites can be measured and established to correlate to certain biological effects, such as a mechanism of toxicity or a desired treatment effect. Furthermore, monitoring the regular metabolic function of subjects under investigation is a powerful tool for detecting individual variability and idiosyncratic responses or can be implemented in the form of a control model. Similarly, alterations in the metabolism profile can be used to establish differences in the metabolic baseline or genetic background of the subjects. Most published approaches have so far focused on two-class distinctions. A classification approach for multiple classes is exemplified by a mechanism-of-action classification method for many herbicides *(17)* or by the Comet consortium, a large multisite study to investigate toxicity patterns in animal studies *(18)*. Earlier, small-scale studies have shown that if animals are treated with known toxins at doses that produce severe toxicity, certain metabolite concentrations appear to show distinct changes that may be correlated to certain pathological findings *(19–21)*. However, it has been shown that confounding effects, such as weight loss, can also explain some alterations in metabolite levels *(22,23)*. Thus, it is emphasized that a well-controlled study design is critical for a correct biological interpretation.

Metabonomics is a technology that leads itself to building multivariate models for classification and prediction purposes. Principal component analysis (PCA) of NMR spectra has become a standard in metabonomics studies *(24–26)*. PCA is a tool used to describe the data in a low-dimensional space. Clusters found in PCA space can often detect the differences between subpopulations of samples, and this technique is particularly amenable to visualize separations between treated and control groups. Other approaches have utilized clustering *(27)* and pattern recognition approaches such as artificial neural networks *(28)* to build classification methods for the mechanism of action of different toxicants. Traditional statistical approaches, like Student's *t*-test, have not yet been well established for metabonomics analyses, but approaches to discover and validate biomarkers call for rigorous statistical treatment, including ANOVA (analysis of variance). We will explore the commonly used techniques, provide in-depth guidance on methods that complement these analyses (such as suggestions for quality control [QC] steps and discussions of common pitfalls), as well as provide additional analyses, visualization methods for biomarker discovery, and methods for metabonomics studies that accompany regulatory filings of drug applications.

An increasing number of research groups now produce metabonomics data and analyses are more routine, generating large data repositories that need to be interconnected with other life and/or postmortem data for the subjects of such studies. Such repositories need to be managed and queried in a comprehensive way.

When first establishing the methodology, it is wise to choose a treatment that will result in a robust response to separate treated from control groups. In practice, often the challenge is to deal with complex study designs and difficult sampling schemes, while aiming to discover biomarkers at low concentration where changes in the signal intensities approach the biological variation between replicates or to deduce the mode of action of a treatment from minute changes in the metabolite profile.

2. Materials

2.1. Infrastructure

A metabolomics effort will include:

1. Sample inventory management.
2. Sample annotation.
3. Laboratory workflow.
4. Data standardization, normalization, and QC.
5. Spectral data storage, archival, and access.
6. Data integration.
7. Data analysis.
8. Biomarker annotation.

It is assumed that an analytical facility and data archiving facilities are available and this chapter will focus on data processing and data analysis. All analyses described here (assuming study sizes of up to several hundred samples) can be executed on a dedicated PC work station if equipped with a fast processor and approx 1 GB of memory. For larger projects, with several thousands of samples, more powerful hardware will be appropriate. Commonly used spreadsheet programs are limited in their utility for analysis of large amounts of multivariate data and no single software package fits all needs, but a combination of several well-chosen packages usually gets the job done, albeit with the need to transform the data between appropriate formats and accurately track all of the steps (**Note 1**).

Detailed familiarity with a range of software tools will be most advantageous and there are a variety of software packages available in addition to those mentioned here. A programming language for reformatting of data (e.g., Perl, freely available at www.cpan.org) and a statistics package (e.g., R, www.r-project.org) for data preprocessing are necessary basic tools. Less coding is required when using some commercial data analysis and data visualization packages. For example, Partek Pro (Partek, Inc., St. Louis, MO) is particularly strong for ANOVA analysis, whereas SimcaP (Umetrics, Umeå, Sweden) has an excellent implementation of PCA and PLS algorithms. Some labs may have expression profiling software (e.g., Genespring [Agilent Inc., Palo Alto, CA]) available that work well on huge datasets where most other PC software tools will fail or become too slow to be of practical use. More chemistry-oriented labs may have access to QSAR program packages that have many useful tools included.

Each lab will strive to establish a wide range of methods and choose the most appropriate technique for each application. To begin, free software tools, the tutorial provided, and commercial-software demos provide opportunities to learn and evaluate a range of methods. For the purpose of demonstrating the most common analyses, we have developed a tutorial written for the R statistical package that includes all data preprocessing steps (PCA and other data analyses, and some basic data visualization) to serve as a tutorial to accompany this chapter.

Data management, in its simplest form, maintains all data in tables as comma or tab-separated ASCII values. Working with such tables is widely applicable and most suitable for labs working with a limited number of studies and a limited number of scientists. Two sources of data are encountered: sample-related information and spectroscopic observations. A sample data table contains a row for each sample, which specifies the spectrum file name, a unique identifier, and factors representing the experimental design (such as treatment, dose, gender, time of collection, and others). Any additional information, such as in-life data (body weight, physical evaluation), or additional end points from the experiment (e.g., clinical chemistry, histopathology) can be added as additional columns to this table and used in the analysis. The second source of data is the spectroscopic observations, in the form of values for integrals from the spectroscopic experiment, which are converted after suitable transformation into ASCII tables with one row per spectrum. Such data tables are suitable to be read into most data analysis packages and statistical analysis programs (**Note 2**).

2.2. Buffers

1. Hoagland solution for growing corn seedlings: prepare Hoagland solution fresh from the following stock solutions that should be kept protected from light and refrigerated at 4°C: 12 mL FeEDTA·Na (5 g in 100 mL, 0.13 M), 2.4 mL KH$_2$PO$_4$ (13.6 g in 100 mL, 1 M), 24 mL MgSO$_4$·7H$_2$O (24.65 g in 100 mL, 1 M), 60 mL KNO$_3$ (10.11 g in 100 mL, 1M), 60 mL Ca(NO$_3$)$_2$·H$_2$O (18.21 g in 100 mL, 1 M) and 60 mL MES buffer (2-[N-morpholino]ethanesulphonic acid) (39.04 g in 1 L, 200 mM), and 12 mL micronutrients stock solution (*see* **item 2**) diluted to 12 L in deionized water.
2. Micronutrient solution: dissolve 2.86 g H$_3$BO$_3$, 1.81 g MnCl·4H$_2$O, 0.22 g ZnSO$_4$·7H$_2$O, 0.08 g CuSO$_4$·5H$_2$O, and 0.02 g 85% MoO$_3$ solution (molybdic acid solution) in 1 L deionized water.
3. 0.25 N HCl solution for plant tissue extraction.
4. 3X Phosphate buffer (PBS) for NMR of urine: 0.2 M phosphate buffer solution, (2.82 g Na$_2$HPO$_4$ and 2.4 g NaH$_2$PO$_4$), 3 mM 3-(trimethylsilyl)-propionic acid-d$_4$, sodium salt (TSP, 0.0516 g C$_6$H$_9$D$_4$NaO$_2$Si,), and 3 mM sodium azide (0.0195 g NaN$_3$) dissolved in 100 mL of a mixture of 66% H$_2$O and 33% D$_2$O.
5. Saline solution for serum NMR: prepare 0.9 % (w/v) solution of NaCl in a mixture of 33% D$_2$O:66% H$_2$O (9 g NaCl in 1 L) with 3 mM TSP-d$_4$ (0.516 g).
6. Methanol-d$_4$ for protein precipitation on cell preparations.
7. Solution acetonitrile-d3: D$_2$O 50:50 (v/v) with 3 mM TSP for fecal pellets extraction.

3. Methods

3.1. Process Outline

A metabonomics experiment typically consists of, or includes, the following steps:

1. Planning and experiment design.
2. In-life phase during which (or after which) samples are collected.
3. Sample processing.
4. Data acquisition.
5. Spectral data processing.
6. Data transformation, scaling, and normalization.
7. Data analysis and interpretation.

All steps should be subjected to QC measures and data management issues need to be dealt with.

3.2. Experimental Design

Experimental design considerations will focus on the scientific question being addressed and the necessary statistical requirements to establish the analysis. There are two possible approaches:

1. A classification or profiling approach aims to distinguish samples based on their metabolomics pattern or profile, often without identifying the cause of the separation.

2. A "biomarker" approach that aims to identify individual compounds in the profile that have altered concentrations because of the study factors and may be related to the mechanism of action.

The experimental design step will define the subject's parameters unique to the study (age, gender, species, strain, diet, and others), treatment regimen, negative (vehicle) and positive controls (**Note 3**), time of sample collection, and determine, by reference or pilot experiments, the number of replicate samples (**Note 4**) and analytical repeats (*see* **Subheading 3.4.**). The experimental design should also consider inclusion of an independent validation experiment. To establish a biologically meaningful result a series of questions can be discussed during the design phase and may need to be addressed in pilot experiments.

1. Would any particular outcome clearly relate to the hypothesis or would alternative interpretations be possible (**Note 5**)?
2. Are there relevant positive and negative controls?
3. Is there a range in the severity of the response?
4. Are there controls that track the spectrum of responses such as efficacy of a drug vs its toxicity?
5. Are alternate chemotypes included to distinguish compound-specific (e.g., ADME effects) from more general mechanistic effects?
6. How can the possibility of confounding effects be controlled?
7. Which tissue is most likely to show a direct or surrogate response?
8. Are the metabolites that are expected to change present in sufficient concentration to be detected by the analytical methods under consideration?
9. What other end points need to be measured or could aid in the interpretation (expression profiling, clinical chemistry, physiological end points, efficacy or growth markers, and so on)?
10. Is the vehicle going to cause a disturbance (**Note 6**)?
11. Is the treatment itself altering the spectra through the presence of drug-related components (DRCs) (**Note 7**)?

3.3. Sample Collection and Preparation

Treatment protocols are specific to a particular study and are not discussed in detail. Sample collection requirements are also highly specific to the particular study. Variations from standard protocols to include metabonomics in a study may include considerations for the most suitable vehicle (**Note 8**), the use of deuterated compounds and reagents, or avoiding some commonly used reagents, like EDTA or ammonium-containing buffers. Sample preparation protocols are chosen to produce highly consistent data with a limited number of steps (**Note 9**).

3.3.1. Plant Tissue Metabonomics

3.3.1.1. Hydroponic Culture of Zea mays Seedlings for Metabonomics

Zea mays seeds are set to germinate in paper towel rolls in tap water for 5 d in a controlled growing chamber. The environment is adjusted to "summer conditions" (day/night ratio of 14/10 h, regulated temperature of 27°C, and humidity of 70%). After germination the seedlings are visually inspected. Some of the seedlings may not have germinated at all or have only short roots. The delayed growth will not allow for enough material at harvest time. Seedlings that are homogeneous in size and appearance are selected, set in 50-mL amber bottles in 25-mL Hoagland nutrient and grown for five more days, after which they have reached the three-leaf stage. It is convenient to set 20% more seedlings than are needed for the experiment as some seedlings may not further develop in the hydroponic solution.

Twenty milliliters of a stock solution of herbicide in acetone is added to the hydroponic solution or applied to the second leaf. Some herbicides are absorbed through the roots, and should be applied directly into the hydroponic solution. Contact herbicides should be applied to the leaf. The concentration of herbicide depends on the efficacy of the compound or formulation and should be sufficient to stunt the plant growth. Control plants should be treated only with the vehicle, in this case, acetone. Plants are returned to the growing chamber.

3.3.1.2. Plant Tissue Collection

Twenty-four hours post-treatment the plants are harvested by excising between the coleoptile and the first-leaf collar. This meristematic tissue is in active, fast growth and metabolic changes occur in this tissue at the highest rates, in comparison with the rest of the organism. After 24 h the plants may show only slight growth stunting in response to the treatments. The first-leaf sheet is separated and discarded and the rest of the tissue (approx 250–300 mg per plant) is collected, flash frozen in liquid nitrogen in a cryogenic 3-mL tube, and stored at –80°C in a freezer until further use.

3.3.1.3. Liquid Extraction of Plant Tissue

Precool mortars and pestles with a small amount of liquid nitrogen. The frozen plant tissue is then pulverized in a mortar (under liquid N_2). Frozen material pulverizes to a very small particle size, relative to wet material. Add 2.4 mL of HCl solution (0.25 N), continue mixing with the pestle, transfer into a 2-mL microcentrifuge tube, and centrifuge at 14,000g, 4°C, for 60 min. NMR samples are prepared from 0.5 mL of the supernatants and 0.2 mL D_2O (with TSP) and kept on ice until NMR measurement.

3.3.2. Cell Extractions

Cells from monolayer tissue culture (hepatocytes, epithelial cells, and others) should be carefully harvested to avoid lysis. For a NMR sample to be measured in a 3-mm NMR tube (volume ~180 μL) using a cryoprobe, a minimum of 6×10^6 cells gives an acceptable signal to noise (comparable to the signal-to-noise ratio of metabolite NMR signals in rat urine) after 512 scans.

For the harvest procedure, nonenzymatic cell detachment products such as Cellstripper® produce the best results for NMR spectroscopy. Instructions for detachment, as given by the manufacturer, are: prewarm Cellstripper to incubator temperature. Remove the spent medium from the culture vessel (flask, Petri dish, and others). Add a small amount of dissociation solution to the vessel without disturbing the monolayer. This is best performed by slowly adding the solution to the side of the flask opposite the monolayer or to the side of a Petri plate. Gently swirl the vessel to cover the monolayer with the solution. Discard the solution from the vessel. Add a small amount of Cellstripper to the cells again and leave a small amount of solution in the vessel, just enough to cover the monolayer. Incubate the cells at 37°C, observing microscopically, until the cells begin to round up. Tapping the side of the vessel may facilitate removal of difficult cell lines. After detachment, disperse the cells into suspension by pipetting repeatedly.

The cells are then washed three times with isotonic phosphate buffer to remove any remaining nutrient solution as well as the Cellstripper solution, as these produce resonances in the NMR spectrum that will interfere with the signals of the endogenous metabolites. The washes are accomplished by adding 0.5 mL of PBS to the cell suspension, gently mixing by pipetting a couple of times and centrifuging for 5 min at 1000g. Remove and discard the supernatants. Pellets are the frozen and kept at −80°C until lysis and preparation for spectroscopy.

The lysis is performed through two thaw-freeze cycles in D_2O as follows. Defrost cell samples adding 100 μL D_2O with 0.1% sodium azide and vortex. Refreeze in dry ice for 30 min, then thaw to room temperature, vortex, and centrifuge for 10 min at 4°C and 12,000g. Recover the supernatants (S1) and wash the pellets once with D_2O solution, centrifuge, and add the supernatants to the supernatants S1.

Deproteinization of the cell preparation is achieved by adding two volumes (300 μL in this protocol) of cold MeOD-d_4 (kept on ice at ~0°C) and letting stand on ice for 10 min. The samples are then centrifuged for 15 min at 4°C and 12,000g. The supernatants are recovered and concentrated in a speed-vac until dry (~2 h). The use of a lyophilizer is not recommended because some volatiles may be lost in the process. The samples can be then stored frozen at −80°C until NMR measurements are performed.

The samples are reconstituted in 180 μL 200 mM phosphate buffer in D_2O into a 3-mm NMR tube for spectroscopy.

3.3.3. Urine

Urine of rodents should be collected in wire-bottom metabolic cages into chilled tubes. A solution of sodium azide, added to the collection tubes to a final concentration of 0.1%, will stop bacterial degradation of metabolites. The cages are washed once a day. For long-term studies, when rodents are housed in shoebox cages, and the urine collection is done only sporadically, it is important to let the animals acclimate to the metabolic cages for at least 48 h, prior to collecting the samples, because the metabolic profile of the urine reflects changes in environment, as well as any other stress-related changes. After collection, the samples are centrifuged at 4°C, 2500g for 10 min, and the supernatants collected and frozen at –80°C until NMR measurement. Urine of larger animals (dogs, primates) can be collected by catheterization or cystocentesis and the previously mentioned procedure used to store the samples. Particular attention should be used during the catheterization or cystocentesis process not to contaminate the urine samples with blood. Urine can also be collected, postmortem, directly from the bladder.

For NMR spectroscopy, 0.4 mL of thawed urine is mixed with 0.2 mL of 0.2 mM PBS in D_2O with 3 mM TSP.

Human urine is more diluted than that of rodents and concentration of human urine is suggested. A 3-mL aliquot is centrifuged and freeze-dried. It can be stored frozen and reconstituted in 0.3 or 0.5 mL D_2O or buffer, with TSP added as frequency reference prior to analysis *(29)*.

3.3.4. Serum

Blood should be collected in Vacutainer® serum separator tubes (SST™) according to the manufacturer's protocol, usually inverting the tube gently five times, letting the blood clot for 30 min, and then centrifuging for 10 min at 1000–1300 rpm at 4°C. The SSTs do not introduce any extraneous components or signals in the proton NMR spectra, Deprez et al. *(30)* also suggest Sarstedt™ tubes as suitable. Plasma preparations using Vacutainers with anticoagulant agents, such as citrate or EDTA, are not appropriate for NMR-based metabonomics.

The supernatant is carefully retrieved after the centrifugation step and frozen at –80°C until NMR spectroscopy measurements are made. Serum samples should not be left indefinitely in the freezer. Enzymatic activity and biochemical changes may continue, although at a much slower pace, even at ultra-low temperatures. Serum samples should be used preferably within 6 mo.

For NMR spectroscopy, 0.4 mL of serum is mixed with 0.2 mL saline solution (0.9% [w/v] NaCl in D_2O) with 3 mM TSP.

Deproteinization of plasma *(30)*: add an equal volume of acetonitrile to 0.5 mL plasma, precipitate for 5 min, centrifuge 5 min at 13,500*g*, remove solvent using a stream of nitrogen, freeze-dry, and reconstitute with D_2O or PBS.

3.3.5. Feces

Extraction of fecal pellets from rats for metabonomics can be performed as follows. Fecal pellets samples are collected in the morning before changing the bedding in shoebox cages, or in metabolic cages.

For extraction, add 2 mL of acetonitrile-d3 solution: D_2O 50:50 (v/v) with 3 m*M* TSP to two to three rat fecal pellets per rat per time-point in 2-mL microcentrifuge tubes.

Homogenize (with a microhomogenizer) for 10 s, vortex for 10 s, and then set in an ultrasonic bath for 5 min at room temperature.

After this last step the samples are centrifuged at 12,000*g* and 4°C for 20 min. Collect the supernatants for NMR measurements. The supernatants can be stored at –80°C until further use.

3.3.6. Bile

Rat bile can be collected through cannulation (surgical procedure not described here). The volume of a bile sample used for metabonomics is 0.4 mL per sample per animal per time-point. Add 0.2 mL pure D_2O with TSP (no buffer, to avoid destroying the micellular structures), vortex for 10 s, and transfer into a 5-mm NMR tube for measurement using normal water suppression techniques and Carr–Purcell–Meiboom–Gill (CPMG) sequence.

A second set of measurements is done after a deproteinization procedure that also extracts most of the lipophilic components. Samples are diluted with an equal volume (0.6 mL) of acetonitrile-d3, vortexed for 10 s, and then centrifuged for 20 min at 12,000*g* and 4°C. The supernatants are recovered for NMR spectroscopy and can be kept frozen at –80°C until further use.

3.4. NMR Data Acquisition

Most of the NMR-based metabonomics studies rely on one-dimensional (1D) ^1H NMR spectroscopy. The use of high-field NMR spectrometers is typically standard. Studies that aim toward pattern recognition, where the spectral information is commonly binned into low-resolution bins do not require the highest resolution, but high resolution ($\geq$600 MHz) and highest sensitivity (e.g., use of cryogenically cooled probes) will greatly enhance the detection limit and can be critical to uniquely identify a biomarker. Multidimensional and heteronuclear NMR techniques have proven useful to identify metabolites or to reduce the overlap present in 1D NMR. Because most samples will be aqueous systems, water suppression is required. The most suitable NMR technique will minimize the residual water signals without introducing baseline and phase distortions and maximize robustness and insensitivity toward changes in sample composition, (in particular salt and pH variation) and probe tuning. Most commonly used are presaturation of the water resonance often using a first increment of a "NOESY" pulse sequence

$$\left[\text{relaxation delay}(\text{cw}) - 90^0_{x,-x} - t_0 - 90^0_x\, \tau(\text{cw}) - 900^0_x - \text{Acquisition}_{x,-x} \right] \quad (1)$$

which is applicable to urine, feces, and (protein-depleted) cell lines. A CPMG pulse sequence

$$\left[\text{RD}(\text{cw}) - 90^0_x - (\tau - 180y - \tau)_n - \text{AQ}_x \right] \quad (2)$$

can be useful, (bile and serum) to deplete the relaxation-broadened protein signals. Optimized methods specifically tailored to improve automated data processing and improved robustness against variations in sample pH and salt content have been developed *(31)* and a detailed comparison between these methods is forthcoming *(32)*. We typically use 256 scans for the acquisition of most biofluids on a 600-MHz spectrometer. CPMG pulse trains have reduced signal intensity for which we compensate by using 512 or more scans (**Note 10**).

3.5. NMR Signal Transformation

1. Apodization: line broadening with a factor of 0.5 Hz is typically used. If the free induction decay is truncated to reduce the size of the data matrix instead of the more commonly used resonance binning, alternate window functions will be necessary to avoid truncation artifacts during Fourier transform.
2. Fourier transformation: with the advance of digital NMR instruments and numerous variations on the data acquisition processes, the vendor's NMR processing software may provide the most robust and suitable algorithm for this processing step.
3. Phase and baseline correction (**Note 11**).
4. Chemical shift referencing: typically using TSP as internal standard (**Note 12**).
5. QC: inspect individual spectra for errors in automation, auto shim failures, and so on. Rerun failed samples or manually reprocess where necessary.
6. Integration (**Note 13**).
7. Data export and reformatting: converting the NMR data from the spectrometer manufacturer's proprietary format into a commonly readable ASCII representation like JDX is a readily available possibility (**Note 14**) that is compatible across all instrument manufacturers and many NMR analysis programs.
8. Convert the integrated data into a two-dimensional (2D) data matrix, with each row representing a spectrum, and the columns representing resonance integrals or bin intensities is the most widely acceptable format. Custom Perl scripts are suitable for this task unless a database engine is used for managing the data.
9. Archive the free induction decays (and spectra, if desired).

3.6. Data Preprocessing

Data preprocessing is an often neglected but very critical step in the process to create a dataset for analysis. The main focus is to avoid or to remove any systematic errors and statistical bias.

1. Prepare the sample spreadsheet, create additional columns for later data manipulation within the various statistical programs, and export as a .csv file or into a database (**Note 15**).
   - QC: calculate cross-tabulation of factors, check for typos, and correct any inconsistencies.
   - Software: Excel, SQL, Open office.
2. Merge NMR data with sample information.
   - QC: Flag missing spectra.
   - Software: Perl, R.
3. Scale the NMR data, alternatively by (1) reference to an exogenous standard (possibly the NMR reference standard). (2) Reference to an endogenous standard (e.g., creatine), (3) reference to total or partial integral (most commonly used), and (4) linear regression (**Note 16**).
   - QC: Range, histograms, ANOVA on scaling factors of scaling factors (*see* **Note 17**).
   - Software: Perl, R.
4. Calculate derivative spectra such as mean spectra and standard deviation spectra for each group. Mean and standard deviation spectra for each treatment group and difference spectra and other derivatives that may aid in the inspection and interpretation, are more meaningful than randomly picked "representative" spectra, and are useful for presentation purposes. Depending on the variability of the data, and the presence of possible outliers, the use of robust methods *(33,34)* to calculate the various statistical measures should be considered.
5. Calculate and analyze QC measures (**Note 18**).
   - Pearson correlation between spectra (**Fig. 1H**) and between spectra of each group and their group mean.
   - Inspect spectra within the context of the treatment groups and perform a first pass PCA analysis for QC purposes: identify possible outliers (by inspection, by PCA score, or by residual error of the PCA).
   - Follow up on possible technical outliers, fix or document possible errors and outliers that will be or may need to be removed.
   - Are outliers caused by sample handling difficulties? Do some samples appear to contain impurities (e.g., feed, bedding, blood contamination, sample degradation)? Are there any samples that appear in the "wrong" treatment group indicative of potential sample mislabeling?
   - Inspect spectra and PCA loadings, identify highly variable signals. Identify vehicle and exogenous (drug and drug metabolite-related) signals. If multivariate analyses steps are planned, it may be useful to create a dataset that has the regions with vehicle and DRCs removed, or better, (to avoid breaks in the

ppm axis) the respective intensity values replaced by imputed values (or "noise"; setting regions to zero is not recommended). Are there any indications of variable exposure (based on vehicle or DRCs signals, or other analysis)?

6. Repeat scaling and QC (**steps 3–5**) if necessary. Exclude any regions identified as possibly treatment or drug-related or as highly variable, as identified in **step 4** when calculating the scaling factors. Determine whether additional, or alternative, scaling steps may be required. Determine and evaluate appropriate methods.

7. Create (additional) normalized datasets. For PCA and similar multivariate analyses, some software programs have built-in normalization schemes, typically mean centering, univariate scaling, and log transform. Scaling by the root of the standard deviation is less common but can be helpful. We recommend scaling all data by the standard deviation (or its root) calculated from a single treatment group (typically the control group) or the average standard deviation spectrum across all groups, similar to the VAST *(35)* scaling procedure, rather than using the standard deviation calculated across all groups, to avoid reducing signal intensities overproportionally where treatment effects are present. For NMR signal integrals, transformations to approach a Gaussian normal distribution are not necessary.

8. Archive the "processed" datasets.

3.7. Data Analysis

There are a large variety of methods available for the analysis of the NMR data (*see* e.g., http://www.itl.nist.gov/div898/handbook/ for an introduction to many of the statistical concepts). Depending on the circumstances, the actual scientific objective, availability of particular data analysis tools, and familiarity with particular analysis techniques will affect the analysis process. In general, robust, distinct treatment effects can be successfully described with most techniques, and a pilot project can help to establish, learn, and optimize each method. In practice, we often find that biologically important effects are not always obvious and may require experience and familiarity with the methods, their particular strengths, weaknesses, and pitfalls. Following is a list of possible techniques, some of which are further discussed in **Subheading 4**. In particular for studies with multiple factors, each having several levels, visualization of the analysis is often nontrivial and may require considerable efforts.

1. Visual inspection of the spectra: (**Fig. 1I,B**).
   - Select subsets of data, color data by different treatment factors (**Fig. 1I**).
   - Plot mean spectra for each group, stack plots, difference spectra (**Fig. 1B**).
2. ANOVA/*t*-tests:
   - Develop a model to describe the experiment, fit the spectra to the model. Plot $-\log P$ vs chemical shift for visualization (**Fig. 1B**). Post-hoc analyses may include Dunnett's test or pairwise Student's *t*-test. Rule out possible systematic errors resulting from phase, baseline effects, signal overlap, and others.

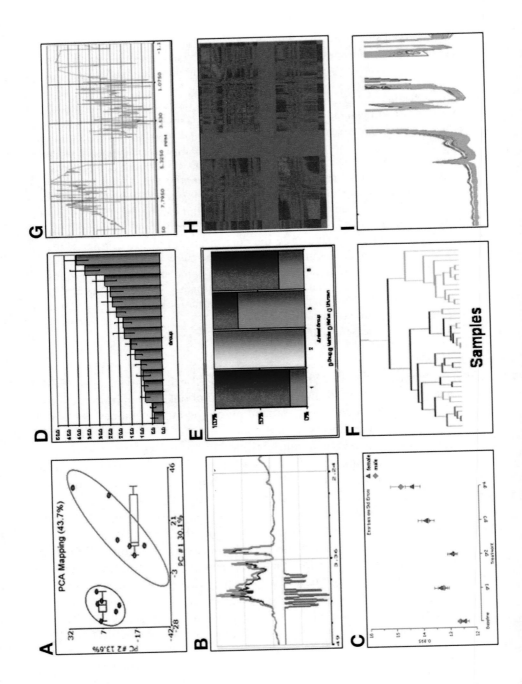

260

- If there are multiple markers, a PCA scores plot using only the markers selected by ANOVA is useful for visualization. Select the most significant markers for each factor using a multiple testing correction method, such as false discovery rate.
- Integrate over all signals of each compound of interest, and calculate ANOVA for the individual compounds.
- Develop a discriminate model using forward selection for multiple chemical shift values for class prediction purposes. Apply a multiple testing correction method such as false discovery rate for p-value estimates.
3. PCA: describe data in low-dimensional space; classify samples (**Note 19**).
   - PCA diagnostics include: scores, loadings, percent-explained variance, convergence, residual error, and cross validation. Examine potential outliers as determined by residual error (e.g., DMODX in Simca) and in factor (score) space.
   - Exclude extremes and recalculate if necessary, or use robust methods to calculate the correlation matrix. Omitted (outlier) vectors can and should be projected back into the PCA space.
   - Determine the number of significant principal components (PC) and PC convergence. Plot loadings as a function of chemical shift. Do loadings correlate with NMR signals; are there any artifacts (e.g., baseline roll) that dominate the PCA loadings (e.g., **Fig. 1G**)?
   - Analyze PCA scores plots: do treatment factors appear to create clusters of samples in PCA space? Perform ANOVA for each PC to determine statistical significance of components as descriptors of the experiment. Calculate the Hotelling's T^2 ellipse for each treatment group (**Fig. 1A**).
   - Determine which loadings contribute with the PC if there is a particular PC axis that is tightly associated with a study factor. Perform ANOVA on selected signals, or on signal integrals summarized across identified resonances of individual compounds. Do these signals or compounds, each by itself or in combination, create a discriminant model?

Fig.1. *(opposite)* Illustration of some data visualization methods for metabonomics. (**A**) Scatter plot of principal component analysis scores, with Hotelling's ellipses (at 2σ) and box plots for principal components (PC)1. (**B**) Plot of mean spectra for two treatment groups and Bonferroni-corrected p-values (bottom) curve. (**C**) Reaction coordinate vs treatment group for two gender groups. (**D**) Bar graph of the concentration of a metabolite as a function of group. (**E**) Column plot of a prediction result. (**F**) Sample tree calculated from the hierarchical clustering of spectra. (**G**) Plot of PC loadings as a function of chemical shift. (**H**) Pearson correlation matrix, with chemical shift as the axes demonstrating correlation between resonance integrals. In this example, correlation between large spectral regions indicated a baseline problem. (**I**) Expansion line plot depicting the superposition of nuclear magnetic resonance spectra, colored by treatment group. Plots **G,H,I** demonstrate processing artifacts from a bias in the automated phase and baseline correction.

4. PLS, PLS-DA:
   - PLS is a method analogous to PCA, but uses the class information to calculate the loadings, maximizing the distance between the classes. It can be useful if major components are dominated by individual variability or to isolate multiple study factors. Requires validation of the components to avoid danger of overfitting (*see* **step 7**). Plot and analyze visually scores and loadings, analyze residuals and cumulative variable influence, plot observed vs predicted factor values, plot scores predicted for validation and tests sets, plot predicted class membership (**Fig. 1E**).

5. Clustering methods:
   - Calculate cluster trees along both the sample and the chemical shift dimension (e.g., source: normalized intensity data; distance measure: correlation matrix).
   - Clustering in chemical shift space can identify resonances that are correlated to one another (**Fig. 1H**) (protons from the same compound, or from metabolites that are co/anti-regulated. This approach is limited by resonance overlap, and works best with high-resolution data).
   - Clustering in sample space can measure relatedness between samples, and will possibly show relations among study factors (**Fig. 1F**) but measures overall spectral similarity and is often less sensitive than PCA for predictive modeling. Clustering is often useful to find outliers and systematic bias.
   - Clustering can be combined with ANOVA or other methods to first select the "important" resonances for clustering.
   - Clustering of PCA scores is less prone to subjective judgment than graphical defining clusters in a PCA scores plot.

6. Artificial neuronal networks (ANN), support vector machines (SVM), genetic programming (GP), and so on:
   - A variety of very powerful methods for class predictions have been described and can be useful for automated classification. ANN are particularly useful when large numbers of factors and samples are involved and a general class prediction is desired. For neuronal networks, the Stuttgart Neural Network Simulator (SNNS, http://www-ra.informatik.uni-tuebingen.de/SNNS/) is a very powerful and versatile package that is freely available, and its use in metabonomics has been exemplified (*17*). Similarly, genetic programming has been demonstrated to be a sensitive methodology finding combinations of markers for class prediction (*35*). So far SVM and GP seem to be developed for two-class distinctions, and some commercial applications are available.

7. Validation:
   - All classification methods rely on validation by an independent test set. "Independent" in this context should be very narrowly defined and should separate each step in the process, including all data preprocessing and scaling processes. Leave-one-out cross-validation and bootstrapping can help provide estimates on *p*-values in ANOVA analysis but are of little use for classifica-

tion approaches, which require that a complete treatment group or batch be omitted from the training.

3.8. Data Visualization

Data visualization methods are critical at all stages of a metabonomics analysis. The large amount of data produced in an '-omics' experiment is almost impossible to describe adequately with words or numerical tables. The most common visualizations found in the literature are the representation of one or a few representative spectra, and score and loadings scatter plots from a PCA analysis. Use of data visualization during QC, and advanced techniques to evaluate results from uni- and multivariate analysis together with their error estimates with respect to each other and to the original spectral data are most helpful. **Figure 1** illustrates a variety of graphs in an example portfolio.

1. Prepare a compilation of results from various analyses previously described and from other end points to interpret results in context, visualize data interactively. Two complementary data matrices are typically obtained:
    a. A sample-centric matrix that contains PCA scores, cluster group assignments, and other classification results that can be correlated to other end points and treatment effects (**Fig. 1A**).
    b. A data matrix that contains variable-centric data like PCA loadings, ANOVA-p-values, and others. Spectrometrists will be comfortable with plotting these results against a chemical shift axis, which serves as a means of identifying the markers. This type of display can also help to align a loading or p-value with a particular resonance (**Fig. 1B**).
    Because most analysis will be performed on a binned or otherwise reduced dataset, it is important to project findings on particular regions or biomarkers back to a full-resolution spectrum. Is the peak clearly associated with a single compound, or are there resonance overlaps, variations in chemical shift values (e.g., pH variations)?
2. For identified biomarkers: plot individual resonance intensities (**Fig. 1C**). Are all individual resonances of a metabolite in concordance? Can the metabolite be uniquely defined? LC-NMR and 2D NMR methods may be necessary to answer some of these questions. Traditional bar graphs with error bars and an indication of which changes are statistically significant are useful (**Fig. 1D**).
3. Inspect the raw spectra using stacked plots of all spectra (**Fig. 1I**), or mean, standard deviation, or difference between means (**Fig. 1B**). Scatter plots of mean spectra vs each other can also be helpful to emphasize fold changes. Selecting a single "representative" spectrum for a class can be misleading.
4. PCA scores are displayed as 2D and 3D scatter plots. Clever use of colors and symbols may be necessary to display multiple factors. A sample sheet with ample columns having various levels of plot labels will be of great help for this purpose. Separation of data into different figures may help reduce overcrowding. Replace multiple values by the mean and its standard deviation. Standard deviation in PCA space can be displayed via Hotelling's T^2 ellipses.

3.9. Follow-Up and Validation

1. Postanalysis NMR experiments like 2D correlations, 1D selective TOCSY experiments, and adding small amounts of a known standard sample into the biological sample (also known as "spiking") are crucial to the unique identification of components.
2. Relating the resulting finding into the biological context will become the core of the interpretation.

4. Notes

1. Excel, Openoffice, and others, limit the number of columns to 256, lack many important algorithms, and are limited in their ability to visualize complex data structures, but serve well in collecting results from the various steps. We warn against the use of the copy and paste functionality when handling large data matrices because this may lead to the loss or alteration of data. Using file import/export of ASCII data tables (see Note 2) or a database interface is safer.
2. Although the use of ASCII tables produces a format that is compatible with virtually every data analysis package, and facilitates data exchange between the different analysis packages, it is important to keep in mind that such a format typically introduces a truncation of the numeric precision. It is, therefore, necessary to establish a numeric format that captures the dynamic range, and at the same time, is at least one order of magnitude more precise than the experimental noise. It is not recommended to set negative values, or values in excluded regions to zero to avoid errors in the determination of the data variance. Some analysis programs provide the option to read data directly from an instrument format; however, sample meta-data are often not imported when importing data by this direct route.
3. Experimental design considerations: statistically related design considerations will include the number of treatments or groups, the number of replicates, and the randomization strategies. Those statistical requirements will need to be balanced against practical constraints, like the need for acclimatization periods and control of environmental influences. The desire to reach fully balanced designs often results in a large number of (vehicle) control samples that may not always be necessary. On the other hand, the influence of batch effects, or the need of relevant controls to separate compound-specific effects and class effects are often underestimated. For larger studies, a random block design, i.e., spreading replicates across batches will increase the power of the experiment.
4. Replicates: urine is a more variable biofluid than serum and 6–10 replicates per group are useful. Some treatments or disease states (e.g., polyuria) induce diluted urine that results in reduced sensitivity and often causes problems with data processing (because of the altered magnetic properties). Such effects, when anticipated, can be partially compensated for by concentration of the samples, increasing the number of NMR scans, or increasing the number of animal replicates for these groups. Also, if the use of multivariate methods, such as PCA, is

planned, having a very small number of samples will most likely lead to a loss in sensitivity.

5. Connor et al. have elegantly demonstrated that some treatments will cause altered urinary metabolite profiles through the alteration of feeding behavior and confound the interpretation. Similarly, we have found that treatments that alter the acid–base balance will cause changes in the amount of some urinary metabolites, e.g., citrate, that are used by the kidney to stabilize the pH of the urine.

6. Some vehicles can alter the metabolic response profile. A common vehicle used in drug evaluation studies is PEG-400. It gives rise to large undesired signals in urine. More disturbingly, it induces a particularly strong metabolic effect, and may alter the response profile of a compound under study. Furthermore, it is not suitable for LC–MS analysis. Other vehicles, like corn oil, can induce short-term responses. Saline solution and methoxycellulose do not appear to influence the metabolic profile of urine. Similar considerations are necessary for the route and time of administration.

7. Many toxicant-related studies have focused on investigating biological mechanisms and responses. The appearance of the toxicant or its direct metabolites can cause an undesired effect on the multivariate data analysis when present in the spectra of a sample. Isotope labeling (coupled with a suitable filter inserted into the NMR pulse sequence) and perdeuteration strategies can be considered to "remove" these resonances from or identify them in the spectra. Similarly, if an effector is used, e.g., an antibiotic to switch on a gene in a transformed cell line, it is necessary to assess if this effector by itself has an effect, or if there is a baseline expression of the gene under study.

8. Sample collection: specifically for urine collections in rats, the use of metabolic cages with refrigerated collection compartments is often recommended but not necessary if other precautions are taken to avoid degradation and bacterial contamination. For urine, an accurate measure of the pH at the time of collection is recommended.

   Because many organisms show a significant alteration in the metabolic profile as a function of environmental conditions, recording and controlling those factors may be important for a study where metabonomics is one of the end points. The use of growth chambers for plants, time of the day of the sample collection for animals, and others, will be important factors for a successful metabonomics analysis. Similarly, individual measures of pharmacokinetic parameters for a drug treatment, or RNA or protein levels in genetic, transfection, or knockout studies may aid in the interpretation of the data.

9. There is an imminent danger that small artificial variations can introduce group effects that may skew the data analysis. It is most critical that the sample collection and processing is executed to minimize variation and that all experimental parameters are controlled carefully.

10. NMR is a highly reproducible analytical technique and the electronic noise and variability between replicates is typically very small compared with variation between replicates. For NMR, analytical repeats do not offer a gain in statistical

power (when compared at constant experiment time) because any potential gain in statistical power is offset by the reduced number of scans for a sample because of the loss of time spent with re-equilibrating and reshimming the samples; however, an increase in information can sometimes be gained if the period for data acquisition is split to acquire spectra with different pulse sequences. For example, the combination of CPMG and presaturation water suppression is recommended for serum. The spectra can be added or analyzed separately. This may increase the information content obtained in the experiment owing to the complementarity of the information collected.

11. In contrast to "regular" NMR spectroscopy, the "best" phase, baseline, and others, are less of a factor than the consistency of these steps. For example, a small phase error may not cause a problem when comparing intensity changes across many samples as long as all spectra have the same error; however, even minor phase variations can cause distortions at the flank of an intense signal that will be larger than the intensity of a low concentration metabolite. Similarly, visually unnoticeable variations in the baseline will cause large distortions in the data matrices, in particular when employing univariate scaling. Unfortunately, phase and baseline correction are a function of the sample composition: changes in the dielectric properties of a sample, e.g., salt content, will cause a change in the NMR probe tuning, which in turn affects the phase of the NMR signal. We find the NMR phase values vary by approx 1–5° across large studies, and residual variations between spectra after phase correction to be as much as 0.5–1.0°. These variations are detected in the statistical analysis, and we have observed separations in the PCA between treatment classes predominantly caused by small baseline rolls that were not discovered during the visual inspection of the spectra.

    Treatments and animal groupings that have large effects on protein (e.g., old vs young male rats) or salt content (e.g., polyuria), or urine volume (females vs males), and others, are prone to present systematic errors. These artifacts can be detected by using a variety of methods and a range of data visualization steps.

12. TSP binds to proteins and (e.g., in serum) TSP can be broadened. Referencing against a prominent metabolite with a known chemical shift value that is largely pH and temperature independent can be used.

13. Spectra integration: a commonly used protocol for the integration of NMR employs fixed "bins" of 0.04 ppm width in the range between 10 and 0.02 ppm. The method was developed (24) and optimized for urine spectra of rats for analysis of toxicity patterns and has the advantage that it captures some of the major signals of urine NMR spectra in a single NMR bin, reduces the complexity of the spectra, and is relatively insensitive to small chemical shift variations and referencing inaccuracies. It also reduces the size of the data matrix to be compatible with the column number limits of commonly used spreadsheet programs and facilitates fast data processing. Another advantage is that spectra from different datasets can be compared with one another, even when some of the acquisition parameters change from spectrum to spectrum or batch to batch. The disadvantage is that many bins contain more than one metabolite and this

fact will reduce the sensitivity for detecting changes in minor metabolites. Also, intensity values of a single signal may be split between bins, and small chemical shift variations may still cause a signal to swap bins between different samples. Using fixed bin sizes also requires data interpolation algorithms that are not commonly available. We prefer smaller, fixed bin sizes for large-scale applications to define signatures and metabolite profiling patterns, and we commonly use a first pass PCA analysis for QC purposes based on a bin size of approx 0.02 ppm. "Smart bucketing" that tries to avoid splitting signals into separate bins has been implemented in some commercial software packages (ACD) as a solution to this issue. For more in-depth analysis, when we are seeking biomarkers to investigate mechanistic questions, we define integration limits using a stack plot of all spectra that passed the QC process. This process avoids some of the disadvantages of fixed bucketing approaches, like bin swapping and peak splitting, and provides us with a relatively small and "clean" data matrix, with signals of isolated multiplets summarized to a single resonance integral. Further improvements can be achieved using line deconvolution methods.

14. For Bruker NMR instruments with a macro that contains:

    sprintf(OUT,"%s/%s_%d.dx",path,name,expno);TOJDX(OUT,1,1,"*","*",user)

    An example of an ACD processing script is available upon request.

15. The analysis of the study meta-data for inconsistencies can, as a minimum, point out potential errors. For this purpose, compiling cross tabulations of the various study parameters serves as a simple, but relatively efficient, method to identify obvious data errors: are all expected samples present and organized in the correct group, are animals not duplicated, changing treatment groups or gender, and so on? If there is a particular coding or sequence maintained during collection: is this sequence consistent? These questions can be explored using the Excel "pivot table function," or, when using a database with sample annotation, by using the "group by" statements in SQL. Furthermore, it is prudent to check any transcribed data in a final datasheet against the raw data sources. For numeric data, calculating statistical values or plotting of histograms or similar visualization techniques is often a fast way to identify missing data, and outliers or values in error.

16. Scaling of spectral data: sometimes, prior experience or clinical chemistry results will suggest to utilize ratios between certain metabolites, such as the citrate/creatinine ratio, which can similarly be calculated from the NMR peak areas. Absolute concentrations can be determined using an internal reference added at a known concentration; however, at least for urine, it is generally found that there is a large variation in the urine volume between individuals at collection time-points, that leads to large fluctuations in metabolite concentrations that do not correlate well with any treatment effects. Thus, more commonly, it is assumed that the overall metabolite amount is constant and the data can be scaled to minimize the overall difference between the spectra. Scaling each spectrum to a constant total integral produces intensity values that are proportional to the total amount of metabolites. This method is very easy to implement and can scale spectra independently from

the dataset. This method removes variability owing to a variety of parameters introduced by the analytical technology, but is limited by the initial assumption of having constant total metabolite amounts. If large alterations in some resonances are found after a first scaling pass, the most variable signals should be excluded for calculating the multiplier and the spectra should be rescaled.

In particular, when very small changes between treatment groups are observed, and when there are substantial alterations in the composition of the analytes from different subjects, we observed significant residual bias after using the previously listed scaling methods. We found that the consistency between the spectra can be further improved when using linear regression (or robust linear regression) methods. After initial scaling by total integral (and removal of obvious outlier data if necessary), we calculate the global mean (or median) spectrum and fit each individual spectrum to this reference. The intercept provides a further zero-order baseline correction and the slope serves as the scaling factor.

17. A group effect on scaling (or on other meta-data, like the NMR phase correction values) by itself is not a problem, but it should be seen as a warning sign to watch for possible bias in the processing. We found that those artifacts are commonly introduced when some groups in the study produce samples that have distinct physicochemical differences, (such as changes in total urine volume, pH, osmolarity, protein content, and others). As a test for correctly scaled data, a statistical test such as a Student t-test should result in very few or no significant changes between groups of intensities in the noise regions, and most significant changes should be correlated with distinct NMR signals.

18. QC: a critical step during execution of each experiment is a comprehensive QC. The large number of samples processed, and with many steps performed manually during animal treatment (and sample handling) can (and in practice will) cause sample mislabeling and transcription errors, including typos and inconsistencies in labeling.

For spectral data, a plot of all spectra in the form of an overlay or stacked plot is often an excellent way of identifying outliers or data in need of reprocessing. Are all spectra correctly referenced and aligned? Is there any indication of residual pH variations? Is the phase/baseline correction applied consistently across all spectra? Are there any spectra that have unusually broad lines (NMR shim problem/large amount of NH_4^+?), low signal intensity, unusual additional signals, or missing signals? If there are drug or vehicle signals identifiable in the samples: do all samples within the same treatment group have a similar intensity for those signals or are there possible dosing errors?

After scaling, a PCA analysis can identify potential outliers: are there samples far outside the bulk of the samples in a scores plot? (Use the Hotelling T^2 values.) Is there a large error between the original data and those back calculated from the PCA loading and score matrices? (DMODX plot in Simca, error matrices in other programs.)

Pearson R^2 values of each spectra against the median spectrum of all spectra or of each group. Atypical and low R^2 values (within a group) are indicative of possible QC problems. Typically, R^2 values between 0.95 and 1 are observed within replicate urine samples, and more than 0.99 for serum samples. Does a hierarchical clustering of the correlation matrix cluster samples mostly by groups, or are there any obvious outliers?

19. PCA is sensitive to the scaling and normalization methods used, and suffers from potential variation in chemical shift position resulting from pH and temperature variations. Compensating for the variation in dynamic range is important for finding changes in minor metabolites but will often lead to an emphasis of baseline variations.

References

1. Lindon, J. C., Holmes, E., and Nicholson, J. K. (2004) Toxicological applications of magnetic resonance. *Prog. Nucl. Mag. Reson. Spectros.* **45,** 109–143.
2. Colatsky, T. J. and Sumner, S. (2003) Metabolic profiling and biomarker discovery. *Curr. Opin. Investig. Drugs* **4,** 262–263.
3. Robertson, D. G. (2005) Metabonomics in toxicology: a review. *Toxicol. Sci.* **85,** 809–822.
4. Lindon, J. C., Holmes, E., Bollard, M. E., Stanley, E. G., and Nicholson, J. K. (2004) Metabonomics technologies and their applications in physiological monitoring, drug safety assessment and disease diagnosis. *Biomarkers* **9,** 1–31.
5. Czuba, M. and Smith, I. C. (1991) Biological and NMR markers for cancer. *Pharmacol. Ther.* **50,** 147–190.
6. Odunsi, K., Wollman, R. M., Ambrosone, C. B., et al. (2005) Detection of epithelial ovarian cancer using 1H-NMR-based metabonomics. *Int. J. Cancer* **113,** 782–788.
7. Griffiths, J. R. and Stubbs, M. (2003) Opportunities for studying cancer by metabolomics: preliminary observations on tumors deficient in hypoxia-inducible factor 1. *Adv. Enzyme Regul.* **43,** 67–76.
8. Brindle, J. T., Antti, H., Holmes, E., et al. (2002) Rapid and noninvasive diagnosis of the presence and severity of coronary heart disease using 1H-NMR-based metabonomics. *Nat. Med.* **8,** 1439–1444.
9. Moolenaar, S. H., Engelke, U. F., and Wevers, R. A. (2003) Proton nuclear magnetic resonance spectroscopy of body fluids in the field of inborn errors of metabolism. *Ann. Clin. Biochem.* **40,** 16–24.
10. Bock, J. L. (1989) Nuclear magnetic resonance in the clinical laboratory. *Am. J. Clin. Pathol.* **91,** S19–S26.
11. Constantinou, M. A., Papakonstantinou, E., Spraul, M., et al. (2005) 1H NMR-based metabonomics for the diagnosis of inborn errors of metabolism in urine. *Analytica Chimica Acta* **542,** 169–177.
12. Constantinou, M. A., Papakonstantinou, E., Benaki, D., et al. (2004) Application of nuclear magnetic resonance spectroscopy combined with principal component analysis in detecting inborn errors of metabolism using blood spots: a metabonomic approach. *Analytica Chimica Acta* **511,** 303–312.
13. German, J. B., Roberts, M. A., and Watkins, S. M. (2003) Personal metabolomics as a next generation nutritional assessment. *J. Nutr.* **133,** 4260–4266.

14. Himmelreich, U., Somorjai, R. L., Dolenko, B., et al. (2003) Rapid identification of Candida species by using nuclear magnetic resonance spectroscopy and a statistical classification strategy. *Appl. Environ. Microbiol.* **69,** 4566–4574.

15. Fiehn, O., Kopka, J., Dormann, P., Altmann, T., Trethewey, R. N., and Willmitzer, L. (2000) Metabolite profiling for plant functional genomics. *Nat. Biotechnol.* **18,** 1157–1161.

16. Fiehn, O. (2002) Metabolomics: the link between genotypes and phenotypes. *Plant Mol. Biol.* **48,** 155–171.

17. Ott, K. H., Aranibar, N., Singh, B., and Stockton, G. W. (2003) Metabonomics classifies pathways affected by bioactive compounds. Artificial neural network classification of NMR spectra of plant extracts. *Phytochemistry* **62,** 971–985.

18. Lindon, J. C., Nicholson, J. K., Holmes, E., et al. (2003) Contemporary issues in toxicology the role of metabonomics in toxicology and its evaluation by the COMET project. *Toxicol. Appl. Pharmacol.* **187,** 137–146.

19. Holmes, E., Nicholson, J. K., Bonner, F. W., et al. (1992) Mapping the biochemical trajectory of nephrotoxicity by pattern recognition of NMR urinanalysis. *NMR Biomed.* **5,** 368–372.

20. Nicholson, J. K., Connelly, J., Lindon, J. C., and Holmes, E. (2002) Metabonomics: a platform for studying drug toxicity and gene function. *Nat. Rev. Drug Discov.* **1,** 153–161.

21. Robertson, D. G., Reily, M. D., Sigler, R. E., Wells, D. F., Paterson, D. A., and Braden, T. K. (2000) Metabonomics: evaluation of nuclear magnetic resonance (NMR) and pattern recognition technology for rapid in vivo screening of liver and kidney toxicants. *Toxicol. Sci.* **57,** 326–337.

22. Bollard, M. E., Stanley, E. G., Lindon, J. C., Nicholson, J. K., and Holmes, E. (2005) NMR-based metabonomic approaches for evaluating physiological influences on biofluid composition. *NMR Biomed.* **18,** 143–162.

23. Connor, S. C., Wu, W., Sweatman, B. C., et al. (2004) Effects of feeding and body weight loss on the 1H-NMR-based urine metabolic profiles of male Wistar Han rats: implications for biomarker discovery. *Biomarkers* **9,** 156–179.

24. Holmes, E., Foxall, P. J. D., Nicholson, J. K., et al. (1994) Automatic data reduction and pattern recognition methods for analysis of 1H nuclear magnetic resonance spectra of human urine from normal and pathological states. *Anal. Biochem.* **220,** 284–296.

25. Lindon, J. C., Holmes, E., and Nicholson, J. K. (2001) Pattern recognition methods and applications in biomedical magnetic resonance. *Prog. Nucl. Magn. Reson. Spectros.* **39,** 1–40.

26. Eriksson, L., Antti, H., Gottfries, J., et al. (2004) Using chemometrics for navigating in the large data sets of genomics, proteomics, and metabonomics (gpm). *Anal. Bioanal. Chem.* **380,** 419–29.

27. Beckonert, O. E., Bollard, M., Ebbels, T. M. D., et al. (2003) NMR-based metabonomic toxicity classification: hierarchical cluster analysis and k-nearest-neighbour approaches. *Analytica Chimica Acta* **490,** 3–15.

28. Aranibar, N., Singh, B. K., Stockton, G. W., and Ott, K. H. (2001) Automated mode-of-action detection by metabolic profiling. *Biochem. Biophys. Res. Commun.* **286,** 150–155.

29. Lenz, E. M., Bright, J., Wilson, I. D., et al. (2004) Metabonomics, dietary influences and cultural differences: a 1H NMR-based study of urine samples obtained from healthy British and Swedish subjects. *J. Pharm. Biomed. Anal.* **36,** 841–849.

30. Deprez, S., Sweatman, B. C., Connor, S. C., Haselden, J. N., and Waterfield, C. J. (2002) Optimisation of collection, storage and preparation of rat plasma for 1H NMR spectroscopic analysis in toxicology studies to determine inherent variation in biochemical profiles. *J. Pharm. Biomed. Anal.* **30,** 1297–1310.

31. Araníbar, N., Ott, K.-H., Mueller, L., Contel, N., and Roongta, V. (2003) *Experimental Nuclear Magenetic Resonance Conference,* Savanna, GA. March 30–April 4, 2003.

32. Araníbar, N., Ott, K.-H., Roongta, V., and Mueller, L. (2006) *Anal. Biochem.,* in press.

33. Keun, H. C., Ebbels, T. M. D., Antti, H., et al. (2003) Improved analysis of multivariate data by variable stability scaling: application to NMR-based metabolic profiling. *Analytica Chimica Acta* **490,** 265–276.

34. Walczak, B. and Massart, D. L. (1995) Robust principal components regression as a detection tool for outliers. *Chemometrics and Intelligent Laboratory Systems* **27,** 41–54.

35. Kell, D. B. (2002) Metabolomics and machine learning: explanatory analysis of complex metabolome data using genetic programming to produce simple, robust rules. *Mol. Biol. Rep.* **29,** 237–241.

Practical Aspects of Uniform Stable Isotope Labeling of Higher Plants for Heteronuclear NMR-Based Metabolomics

Jun Kikuchi and Takashi Hirayama

Summary

Analytical methods for probing plant metabolism are taking on new significance in the era of functional genomics, metabolomics, and systems biology. Nuclear magnetic resonance (NMR) is becoming a key technology in plant metabolomics. Stable isotope labeling of cultured cells and higher organisms has been especially promising in that it allows the use of advanced heteronuclear NMR methodologies through a combination of in vivo and in vitro measurements. This new approach provides much better resolution of the metabolite mixture signals in the multidimensional NMR spectra than does the conventional one-dimensional ^{1}H-NMR previously used in plant metabolomics. In this chapter, we describe the practical aspects of two key NMR technologies: uniform stable labeling of plants and in vitro heteronuclear NMR.

Key Words: Stable isotope labeling; plant metabolomics; *Arabidopsis thaliana*; nuclear magnetic resonance; chemical shift; root uptake; photosynthesis.

1. Introduction

Novel methods for the measurement of the components of living systems are providing rapid advancements in life science. In the era of the metabolome (analysis of all measurable metabolites), a mass spectrometry (MS)-based approach is considered to be the major technology (*1–3*), whereas nuclear magnetic resonance (NMR)-based methods are considered a minor technology because of low sensitivity. However, the NMR-based approach can be refined to take advantage of the strengths inherent in NMR measurements, such as high reproducibility, the ability to make noninvasive (or at least nondestructive) measurements, selectivity of nuclear environments, and the validity of structure analysis of diverse biomolecules (*2,3*). These advantages can be achieved by

From: *Methods in Molecular Biology, vol. 358: Metabolomics: Methods and Protocols*
Edited by: W. Weckwerth © Humana Press Inc., Totowa, NJ

uniform stable isotope labeling of organisms, which allows the application of the multidimensional NMR methods that have been used in protein structure determination *(4,5)*. Here, we describe the practical aspects of uniform stable labeling of plants and in vitro heteronuclear NMR.

1.1. Chemical Structure Determination by Heteronuclear NMR

MS signals indicate the molecular weight and provide some indication of the component molecular weights of each compound, but NMR gives information about the chemical structure of each compound as a function of chemical shifts *(6)*. **Figure 1** is a schematic representation of how different capillary electrophoresis–MS and NMR spectra give information of a solution containing Val and Glu. The MS spectrum provides one signal per compound (**Fig. 1A**), whereas the NMR spectrum (**Fig. 1B**) has information corresponding to the number of chemical groups. **Figure 1B** shows the expanded aliphatic region of the ^{13}C-heteronuclear single coherence spectroscopy (HSQC) spectrum *(7)*, with methyl, methylene, and methine signals appearing separately from high- to low-field regions (**Note 1**). In HSQC NMR spectra, NMR signal intensities reflect the number of carbon atoms attached to protons, assuming that each constituent is present in an equimolar ratio. For example, the two methyl signals (Hγ, Hγ') of Val indicate a value three times higher in intensity than methylene (Hβ) or methyne (Hα) signals. Multidimensional NMR spectra can also segregate mixed signals into different dimensions, such as a ^{13}C chemical shift (**Note 2**). **Figure 1C** is a schematic representation of a two-dimensional (2D) ^{1}H-^{13}C-HSQC spectrum of the solution containing Val and Glu. Each ^{1}H-^{13}C cross peak can spread out in two dimensions as functions of ^{1}H-^{13}C and ^{13}C chemical shifts. The cross peaks are indicated as contour signals so that the volume of the contour is reflected as the intensity of one-dimensional (1D) ^{1}H-NMR. Since NMR signals are highly reproducible, quantitative assessment of each metabolite in a sample is highly reliable, whereas MS signals can be less reliably quantitative owing to the matrix effect (i.e., "ion suppression" or "ion enhancement") *(8,9)*. In addition, 2D HSQC experiments have the advantage of detecting subtracted signals quantitatively because of their high reproducibility, whereas MS (especially in liquid chromatography–tandem mass spectrometry) sometimes suffers from matrix effects in terms of signal quantification. As previously indicated, introduction of ^{13}C chemical shifts in a second dimension offers significant improvement in the signal distribution of metabolite mixtures. A minor problem is the low abundance of ^{13}C nuclei (1.1%). However, this weak point can be overcome by stable isotope labeling of NMR samples *(10)*. Stable isotope labeling has the benefit of not only providing enhanced ^{13}C-signals, but it also allows the application of reliable NMR to the study of metabolism in plant systems. Therefore, we will describe our original protocols of these technologies (**Note 3**).

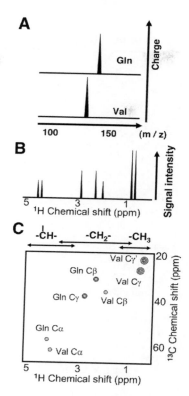

Fig. 1. Schematic representation of mass spectrometry and nuclear magnetic resonance spectra of an equimolar mixture of Gln and Val. (**A**) CE/MS (**B**) 1D ¹H-NMR (**C**) 2D ¹³C-HSQC.

2. Materials

2.1. Growth on Agar Media

1. MS agar plate. According to Murashige and Skhoog *(11)*, for 1 L combine 4.3 g plant salt mixture (Wako Pure Chemical Industries, Osaka, Japan), 20 g sucrose, and 0.5 g MES. Adjust pH to 5.8 with KOH. After the addition of 8 g bacto agar (Becton, Dickinson, and Co., Sparks, MD), sterilize by autoclave. After autoclaving, pour into plastic Petri dishes (25–30 mL per dish), 90 × 20-mm (Ina-Optika, Osaka, Japan).
2. Prepare seed sterilizing solution: 50%(v/v) of sodium hydrochlorite solution (5% solution; Wako Pure Chemical Industries) in water. Dissolve Triton X100 at a final concentration of 0.05%. Keep at 4°C.
3. Sterilize water for washing seeds.

Table 1
Composition of JPL Media Used in the Study

JPL medium		JPL-C		JPL-M	
• JPL-M	800 mL	• $FeSO_4 \cdot 7H_2O$	2.78 g	• JPL-A′	37.5 mL
• JPL-0	100 mL	• Na_2-EDTA·$2H_2O$	3.72 g	• JPL-B	0.375 mL
• JPL-S	100 mL	• Autoclave		• JPL-C	2.5 mL
				• Adjust pH 5.7	
JPL-A′		JPL-D		with KOH	
• KNO_3	65.5 g	• Myo-inositol	40 g	• Autoclave	
• $CaCl_2 \cdot 2H_2O$	4.4 g	• Glycine	0.8 g		
• $MgSO_4 \cdot 7H_2O$	3.7 g			JPL-O	
• KH_2PO_4	1.7 g	JPL-VT		• Casein hydrolysate,	
• Autoclave		• Nicotinic acid	0.5 g	vitamin free	1 g
		• Pyridoxine·HCl	0.5 g	• JPL-D	2.5 mL
JPL-B		• Thiamine·HCl	0.4 g	• JPL-VT	1 mL
• H_3BO_3	6.2 g			• Adjust pH 5.7	
• $MnSO_4 \cdot 4H_2O$	22.3 g	JPL-P		• Autoclave	
• $ZnSO_4 \cdot 7H_2O$	10.6 g	• KH_2PO_4	5.3 g		
• KI	0.83 g	• $Na_2HPO_4 \cdot 12H_2O$	21.8 g	JPL-S	
• $Na_2MoO_4 \cdot 2H_2O$	0.25 g	• Autoclave		• Sucrose	150 g
• $CoCl_2 \cdot 6H_2O$	25 mg			• JPL-P	10 mL
• $CuSO_4 \cdot 5H_2O$	25 mg	NAA[a] solution		• NAA solution	10 mL
• Autoclave		• NAA[a] 186.2 mg in EtOH		• Autoclave	

Note that all mediums listed are for 1 L.
[a] NAA, α-Naphthaleneacetic acid (Sigma-Aldrich).

2.2. Growth on Synthetic Soil

1. Prepare solutions: 1 M KNO_3, 1 M potassium phosphate (pH 5.5), 1 M $MgSO_4$, 1 M $CaCl_2$, 20 mM Fe-EDTA, and micronutrients solution (70 mM H_3BO_3, 14 mM $MnCl_2$, 0.5 mM $CuSO_4$, 1 mM $ZnSO_4$, 0.2 mM $NaMoO_4$, 10 mM NaCl, and 0.01 mM $CoCl_2$).
2. Nutrient solution: add 5 mL of 1 M KNO_3, 2.5 mL of 1 M KPO_4, 2 mL of 1 M $MgSO_4$, 2 mL of 1 M $CaCl_2$, 2.5 mL of 20 mM Fe-EDTA, and 1 mL of micronutrients solution to 985 mL of water.
3. Mix vermiculite and perlite (1:1 vol) and wash with water several times.

2.3. T87 Cell Culture

1. Prepare JPL medium solutions listed in **Table 1**.
2. Sterilize Erlenmeyer flasks with a cap.
3. CIM agar plates. For 1 L: combine 3.1 g Gamborg's B-5 salt mixture (Sigma-Aldrich Japan, Tokyo, Japan), 1 mL Gamborg's vitamin solution (Sigma-Aldrich), 30 g sucrose, 0.2 mL of 1 mM α-naphthaleneacetic acid (Sigma-Aldrich) in ethanol, and 0.5 g MES. Adjust pH to 5.7 with KOH. After adding 6 g of bact agar, sterilize by autoclave. Pour into appropriate plastic Petri dishes or containers for plant culture.

3. Methods

3.1. Plant Systems

Arabidopsis thaliana has become the pre-eminent model plant species for genetics, molecular biology, genomics, and host–pathogen interactions. We have chosen *Arabidopsis* because reliable and standardized laboratory growing conditions have been established, the complete genome has been sequenced and is accessible, and a large transcriptome database is available. These resources are extremely valuable for explaining changes in the metabolic profile at the molecular level. Because of the high degree of sensitivity provided by NMR, it may be possible to detect differences in the metabolic profiles of different *Arabidopsis* ecotypes (e.g., Columbia, Landsberg, and Nossen). *Perilla frutescens* L. Britton var. *crispa* (Lamiaceae; Shiso, Purple Mint) is a plant commonly grown for its oil in industrial uses and as a garnish.

We also use cultured *Arabidopsis* cell line T87. In some cases the physiologically uniform samples provided by cultured cells are very useful for metabolite analysis. For metabolite analysis to be meaningful, it is important to carefully control the environmental condition of plant samples. However, it should be noted that cultured cells are limited in that they provide only general information about plant physiology, and do not provide a reliable source of tissue- or organ-specific functions. Therefore, metabolite data obtained using cultured cells should be considered as a special case.

3.2. Plant Growth on Solid Agar Plates

3.2.1. Small Scale (Seeds Less Than 50 mg)

1. To sow seeds on solid agar plates, the surface of seeds should be sterilized. Pour the seeds into an Eppendorf tube and add 500 µL of the sterilizing solution into the tube containing the seeds. **Note:** if seeds are badly contaminated with bacteria or fungi, washing with 70% ethanol can be applied before this treatment.
2. Voltex for 1 min and keep for 5 min at room temperature.
3. Centrifuge at 800*g* for 30 s to spin down seeds.
4. Remove the solution as much as possible.
5. Add 1.5 mL of sterile water and shake tube vigorously.
6. Centrifuge at 800*g* for 30 s and remove the solution from the tube as much as possible.
7. Repeat **steps 5** and **6** at least two more times (more seeds requires more wash).
8. Pick up seeds with water using a bore pipet-chip or a 1 mL chip, pour on the agar plate, and spread the seeds with the chip. In a few tens of seconds, seeds are settled down on and attached to the surface of the agar plate. Then, remove the excess water. Or, after the last wash with water, remove the water as much as possible. Add 0.7% low-melting agarose (geling temperature 24 to 28°C, Invitrogen Japan, Tokyo, Japan) cooled to room temperature, and pour melted agarose with seeds onto the agar plate.

9. Keep plates with seeds in 4°C for 4 d for stratification.
10. Place the plates under appropriate conditions. Usually we use a growth chamber that can control the temperature and light cycle.

3.2.2. Large Scale (Seeds More Than 50 mg)

1. Measure *Arabidopsis* seeds. Roughly 125 to 150 mg represents 5000 seeds. Pour the seeds in a 15-mL disposable centrifuge plastic tube with a screw cap. Add 5 mL of the sterilizing solution into the tube containing seeds. **Note:** if seeds are badly contaminated with bacteria or fungi, washing with 70% ethanol can be applied before this treatment.
2. Voltex for 1 min and keep for 5 min at room temperature.
3. Centrifuge at 800*g* for 30 s to spin down seeds.
4. Remove the solution as much as possible.
5. Add 10 mL of sterile water and shake tube vigorously.
6. Centrifuge at 800*g* for 30 s and remove solution as much as possible.
7. Repeat **steps 5** and **6** at least two more times.
8. Remove water as much as possible. Add 0.7% low-melting agarose (geling temperature 24 to 28°C; Invitrogen Japan) cooled to room temperature, and pour melted agarose with seeds onto agar plates.
9. Keep plates with seeds at 4°C for 4 d for stratification.
10. Place the plates under appropriate conditions. Usually we use a growth chamber that can control the temperature and light cycle.

3.3. Plant Growth on Soil

1. Put the soil in a pot or an appropriate growing box. Pour the nutrient solution into the soil.
2. In the case of starting from seeds, seeds should be stratificated to induce germination. Usually, we treated seeds before sowing on soil. Pour the seeds in a tube, add water, mix vigorously, and place the tube at 4°C for 4 d.
3. Or, transfer germinated seedlings or grown plants grown on solid agar plates to soil. Make a hole on the surface of the soil and put the roots of the plants in the hole and bury it carefully. Cover the pots or boxes with plastic wrap to avoid drying until plants start to grow (about several days).
4. Place the pot or box under appropriate conditions.
5. Plants are supplied nutrient solution every week.

3.4. Arabidopsis *T87* Cell Suspension Culture

The method and the growth condition of T87 cell culture have been described by Axelos et al. *(12)*.

1. Prepare the JPL medium in flasks (20 to 100 mL of JPL medium in 100–500 mL flask).

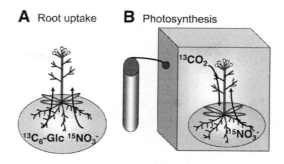

Fig. 2. Schematic representation of uniform labeling methods. (**A**) Both ^{13}C and ^{15}N nuclei can be incorporated from root uptake when grown on agar plates containing ^{13}C- or ^{15}N-labeled compounds. (**B**) Carbon nuclei are incorporated from ^{13}CO$_2$ through photosynthesis, whereas ^{15}N nuclei are from roots.

2. To avoid taking aggregated cells, 10–20 mL of 7- to 10-d-old cell culture is passed through sterilized 0.5-mm nylon mesh. **Note:** this step may not be necessary for every inoculation.
3. Inoculate the 7- to 10-d-old cell culture into new JPL medium. Grow them at 20–23°C with rotary shaking at around 100 rpm. **Note:** T87 cells can also be grown on the solid CIM agar plate as callus.

3.5. Stable Isotope Labeling by Root Uptake

Uniformly labeling living samples with stable isotopes such as ^{13}C or ^{15}N can be achieved by supplying compounds containing those isotopes as nutrients. Labeling whole plants is straightforward and efficient because plants absorb ^{15}NO$_3$ and ^{15}NH$_4$ very efficiently through their roots (**Fig. 2A**). In addition, plants can also absorb sugars or amino acids, thus, it is possible to label plants with isotope-tagged compounds and to observe metabolites produced from those compounds. Cultured cells also take up many sugars efficiently.

For ^{15}N labeling, the nutrient solution is prepared by substituting KNO$_3$ with K^{15}NO$_3$ (Cambridge Isotope Laboratories, Inc., Andover, MA). With ^{15}N as the sole nitrogen source, nearly 100% efficiency of labeling mature tissues is achieved. ^{15}N-labeled seedlings can be obtained from the seeds of ^{15}N-labeled plants because early stage seedlings use nutrients stored in seed. Plants also can be grown on solid media containing the ^{15}N-nutrient solution instead of MS salts.

^{13}C$_6$-glucose is the most useful substrate for labeling plants with ^{13}C by root absorption. Plants prefer sucrose as a carbon source, but ^{13}C-sucrose is either not available or is very expensive. Seeds are germinated and grown on MS agar plates containing 0.5–1% ^{13}C$_6$-glucose (Cambridge Isotope Laboratories,

Inc.) instead of sucrose, but it is difficult to obtain progeny from plants grown in a plate.

3.6. Stable Isotope Labeling of Cultured Cells

Cultured cells can be labeled by growth on JPL medium without sucrose, but amended with filter-sterilized $^{13}C_6$-glucose to a final concentration of 0.5–1%. T87 cells can grow in glucose medium but the growth rate, cell color, and cell shape can be affected.

3.7. $^{13}CO_2$ Labeling by Photosynthesis

Labeling plants with $^{13}CO_2$ is relatively more difficult than with ^{15}N because it requires a chamber to expose plants to the gas. We use an acrylic chamber (**Fig. 2B**). Plants growing on soil are labeled in a chamber filled with $^{13}CO_2$ air (340 ppm; Shoko Tsushou, Tokyo, Japan).

When labeling times are limited to a few minutes to 1 d, it may not be necessary to worry about environmental conditions, such as humidity or accumulation of volatile plant hormones. In that case, the chamber can be simple, for example, a compact disc case can be used (*13*). However, uniform tissue labeling requires long-term growth in a closed chamber. In this case, high humidity and the accumulation of volatile plant hormones, such as ethylene, will affect the plant growth and metabolism. Ideally chamber air is changed frequently to prevent the buildup of excessive moisture and volatile compounds. However, changing the air removes the isotope-tagged gas, thus increasing the cost and reducing labeling efficiency. In order to maintain optimal growth conditions, we designed a chamber that contains the labeled gases but maintains adequate growth conditions (**Fig. 3**). It is equipped with fans to recirculate air, a dehumidifier, and space for photocatalytic filters. Ethylene is reduced by photocatalytic oxidation with TiO_2, so placing photocatalytic-active compounds in the air-flow path of the chamber should reduce the effect of volatile compounds. However, maximization of labeling efficiency requires the consideration of growth conditions, plant developmental stage, and duration of labeling.

3.8. NMR Sample Preparations

1. The NMR sample can be used for both wet and dried states of the target plants. To avoid individual differences owing to water content, we prefer to use freeze-dried plant samples.
2. Samples from **step 1** should be transferred into a 2-mL Eppendorf tube and weighed by a balance. Generally, 2–10 mg of dried plant samples are used for extraction.
3. These samples are homogenized by using auto-mil (Tokken Inc., Chiba, Japan [http://www.tokken.jp]).

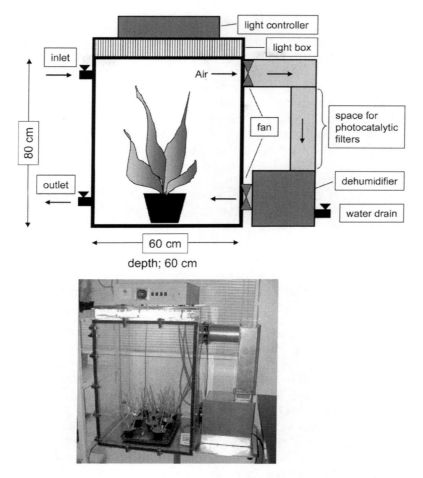

Fig. 3. Plant growth chamber designed for $^{13}CO_2$ labeling. The chamber is equipped with fans for air circulation, nozzles for gas change, and a dehumidifier. The chamber also has space for photocatalytic oxidation filters for reduction of volatile plant compounds, such as ethylene.

4. Add 0.5 mL extraction buffer into the 2-mL Eppendorf tube.
5. The sample solution should be stirred at 1400 rpm using thermo-mixer (Eppendorf Co. Ltd.) for 5 min and kept at 50°C.
6. The extracted sample solutions are centrifuged at 12g for 5 min.
7. High-molecular compounds, such as proteins and polysaccharides, dissolved in supernatant are removed by centrifugal filter (Microcon YM-5, Millipore Co. Ltd., Bedford, MA).
8. Filtered solution is transferred into a 5-mm φ-NMR tube using a pipet.

3.9. The Heteronuclear NMR Experiments **In Vitro**

1. The NMR sample tube should be inserted into a NMR superconducting magnet for 5 to 20 min before the experiments at desired temperature. In our case, the NMR probe head (NMR sample inserted) is usually kept at 50°C. Within this period, NMR sample solution can be well equilibrated.
2. Radiofrequency tuning and matching of the NMR probe should be performed at 500 MHz for ^{1}H and 125 MHz for ^{13}C in the case of a 500-MHz NMR spectrometer.
3. NMR shimming should be performed for the z-axis (direction to B_0 of superconducting magnet) and x,y-axis (radial direction to the B_0).
4. Determine the ^{1}H frequency of the residual water signal by a one-pulse 1D-^{1}H-NMR experiment.
5. Pulse length of the ^{1}H resonance is easily changeable in regard to the dielectic properties of the NMR sample. Therefore, ^{1}H–$\pi/2$ pulse should be determined by null-point at the 2π pulse.
6. Run the 1D ^{1}H-NMR experiment by residual water suppression pulse-sequence such as Watergate *(14)*.
7. Run the other nD-NMR experiments according to the desired pulse sequences, such as 2D ^{13}C-HSQC, 2D ^{15}N-HSQC *(15)*, and 3D ^{13}C-HCCH-COSY *(16)*, etc.

4. Notes

1. Example of the heteronuclear NMR experiments. **Figure 4A** shows the 2D ^{13}C-HSQC spectra of *A. thaliana* and *Perilla frutescen* var. *crispa* using a 500-MHz NMR spectrometer equipped with a triple axis gradient. Both plants were grown on soil and labeled with ^{13}CO$_2$ for 3 wk. DMSO extracts provide well-resolved 2D ^{13}C-HSQC spectra in comparison with previously reported 1D ^{1}H-NMR patterns *(17,18)*. As indicated in **Fig. 1**, ^{1}H and ^{13}C chemical shifts indicate differences in the methyl, methylene, and methine groups from high-to-low field. Aromatic signals are folded in the ^{13}C dimension from 100 to 160 ppm. Related compounds tend to form signals in isolated regions, as indicated in **Fig. 4**, including lipids (thick line), organic acids (thin dotted line), sugars (hashed lines), olefins (thick dotted line), and aromatics (thin dotted line). Since the chemical shifts represent physical parameters, these values are exactly same in all NMR instruments.
2. The 2D ^{13}C-HSQC spectrum of *A. thaliana* is relatively richer in lipid signals than other compound-type regions, but *P. frutescen* var. *crispa* contains a variety of sugars. Because ^{13}C-NMR chemical shifts are sensitive to differences in chemical structure but insensitive to the experimental environment, such as solvent effects *(19)*, 2D HSQC-type spectra offer exceptionally useful information for assignment of individual chemical groups. Thus, the construction of a database of 2D HSQC spectra of predominant metabolites would provide a useful tool in metabolomics.
3. Patterns formed by 2D ^{13}C-HSQC spectra should be a reliable indicator of metabolic states in a plant, and could provide an accurate and reproducible profile of metabolism in time-course experiments, or when plants are subjected to drought,

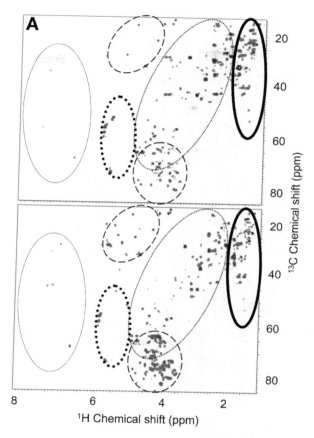

Fig. 4. (**A**) 2D ¹³C-HSQC spectra of the DMSO extracts of *Arabidopsis thaliana* and *Perilla frutescens* var. *crispa*. The spectra were measured on a Bruker DRX-500 spectrometer equipped with a ¹H inverse probe with triple axis gradient. A total of 128 complex f1 (¹³C) and 512 complex f2 (¹H) points were recorded with 32 scans per f1 increment. The spectral widths were 12,000 Hz and 9500 Hz for f1 and f2, respectively. Circles are approximate indications of regions for lipids (thick line), organic acids (thin dotted line), sugars (hashed lines), olefins (thick dotted line) and aromatics (thin line).

(Continued on next page)

predation, disease, or other stresses. This technique may also be used for comparisons of closely related plants in response to environmental factors, and could play a role in validating plant identification. In order to show accuracy of these metabolic patterns formed in 2D ¹³C-HSQC spectra, 370 assignments next to the signals of uniformly ¹³C-labeled T87 cells are represented in **Fig. 4B**. These signal assignments were mainly performed by referencing standard chemical shifts individually observed at same conditions.

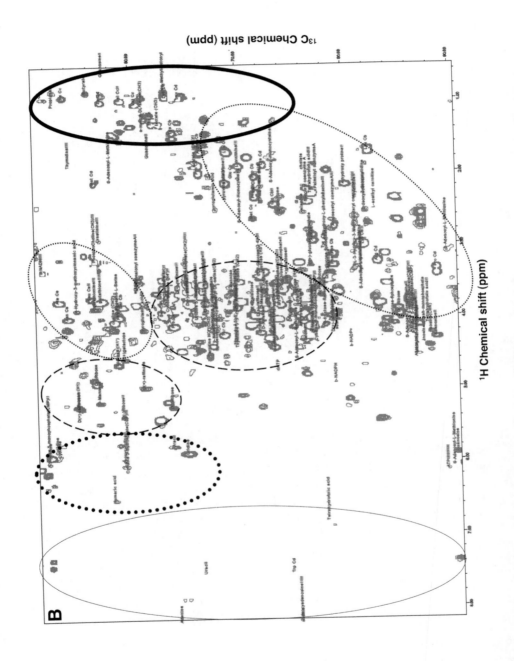

284

Acknowledgments

This work was supported in part by RIKEN GSC Internal Collaborations (no. 830-56625), by CREST (no. A88-54366), Japan Science and Technology Agency to J.K. and T.H. We also acknowledge Grants-in-Aid for Scientific Research (no. 15710171, to J.K.; no. 15570045, to T.H.) from the Ministry of Education, Science, Sports, and Culture of Japan.

References

1. Villas-Boas, S. G., Mas, S., Akesson, M., Smedsgaard, J., and Nielses, J. (2005) Mass spectrometry in metabolome analysis. *Phyl. Trans. R. Soc. Lond.* B **359,** 857–871.
2. Kikuchi, J., Shinozaki, K., and Hirayama, T. (2004) Stable isotope labeling of Arabidopsis thaliana for a hetero-nuclear NMR-based metabolomics approach. *Plant Cell Physiol.* **45,** 1099–1104.
3. Kikuchi, J. and Hirayama, T. (2006) Hetero-nuclear NMR-based metabolomics. *Biotech. Agri. Forestry* **57,** 94–101.
4. Kikuchi, J., Iwahara, J., Kigawa, T., Murakami, T., Okazaki, T., and Yokoyama, S. (2002) Solution structure determination of the two DNA-binding domains in the *Shizosaccharomyces pombe* Abp1 protein by a combination of dipolar coupling and diffusion anisotropy restraints. *J. Biomol. NMR* **22,** 333–347.
5. Fukushima, K., Kikuchi, J., Koshiba, S., Kuroda, Y., and Yokoyama, S. (2002) Solution structure of the C-terminal domain of DEF45/ICAD. A structural basis for the regulation of apoptotic DNA fragmentation. *J. Mol. Biol.* **321,** 317–326.
6. Claridge, T. D. W. (1999) *High-resolution NMR techniques in organic chemistry.* Elsevier Science, Oxford, UK.
7. Vuister, G. W. and Bax, A. (1992) Resolution enhancement and spectral editing of uniformly ^{13}C enriched proteins by homonuclear broadband ^{13}C -^{13}C decoupling. *J. Magn. Reson.* **98,** 428–435.
8. Mallet, C.R., Lu, A., and Mazzeo, J. R. (2004) A study of ion suppression effects in electrospray ionization from mobile phase additives and solid-phase extracts. *Rapid Commun. Mass Spectrom.* **18,** 49–58.
9. Mei, H., Hsieh, Y., Nardo, C., et al. (2003) Investigation of matrix effects in bioanalytical high-performance liquid chromatography/tandem mass spectrometric assays: application to drug discovery. *Rapid Commun. Mass Spectrom.* **17,** 97–103.

Fig. 4. *(opposite)* **(B)** 2D ^{13}C-HSQC spectrum of *Arabidopsis* T87 cells. The spectra were measured on a Bruker DRU-700 spectrometer equipped with a ^1H inverse cryogenically cooled probe with *z*-axis gradient. A total of 128 complex f1 (^{13}C) for 7000 Hz and 512 complex f2 (^1H) points for 11,200 Hz were recorded with 32 scans per f1 increment, respectively.

10. Kikuchi, J., Asakura, T., Hasuda, K., et al. (2000) An advantage for use of isotope labeling and NMR chemical shifts to analyze the structure of four homologous IgG-binding domains of *Staphylococcal* protein A. *J. Biochem. Biophys. Method* **42**, 35–47

11. Murashige, T. and Skoog, F. A. (1962) A revised medium for rapid growth and bioassays with tobacco tissue culture. *Physiol. Plant* **15**, 473–497.

12. Axelos, M., Curie, C., Mazzolini, L., Bardet, C., and Lescure, B. (1992) A protocol for transient gene expression in *Arabidopsis thaliana* protoplasts isolated from cell suspension cultures. *Plant Physiol. Biochem.* **30**, 123–128.

13. Cegelski, L. and Schaefer, J. (2005) NMR determination of photorespiration in intact leaves using in vivo $^{13}CO_2$ labeling *J. Magn. Reson.* **178**, 1–10.

14. Piotto, M., Saudek, V., and Skelener, V. (1992) Gradient-tailored excitation for single-quantum NMR spectroscopy of aqueous solutions. *J. Biomol. NMR* **2**, 661–665.

15. Grzesiek, S. and Bax, A. (1993) The importance of not saturating H_2O in protein NMR. Application to sensitivity enhancement and NOE measurements. *J. Am. Chem. Soc.* **115**, 12,593–12,594.

16. Kay, L. E., Xu, G. Y., Singer, A. U., Muhandiram, D. R., and Formankay, J. D. (1993) A gradient-enhanced HCCH-TOCSY experiment for recording side-chain ^1H and ^{13}C correlations in H_2O samples of proteins *J. Magn. Reson.* **B101**, 333–337.

17. Ott, K.-H., Aranibar, N., Singh, B., and Stockton, G. W. (2003) Metabolomics classifies pathways affected by bioactive compounds. Artificial neural network classification of NMR spectra of plant extracts. *Phytochemistry* **62**, 971–985.

18. Choi, H.-K., Choi, Y. H., Verberne, M., Lefeber, A. W. M., Erkelens, C., and Verpoorte, R. (2004) Metabolic fingerprinting of wild type and transgenic tobacco plants by ^1H NMR and multivariate analysis technique. *Phytochemistry* **65**, 857–864.

19. Kikuchi, J. and Asakura, T. (1999) Use of ^{13}C conformation-dependent chemical shifts to elucidate the local structure of a large protein with homologous domains in solution and solid state. *J. Biochem. Biophys. Method* **38**, 203–208.

Index